SKY'S LIMIT

FROOME, WIGGINS
and the Quest to Conquer the Tour de France

RICHARD MOORE

INCLUDES THE 2013 TOUR DE FRANCE WIN

HarperSport
An Imprint of HarperCollins*Publishers*

First published in 2011 by
HarperSport
An imprint of HarperCollins*Publishers*
77–85 Fulham Palace Road,
Hammersmith, London W6 8JB

This updated edition published 2013

www.harpercollins.co.uk

1 3 5 7 9 10 8 6 4 2

A catalogue record of this book is
available from the British Library

ISBN 978-0-00-754993-1

Printed and bound in Great Britain by
Clays Ltd, St Ives plc

MIX
Paper from
responsible sources
FSC C007454

Find out more about HarperCollins and the environment at
www.harpercollins.co.uk/green

CONTENTS

THE START OF THE JOURNEY

'They'll use technology that we're all going to look at and go, "Woah, I never saw that before."'

Lance Armstrong

Rymill Park, Adelaide, 17 January 2010

It's a sultry hot summer's evening in downtown Adelaide, and, at the city's Rymill Park, a large crowd begins to gather. Families line a cordoned-off rectangular 1km race circuit, around the perimeter of the park, while the balconies of pubs fill up with young people drinking beer out of plastic cups.

The road cycling season used to start six weeks later in an icily cold port on the Mediterranean, with the riders wrapped in many more layers than there were spectators. But the sport has changed in the last decade: it has gone global. And no event demonstrates that to the same extent as the season-opener: the Tour Down Under.

This year, though, there is another harbinger of change. Possibly. Wearing a neatly pressed short-sleeved white shirt, long black shorts and trainers, rubbing sun cream into his shaved head as he paces anxiously among the team cars parked in the pits area, is a man who bears more than a passing resemblance to a British tourist. It's Dave Brailsford.

In his native Britain, Brailsford has gained a reputation as a sporting guru. Since 2004 he has been at the helm of the British Cycling team, which, at the Beijing Games in 2008, he led to the most dominant Olympic performance ever seen by a single team. But that was in *track* cycling, not road cycling. Road cycling – continental style – is a whole new world, not just for Brailsford but for Britain, a country that has always been on the periphery of the sport's European heartland.

There have been British professional teams in the past. But they have been, without exception, doomed enterprises, Icarus-like in their pursuit of an apparently impossible dream. The higher they flew – to the Tour de France, as one particularly ill-fated squad did in 1987 – the further and harder they fell. And the more, of course, they were burned in the process. In fact, it seems oddly fitting that after more than a century of looking in on the sport with only passing interest, and limited understanding, Adelaide in Australia, on the other side of the world, marks Brailsford and his new British team's bold entry into the world of continental professional cycling.

Bold is the apposite word. Everything about the new team, Team Sky – from their clothing, to their cars, to the brash and glitzy team launch in London just days earlier – screams boldness and ambition. They don't just want to *enter* the world of professional road cycling. They aspire to stand apart; to be different. And by being different, and successful, they aspire to change it, almost as the team's sponsor, British Sky Broadcasting, has changed the landscape of English football over the past two decades; almost as Brailsford and his team 'changed' track cycling, not merely moving the goalposts, but locating them in a different dimension.

Team Sky is Brailsford's creation, along with his head coach and right-hand man, Shane Sutton. Sutton, a wiry, rugged, edgy, fidgety Australian, is the joker to Brailsford's – with his background in business and his MBA – straight man. They are as much a double act as Brian Clough and Peter Taylor, the legendary football management team. And similarly lost without each other. Here in Adelaide, an hour before the first race of the season, and the first of Team Sky's existence, Sutton is missing. Brailsford keeps checking his phone and finally it beeps. 'The eagle has landed,' reads the text message. Sutton's delayed flight from Perth has arrived. Brailsford looks relieved. 'Well, Shane needs to be here for this,' he says.

Sutton arrives. Has he brought champagne, ready to toast the occasion? 'Nah, none of that bullshit,' he replies testily. He is wearing the same team-issue outfit as Brailsford; but if Brailsford looks like a businessman on holiday, Sutton, in his white shirt and long black shorts, has the mischievous, scheming air of a naughty schoolboy. Brailsford reaches into the giant coolbox parked in the shadow of the team car and pulls out a couple of cans of Diet Coke, tossing one at Sutton. They open their cans, take a swig, and wait for the action, which is just minutes away.

Brailsford has hurried back to Rymill Park from the team's hotel, the Adelaide Hilton, where he gave the seven Team Sky riders – Greg Henderson of New Zealand, Mat Hayman and Chris Sutton of Australia, Russell Downing, Chris Froome and Ben Swift of Britain, Davide Viganò of Italy – a pep-talk. Earlier, the riders had been presented on stage by the TV commentators, Phil Liggett and Paul Sherwen. 'I never thought I'd see the day we'd have a British team in the ProTour,' said Sherwen. The ProTour is cycling's premier league of major events.

Though all experienced professionals, most of whom have competed for big teams, the seven Team Sky recruits find themselves riven with nerves as they prepare for their debut. The dead time between the presentation of the teams in the middle of Rymill Park and the start of the race acts as a black hole into which spill fears, doubts and anxieties. 'We were all nervous, just sitting around, waiting,' Mat Hayman will recall later. 'Pulling on the new kit, being given this opportunity to be part of this new team … We all know what's gone into this team: more than a year's work, so much thought and organisation. We're excited about it, too, because we've all bought into what Dave and Shane and Scott [Sunderland, the senior sports director] are trying to do. And we all said that it had been a while since everyone had been so nervous about lining up.'

Just before they left the hotel, to pedal the 10 minutes to Rymill Park, Brailsford addressed them. 'This is a proud moment for me,' he said. 'And it's a unique occasion. We're only going to make our debut once. This is it, lads. It's a privilege. Enjoy it.'

Brailsford had been in Adelaide for 48 hours ahead of the big kick-off, with Sunday evening's circuit race followed, two days later, by the six-day Tour Down Under. He had checked into the Hilton late on Friday evening and then wandered into the hotel lobby. 'I'm a worrier,' he said. 'I always worry. I'm always wondering, what if we'd done this, or that. I'm sure that'll never change, but I'm confident that we've done everything we could to prepare. It's a huge moment. I'm excited.' But he sought to add a note of caution. 'You can't go from having a group of individuals come together in Manchester to an elite team in six weeks,' Brailsford pointed out. 'It's a process.'

Despite the late hour, Brailsford drank a coffee, then another. And he kept talking, stopping only to yell at Matt White, the director of a rival team, Garmin-Transitions, as White walked through the lobby. 'Hey, Whitey!' he yelled, though White didn't appear to hear him. 'Whitey!'

Brailsford seemed out of his comfort zone, which, for several years, has been the centre of a velodrome, surveying his riders as they circle the boards of the track, talking to his coaches, in conference – arms folded – with Shane Sutton. With Team Sky, Brailsford's job title is team principal, which seems a bit vague (and, again, *different*), other than in one important respect: he's the man with overall responsibility. But on the ground, during races, the sports directors will call the shots. Here in Adelaide the man in that role is one of the team's four sports directors, Sean Yates, an experienced British ex-professional; indeed, a former stage winner and wearer of the yellow jersey in the Tour de France. Yates has been overseeing the team's training all week in Adelaide.

It is clear that Brailsford, having just arrived, isn't quite sure yet of his role. This is not his world; not yet. He wants to focus, however, on the bigger picture; on the many races in the early part of the season, and the spring Classics, all leading up to Team Sky's major target, the Tour de France, where they will be aiming to support their leader and homegrown talisman, Bradley Wiggins, in his bid for a place on the podium in Paris.

'People keep asking, "What would be a good race for us here, or what would make a good season?"' says Brailsford. 'The important thing is to try and not underperform. We're trying to create an environment in which the riders can perform to the very best of their ability. So if they underperform, we're doing something wrong.'

In Rymill Park the first-day-of-term feeling means an intoxicating sense of excitement combined with nervous anticipation; of new teams and new outfits; of glistening new bikes; of gleaming legs, unblemished by the scars and road rash that will disfigure them in the weeks and months to follow; of excitable Australian fans, who in previous years have only been able to watch the great European stars of the sport on television, and at night. Everything is shiny and new, except for

38-year-old Lance Armstrong, leading his new RadioShack team into the second year of his comeback.

In the pits, immediately after the first bend of the 1.1km circuit, the team cars are lined up, side by side, with the Team Sky vehicle – a Skoda, supplied by the sponsor, rather than their usual Jaguar – flanked by Française des Jeux and Astana, then Garmin-Transitions and HTC-Columbia. Brailsford and Sutton slap their riders on the backs and whisper encouraging words as they leave the shaded area behind the car and pedal to the start.

'We've got a game plan,' says Brailsford as he and Sutton perch on the bonnet of the car. Planning to the nth degree is what Brailsford is most famous for. But he and Sutton look apprehensive and on edge as they await the countdown and the firing of the gun.

In contrast is Bob Stapleton. As the owner of the rival HTC-Columbia team, Stapleton's position is similar to Brailsford's. Stapleton is the man in charge, but he has always appeared relaxed in that role. Typically, he can be found hovering around the fringes of his team in the mornings, chatting easily to journalists. Like Brailsford, Stapleton tends to be viewed as something of an outsider in a sport which has a reputation for being resistant to, and suspicious of, outsiders. He was a millionaire businessman in his native California before being parachuted in to clean up and manage one of the world's top teams in 2006. But since then he seems to have overcome any suspicion or hostility. His manner is amiable and open: that must help. But it helps even more that his team, HTC-Columbia, is successful, and wins more races than any other.

Now, as the first race of the 2010 season gets underway, Stapleton wanders away from his own team car and strolls towards Brailsford and Sutton. But he doesn't quite make it that far, stopping and sitting on the bonnet of the Astana team

car, whose staff, in animated conversation, are sitting on the
tailgate, facing away from the action. (Such apparent disinter-
est among people working at this level of the sport can be
fairly typical, if slightly unusual at the first race of the season.
It suggests a certain complacency in some teams, which
Brailsford has already identified as an opportunity.)

In his Columbia clothing – gentle beige and pastel turquoise
– Stapleton, as he smiles and asks, 'Mind if I join you guys?',
and settles on the bonnet of the Astana car to watch the action
unfold, appears as laidback as a millionaire Californian cycling
enthusiast who has been able to indulge his passion for cycling
by running his own team. Which he is. His sports director,
Allan Peiper, cuts a less relaxed figure by the HTC car, an
earpiece and microphone connecting him to his riders, and
making him look like a bouncer in a rowdy football pub.
Sutton and Brailsford are sitting on the bonnet of the Team
Sky car, with Sean Yates in close attendance. But Yates is not
linked up by radio to his riders. 'Our boys know what they're
doing,' says Sutton.

What they appear to be doing, in the early part of the race,
is remaining as invisible as possible. Attacks are launched – the
young Australian Jack Bobridge is particularly aggressive –
and brought back by a peloton that seems to be quickly into
the speed, and rhythm, of racing. But at half-distance a break
goes clear and stays clear. It includes Lance Armstrong. 'He's a
guy with a lot going on this year,' observes Stapleton crypti-
cally (though also presciently).

Armstrong is joined by four other riders, and they work
well as a quartet, building a lead that stretches to almost a
minute over the peloton. Still Team Sky, in their distinctive,
predominantly black skinsuits, are anonymous, hiding somewhere in the middle of the pack. Brailsford and Sutton remain
perched on the bonnet of the car, apparently content that the
plan is being followed, though there's a moment of panic

when Ben Swift appears after the bunch has passed, the spokes having been ripped out of his rear wheel by a stray piece of wire. The young British rider is given a spare bike, pushed back on to the course, and quickly rejoins the bunch.

While Brailsford and Sutton focus on the race, Stapleton watches with what appears to be amused detachment. He wonders aloud whether, without ProTour status, this circuit race in central Adelaide – really only a curtain-raiser to the main event, the Tour Down Under – even *counts* as the first race of the season.

'If we win, it is the first race of the season,' decides Stapleton, with a twinkle in his eye, after giving it some thought. 'If we don't, it doesn't matter.'

The Armstrong break is allowed to dangle out in front long enough for the crowd to start to believe that the American might win. But with four laps to go Stapleton's HTC squad hits the front, a blur of dazzling white and yellow leading the peloton as they fly past the pits area, travelling noticeably, and exhilaratingly, faster.

'Oh yeah, now we go,' says Stapleton. Shadowing Stapleton's team, though, are five Team Sky riders, packed equally tightly together. And shadowing is the word: in their dark colours they look sinister, menacing.

On the next lap HTC still lead, Sky still follow. But the next time, with two to go, the speed has gone up again, and the HTC 'train' of riders has been displaced from the front: now it's Sky who pack the first six places, riding in close formation, with Greg Henderson, their designated sprinter, the sixth man. 'That's all part of the plan,' says Stapleton with a chuckle.

True enough: HTC surge again, swamping Sky. And in previous seasons that would have been it: game over. But Mat Hayman leads his men around HTC and back to the front; then he leads the peloton in a long, narrow line for a full lap. Once Hayman has swung off, HTC draw breath and go again, but Sky have the momentum now, and they're able to strike back. On the final lap, the two teams' trains are virtually head to head – they resemble two rowing crews, as separate and self-contained entities – until the final corner, when HTC's sprinter, André Greipel, commits a fatal error: he allows a tiny gap to open between his front wheel and the rear wheel of his final lead-out man, Matt Goss. It is a momentary lapse in concentration, or loss of bottle by the German, but the margins are tiny at this stage of the race, and there isn't time for Greipel to recover. Henderson has been sitting at the back of the Sky 'train', watching his handlebar-mounted computer read 73kph ('I thought, "Holy shit! I've never been in such a fast lead-out train"'), and now, as they enter the finishing straight, Henderson's lead-out man, Chris Sutton, dives into the gap created by Greipel's hesitation. And as Goss begins to sprint, Sutton and Henderson strike.

On the final lap Brailsford and Sutton leapt from the bonnet of the car as though the engine had been turned on. They sprinted to the first corner, where a big screen had been set up, and they watched as Henderson and Sutton sprinted for all they were worth up the finishing straight, passing Goss, and both having time, just before the line, to look round and sit up, their hands in the air, to celebrate a fairly astonishing one-two.

Brailsford and Sutton punch the air and embrace each other, before Brailsford disappears into a huddle of journalists. But Stapleton appears and stretches over to shake hands. 'You guys can see,' says Stapleton, 'I was the first to congratulate him. Congratulations, Dave, that was terrific.'

Even the languid, laidback Sean Yates is overjoyed. He high-fives the riders as they return to the car. 'I think other teams will look at that and think, they've just rocked up, put six guys in a line, they looked fucking mean, and they won the race,' says Yates.

'Textbook,' says Sutton. 'But I've never seen Dave so stressed. With a lap to go I gave him my stress ball. He was pumping it like nobody's business. Look, I'm here because Dave wanted me to fly over and be here. We shook hands at the start of this race, and said this is the start of the journey, but this is about other people's expertise. They've done the hard yards. But being part of this,' adds Sutton as he turns to embrace his nephew, the second-placed Chris, 'is absolutely fantastic.'

Brailsford and Sutton also know the value of a good start to any campaign. They think back to Beijing, to day two of the Olympics, when Nicole Cooke won a gold medal in the women's road race. It was a performance that galvanised the track team, inspired them and injected momentum, before they themselves went out and won seven gold medals. But what is most encouraging about the one-two in Rymill Park – for all that it is *only* a criterium; for all that it is only the *hors d'œuvre* to the Tour Down Under – is that it involved the execution of a plan; and that, in taking on HTC-Columbia in setting up a bunch sprint, they had beaten the world's best exponents of this particular art.

It was encouraging. But Brailsford was more than encouraged; he was buzzing. Already aware that there had been some sniping, and lots of scepticism over his stated plans and ambitions, not least his intention to do things *differently*, he now hits back: 'Some people seem to think we ride round in circles [in velodromes] and don't know what we're doing, but we know what lead-outs are, and we know what sprinting is about from the track.

'Some people are saying this team's all about marketing, flash and razzmatazz, and all the rest of it,' he continues. 'But we'd talked that finish through. That's what we do. The race was predictable. Not the win, but the pattern the race would follow – a break going, and being brought back at the end. We knew what was going to happen, and that it'd come down to the last couple of laps. So you plan for that. You have to have a plan.'

And nobody could argue: day one had gone to plan.

CHAPTER 1

CRITICAL MASS

'I thought, bloody hell, what are you supposed to do? Sit up? …
This is the Tour de France – you don't sit up.'

Bradley Wiggins

Bourg-en-Bresse, 13 July 2007
It had been a typical flat, early stage of the Tour de France.
Typical, that is, unless you happened to be British.

Stage six, 199.5km from Semur-en-Auxois to Bourg-en-
Bresse, rolled through flat but beautiful Burgundy country-
side, past golden fields, sprawling stone farms and proud
châteaux. But amid the usual flurry of attacks in the early kilometres, from riders eager to feature in the day's break, one
man went clear on his own.

He was up near the front of the peloton, ideally positioned for the waves of attacks. He followed one of those
accelerations, then looked around to see that he had four
riders for company, with daylight between them and the
peloton. A gap! Perfect. And so he put his head down, tucking into a more aerodynamic position, and pressed hard on
the pedals, making the kind of effort that had propelled him
to his Olympic and world pursuit titles. When he turned
around again he saw that he was alone. He wasn't sure what
had happened, whether his companions had been dropped

or given up. And he wasn't sure what to do. So he kept going.

Bradley Wiggins, riding for the French Cofidis squad, carried on riding alone, elbows bent, beak-shaped nose cutting through the wind, long, lean legs slicing up and down to a relentless beat, for kilometre after kilometre after kilometre. While the peloton ambled along behind him, content to let the solitary rider up front flog himself, the Englishman built a lead that stretched to an enormous 16 minutes. At that point there was around 9km, or 6 miles, between him and the others. It was an unusual way to do it. And it was probably doomed to failure. But Bradley Wiggins was finally making his mark on the Tour de France.

The previous year, when the then 26-year-old Wiggins had finally ridden his first Tour, he was one of only two British riders in the race, the other being David Millar, returning from a two-year suspension for doping. Wiggins seemed like a square peg in a round hole. He was the Olympic pursuit champion, a track superstar and a road nobody. For five seasons, since turning professional with the Française des Jeux team as a raw 21-year-old in 2002, Wiggins had drifted around some of the most established, most traditional teams in the peloton – from FDJ to Crédit Agricole – before moving on to a third French outfit, Cofidis, in 2006.

To observers, road racing seemed more like a hobby than a profession. It was what Wiggins did when he wasn't preparing for a world championship or Olympic Games. He was fortunate to be in teams that indulged him in his track obsession; or perhaps they just didn't care, and could afford to write off his salary – starting at £25,000, rising to £80,000 – or regard it as a small investment in the British market. Although any interest his teams' sponsors – the French national lottery, a French bank and a French loans company – had in the British market must have been, at best, negligible.

Most mornings during his first Tour, Wiggins would leave the sanctuary of his team bus. He would swing his leg over his bike and weave through the crowds to the signing-on stage. Then he would head for the Village Départ, where entry is restricted to guests, VIPs, accredited media and riders – though in the era of luxury team buses, few riders deigned to appear. Wiggins was different. He liked to read the British newspapers and drink coffee with British journalists in the Crédit Lyonnais press tent.

About halfway through his debut Tour, as he waited one morning in the Village Départ for his wife, Cath, who was over to visit, Wiggins was asked how he was finding the race. 'Um, I think I can win this thing,' he said. He missed a beat before cracking a wry, self-deprecating smile. The idea was ridiculous. It confirmed his image – and indeed his self-image – as an outsider.

Not that he was a disinterested outsider. Wiggins' knowledge of the Tour de France, his respect for it, and his awe of its champions, was obvious; he just didn't seem to understand what he, Bradley Wiggins, was doing there, or what, if anything, he could bring to the party. Rather, he resembled an English club cyclist parachuted into the biggest race in the world; he seemed oblivious to, or in denial of, his talent.

On another occasion Wiggins sat drinking coffee and reading the papers a little too long. One of his Cofidis directors came hurrying over, shouting: 'Brad! Allez!' The race had left without him. Amid scattered newspapers and upturned cups of coffee, Wiggins shot up, grabbed his bike, pedalled hastily across the grass and bumped on to the road just in time to join the tail end of the vast, snaking convoy of vehicles that follows the race, working his way through that and finally into the peloton to survive another day. After three weeks he finished 123rd in Paris. But to the extent that any rider who finishes the Tour can do, he left no discernible trace.

In 2007, his second Tour is proving a little different. He finishes fourth in the prologue time trial, and, with his great escape on stage six to Bourg-en-Bresse, Wiggins is at least getting himself noticed. For five hours he hogs the TV pictures, which depict him toiling for mile after solitary mile. The landscape flashes past, but it is as though Wiggins, in his post box red Cofidis kit, is part of it. Several observers remark on his style, his smoothness, his élan. *'Il est fort,'* they say, *'un bon rouleur.'*

Halfway through the stage Wiggins' lead over the peloton is down to 8 minutes, 17 seconds, still a considerable margin. He continues to look strong; the effort effortless. And among some of the journalists gathered around monitors in the press room a theory emerges as to the motivation for his lone attack. The clue is in the date: 13 July. It's 40 years to the day since Britain's only world road race champion, Tom Simpson, collapsed and died on Mont Ventoux, while riding the 1967 Tour. Wiggins is a patriot with a keen sense of cycling history; the type who could tell you not only the date of Simpson's death, but what shoes he was wearing.

So that explains it: Wiggo's doing it for Tom.

Approaching Bourg-en-Bresse, it even seems that he may defy the odds – and the sprinters' teams, now pulling at the front of the peloton as they pursue their quarry – and hang on to win. But as he rides into the final 20km – stopping briefly to replace a broken wheel, throwing the offending item into the ditch as his team car screeches to a halt behind him – and Wiggins hits a long, straight expanse of road, the wind picks up. It blows directly into his face, and presents a serious handicap. The peloton can always move significantly faster than a small group or single rider; but especially into a headwind.

As Wiggins passes under the 10km to go banner, his lead having disintegrated, he is a dead man pedalling. The peloton leaves him dangling out front before casually swallowing him up with 6km to go. One of the helicopter TV cameras lingers on Wiggins as riders stream past and he drops through the bunch, and straight out the back.

Tom Boonen of Belgium wins the bunch sprint and is swamped by reporters and TV crews as he slows to a halt beyond the finish line. Other riders attract their own mini-scrums. Finally, after a long 3 minutes, 42 seconds, Wiggins appears – the 183rd and last man to cross the line. As he comes to a weary halt and wipes his salt-caked face with the back of his mitt he also attracts a mini-scrum.

So was it for Simpson? 'Sorry?' replies Wiggins. Today is the anniversary of Simpson's death, he is told.

'Nah, nah. I didn't realise,' he shrugs. 'But it is my wife, Cath's, birthday. She'll be watching on TV at home with the kids. I suppose it was the closest I could get to spending the day with her.'

To the journalists' disappointment, he admits that it wasn't planned. 'There were five of us in a little move at the start, I pulled a big turn, looked round and saw I was on my own. You don't choose to end up on your own like that, it just happens. I thought, bloody hell, what are you supposed to do? Sit up? … This is the Tour de France – you don't sit up. So I thought I'd continue. When I got a minute I thought there'd be a coun- terattack and some bodies would come across to me, but that never happened. So I just kept going.

'When I got 10, 15 minutes, I thought maybe it could happen and I could win the stage. Even at 15km to go I thought it might happen, but it was that bloody headwind towards the finish. I was still doing 45kph, but I knew they'd be doing 52 or 53. At 10km I knew really that I had no chance with that headwind.'

Still, it was a day on which Wiggins could look back with pride. And he'd earned himself a first-ever trip to the podium, the steps of which drained the last ounces of energy from his legs, to receive *le prix de la combativité* – the day's award for most aggressive rider.

Two places in front of Wiggins, having also been dropped by the main pack as the speed picked up towards the finish, another British rider had gone past as we waited for Wiggins. He was young, it was his debut Tour, but grave disappointment was etched on his face in the form of an angry scowl. It was Mark Cavendish, and his much-anticipated debut in the biggest race in the world was one of the main reasons for the appearance in Bourg-en-Bresse of Dave Brailsford, the British Cycling performance director.

An hour later, with the dust settling on the stage and the finish area being noisily dismantled by members of the Tour's vast travelling army of workers, Brailsford sits in a bar and reviews the day. While his companions drink beer, he orders mineral water. 'I'm in training,' he explains. 'I'm riding l'Etape du Tour [a stage of the Tour, the popular mass participation ride] with Shane.'

Until now, Brailsford, though he has become a familiar figure at track cycling events, has not been a regular visitor to the Tour de France. But there's a good reason for that: it falls outside his remit. Three years earlier he had inherited the track-focused programme, known as the World Class Performance Plan, devised by his predecessor, Peter Keen. As Brailsford sits down in Bourg-en-Bresse he can reflect that Keen's World Class Performance Plan is exactly a decade old; what he cannot see, other than in his wildest dreams, is that in 13 months it will come to glorious fruition at the Beijing Olympics.

Something else is afoot here in Bourg-en-Bresse, however, and it has nothing to do with Beijing, and it has nothing to do with track cycling. Brailsford, even as he basks in the afterglow of his team's domination of the recent World Track Cycling Championships in Palma, and plots the 13 months to Beijing with the kind of supreme confidence that can only come from such domination, appears to be looking beyond all that, to some distant, imagined horizon. You can see it in his piercing blue eyes; they blaze with enthusiasm and sparkle with the excitement of a child catching a first, thrilling glimpse of … well, of the Tour de France.

As he outlines his dream, his enthusiasm intensifies; in fact, the plan seems to be progressing rapidly and taking shape in his imagination right here, under the large canopy of a tree, just outside a bar in Bourg-en-Bresse.

There have been several catalysts, says Brailsford, which all add up to 'a critical mass', or a tipping point. 'That was a good effort from Brad today,' he says. 'Good to see him having a go.' But Wiggins' big day out had been the icing on the cake – or the cherry on the icing on the cake. A few days earlier, Brailsford and a million or so others had been in London for the Tour's first-ever Grand Départ on British soil. The Tour had got underway with a prologue time trial around the British capital, passing the Houses of Parliament, Buckingham Palace and Hyde Park, before, the next day, a road race stage took them to Canterbury along roads lined the entire way with spectators. It had been extraordinary – a weekend in which you'd have been forgiven for thinking that London was cycling's spiritual home – and which prompted Christian Prudhomme, the Tour director, to eulogise London and Britain in a way that no Frenchman had done since Napoleon III. 'I do not know when we will come back,' said Prudhomme. 'But one thing is certain: it is not possible for us not to return.'

Yet Brailsford feels that something even more significant than the London Grand Départ is brewing. Five British riders are riding – the biggest British participation since the last British team to ride the Tour, the ill-fated ANC-Halfords squad, took part in 1987. And among those five riders are two highly promising youngsters, Mark Cavendish and Geraint Thomas.

This has got Brailsford thinking. Twelve months after watching the then 19-year-old Cavendish win a gold medal at the World Track Championships in Los Angeles, Brailsford and Sutton found themselves at the Commonwealth Games in Melbourne. It being the Commonwealth Games, at which riders compete for the home nations rather than for Great Britain, Brailsford and Sutton were not as occupied, or under as much pressure, as they'd usually be during a major championship. They spent a fair amount of time sitting together in the stands, watching Cavendish win another gold medal on the track, this time for the Isle of Man, and they discussed the future. They cast their minds back to the Manchester Commonwealth Games in 2002, and forward to the Delhi Games in 2010. In between, of course, were the Olympics. But a sense of repetition, of being locked into a cycle of major games, was evident. Because that is the limitation of track cycling: it's all about the major games and world championships; there is no velodrome-staged equivalent of the Tour de France or Giro d'Italia, or Tour of Flanders or Paris-Roubaix. These road races are the monuments of the sport; where the history, the prestige and the money is. 'We were thinking,' Sutton said later, 'that we can't keep doing this forever. We've got to do something different.'

The conversation went no further. But 10 months later, back in Los Angeles for a track world cup meeting, Brailsford and Sutton once again found themselves with time to kill, and again they began to project beyond Beijing. Ironically, this owed to a stroke of misfortune for one of the latest of the talented young British riders to emerge, Ben Swift. Swift had been due to ride the madison with Rob Hayles, but he crashed and broke his collarbone. 'Shane and I had a lot of time on our own and a lot of time to chat,' Brailsford said, 'and we inevitably got to talking about future plans.'

And so to Bourg-en-Bresse, and the bar in which Brailsford is sipping water as the late afternoon turns to evening. What is always most striking about Brailsford is his enthusiasm; his shoulders hunch, and he cups his hands in front of his face, almost like the rugby player Jonny Wilkinson preparing for a goalkick; then he moulds those hands into constantly shifting shapes as he talks. 'I was inspired by London,' says Brailsford, 'but this is something I've been thinking about for a long time, and I feel that the time's coming for a British pro team.'

'Here,' he clarifies. 'In the Tour de France. From a personal point of view, if someone asked me what I wanted to do next, that would be it. We had a gut feel that Cav [Cavendish] and Geraint would come through at this level, but thinking it and seeing it are two different things. When I saw Geraint leave the start house for the prologue in London it was that moment of realising that it's not just something we're thinking about. I see Cav and Geraint now and think: it's on.'

Brailsford outlines how such a team could work, in particular with regard to funding. Because what he's talking about would need serious backing, with a sponsor able and willing to pump millions into the project. 'The type of partner we'd be looking for would be British. It would be a British initiative. We'd be all about innovation and about doing it clean. In the first instance it would be about being competitive: that'd be our aim. But ultimately you'd want to win. You wouldn't run a pro team if you didn't want to win. It wouldn't fit our mentality not to aim to win.

'The money? It's difficult to be clinical about it, but there's a huge amount of money floating around the City, and a very small circle of people managing a huge amount of money. If you're in that circle … it's not finding money that's the obstacle. I don't think so. I mean, all the teams here are investing between £3m and £8m a year. It's a shed load of money, and they're all committed for four years, but if there weren't decent returns on that, they wouldn't be doing it, would they?'

But how would Brailsford do it? Would he combine running a Tour de France team with his current job, as British Cycling's performance director? 'It'd have to be done as a private enterprise – or as part of the governing body, which would be a first,' he says. 'No other governing bodies run a pro team. But not many countries have the kind of funding structure for elite sport that Britain has.'

One of the reasons for Brailsford being here at the Tour, he explains – and apart from riding l'Etape du Tour in a few days' time – is to negotiate some of the British riders' contracts. He is almost, it seems, acting as their agent, which is curious. But this too has highlighted a problem – or an opportunity. The problem is that the riders are contracted to, and under the control of, teams that operate independently of British Cycling, and with fundamentally different – even opposed – priorities. They are not, for example, remotely interested in the Olympics. Which is a problem for Brailsford, and a frustration. The riders in question, with Cavendish and Thomas to the fore, have been nurtured and developed by British Cycling. Brailsford wants to bring them back under an umbrella that he is holding.

'The lads here know I want to do this [set up a pro team] and they're all absolutely mad for the idea,' says Brailsford. 'I'm here negotiating their contracts for them; so I know what's in their contracts. And I know – or I'm learning – how the teams are structured and how they operate.

'We've got a set philosophy about doing things at British Cycling,' he continues, 'with the riders at the centre. But look at a lot of teams here at the Tour – that's not how they operate.

Between races they don't even see their riders. They don't know where they are, never mind what they're doing. It's bonkers.'

It is also, thinks Brailsford, one reason why a doping culture is so prevalent in professional road cycling; the theory being that expectation/pressure coupled with absence of care/responsibility equals ideal conditions for such a culture to develop. He'd do it differently, he says. 'If we did anything it'd be 100% clean. We've got this young generation coming through, riders who don't want to cheat. And there's wider enthusiasm; untapped potential. We saw it in London and on the road to Canterbury; the crowds, screaming by the roadside … despite all the doom and gloom and the negativity around the doping stories.'

And what about the older guard – Wiggins and the reformed doper David Millar? Would they be involved? 'You'd like to think it'd be possible to do this before they've retired,' says Brailsford. 'I want to bring together lots of different elements in cycling in Britain. Instead of factions, let's get behind this thing and see what we can do.

'It's dependent on these riders progressing and coming through,' he adds. 'We're not going to do it until the riders are good enough to do it; until we have the critical mass of British talent we can't do it. It's unlikely you're going to get 25 British riders, but you need the critical mass; we wouldn't do it with an international team. But knowing what I do of the young lads coming through, there's plenty of talent. That's not the issue.

'And with Cav, we've got a winner. He's your goalscorer.'

Brailsford mentioned doping, and doing it clean. The British track team had proved it could be done: there was no mud sticking to them, yet they were winning left, right and centre.

But it was quite different to the road; track cycling didn't have the ingrained doping culture of road cycling, which was precisely why Brailsford's predecessor, Peter Keen, had decided, back in 1997, to ignore the road.

Blond-haired and boyish, and blessed with infectious enthusiasm, Keen, when he was appointed performance director, was acclaimed as a visionary. He was the sports scientist who had coached Chris Boardman to an Olympic gold medal – the first by a British cyclist in 84 years – in Barcelona in 1992, and subsequently helped Boardman with the difficult transition from track to road racing, going from his Olympic and world pursuit titles, and world hour record, to winning the prologue time trial and wearing the yellow jersey at the Tour de France.

But in 1997 Keen accepted an even bigger challenge: to turn round the fortunes of the British Cycling team. For the first time, the sport had money, thanks to lottery funding. Keen was given an annual budget of £2.5m and charged with drawing up a plan that could transform Britain's cyclists from mediocrity to … well, just about anything would be an improvement on performances that, with the odd exception (Boardman, Graeme Obree, Yvonne McGregor), ensured Britain occupied the lower tiers of world cycling.

Keen's proposals, to focus the country's efforts, and funding, exclusively on track cycling, were radical and controversial. But he had thought about it long and hard, and he felt that he had little choice; that to try and produce a road team that could compete with the best in the world would be pointless. 'My view at the time,' Keen told me in 2007, 'was that men's professional road cycling was almost completely dominated by an underlying drugs culture. And … in the context of the programme I was charged with creating, having a drugs system, or even a tolerance of a drugs system, was just not an option.

'The idea that you could *plan* for men's road racing success at world level ... to me it couldn't be done,' continued Keen, for whom planning is like breathing. 'It seemed to me that the furthest we could go with road racing for men was to create a development programme where we could take promising young riders to that line in the sand – of what I'd call performance credibility – and then say, "If that is the world you want, as far as we understand it, then off you go and good luck."'

As he spoke, Keen measured his words carefully, but the implications and subtext to what he was saying were as devastating as they were damning. That phrase, 'performance credibility', had particular resonance, not least because of Keen's intimate knowledge of the sport. He was speaking not as an outsider, but as someone whose protégé, Boardman, was now part of the world he was describing. Although Boardman had showed flashes of brilliance in road races, the highlight perhaps being his second place – to five-time Tour de France winner Miguel Indurain – at the 1995 Dauphiné Libéré, his potential on the road appeared to be limited. By what? His limitations over the longer distances, or the three-week duration of the Tour de France? Or his refusal to take drugs? Keen wouldn't say explicitly. But he might have said that Boardman's performances fell within the realms of 'performance credibility', and left it at that.

Nevertheless, for many, Keen's track-focused plan was tantamount to treason. Ignore road cycling? Pretend the Tour de France doesn't exist? He was trampling on the dreams of all those – the overwhelming majority of cycling fans – who are drawn to the sport by the glamour and excitement of the greatest race in the world.

Keen argued that he had no choice; he was under pressure to produce a return on the new funding under the terms dictated by the distributors of lottery cash. UK Sport was the agency charged with sharing out the money among all the governing bodies, but the cash came with conditions attached and targets to be reached. For UK Sport, the challenge was this: how to set comparable targets across all sports. The answer was to focus on world championships and Olympics. Sports would be assessed and evaluated purely on their performances in these events. Olympic and world medals would effectively write lottery cheques. Conversely, no medals would see funding reduced.

In cycling, the maths was simple. At the Olympics there were 12 gold medals available on the track, just four on the road (and two in mountain biking); and it was the same at the world championships. Keen concluded that a British rider could win the Tour de France or the Paris-Roubaix Classic and become a household name in mainland Europe, but it would count for nothing as far as UK Sport was concerned. So he had no choice: the bulk of the money had to be directed towards the track.

But Keen went further than that. As he settled into his office in the Manchester Velodrome in 1997 – having first visited a used furniture shop to buy a desk and chair – he pored over files describing road races all across Europe to which British teams were invited every year. And every year they went, invariably to be soundly thrashed by their continental rivals, blowing holes in the budget with no tangible return. As far as Keen was concerned it was madness. Even worse, it was pointless. So he took a more radical step than merely cutting funding for a men's senior road squad: he took his axe to it. In the British cycling revolution, at least in its first phase, it was not – to paraphrase Lance Armstrong – all about the bike. It was all about the track.

*   *   *

Ten years later, even as Brailsford, who took over from Peter Keen in 2004, spoke in Bourg-en-Bresse with such breezy optimism of running a clean team and entering the Tour de France, the omens seemed less than encouraging.

In fact, Keen's prescience had proved remarkable, and his decision not to fund a road programme eminently sensible. A year after he drew up his World Class Performance Plan, with its track focus, a major doping scandal erupted at the 1998 Tour de France. It blew the lid on the scale of organised, endemic doping at the highest level of professional road cycling. The so-called 'Festina affair' – involving the world's number one team – proved to be merely the start, however. It was followed, over the following years, by a drip-drip-drip of doping allegations, revelations and scandals.

Drip-drip-drip they went, like an irritating leak that isn't quite bothersome enough to actually fix. Finally, in 2006, came the next deluge: an international blood doping ring uncovered by a Spanish investigation, which removed the favourites, Ivan Basso and Jan Ullrich, on the eve of the Tour de France. This, coupled with a positive test for the eventual winner of that year's Tour, Floyd Landis, seemed, finally, like it could be the tipping point, and the catalyst for change. If the first step to changing is to admit you have a problem, then such a step appeared to be taken towards the end of 2006, cycling's *annus horribilis*, when the sport's world governing body, the UCI, commissioned an independent audit to discover the extent of the doping problem: a small step, but a significant one for an organisation that stood accused of burying its head in the sand, or, worse, being complicit in the problem. Meanwhile, and under pressure from the World Anti-Doping Agency (founded in response to the Festina affair), the number of anti-doping tests were stepped up; and the first steps were taken by the UCI to establish 'biological passports' for riders. When these were finally introduced, for the 2008 season, they were hailed as being at the vanguard of anti-doping.

But in Bourg-en-Bresse, as Brailsford spoke about lifting the 'doom and gloom and negativity around the doping stories', his optimism was to prove premature. The 2007 Tour was hit by a series of catastrophic scandals, from the yellow jersey Michael Rasmussen's series of missed drugs tests before the race had started, to double stage-winner Alexandre Vinokourov's positive test for an illegal blood transfusion.

'La mort du Tour,' read the front page headline of the French newspaper *Libération*, in thick black letters, above the ghostly silhouette of a racing cyclist, as the Tour stumbled towards the finish in an ever-thickening fog of drugs-related scandals. *France Soir* even devoted its entire front page to an official-looking 'death notice', announcing the passing of the Tour de France on 25 July 2007, in Orthez, 'at the age of 104 years, as a result of a long illness'. The paper stated that 'the funeral will be held in a strictly private circle'.

Wiggins, who had consistently spoken out against doping – and, indeed, offered this as one reason why he had continued to focus his efforts on the track rather than the road – even found himself indirectly implicated when a Cofidis teammate, Cristian Moreni, tested positive for testosterone in the final week. Moreni was arrested at the summit of the Col d'Aubisque, the gendarmes having waited for him as he finished the 228km stage before carting him off in his cycling kit, while the rest of the Cofidis team, including Wiggins, were given a police escort off the mountain.

Speaking an hour later from a police station, Wiggins admitted he had found the situation 'scary': 'I don't want to be caught up in this in any way. It makes you think about your future as a professional. What is the point? I could be doing better things than pissing about like this. But then you think, why shouldn't I continue doing something I get a lot of pleasure out of?'

Not that Wiggins had a choice about continuing in the 2007 Tour, with the organisers requesting their withdrawal and Cofidis obliging. Wiggins was disgusted with Moreni, with his team and with the Tour. He couldn't bear to wear his Cofidis leisurewear to Pau airport, so he borrowed a T-shirt belonging to David Millar (ironically, Millar's team, Saunier Duval, later lost a rider, Iban Mayo, to a positive test). Wiggins stuffed his Cofidis clothing in a bin at the airport and never competed for the French team again.

By this point, Mark Cavendish had been withdrawn by his T-Mobile team, who were keen not to overburden their hot young prospect, but Geraint Thomas was still riding, and riding strongly. The youngest rider in the race made it to Paris, in 139th place. He was second from last, but he appeared to have something to spare, and he cut a relaxed figure in the mornings before stage-starts, apparently unfazed by what was going on around him, his mood consistent and his understated humour intact. David Millar compared him to 'one of the penguins in *Madagascar*.' He meant the animated film, 'where the penguins appear all cute and cuddly, but that disguises a core of steel and a real malevolent streak.' The highlight of Thomas' Tour had been an early stage into Montpellier, when the Welshman led the peloton at high speed in the closing kilometres, helping to set up his South African teammate, Robbie Hunter, for the sprint victory. It underlined his ability, his class.

The potential of Thomas and Cavendish, strongly hinted at during their debut season in the professional ranks in 2007, gave Brailsford grounds for optimism and acted as a counterweight to the 'doom and gloom' that, to so many other fans and observers of professional cycling, seemed so pervasive. But with the sport at such a low ebb – reaching its lowest point, perhaps, in December 2007, when the German communications giant T-Mobile withdrew their backing of Cavendish's team – Brailsford might have argued that the time was right to get involved. It could be called the logic of the property market: buy when the prices are low.

Nine months after Bourg-en-Bresse, Brailsford's search for a backer for his plans to set up a professional road team began in earnest. The road team would be phase three of the British cycling revolution (phase two had produced Thomas and Cavendish, and will be discussed in the next chapter). It seemed a big ask: Brailsford was looking for a British sponsor prepared to fork out around £10m a year. 'Dave had been in negotiations with British Cycling over his contract,' says Shane Sutton, 'and bringing in a pro team was part of his re-negotiations, so after the Manchester World Track Championships [in March 2008] Dave said to me: "You run the Olympic [track] team, and I'll go out and source some money." Dave was in meeting after meeting in London; sometimes I went, too. It was good; it gave us a feel for what we wanted.'

One of those meetings was with executives from British Sky Broadcasting. 'With Sky,' says Sutton, 'it wasn't a case of us selling it to them. I think it was more that they looked at what we were doing, and thought: we need to get hold of these guys who are running cycling.' In fact, the meeting with Sky was driven by Sky, who – according to one insider – 'came to us and had a really clear vision of what they wanted to do and how they were going to achieve it.' Jeremy Darroch, the BSkyB chief executive, told *Management Today* magazine in March 2010 that he'd been actively seeking a sport to back, which was 'very much open to all, where it didn't matter if you were a man or a woman, whether you were young or old. I'd heard about what Dave was doing and I was impressed.'

But as much as Brailsford and Sutton, it was Thomas and Cavendish – especially Cavendish, the 'goalscorer' – who seemed to hint at a future in which, as well as on the track, British cyclists also won on the road, maybe even at the Tour de France. Thomas and Cavendish, and others like them, were the rays of sunlight penetrating the gloom. They were the riders who, unlike Bradley Wiggins and the other talented British riders who had never seemed to quite fulfil their potential on the road, could put Britain on the map of continental road cycling.

'We're very confident we've got a conveyor belt of young talent working now,' said Brailsford in Bourg-en-Bresse. 'We always thought that's what would happen, and I think we're seeing it now.'

This 'conveyor belt of talent' was also known as the British Cycling Academy.

CHAPTER 2

THE ACADEMY

'I didn't want them sitting on their fat backsides with a PlayStation or drinking coffee, because this is a job.'

Rod Ellingworth

Quarrata, Italy, April 2010

Hidden away on a street that lies off the main road in the tiny Tuscan town of Quarrata sits what looks like a family home, indistinguishable from all the other family homes that surround it. Apart from one thing. In the drive, semi-hidden from the street and running down the side of the two-storey building, sit two vehicles: a silver estate car and a van, both decorated in swirling red, white and blue, and the words, 'Great Britain Cycling Team'.

Entering the house via the drive and through a side door, you come into a large workshop. A row of Pinarello bikes hang by their front wheels from hooks on the wall, and a mechanic breaks off from working on a time trial machine that appears to be suspended in mid-air – actually it's fitted to a bike stand – to point silently to an adjoining door. This leads into a living room dominated by an enormous flat-screen TV showing MTV, with the sound muted. And in the corner is a desk, behind which, with his back to us, sits Max Sciandri, in a scruffy navy sweatshirt and jeans, tapping into a Mac laptop, a huge and messy-looking year planner on the wall above.

The Anglo-Italian – born in Derby, raised in Tuscany – is coach to the British Cycling Academy, based in this house in Quarrata. Sciandri also lives in Quarrata, in a much larger house on the outskirts of the town. 'It's a great house,' says the retired professional – of his own sprawling place, not this more modest one. 'Lance [Armstrong] came with Sheryl Crow,' says Sciandri, quickly overcoming any reluctance to name-check one of his former teammates. 'Sheryl loved my house. And she must have seen some houses …'

Today, Sciandri has sent the five Academy riders on a two-hour recovery ride. He conducts a tour of the house. 'I'll show you some rooms, hopefully they're clean.' But after climbing the stairs, and before we come to the shared bedrooms, we are confronted by a mural. 'Swifty [Ben Swift] started the wall,' says Sciandri as we pause in awed admiration before it.

'The wall' is the extraordinary legacy of the riders who have now been through the British Cycling Academy; a collage of cycling photographs cut from magazines. It contains hundreds, possibly thousands, of images, mainly featuring the stars of the current peloton, though with some old-timers in there – even, if you look hard, Sciandri himself. 'Yeah,' he laughs dismissively. 'But they're too young to remember my career. I don't talk about it.'

Sciandri, in his strong Italian accent (which has more to do with the cadence of his speech than his pronunciation), explains how the Quarrata base came about. 'I called Dave [Brailsford] at the end of 2005 and I said, "Dave …"' Then he stops himself. 'You could see that British Cycling had so much potential,' he tells me. 'It was just bursting, waiting to grow. It's like a tree – you can't put it in a pot. It was bursting out of its pot; it didn't have anywhere to go. It needs to go on a hill, you know? So I said to Dave, "Let's do something in Italy." I wasn't ready to be a team director. Cycling had been my life, I'd done my years and I needed to step back, but I knew I wanted to be involved somehow.

'Rod [Ellingworth] was appointed as the coach to the Academy, so I stepped back a bit. But I helped them set up here in Quarrata; I helped them get into races, because it's not that easy in Italy – you need to have been around a bit; you need to know the right people, you know?'

While Sciandri is talking he is interrupted by a clip-clop-ping sound. The riders have returned and are walking across the hard floor of the workshop in their cleated cycling shoes. 'Luke, Tim … Chris, Erick, Andy,' says Sciandri as they file in with their GB cycling kit, peeling gloves from freezing hands and, at Sciandri's prompting, extending them to shake.

'We got caught in a bit of snow and turned around,' one of them tells Sciandri.

'Turned round straight away,' says another.

They disappear to the shower area (in one of the many modifications to the house, there are five shower cubicles in a large wash area). But 15 minutes later we are interrupted again, this time by the sound of a gun being fired: a computer game is in progress. It means that Sciandri has to raise his voice to be heard above the sounds of gunfire and violence.

'You don't know who's going to make it when they come here,' Sciandri is saying above the din, 'but everyone gives you something right away, you know? Cycling's hard, and a lot of these boys are really young, and they change a lot physically.' Almost paternally, he adds: 'You see them when they get here; they're little kids, their legs are not formed yet, and then they start doing four to five hour rides, stage races of eight days, and they change. They grow up.'

* * *

The following advert appeared in late 2003:

> 'Wanted: ambitious Under-23 male endurance cyclists to join
> residential Olympic Academy. The Academy will be full time and
> based in Manchester. Academy members will have the opportunity
> to be selected for [track] World Cups, six-day and other
> international track competitions. To survive and/or progress young
> riders will need to live and breathe cycling and devote their next
> years to the achievement of challenging goals. Strong work ethic
> required. Apply to British Cycling, The Velodrome, Manchester.'

The man charged with setting up the new Olympic Academy
was a former professional rider, Rod Ellingworth. Ellingworth
had raced for an amateur club in France, but his dreams of
turning professional with a continental team didn't material-
ise. He returned to the UK and joined a domestic team, sponsored by Ambrosia creamed rice. But after retiring, in 2002, he
seemed to discover his true vocation, embarking on a career as
a coach with one of British Cycling's satellite talent schemes
for young riders. In March 2002 he was appointed coach to the
south-east of England Talent Team.

The next winter, 2002–03, Ellingworth organised a weekend
event for the talent teams – representing Scotland, Wales, two
from the north of England, the Midlands and two from the
South of England – at the Manchester Velodrome. 'I called it
coach-led racing,' explains Ellingworth. 'I asked each of the
talent teams to send their best two riders; I also had the
national junior squad there, and the Under-23 team. So we
had the entire development group in the one room. And we
did three days of bike racing: a big warm-up session then
scratch, points and madison racing on the track. But for each
race I'd give them specific jobs to do; different jobs. I'd tell 'em:
"Your job is to rip this bike race up." "Your job is to control the
bike race." "Your job is to wait for a sprint finish."

'We filmed every race,' adds Ellingworth. 'Then they watched it on a cinema screen – that was good. But for each race I'd be trackside, controlling the bike race. That's what I mean by coach-led.'

Ellingworth's approach caught the eye of Peter Keen and Dave Brailsford, who by then were working on a plan to establish a school, or academy, to spot and nurture talent at a younger age. (Or potential: 'We look for potential, not talent,' as one of the British Cycling coaches told me.) It was a project that would move the British cycling revolution into its second phase, creating a conveyor belt of young talent to feed into the senior teams. Although it was set up to accommodate Under-23 riders, it was decided that it should be pitched at riders who'd recently turned senior, the 18–20-year-olds; an age at which riders are especially vulnerable to giving up, lured by competing attractions such as alcohol and the opposite sex.

John Herety, a former professional road cyclist who had acted as Britain's road manager since 1997, approved of Ellingworth's appointment. 'Rod was someone I knew very well from when he raced,' says Herety. 'He perhaps didn't have the engine to make it at the very highest level, but he knew how to race, and he was one of these riders who maximised what he had. He was extremely knowledgeable about racing, on track and road. He was very strong on tactics. And he had a very strong work ethic.'

'When Rod was asked to set up this new Under-23 Olympic Academy, he asked for ideas, but that was typical Rod: he was constantly asking questions,' continues Herety. 'He had clear ideas himself about how the Academy should be run; he was of the opinion that we needed total control over the riders. He looked at the Australian model and decided the only way to do it was to get hold of them very young, then break down all the component parts of being a professional, and try to equip them with the necessary skills. He was very, very hands on. Almost 24/7; it was extreme, certainly compared to what we'd been used to. I couldn't have done it like that. But he had a plan, a vision. He knew where he wanted the Academy riders to be in a year's time.'

The vision for the Academy was that it would be a talent school – a hothouse – for male track endurance riders. The fact that it was prefixed by 'Olympic' underlined where its priorities lay. However, even if the official focus was on track racing, the Academy had the potential – as Herety and indeed Ellingworth well knew – to produce talented road riders. Herety even goes as far as to suggest that this was its main, though not explicit, objective: that road success was the secret agenda. 'It's a fact,' says Herety, 'that track endurance racing, if you look at history, produces great road riders.

'You get a better rider if he's been through a track programme,' Herety continues. 'It's the discipline: the twice-daily training sessions; and the structure. If they had a track session at 9am, they had to be there at 9am. Too many road riders from my era would get up at 9.30, look out the window, see that it's raining, and think, oh well, I might go out at 10.30. The Academy, in Rod's mind, would be like a school. It would be structured, and riders would have to buy in, or the whole group would be penalised.'

Expanding on what he means by the potential of a track programme to produce top road riders, Herety explains: 'It's the skills that you get from track racing, which you don't really develop – or not so easily – on the road.' He is talking about bike-handling and race craft, and more generally the kind of skills you can only hone by riding in a fast-moving group of riders, on a steeply-banked track, on a bike with no brakes, no gears, and nothing except your own skill, balance and nerve to keep you upright and out of trouble. 'If you were really fast on the road you could maybe get away with the skills deficit you'd have from not riding the track, but it would limit you,' says Herety. 'So the skills acquisition side was really important. And Rod was really big on that.'

Yet Herety also argues that track training and racing on its own couldn't produce the complete rider. It might equip a rider with skills and speed, as well as lending structure and fostering discipline, but it didn't involve enduring five or six hours in the saddle, in all weather conditions. 'To be honest, our lads needed toughening up,' says Herety. 'The track was giving them the skills and the speed, but it wasn't making them really tough. Even if they did three sessions a day, they still needed the depth of endurance that you only get from spending hours in the saddle. Rod was a big believer in that, too.'

Herety continues: 'When the Academy was set up, the emphasis appeared to be on track racing. It was sold to the bosses [the lottery distributors at UK Sport] that way; but, in a way, it was sold to the riders as something else.'

Why might it be sold to the riders as something other than a track-focused programme? As I noted in the last chapter, track cycling has its limitations. There is no track equivalent of the Tour de France, or Paris-Roubaix, or any of the other events that fire the imagination of so many young cyclists. To attract the best and most ambitious young male endurance cyclists it had to offer more than points races and madison races on the track; it had to offer road racing opportunities, and perhaps even a route, however indirect, to professional racing on the continent.

Its title, the 'Olympic Academy', was misleading – perhaps deliberately so. Not that it mattered to Ellingworth, whose focus was very simple. For him, it didn't matter whether it was a track racing or a road racing academy. 'What I loved about Rod,' says Herety, 'was his enthusiasm. He kept it dead simple, talking about "bike racing". He'd say, "Come on, let's race our push bikes, lads." It was basic, but it allowed him to really connect with the riders. Sometimes we over-complicate things. Rod kept it really simple.'

When it came to the interviews for the first applicants to the Academy, Herety was asked to sit on the panel, alongside Ellingworth and another rider-turned-coach, Simon Lillistone. Herety was there as an observer, he says, 'making sure they followed the protocols laid down by Peter Keen.'

One of the first interviewees presented them with a dilemma. Based on a strict interpretation of Keen's criteria, the candidate in question fell short. 'They weren't going to take him on,' says Herety. He wasn't hitting the 'numbers' in the physiological tests; his scores in tests on stationary bikes were not up to scratch. Performing well in a laboratory was not his forte.

'But he's the only guy who's won 20 races,' Herety told Ellingworth and Lillistone. 'You're only saying "no" to him because he doesn't fit the criteria – but maybe the criteria are wrong.' Ellingworth and Lillistone appealed to Keen, who agreed in this case to apply some flexibility and that the young rider from the Isle of Man should be accepted to the Academy. Herety won the argument: Mark Cavendish was in.

'The first time I met him properly,' says the red-haired, freckled and youthful Ellingworth of his introduction to Cavendish, 'I was stood outside the [Manchester] Velodrome in the car park, and I heard this car hurtling towards me. It was a gold Corsa; it had a "007" number plate and "Goldfinger" written along the top [of the windscreen], and bald tyres. I just thought, Oh my god ...'

In fact, Ellingworth had encountered Cavendish previously, at his coach-led racing weekend the year before. Cavendish was there because he was on the national junior squad. 'All I remembered from that time was that he was this barrel-shaped guy,' says Ellingworth. 'He had a sprinter's position, on this yellow bike, but his set-up was all wrong. He didn't shine. But what I do remember was that he came up to me in the car park afterwards, and said: "That's the best few days I've ever had on the bike. Can I come along to the next one?"'

Ellingworth met Cavendish again when he applied to join the Academy. Eight applicants were invited to be interviewed for the initial six places. 'There was one sneaky question,' says Ellingworth. 'We asked, "How did you get here today?" I thought it would tell us if they'd been paying attention; and some of them, who'd been driven by their parents or a mate, didn't have a clue. But Cav was good; he could name every road.

'The thing about him was that, while a lot of guys were telling us what they thought we wanted to hear, Cav said things with more passion, and he was dead upfront. He'd been working in a bank and hadn't been doing much training. He'd put on a bit of weight and he was struggling to get it off – he was upfront about all that.

'I remember ringing him afterwards, telling him he'd made the cut. He said, "I promise I'll never let you down." I said, "I just need you to work really hard."'

A priority for Ellingworth, landed with a squad of six boys barely out of adolescence – Cavendish, Matt Brammeier, Ed Clancy, Bruce Edgar, Christian Varley and Tom White – was to establish some early principles. 'I wasn't too bothered about the bike riders,' Ellingworth says. 'My view was that we had to get the structure in place.'

That structure involved a daily routine, which, in year one, and on a typical day in Manchester, where they were based, went as follows: 7.30am, report to velodrome; 8–11.30am, road training; midday, lunch; 1–3pm, French class; 3–6pm, track training; 6pm, home.

Then there was the racing. 'I pitched it high when we worked out the racing programme, in terms of its intensity,' says Ellingworth. 'It was just a gut feeling, but I was thinking that they had to do at least 80, 90 races a year, whether track or road. It didn't matter which it was. I just wanted them to be thinking, and talking, about bike racing. So they'd be coming home in the car, talking about the bike race. Cav in particular: he'd be dissecting it. "Did you see that attack? Did you see that guy fall?" But that, for me, was them learning. The previous year they'd only done 22, 23 days of racing. That was only 22, 23 days of learning. It wasn't enough.'

In this sense, Ellingworth's principles derived from road racing, where a diet of regular racing is *de rigueur*. 'It was track and road all year round,' he explains. 'We'd mix and match. But the main emphasis was skills and drills. I wanted to get their skill levels so high; because no one else in the world was working on those things in this way, in a training academy type environment.'

It wasn't just cycling. 'As well as the French lessons they did nutrition courses,' says Ellingworth. 'I used to set them homework, too – little essays. A thousand words on life in the Academy, or a thousand words on [Australian professional] Stuart O'Grady, or whatever. Most of them did those on a computer, which was good – it gives you the word count straight away.

'Cav wrote his out by hand,' Ellingworth continues, smiling knowingly. 'I thought: he's going to think I'm not going to count how many words he's done.

'Well, the thing was,' Ellingworth adds, 'I wasn't interested in the content. All I was interested in was that they'd followed instructions and organised themselves to do what I'd asked them to do. They could've written "blah-de-blah" as far as I was concerned, as long as they wrote it a thousand times. Routine, discipline, and organising your time: that's what I was looking for. It's like a bike race. You don't come and say: "I'm going to start riding now." It's when *I* say; not when you feel like it.

'So I counted how many words Cav had written: 853. Did I let him have it. I made him do it again. To be fair, he laughed. He said he knew it wasn't a thousand.'

In the first year of the Academy, 2005, the racing programme was primarily in the UK, with the Academy riders – who raced under the Persil banner, the washing powder company being a British Cycling sponsor – fed a diet of Premier Calendar road races. The elite Premier Calendar series included a long-established event, the Girvan Three-Day over the Easter week-end, and Ellingworth's team made a strong early impression by winning stage one, courtesy of Cavendish.

For Ellingworth, though, the education extended beyond racing; it covered attitude, too, and conduct. Cycling – road racing especially – is riddled with little acts that are officially outlawed, but often subject to officials and other teams turning a blind eye. If, for example, a rider is off the back of the peloton – after a puncture or crash – then he will often regain contact by tucking in and sheltering behind the cars that form the convoy behind. That was okay in Ellingworth's book, as long as it was for a legitimate reason, such as a puncture or crash. 'There was to be no cheating,' says Ellingworth. 'No getting in the cars if you'd been dropped; and definitely no holding on to the car. If you got dropped, you got dropped.'

The weekend of the Girvan Three-Day also underlined, for Ellingworth's squad, their mentor's work ethic. 'The Girvan finished on the Monday, and on the Tuesday I had them back on the track,' he says. 'I took them to Belgium soon after that. We did 10 days of 'kermesses' [kermesses being road races on circuits typically 5–15km in length, covered numerous times, of which there can be several a day in Belgium at the peak of the season] and I got them doing a kermesse one day, a rest day the next, then another kermesse, another rest day, and so on. But the rest days would be three to four hours on the bike – nice and easy, with a café stop at the end, but that time on the bike was important.

'There was one day in Belgium when I told them: "I want you to do three hours non-stop, then have a café stop at the end of your three hours and tootle back." I usually followed them in the car but on that day I stayed back to do a bit of work.

'About four-and-a-half hours later they appeared back. That seemed fine: they'd done their three hours, they told me, then stopped at a café. But later, as we were all having dinner, Cav had a camera, and he was showing all these pictures. And I happened to catch sight of one of the pictures. It showed them sitting in a café in a town centre. Well, I recognised the town and it wasn't anywhere near where we were staying.

'I was furious. I told them, "Don't bullshit me." And I made them get changed and go out and do another four hours hard. At night, with me following in the car.'

The next month, when they went to ride in a round of the British Under-23 series in Cornwall, Ellingworth issued his riders with their instructions at the start. As the riders representing the Academy – supposedly the cream of the Under-23s – they were expected to dictate the race. And Ellingworth wanted them to do exactly that; or at least try to.

'I do not want a break to go clear in the first part of this race without one of us in it,' Ellingworth told them. 'If a break goes in a tough section, and we're not *good* enough to go with it, that's okay. But if it goes and we miss it because we're not concentrating – that's different.'

A break escaped within three miles of the race starting. The six Academy riders all missed it. What's more, one member of that early break, the Scottish rider Evan Oliphant, held on to win. 'We were chasing all day, because they thought they were too big, too good,' says Ellingworth. 'I was watching them off the line, and there they were: the Persil guys, the Academy boys, laughing and joking. And then they miss the break because they're not paying attention. So at the finish, in full view of all the other riders who were packing up, I lined them up. And I asked each of them: "Did you see the break go?"

'"Yes," said the first one. I went along the whole line: "Did you see the break go?" "Yes."

'"Right," I said, "why did you miss it?" They were quiet; said nothing.'

'I said, "Get in the car; don't say a fucking word to me all the way home." And they didn't.

'We drove from Cornwall to Manchester, got back at 11.30 at night. They were unloading their bikes and I said, "Right all of you, 8.30 tomorrow morning be here and ready for a long bike ride." They turned up and I made them do five hours of "through and off"' – a style of riding that simulates a break in a road race, team time trial or team pursuit, where riders form an ever-rotating chain, taking turns at the front, keeping the speed high. 'I said: "Come on guys, if you were in a pro team you'd lose your job for what happened yesterday. If your job is to get in the break and win the race and you don't do it, you'll lose your contract."

'I was just,' adds Ellingworth almost forlornly, 'trying to prepare 'em.'

Ellingworth has a bank of such stories, which paint him, inevitably, as a hard taskmaster and disciplinarian. With his red hair, you might imagine that he possesses a fiery temper, too. But that assumption would be incorrect. Mild mannered would be a more accurate description. Ellingworth's approach, and his method, saw him deploy far more subtle – and far more effective – tactics than wielding a big stick. 'I never got mad at 'em,' he claims. 'Never raised my voice.'

John Herety backs this up: 'He didn't shout and scream. He kept everything in-house. Rod had a bit of Alex Ferguson about him in that respect. You look at Ferguson – he's supposedly a legendary disciplinarian, really tough. People talk about it; he has that reputation; but you don't see it. From what I saw of Rod, he told them: "You will be there at this time." I know he issued punishments – he'd have them cleaning the staff cars, or working with the mechanics for a day, or he'd make them do laps of a circuit near where I lived – but it was all done quietly and kept in-house; he didn't get angry. He didn't use a big stick. The way he instilled discipline was very clever.'

It was also consistent with the culture at British Cycling, particularly the culture that developed under Dave Brailsford when he took over from Peter Keen as performance director. Brailsford, who worked in the cycling industry, had answered a plea from Keen in the winter of 1997 for bikes and clothing, and then become involved in the business side of running Keen's lottery-funded programme. 'What Peter saw in Dave was someone very good with budgets, spreadsheets and all that kind of thing,' says Herety. 'Peter was bright – he could do spreadsheets – but he didn't like them. Peter was also fantastic as a visionary, but he wasn't brilliant in his relationships with people. Dave started working at the Manchester Velodrome [becoming operations director, effectively Keen's number two], and he and Pete got closer. As time went on their desks got closer and closer.'

When Keen eventually decided to move on, in 2004, Brailsford stepped into his shoes. 'It brought about a sea change,' says Herety. 'What changed completely was the way the staff interacted with the senior management team. Dave was a lot easier to talk to. Peter was quite distant and aloof. He hadn't worked in business or with other people; he had been a scientist and a lecturer in a university, where he hadn't had to listen to what other people said. But that's what Dave was good at. And he's good at empowering people.'

Brailsford's journey to the top of British cycling had been circuitous: he went to race in France as a teenager, staying for four years in the St Etienne area, but achieving only modest results, failing in his dream of turning professional and one day riding the Tour de France, and returned to study for an MBA at Sheffield Business School. But he was keen to remain involved with cycling, and his path crossed Herety's in 1993, when he answered another plea: to act as *soigneur* to a small professional team managed by Herety (and sponsored by a Rotherham nightclub).

Brailsford's qualifications as a *soigneur* – the main responsibility being to massage the riders' legs – were unclear, though Herety admits he adopted, by necessity, a beggars-can't-be-choosers approach to staff recruitment. 'If you had a massage table and a tub of baby oil, you were in,' he jokes. But he must have made a good impression. Later that season, Brailsford was invited to act as *soigneur* to the British team at the World Championships in Norway.

Herety also recommended Brailsford for a job with an Essex-based bike manufacturer, Muddy Fox. 'He went for an interview for the job of UK sales manager,' says Herety. 'And he walked out of that interview as European sales manager. I'm not sure they were even interviewing for that position. But Dave talked himself into it. And he went from there ...'

As performance director at British Cycling, Brailsford strived to create a supportive environment, in which people – coaches, athletes – felt they could have a say, and influence decisions. That didn't mean there were no rules or discipline; but his approach, he explained, was 'more carrot than stick'. As he said in 2007: 'I don't believe in stick, but that doesn't mean to say we're soft. If our lads walk into training five minutes late, we say, "Sorry, thanks for coming but off you go, home." But bawling at people creates a sense of fear and I don't believe that brings the best out of people.'

The Academy, under Ellingworth's stewardship, but with Brailsford taking a very close interest, was run along similar lines, though perhaps, as Ellingworth acknowledges, with a greater emphasis on 'strong leadership'. He says that most of the riders thrived in an environment in which rules were rigidly applied. 'Cav kind of liked it, I think,' says Ellingworth. 'Some are like that. It was a dictatorship style, that first year or two, I suppose. But I like that too. Look at my boss, Dave Brailsford. He can be a hard bastard; he can be real ruthless. But I like that sort of leadership, as long as you're fair. As Brailsford said to me: our job as coaches is to make these guys better, not to eliminate them. But it had to be tough. It's like being in the army; okay, they're not going to war, but they're out there racing flat out against every nation in the world, pushing and shoving and competing. You don't want guys wimping out.

'I was strict with some of the rules', Ellingworth continues. 'Punctuality was a big one. "The wheels are turning at 9am" is what I'd always say. If they were late, I said, "Right, you're cleaning all the bikes after." So after 160, 170km, they had to clean the bikes. The mechanics [whose normal job it was] loved it.'

In the early years of the Academy – before the setting up of the base in Quarrata – the riders were based in two houses in Manchester, one near the city's university, the other in the grittier area of Fallowfield. As members of the Academy they had an allowance of £6,000, the money coming from lottery funding, but half went straight back to the governing body, to cover the rent on the houses. Managing their money – they lived on £58 a week – was part of the education, says Ellingworth.

As Cavendish wrote in his 2009 book, *Boy Racer*, the Academy provided a University of Life type experience: 'In that first year we learned a hell of a lot about bike racing, but more about ourselves and, I suppose, even more about life in general.' When asked if he feels he 'missed out' by not attending a proper university, Cavendish responds: 'If university life was about booze and drugs and skipping lectures, then, yeah, I missed out. If it was about having a laugh and living with two mates who cooked bad food and turned the place into a shit-hole on a daily basis, then, no, I think life with Bruce and Ed [in the Fallowfield house] was a fairly decent substitute.' (It's unlikely that the rooms were as much of a 'shit-hole' as Cavendish claims. Ellingworth conducted random 'room tests': 'I wanted them to learn that, if they'd been away racing, it was nicer to come back to a place that was neat and tidy.')

Though the first six Academy riders had been offered a two-year berth, not all survived. 'One rider left because he wouldn't listen to instructions,' says Ellingworth. 'It could be the smallest thing: handlebar tape dragging off his bars. I kept telling him: "Sort your bar tape out – you're representing Britain, look neat and tidy." He also punctured three or four times in a few days and never went to the velodrome to get new inner tubes. He'd get up in the morning, the ride would be going at 9am, and he'd be sorting it then.

'Some didn't make it, but that's normal,' continues Ellingworth breezily. 'You'd expect that with a group of 19- or 20-year-olds. But I think that if someone stops at that age it proves they don't want to be cyclists. If you really want to be a cyclist, if you really believe you can do it, you'll keep at it. It's not about money; it's about whether they *want* to do it. And the guys who really want to make it can recognise a good opportunity when it comes along. Cav recognised it was a dream situation for him to be in, so he and I hit it off pretty soon. But I take my hat off to someone like Matt Brammeier, who has stuck at it.' (Brammeier moved on from the Academy but continued racing until he suffered a horrific crash in 2007, when he was struck by a cement lorry and broke both legs. He returned to join a Belgian team, switched his allegiance to Ireland and completed a remarkable comeback by signing with Cavendish's HTC team for the 2011 season.)

The Academy didn't work for some, but, as Ellingworth notes, it worked spectacularly for Cavendish. Had it not existed then he would have taken the only possible road to a career as a professional road cyclist; the old road to Europe, as followed by such British luminaries as Brian Robinson, Tom Simpson, Barry Hoban, Graham Jones, Robert Millar and Sean Yates (a road that Ellingworth and Brailsford, when they were cyclists, also followed, with less spectacular results). Fully intending to take that road, Cavendish was working in Barclays Bank on the Isle of Man to save enough money to live abroad and pursue his dream of turning professional. 'I'd always intended to leave Barclays at the end of 2003 to dedicate myself full-time to cycling, hoping that a pro contract would be waiting for me at the end of two or three seasons in the under-23 or amateur category,' he writes in his book. 'Belgium, Holland, Italy, France: they all had a sprawling network of amateur clubs, many with six-figure budgets, top-notch bikes and back-up, international race programmes and often feeder agreements with the best pro teams in the world.'

Cavendish knew how tough that would be: 'In the past, any British youngster who aspired to turn pro had relied on contacts and their own initiative; they'd had to overcome homesickness, loneliness and a language barrier, not to mention the bias foreign teams usually show towards their own riders. A few, really resilient souls had even made it, but they'd done so in spite of, rather than because of, the system.'

With the inevitable turnover of riders there was a new Academy intake at the end of the first year, including a young

Welshman, Geraint Thomas. And in year two, says Ellingworth, it became blindingly obvious to him which riders had the attributes to make it as professionals. 'Cav, Gee [Thomas] and Ed [Clancy] were just different,' he says. 'They stood out.'

'It was something I definitely could only do at that age,' admits Geraint Thomas of life in the Academy. 'I couldn't do it now. But it gave me so much. It taught me about living away from home and looking after myself. It was as much about lifestyle, really. It wasn't about results, it was about learning. Even the guys who didn't make it – I still speak to some of them, and they say that it gave them so much, whatever they ended up doing. One rider, Ross Sander, packed in cycling and moved to America to be with his dad. But I still speak to him once in a while; he'll say the same. We owe a lot to Rod and the Academy.' (It's interesting to note that Sander, like Brammeier, changed nationality, in his case taking out American citizenship. Another talented young rider who didn't appear to fit in to the British system, Dan Martin, did the same, and now represents Ireland. It means that several talented young British riders have not flourished in the British system, rejected it, and are now lost to future British squads.)

'For me personally,' continues Thomas, 'the Academy only reinforced the idea that this was what I wanted – to be a pro cyclist. If you do survive it, and come out of it well, it definitely sets you up nicely for pro bike riding. But there were others, who were forced to realise that it wasn't for them.'

With his trademark wry smile and tendency towards under-statement, Thomas adds: ''Cos it's not an easy sport, is it?'

Like Cavendish, Thomas remains close to Ellingworth. Indeed – and without wishing to provoke gender confusion – there is something of Miss Jean Brodie (Muriel Spark's crea-tion, a charismatic teacher at a girls' school in Edinburgh in the post-war years, and the star of her novel, *The Prime of Miss Jean Brodie*) about Ellingworth. 'Give me a girl at an impressionable age and she is mine for life,' was Brodie's mantra. To those riders whom Ellingworth guided through their early years, he seems to have had a similarly major influence; like the most memorable teachers, he was far more than mere teacher. 'I am in the business of putting old heads on young shoulders' was another Brodie-ism. (But just to be clear: Brodie's fascist undertones are not evident in Ellingworth's approach.)

Ellingworth's greatest strength, says Thomas, is that 'he took no shit really. He'd say, "Get out there and earn your pennies" – that was one of his favourite lines. To me he was like the boss. To Ed he was more of a father figure. To Cav I suppose he was kind of like an older brother. He'd adapt how he was, depending on the rider. He was hard. Sometimes he just kept pushing people and they did crack, but he was good at teaching you how to look after yourself. He was a teacher, really.'

Thomas joined the Academy in time for an extended training camp in Australia. It was the winter of 2004, leading up to the World Track Cycling Championships in Los Angeles in March 2005. The trip to Australia followed the European Under-23 Track Championships in Valencia in August 2004, which represented a low point for Ellingworth. 'I was struggling with the group, they were getting a bit wild – which can happen if you don't control them,' says Ellingworth. It didn't help, perhaps, that the Academy riders were joined by others, including the female squads. Parties, or 'gatherings', were as inevitable as the fact that Ellingworth would catch them. Cavendish's recollection, in *Boy Racer*, of becoming aware of Ellingworth, sitting on the curb of the pavement below and watching them as they threw a party in one of the apartments, is almost enough to send a shiver down the spine. Ellingworth also recalls breaking up a night-time race – not a bike race, but a running race up the fire escape steps – arriving just in time to find Cavendish wheezing and panting up the last flight, while Matt Brammeier waited at the top with a stopwatch. 'They weren't giving me 100%,' says Ellingworth. 'And if they don't give me 100% I get a bit pissed off.'

Australia represented an opportunity to re-introduce the boot camp elements to life in the Academy, particularly since they'd be there for two-and-a-half months. Shane Sutton, now working with the track sprinters, was also there, adding some authority, and helping to oversee the work of an initiative still, of course, in its infancy, and still to produce tangible results.

After being initially based in Sydney they travelled to Bendigo, the town close to Melbourne. 'They flew,' says Ellingworth. 'I drove. It was a 14-hour drive. But when I arrived, not one of 'em asked me how I was doing, or how the trip was. They were so caught up in their own little world. I didn't want them to know anything about me; I just wanted them to show respect. I almost ripped them to pieces for that.'

Things improved. They raced in the well-established Bendigo criteriums – Cavendish winning one – and trained as they'd never trained before. 'They were doing 250, 260km a day on the bike,' says Ellingworth, 'a massive workload. They enjoyed it. And they never stepped out of line. Well, there were a couple of little issues, but nothing serious. They'd be out for three, four hours in the morning, going at 5.30, 6am, to miss the heat. Then they'd do three hours on the track in the afternoon. And then a crit' in the evening! But they were in great form. Absolutely flying.'

But in February, just a month before the World Championships, there was an incident that Ellingworth says he 'always dreaded'. 'When they were out training as a group, without me following them in the car, you did worry a bit, because it'd be so easy to have a situation like the one with Amy Gillett.' (Five months later, in July 2005, Gillett, the

Australian track cyclist, was killed in Germany when the group she was riding in was hit by a car.)

They were out for a three-hour road ride, bowling along in a compact group on an unremarkable stretch of road, when one of the riders happened to go over a piece of metal lying in the road. The metal was tossed into the air by his tyre; and it flew into the front wheel of one of the riders behind. The rider was Geraint Thomas; his front wheel locked dead and he was tossed from his bike, crashing heavily, his chest landing on his handlebars. He was badly injured and taken to hospital, where internal bleeding was diagnosed. Thomas had ruptured his spleen, which had to be removed. He was quickly reassured that he'd make a full recovery, but he was out of the senior World Track Championships in Los Angeles, for which he had – surprising some – been selected to ride the madison, partnering the experienced Rob Hayles.

Cavendish replaced him, though he'd been 'a bit shocked' not to have been selected in the first place. Thomas, he said, 'was the golden child'.

Thomas, who was off the bike for six weeks while he recovered from his injuries, travelled to Los Angeles with Cavendish. 'I had a ticket,' says Thomas. 'I'd stayed in Oz with the Academy lads after the crash, and Shane [Sutton] told me to go and watch the World's, to see what it was all about. When I got there I started to help the mechanics out, because I could move about a bit more, and I could take bikes back and forth for them. But after about two days, I thought: fuck this. If I'm able to carry bikes around I might as well get back on it – so I rode my rollers for half an hour, and didn't help the mechanics any more.'

The event that first Thomas, then Cavendish, had been selected for was the madison, a two-man race in which one rider races while his teammate circles the top of the banking, waiting to be slung (by the hand of his teammate) back into the action. It is perhaps the toughest of the track endurance events, as well as one of the most difficult to follow, with bodies strewn everywhere. Consequently, it is also one of the most dangerous.

But madison training had been a staple of the diet Ellingworth fed his Academy charges. In their endless sessions at the Manchester Velodrome they were put in pairs to ride madison-style drills on an almost daily basis. As far as Ellingworth was concerned, for speed, skill and spatial awareness, there was nothing that could beat the madison. But John Herety was not alone in watching some of these sessions through the cracks in his fingers. 'Rod loved the madison, because he knew that, from a skills point of view, anyone who can ride a madison is going to get it,' says Herety. 'But I was always a bit nervous watching them. The numbers were small, we didn't have *that* many talented riders – the pool of talent wasn't big – so to put them into madisons, well … it was quite dangerous.'

And it *was* dangerous. Ellingworth remembers one session of madison training in which Cavendish suffered a particularly heavy tumble. 'Down he went, wallop! There were a few of 'em came off and slid down the banking. They all got back up, but Cav, who gets on his bike, rides towards me real slow. He was looking a bit funny. I asked him, "You alright?" He unzipped his jersey and he had all these splinters on his chest. Then he pulls down his shorts, and pulls his dick out. And he's got a splinter through his dick! Luckily Doctor Rog [Roger Palfreeman, the British Cycling doctor] was in that day and he pulled it out. Cav took the splinter home in a bag.'

But the hundreds of hours of madison training stood Cavendish in good stead in LA. With the more experienced Rob Hayles – a bronze medallist in the madison with Bradley Wiggins at the previous year's Olympics in Athens – the British pair won the race. At 19, Cavendish was a world champion and he, and the Academy, were on the map. Within a year of setting up, Ellingworth's school of excellence, intended to build Britain's next generation of champion cyclists, had produced its first major result.

When he reflects now on the early years of the Academy, Ellingworth can do so with understandable pride. He does admit to one or two regrets. It should have been more focused, he thinks – rather than doing everything, on the track and road, he thinks they could have prioritised certain events and excelled in them. But it's a minor gripe. The hundreds of races were not just races, they were also 'learning experiences', after all.

With his full head of unruly red hair – sculpted by gel into a spiky style that seems reluctant to follow instructions – and his long, straggly sideburns, Ellingworth looks as youthful as he did when he began to lay down the rules that would govern life in the Academy. He explains: 'One of the biggest ideas I had when I started the Academy was that if you could go through something together, you'd really feel that you'd achieved something; and a few years down the road, you'd come back together. And I can see that. There's this connection. Even between the original Academy guys and the new ones. Cav, Gee and Swifty all go to the Academy house in Quarrata and tell 'em: "You don't have it as hard as we had it."

'But that's how I coach,' Ellingworth adds. 'It's about groups, pulling together, learning together and from each other. I'm not a coach who likes to ram it down their necks.'

The question that Ellingworth cannot answer concerns where he picked up his ideas. Who influenced him? He shrugs. 'I think it's just stuff you do over time. Okay, I never had a top pro career, but you're still racing your bike, you're living out of a suitcase, you're trying as hard as everyone else. You're looking and you're seeing. You understand what it takes.

'No one ever helped me,' Ellingworth continues. 'It was not really people I was inspired by. There was nobody really. They were just ideas I had. And I looked at other models – the Australian Institute of Sport had a great model.'

Eventually, though, Ellingworth comes back to what seems to be his core belief – his central principle. 'I was always interested in a group of people, and the question of what makes them real strong as a group.

'If you have a group of people, what bonds them together, even if they're from completely different parts of the world? When they've done something together and been through something together. I dunno, they could've walked across the country together. They don't know each other at the start. They'll argue; they'll struggle. But they'll be bonded at the end; they'll be like a family; they'll never forget that experience. That's really powerful. And that's what I wanted the Academy to be like.'

Inadvertently or not, accidentally or by design, Ellingworth's British Cycling Academy also heralded a switch of focus and a change of direction for British cycling. If phase one of Peter Keen's British cycling revolution had produced world-class track cyclists, phase two – symbolised by the Academy – seemed to set in motion a conveyor belt of talented young riders who might one day target success on the road, in the great races of Europe: Milan-San Remo, Paris-Roubaix, the Giro d'Italia, Tour de France, Vuelta a España …

Dave Brailsford's dream of setting up a professional road team was a logical extension of that. It was phase three.

CHAPTER 3

GOODBYE CAV, HELLO WIGGO?

'We're the minions.'

Dave Brailsford

Celtic Manor, Newport, 24 July 2008

'He's done what?!'

Shane Sutton and Dave Brailsford were discussing Mark Cavendish. Though they found themselves in the sumptuous surroundings of Celtic Manor, the five-star golf resort in Newport, Wales, their minds were frequently in France. It was difficult for them not to be.

Cavendish, their prodigy, golden boy, natural-born winner, product of the British Cycling Academy and the rider around whom a British professional team would one day logically be constructed, had become the sensation of the Tour de France with four stage wins in his second attempt at the world's biggest race. 'I believe I'm the fastest sprinter in the world,' he had said the day before the Tour started, and he had now proved it. Four times.

The cream of British Cycling thus occupied parallel universes for much of the month of July 2008. In Newport, holed up in Celtic Manor, was the British track team, now in 'lock-down' mode, and almost to a man and woman recording world-class times while training on the nearby Newport

Velodrome, with the Olympics only weeks away. And in France was Mark Cavendish: the hottest property in world cycling.

Following stage 14, on 19 July, Cavendish abandoned the Tour in order to remain fresh and fit for the Olympics. He would ride the madison with Bradley Wiggins in Beijing, though at this point, and unknown to all but a few people, Wiggins' participation in the Olympics was in doubt due to a virus that left him bed-bound for six days.

Brailsford and Sutton had a lot on their plate. The deal with Sky was done, and on 24 July the satellite broadcaster was announced as the new 'principal partner' of British Cycling. A five-year, 'multi-million pound partnership' encompassed every level of cycling, from encouraging participation to grassroots, to talent development, to elite; and every discipline, from BMX to mountain biking, track and road racing. The wider goal was to get Britain back on its bike – to continue a process that London's 2007 Grand Départ may have started, of transforming the country's cycling culture, and encouraging a million more people to ride bikes over the next five years. 'I believe this partnership will create a step change for cycling,' said Brailsford. 'Working together, we can take elite cycling to new heights and get more people involved in the sport at all levels.'

The track sprinters Chris Hoy and Victoria Pendleton – both of whom would go on to win gold medals in Beijing, in Hoy's case three – fronted the launch of the Sky partnership. There was no mention of the sponsorship extending to a professional road team.

But Brailsford and Sutton both knew – despite their later assertions to the contrary – that the partnership with Sky was a forerunner to a professional team. Wiggins knew. And Cavendish knew. All were clear, too, that Cavendish would be the leader, the talisman; the fulcrum of the new team, the plans for which Brailsford had brought forward. In Bourg-en-Bresse he identified 2013 as the likely launch date, following the London Olympics. Yet in May 2008, as negotiations progressed with Sky, Brailsford revised that: the team would hit the road in 2010, he said.

Cavendish's four stage wins at the Tour, which followed two stage wins in the Giro d'Italia, confirmed the wisdom behind a plan that would see Britain's first major league professional team led by the world's best sprinter, and most prolific winner. One of Brailsford's trump cards was Rod Ellingworth, Cavendish's coach. Cavendish rode for Bob Stapleton's Columbia-High Road team – a new team that Stapleton, the Californian millionaire, had salvaged from the ashes of the old T-Mobile outfit, later to become Columbia-HTC, then HTC-Columbia. But Ellingworth was still the man Cavendish turned to, still the big brother figure, who managed his training and gave him tactical coaching. Ellingworth was also the man who, when Cavendish was at the Academy, instilled in him the understanding that, in order to win, he had to lead; and that in order to lead, he had to act like a leader. It meant accepting the responsibility, and handling the pressure, of having eight teammates sacrifice their own chances for him. 'There aren't many who can take on that responsibility,' says Ellingworth. 'But Cav can.'

But in the run-up to the Tour, and before the British Olympic team departed for the Newport holding camp, Cavendish and Sutton, both combustible characters, had one of their fairly frequent bust-ups. It owed to Sutton's repeated assertions, in public and in private, that Cavendish would lead the new British team. Cavendish took exception to the assumption. He felt his involvement was being taken for granted. The upshot was that Cavendish travelled to the 2008 Tour in a fiery, belligerent frame of mind. 'Shane had bawled him out and Cav was asserting his authority,' as one insider puts it. 'The team was to have been built around Cav. But he went to the Tour with a "fuck you" attitude towards Shane and British Cycling.'

And it was this, perhaps, that proved decisive when, midway through the Tour, Cavendish was offered a new two-year contract by Stapleton. It was a contract that would also give his team an option on a third year (taking him into 2011), and it was worth €750,000 a year. When it was offered to him, Cavendish signed it. He told no one.

'He's done what?!'

Brailsford and Sutton were walking across the Celtic Manor golf course when they found out. Cavendish, having arrived in Newport, admitted a little sheepishly to having signed the new contract. When Brailsford and Sutton found out, their reaction was one of shock, disbelief and horror. It would mean – after Beijing – going back to the drawing board.

Then there was Wiggins. In what could almost be a metaphor for his and Cavendish's respective status at the time, while Cavendish was basking in the glory of having won four stages in the Tour, Wiggins was bed-bound fighting a virus.

And when Wiggins wasn't ill, Sutton, who had long acted as a father figure to him, was keen to persuade him to commit to the new team, too.

Wiggins was by now a teammate of Cavendish's at Columbia-High Road. They had ridden together at the Giro in May, Wiggins as a member of Cavendish's lead-out 'train' – the group of teammates that organised themselves at the front in the closing kilometres, forming a team pursuit-style line, with Cavendish positioned at the rear, ready to unleash his sprint in the final 200 metres. It was the kind of riding in close formation, and the kind of fast effort, that Wiggins was brilliant at. Great track rider that he was, he was blessed with the speed and bike-handling skills that only come from hours spent riding in circles around a velodrome. No question, he could be a valuable member of Cavendish's train. And in some respects that made sense for Wiggins, too. At the Giro he appreciated having a specific role and an actual job to do – something he hadn't had in his French teams. But there was a problem: Wiggins did not *want* to become a member of Cavendish's train in a team that he feared would become 'the Cav show'. He did not regard that as 'career progression'.

Wiggins was attracted to the idea of joining David Millar's Slipstream team. While with High Road he could only see a future as a bit part player in the Cav show, with Slipstream (re-named Garmin-Slipstream on the eve of the 2008 Tour) he would be freer to do his own thing (whatever that might be – Wiggins wasn't sure). Garmin offered Wiggins a two-year contract worth €350,000 a year – around €200,000 a year more than he was on at High Road.

And so in Newport, as well as having to fight a virus, Wiggins faced a dilemma. With the Olympics approaching, and Wiggins very publicly aiming for three gold medals – in the pursuit, team pursuit, and finally with Cavendish in the madison – there was always the possibility that success in Beijing could increase his earning power. Then again, in the world of professional road cycling, Olympic track medals might be worth a little, but not very much. In the meantime, the offer from Garmin was good, the security of a two-year deal appealing; but Sutton urged Wiggins not to sign – or to sign for only one year. Brailsford even showed him a fax from Sky, to prove the money would be there to set up the team.

But, to Wiggins – with his wife, Cath, and their young family also weighing heavily on his mind – requesting one year instead of the two on the table from Garmin seemed counter-intuitive. His career to date, in which he'd resolutely focused on pursuit racing for the best part of a decade, suggested he was not, by instinct, a risk-taker. Now, as he prepared to fly to Beijing, probably did not feel like the time to start gambling. He had to make a decision before the Olympics. So in Newport, in early August 2008, Wiggins agreed to spend the next two years with Garmin.

In Beijing, Brailsford and his team were lauded. They won as many gold medals – eight – as Italy won across all sports, and one more than France. Wiggins won two of the three gold medals he'd set his heart on, with the only disappointment – indeed, the entire team's only disappointment – coming in the madison. There, a tired Wiggins, riding his third event, failed to fire, and he and Cavendish were never in the race, finally finishing ninth. Cavendish ended the meeting as the only British track cyclist not to win a medal; and he was disgusted, saying he felt 'let down' by Wiggins and by British Cycling. He wished he'd never pulled out of the Tour de France.

Lanesborough Hotel, London, February 2009

'Morning, gents,' says Dave Brailsford. There are handshakes all round. Then Brailsford sits down and six journalists form a crescent around him, settling into comfortable chairs in a drawing room on the ground floor of one of London's plushest hotels. The Lanesborough is a striking yet understated cream-coloured building overlooking Hyde Park, with Bentleys and Rolls-Royces, engines purring, permanently stationed outside.

There is a slightly awkward silence. Brailsford, in a navy blue British Cycling Adidas tracksuit top, blue jeans and train-ers, is flanked by four men wearing smart suits and ties and polished shoes. One of them introduces Brailsford as the performance director of British Cycling. But we know that. Everyone in Britain now knows that, with Brailsford elevated to the status of sporting guru, and named coach of the year at the BBC's Sports Personality of the Year awards (even though Brailsford is not, and never has been, a coach). He has been visited by Sir Alex Ferguson and his coaching staff at Manchester United; other sports are keen to speak to him, to hear his secrets. Ferguson had sat with Brailsford and Shane Sutton in the former's office at the Velodrome, with Brailsford quizzing the great football manager on his knack of successfully re-building teams as players became old or ineffective. 'Just get rid of the c**ts,' Ferguson told him.

The invitation to come to the Lanesborough had come by phone only 48 hours earlier: 'Be at the Lanesborough Hotel at 10.' But we weren't told why, and nor were we to tell anyone that we'd been invited to a meeting whose purpose we didn't know.

The low winter sun cuts across the room, glancing off Brailsford's head, forcing him to squint. 'Well,' he begins. 'Thanks for coming to this ... em, gathering.' Then he spreads his hands and says: 'We're here to announce Britain's new pro team, and the identity of our sponsor. Sky.'

The dam breaks; and now Brailsford quickly gets into his flow, rubbing his hands enthusiastically, forming them into descriptive shapes. 'My world changes from today,' he says. 'This is new, it's something people haven't seen before. We're setting out to create an epic story – an epic British success story. Now it's down to business: to find out what it's going to take to win the Tour de France with a clean British rider.'

What will the team be called, Brailsford is asked. He seems to hesitate. 'It'll be Team Sky. Yeah, Team Sky.'

And what will the budget be? The men in suits fidget. 'Enough to be competitive,' says one. 'Enough to achieve our ambitions,' says another. Brailsford smiles and shakes his head at the suggestion that they will be the Manchester City of professional cycling – the football club made newly wealthy thanks to an influx of Arab money.

'It's a bit like fantasy football, or fantasy cycling, at the moment,' says Brailsford when asked how far advanced he is in assembling, from scratch, a squad of around 25 riders. 'It's a lot of fun. We've had some fantastic discussions. And we have created a monster database of the top professional cyclists. But at the end of the day it's like *Moneyball*: it's all about doing your homework.'

But what about his aim of winning the Tour with a clean British rider? Never mind Britain's record in the race – three top 10 finishes in 105 years – there is the 'clean' part of the equation. Given cycling's tarnished image, is that possible? 'The perception of cycling is changing,' says Brailsford. 'We need to be agents of change. Our job is to prove beyond doubt that it can be done clean. The legacy of that would be phenomenal.'

Brailsford's mention of *Moneyball* is interesting. *Moneyball* is the 2003 book by Michael Lewis – subtitled *The Art of Winning an Unfair Game* – in which the author spends a season following the Oakland Athletics (A's) baseball team, which consistently punches above its weight, outperforming teams with far bigger budgets. What Lewis discovers, while shadowing the coach Billy Beane and his backroom team, is that the A's have developed a system of recruiting and assessing players that flies in the face of received baseballing wisdom, but which works – and works spectacularly.

The intricacies of Beane's system are too complicated to go into here. One of the central points, though, is that Beane, despite having been a player himself, has done what most insiders in most sports are unable to do; he sees his sport in a fresh, objective way, de-cluttering himself of the experience, prejudices, conventional wisdom and knowledge that tend to be accumulated from years of involvement. He is an insider with an outsider's perspective. Lewis notes that one of Beane's key appointments is a Harvard graduate, someone who has never played professional baseball. Which is a point in his favour, according to Lewis: 'At least he hasn't learned the wrong lessons. Billy had played pro ball, and regarded it as an experience he needed to overcome if he wanted to do his job well.'

This is interesting in the context of British Cycling, and it's easy to see where Brailsford is coming from. For he, too, is an 'outsider' in the world of professional road racing. But it also chimes with something Chris Boardman had told me. For some time now the former professional's job at British Cycling had been to head up the research and development department, the so-called 'Secret Squirrel Club'. It was Boardman's department, or the team of people he oversees, that developed the bikes and equipment used by the British team at the Beijing Olympics, including the rubberised skinsuits which, as soon as the Games were over – and in an example of Brailsford's attention to detail – were recalled and shredded, in case a rival nation got their hands on one and managed to copy them.

In selecting his team of people, Boardman had said his priority was to select those who knew nothing about cycling or bikes. 'There is no one with anything to do with cycling involved in equipment research and development.' And so they were drawn from Formula One and the world of engineering. Boardman's premise was simple: 'Preconceived ideas kill genuine innovation.' He encouraged his team to ask questions which would seem, to anyone involved in the sport of cycling, obvious or even stupid. 'It takes a bit of self-discipline on my part,' Boardman said, 'to work out whether we've reached a dead end with someone, or if I'm stopping [innovation] with my preconceived ideas.' Clearly Boardman regarded his own background, as Olympic and world champion, and Tour de France yellow jersey wearer, as 'experience he needed to overcome if he wanted to do his job well'.

Another thing about *Moneyball*, though, is its emphasis on statistics. This is perhaps what Brailsford was more particularly alluding to in the Lanesborough, especially when he mentioned his 'monster database'. In assessing players, Beane used 'sabermetrics'; that is, the analysis of baseball through objective, statistical evidence.

Brailsford appears to want to do a similar thing in road cycling, using statistics and science – as he has done so successfully in track cycling. This would be a new approach, with professional road cycling as traditional as they come, its teams run by former professional riders, who then hand over to other former professional riders, who then … etc. The pool of people is small; almost, you could say, incestuous.

Brailsford, as he hinted in Bourg-en-Bresse when lamenting the way many teams seemed to be organised and run ('they don't even know where their riders are between races – that's bonkers!'), has perhaps identified this as a weakness; or a 'market inefficiency', to use the language of Michael Lewis in *Moneyball*. Weaknesses and market inefficiencies create opportunities. If a scientific approach doesn't seem to be adopted by other teams, it could be for two reasons: because it doesn't work; or because it hasn't been tried.

There are good reasons for suspecting it might not work. Unlike track racing, which takes place in a relatively controlled and predictable environment, road racing is multi-dimensional and unpredictable. The variables – in weather conditions, the nature of the course, the presence of up to 200 other riders and 20-odd teams – are numerous, even before we begin to decipher some of the unwritten rules and etiquette of the peloton, or the unofficial alliances and 'deals' between riders and teams, which are rumoured to be commonplace.

From a performance point of view, how you evaluate and assess road cyclists seems, in some respects, as complicated as the Enigma code. No analysis can be based simply on finishing positions, for example, since that tells only a fraction of the story. In fact, it might tell *nothing* of the story. Good teams need good *domestiques*, for example. But how do you evaluate a rider whose job it is to look after his team leader? By the number of water bottles he has distributed? By the length, and quality, of the shelter he has provided? What you cannot do is 'measure' the effectiveness of a *domestique* by his order across the finish line. Indeed, it is entirely feasible, sometimes desirable, that a *domestique* does an outstanding job and then doesn't finish the race.

Still, if a more science-based approach hasn't been tried, all the more reason to try it. It would be remiss of Brailsford not to at least explore the possibility. Like Boardman, Brailsford has successfully engaged 'outsiders' – in particular sports scientists with no previous experience in, or knowledge of, cycling – asking them to look afresh at the sport; to ask questions too obvious to be put by 'experts'; to identify 'market inefficiencies'.

But a key member of Brailsford's team has helped in another crucial area, giving his athletes – and indeed coaches – the mental 'tools' to think logically rather than emotionally.

'It's not about switching off emotional thoughts, because that would be impossible,' says Steve Peters, the psychiatrist employed by Brailsford, and now a member of his senior management team, along with Shane Sutton. (Boardman, who had been the fourth member of that team, stepped down after Beijing.) 'It's about bringing emotional thoughts under control,' continues Peters, 'overriding them with logic.'

Peters works with many athletes across many sports, and one of his techniques is to help them identify, and isolate, their 'chimp' – their 'chimp' being the emotional part of the brain. Each of the gold medallists in Beijing spoke with fear of being 'hijacked by my chimp'. They rode in fear of their chimp; or, rather, they rode with their chimp caged. Chris Hoy, the sprinter, said that his tears on the podium after his third gold medal owed to the fact 'I'd kept my emotions in check for the whole five days of competition; that was it all finally coming out.' The tears were the doing of his chimp, unleashed from its cage and running amok.

Also central to Brailsford's *modus operandi* – and the phrase for which he became best known following Beijing – is his 'aggregation of marginal gains'. In fact, Billy Beane in *Moneyball* is similarly preoccupied with taking such a detailed, no-stone-unturned approach. There is another name for it: Kaizen, the Japanese philosophy of constant and continuous improvement.

John Herety mentioned the 'empowering' aspect to Brailsford's management style when he took over from Peter Keen as performance director at British Cycling. This is Kaizen in action: it hands responsibility to everyone within an organisation; from the cleaner to the CEO, everyone is encouraged to participate in the organisation's activities, and to think about and improve their performance. It doesn't have to be a big improvement; just marginal ones. 'We encourage everyone to make a 1% improvement in everything they do,' Brailsford explained. 'Everyone, from the mechanics sticking on a tyre to the riders; their eating, sleeping, resting; everything.'

Central to Brailsford's 'aggregation of marginal gains' and Steve Peters' training of athletes to keep their emotional chimp under lock and key, is a focus on the process. The process is everything. 'There's no point in looking at consequences, because they could be out of your control,' says Peters. 'All you can do … all you can control is the process.'

Brailsford and his team – or most of it – bought into this in the run-up to the Beijing Olympics. Bradley Wiggins, by publicly admitting he was aiming for three gold medals, might have been an exception. When Wiggins failed to do this – winning 'only' two – he seemed slightly disappointed. (Speaking to Peters after the Olympics, he alluded to this in passing, when talking about the difficulties the non-medal winning cyclists were having post-Beijing: 'It's awful for Brad. He did his best and was superb. Double gold – unprecedented, until Chris [Hoy] got his three!')

Brailsford didn't make that mistake. In the run-up to Beijing, and even while the Olympics were on and his cyclists returned with gold medal after gold medal, he steadfastly refused, despite being asked repeatedly, to be drawn into predicting how many golds his team might end up with.

It is this that makes one aspect of the mission statement that Brailsford outlines at the Lanesborough Hotel puzzling, more particularly because it is the big one: the one that will make all the following day's headlines. That stated goal, to win the Tour de France, seems to fly in the face of Brailsford and his team's usual approach. It's an outcome, not a process.

'Control' appears to be another important word to Brailsford. It is a big reason for him wanting to run a professional road team, to bring his top athletes back under the umbrella of British Cycling, to be able to call on them for events – world championships and Olympic Games – in which they compete for the national team, rather than being at the mercy of their pro teams.

As Brailsford now knew all too well, with riders scattered around Europe, 'control' could be difficult to exert even when British riders raced in GB colours. The 2005 World Championships in Madrid had proved that, while also revealing some of the murkier aspects of professional road racing – including the deals and unofficial alliances previously alluded to.

In Madrid, two British riders – Tom Southam and Charly Wegelius – puzzled observers, and indeed the British coaching staff, now headed by Brailsford, by working at the front of the peloton in the early stages of the race. Their efforts were considerable, and did not appear to be in British interests. But there was a good reason for that: they weren't. Though wearing British jerseys, the two were actually working on behalf of the Italian national team.

John Herety, the road team manager at that time, now explains: 'Tom and Charly told me there was the potential for it happening.' Southam and Wegelius both rode for Italian professional teams. 'They were told it'd be in their interests to ride for the Italians. Their motive was not financial, I'm sure of that – it was to keep in with the sinister group of riders who ran cycling in that area [in the north of Italy]. They were looking after their jobs. I didn't like it, I was uncomfortable with it, but …' Herety, who'd ridden as a professional on the continent in the 1980s, and managed teams since the early 1990s, understood the rules of the game, and that, at the world championships, riders from 'lesser' countries would be encouraged, perhaps even obliged, to ride for the country in which they plied their trade professionally.

As Southam explains: 'In any other world championship, up to that point, it would have been the correct thing to do [as a British rider]. It was based on career. I can't speak for Charly, but he was very embedded in Italian culture. His contemporaries, the people he trained with, were in the Italian team. These were the people he worked with and who influenced his career. For me, I was in my second year, I was trying to break into that … circle of riders. I thought I needed to show these guys what I could do.

'The suggestion made to us at the World Championship the previous year was that we should make the most out of this race: to do the best we could for our careers. And I went into Madrid with the same attitude, but the climate had changed and I didn't take that into account. Like I say, in any other world championship it would have been the correct thing to do …'

When Southam says 'the climate had changed,' he is referring to Britain's rising status as a world cycling nation, even if this still owed only to their success on the track, particularly at the previous year's Athens Olympics. As Herety explains: 'One of the big things Dave was trying to create was this belief that we were just as good as everyone else – the Aussies, the Italians, the French, Belgians, Spaniards. This kind of thing had been going on in cycling for years and nobody cared. But the environment was definitely changing. Britain was trying not to be seen as second-class citizens. And so Dave had to be seen to be doing the right thing.'

While Southam and Wegelius were told off (Brailsford phoned Southam in the week after the road race. 'He wasn't unpleasant,' says Southam. 'He just said, "You fucked up"'), the furore that followed Madrid was such that Herety offered to resign as British Cycling's national road manager. 'I was hoping they'd say no,' he says with a bitter laugh. 'But they said, "Okay, then."'

The ramifications of what happened in Madrid were far-reaching, while the episode also provided further retrospective vindication for Peter Keen's original decision not to pour resources into road cycling. Never mind the drugs, it was murky in so many other respects; a game played to its own rules, in a bubble that could resemble a mafia state.

Although Brailsford didn't allude to Madrid when discussing his plans for Team Sky, a key motivation, surely, was to ensure that such a thing didn't happen again. Running his own team could, perhaps, allow him to control what at times seemed uncontrollable.

Martigny, Switzerland, 21 July 2009
Dave Brailsford and Jonathan Vaughters are standing together, but apart from the crowd, in the Village Départ of the Tour de France, locked in conversation. In less than an hour stage 16 of the Tour de France will get underway from the Swiss town of Martigny, crossing the Col du Grand-Saint-Bernard and the

Col du Petit-Saint-Bernard, both enormous Alpine passes, before finishing in Bourg-Saint-Maurice.

They make for an interesting, contrasting pair: Brailsford in British Cycling uniform of blue jeans and polo shirt, the quirkily debonair Vaughters, manager of the Garmin-Slipstream team, in a crisply ironed pale blue shirt, white jeans and brown suede loafers. Vaughters also wears small rectangular, subtly shaded glasses, and has long sideburns, two thin wedges extending down his cheeks towards the corners of his mouth. Since riding with Lance Armstrong in the US Postal team in the late 1990s, Vaughters has cast himself as an outsider, with an original, innovative approach. His team was set up to be different, from their Argyle-patterned strips to the anti-doping culture and the central hub – rather than being strewn across the continent, most of Vaughters' riders live in Girona, Spain. In fact, Vaughters has perhaps stolen a march on Brailsford here. His Garmin team, with its anti-doping ethos and internal testing programme, and its centralised base (unlike other teams, Vaughters knows where his riders are in between races), is doing some of the things Brailsford said he'd do.

Brailsford and Vaughters have much to talk about. Since the pre-Olympic holding camp, in Newport 12 months ago, everything has changed, in particular with regard to Bradley Wiggins. After winning his two gold medals in Beijing, Wiggins, now riding for Vaughters' team, turned his attention, finally, to road racing. And his aspirations seem to extend further than long, doomed solo breakaways. At the Tour's start in Monaco he even admitted that, for the first time in his career, he was aiming for a high overall placing. By 'high', he said, he was thinking top 20. Privately he was thinking top 15, maybe even top 10.

Now, in the final week of the 2009 race, to widespread astonishment, Wiggins sits third overall, just behind Alberto

Contador and Lance Armstrong. On the previous stage, to the ski town of Verbier, his performance was befitting his lofty placing. After his teammates David Millar and Christian Vande Velde set a searing pace to the foot of the mountain, Wiggins rode like someone trying not merely to finish in the top 20, but like someone trying to win the Tour. Here, for the first time, was the sense that Wiggins wasn't merely surviving: he was a major player, instructing his team to set him up, then assuming responsibility for finishing the job off, taking over like only a natural-born leader – or someone at the very peak of their form and confidence – can.

In Verbier, although Contador jumped away to win the stage, Wiggins' fifth place, in the company of climbing specialists Frank Schleck and defending Tour champion Carlos Sastre, and 30 seconds ahead of seven-time winner Armstrong, had left him in third place overall. Only four days remained to Paris. The podium beckoned.

Whatever happened in those final four days it had become clear: Wiggins had managed a metamorphosis of Kafka-esque proportions, in his case from Olympic track star to Tour de France contender. How had he done it? The loss of 7kg clearly helped – his new, pared-to-the-bone physique saw him re-(nick)named: from 'The Wig' or 'Wiggo', he was now 'The Twig' or 'Twiggo'.

Whatever the cause, the implications of his transformation are enormous, especially for the two men locked in conversation in the start village in Martigny. In Newport Wiggins had signed a two-year contract with Garmin, and so Vaughters has Wiggins for the 2010 season. Brailsford, meanwhile, is in the process of scouting and recruiting for Team Sky for 2010. But he is faced with the prospect of running a British team without a British star. Mark Cavendish, on his way to following his four stage wins of the previous year's Tour with six at this year's race, is locked into Bob Stapleton's Columbia-HTC team until the end of 2011. It is difficult to overstate how desperate this situation is. Wiggins and Cavendish are proving two of the stars of the 2009 Tour, both are British, but neither is available to Brailsford's new British team.

Eventually Brailsford breaks off from Vaughters and stops to talk. He describes rider recruitment as 'like a game of poker at the moment'.

'It's a fluid, dynamic situation,' says Brailsford. 'I've been sitting there with my budget most nights, rejigging it on an hourly basis almost, thinking, shit, we can do this, we can't do that. I think we've filled 17 slots. We're getting down to the sharp end now. The element of poker is the question: should we wait to the end of the season and see if any teams collapse, and get some top riders cheap?'

Brailsford describes the 'intelligence gathering' he's been doing, which seems to refer mainly to sussing out whether riders can be trusted; whether they are 'clean'. Indeed, there is a rumour that one prominent rider has been turned down on the basis of suspect data on his biological passport. Brailsford won't confirm this. 'It's not a black and white science,' he says of the analysis of the passports, which monitor a rider's blood and hormone levels over a long period. There is a margin of error, so I can't say for certain that so-and-so is using drugs. But we're taking a no-risk approach.

'When I talk to every agent,' explains Brailsford, 'the first thing I want is consent to see their biological passport. I get all the data sent over to Manchester to get our experts to pick over it. We also look at the history of the guy, his progression over a number of years. All the best bike riders, the clean ones, you see steady progression; you can graph it. The ones whose performances go up in a spike usually test positive. There are no secrets. It's basic stuff; intelligence gathering.

'But yeah, some of the data that comes through – you think, Jeez! I wouldn't say I'm surprised. It just makes me laugh, the audacity of some of them. But like I say, we're taking a no-risk approach.' (I later learn more about one suspect case from Shane Sutton. The rider in question, a top one-day rider, had been offered a contract at the Milan-San Remo Classic in March. 'Then we looked at his [biological] passport,' said Sutton. 'It was all over the place. We just said, "Sorry, mate, see you."' The rider in question subsequently found a place on another big team: possibly a disturbing outcome; or perhaps Brailsford and his team misread his passport. As he says, it's not an exact science.)

Brailsford admits he's been stung by the reaction in some quarters to his stated ambition of winning the Tour with a clean British rider. On both counts, 'British' and 'clean', he has been accused of naivety. 'Everyone says it's impossible to win the Tour clean,' says Brailsford. 'It's been said for a while now. I don't know whether these people think we just stick our heads in the sand in Manchester. We've got some of the best sports scientists in the world. And we use that knowledge and do our homework: we don't just come out with irrelevant comments.

'I think Brad's a case in point,' he continues. 'Bradley Wiggins is clean, and he's here performing with the best in the world. Correct me if I'm wrong, but he could win this bike race. He hasn't changed into a new athlete. He's the same person, taking the same full-on approach to another discipline within the sport. It vindicates our idea that if you take a proper approach – analysing everything, looking at the sports science – then it's possible.

'To be honest,' Brailsford adds, 'for the last couple of years I've been quite confident we'd get a British winner of the Tour de France, and people have said, "Yeah right, you don't know what you're talking about."'

And is Wiggins one of the riders he had in mind as a potential winner?

Brailsford, now standing with his arms folded like a football manager, rocks back on his heels and, with his mouth clamped shut, shakes his head. 'No, no,' he says. 'No, no, no.'

What had he and Vaughters been discussing? 'Actually,' he says, unfolding his arms, 'we were talking about Swiss chocolate.'

Bourgoin-Jallieu, 24 July 2009

In a hot and dusty field in Bourgoin-Jallieu, where stage 19 of the 2009 Tour will start in an hour, reporters and TV crews form a crowd around the entrance to the Garmin-Slipstream team bus, close enough to catch refreshing wafts of the air-conditioning whenever the door opens. Then comes not so much a waft as a blast of something else: the raw punk energy of 'Pretty Vacant' by the Sex Pistols. As soon as it starts it is cranked up, prompting a sing-along inside:

'No point in asking us, you'll get no reply ...'

The bus reverberates to the rhythm, rocking to the movement inside. Matt White, the team's director, steps out, as if to escape the noise. 'Wiggo will be out after this song,' says the Australian, smiling broadly.

When Bradley Wiggins emerges, 24 hours before the biggest day of his career, with his battle for a place on the podium still alive, and set to be decided at the summit of Mont Ventoux on the penultimate day of the Tour, he steps into a swarm of reporters. It is a swarm that has grown day by day, and which is now as chaotic as the crush outside any of the other team buses, with the possible exception of Astana, the team with two of Wiggins' podium rivals, the yellow-jerseyed Alberto Contador and Lance Armstrong. In his comeback year Armstrong would surely not have predicted he'd have to beat a track cyclist for a place on the podium of the Tour de France.

Nobody would have predicted that. But Wiggins has looked strong, Armstrong vulnerable and more erratic than in his pomp. 'Armstrong, fragile troisième,' reads the headline in *L'Equipe* this morning.

The Sex Pistols are Wiggins' choice, and that lyric – 'No point in asking us, you'll get no reply' – has come to seem especially apt. The more Wiggins has grown into his new role as a Tour contender, and the more interest there has been around him, the less comfortable he has seemed. It is one reason, allied to his new star status, for the scrum outside his bus this morning: the less he said, the more prized Wiggo's words became.

But it is in marked contrast to the Tour's first rest day in Limoges, a week into the race, when Wiggins had been expansive, and fascinating. After his performance in the Tour's first mountain range, the Pyrenees, everyone was talking about his weight loss, as though that held the key to his transformation. 'I've worked my arse off for this,' he said in Andorra, after finishing with the leaders at the Tour's first summit finish. It was true: his arse did seem to have vanished.

In Limoges a few days later Wiggins explained how he'd done it, and why: 'I went about it in a really planned way. I worked with Nigel Mitchell [the British Cycling nutritionist] and Matt Parker [the BC endurance coach]. It's been a nine-month process and I did it because I wanted to give the road, and the Tour, a right good crack. Shane Sutton's been telling me I could do it; he instilled that belief and confidence in me.

'After the Olympics, and the party season and making a prat of myself for part of the year, I weighed 83kg. Now I'm 71kg. But that's it; there's no more to come off. It's getting ridiculous now – Nigel's quite worried, I think. But it's worked very well for me. I haven't lost any power. I've been lucky.

'It's been a lengthy process and there were spells when I could put weight on, and others when I could lose it,' Wiggins said. 'A lot of it was changing what I ate, and when I ate, not necessarily eating less. I'd go wheat and gluten free at times. And I'd try not to eat bread. I don't have any sugar any more. That cuts out a lot of calories. I'd have two or three sugars in coffee. And booze – I don't have any beer any more. I forget the last time I had a beer. You get to the point where you don't miss it.'

At this point, Wiggins might not have been comfortable talking about himself as a Tour contender – almost two-thirds of the race remained, including the Alps and Mont Ventoux – but he appeared far from uncomfortable talking candidly and self-deprecatingly about himself, and his almost comical lack of preparation for this Tour. He hadn't reconnoitred the stages to come in the Alps, he admitted. 'Nah, of course I didn't,' he laughed. 'I was doing 10-mile time trials and Premier Calendars [domestic road races] back in England. I didn't really expect to be in this position.'

Yet he had believed that a high overall placing might be possible. Apart from Sutton's encouragement, a catalyst had been the previous year's performance of his Garmin teammate Christian Vande Velde. Vande Velde had been fourth in 2008. 'That was inspiring,' said Wiggins, "cos I know he's clean. It showed me you can do it on bread and water. I mean, I left the Tour in 2007 saying I'd never come back. But watching it on telly last year, seeing people like Christian and Cav, it was a breath of fresh air from the previous years.'

The biggest change, however, was in Wiggins himself. 'I didn't have the work ethic when I first rode the Tour in 2006,' he admitted. 'I was coming off the back of being Olympic champion at the age of 24, and I thought I was it, to be honest. I thought I'd made it. It's only now I realise what cycling's about. With the Olympics, you get swept along, they're great, fantastic, but, in the world of cycling, they don't mean much. You get over-feted for the Olympics.' There were other reasons, though, for sticking to the track, to what he knew. 'Before 2006

I was in a team that I disliked, surrounded by people that disliked me,' Wiggins said. 'And in 2006 I just wanted to do the Tour to say I'd done the Tour. I didn't think I'd come back; I thought I'd lose my contract at the end of 2006, so I just wanted to say I'd done the Tour.

'I grew up in teams where the French had a real funny attitude towards everyone else,' he continued, now hitting his stride – getting things off his chest. 'There was this sense of: "There's no way we can compete with those guys because they're doing other stuff, but we're French and we do it right, and we have croissants and baguettes, and we can sleep at night with a clear conscience and can't control what other people are doing." Even if you were near the top guys on a stage, the attitude was: "That was fantastic, look how well you did." And you were feted for doing quite little things, really.'

Joining Garmin at the start of the season had opened his eyes to a team that 'gives you the freedom to be who you want to be. We're much more of a family, without shouting about it. People want life contracts here. It's just like a close knit friendship, a relaxed atmosphere, and there's no pressure to get results, which suits me.'

As he spoke, in the dining room of a budget hotel on the outskirts of Limoges, Wiggins appeared relaxed and at ease. He slouched in his seat, his long, lanky legs splayed beneath the table, from time to time using his painfully thin arms to help make a point. He tended to avoid eye contact, however. He also remarked testily that he 'had the arse with some journalists,' who kept asking him about doping. 'Lance gave me some advice about the press,' he said. 'But I'm not going to tell you what he told me.'

Whatever it was, Wiggins grew gradually more distant as the Tour wore on and his star ascended. Most mornings he remained in his bus for as long as possible, emerging as the last call was going out for riders to sign on for the day's stage.

Sometimes he had a few words for the waiting press; other mornings he ignored them, hiding behind his Oakley sunglasses and pushing through the crowd as he rode off silently. It was very different to 2006, when he spent mornings drinking coffee, reading newspapers, shooting the breeze. It was true that his circumstances had changed beyond recognition. But was there another explanation? One morning, I mentioned Wiggins' reticence and occasional curtness to Jonathan Vaughters, his team manager. 'He's shy,' said Vaughters. 'It's no more than that; he's really uncomfortable speaking to the press because he's actually very shy.'

'But he's a natural,' I said. 'He's eloquent, and he can be funny. He doesn't seem shy.'

'I was watching him in Limoges,' said Vaughters. 'He was doing a good job of seeming comfortable. But it was an act. I could see his legs under the table – they were shaking.'

Hotel Cadro Panoramica, Lugano, 25 September 2009

Early evening on the roof terrace of the Panoramica Hotel, as the sun sets over Lake Lugano, which nestles deep in the valley below, and Dave Brailsford surveys a pile of white paper sitting on a table, its edges gently lifting with the breeze.

'I can sign those while I talk,' he says to the colleague charged with managing the logistics of setting up Team Sky.

'I'm not sure that's such a good idea,' she says.

They're the riders' contracts for 2010. But they don't include one for Bradley Wiggins. His fourth place in the Tour – missing out on the podium by just 38 seconds to Lance Armstrong – was sealed with a gutsy, even heroic, effort on Mont Ventoux on the penultimate day.

'And so to the Ventoux,' Wiggins had written on Twitter that morning. 'Spare a thought for the great Tom.' Then he rode, with a photograph of Tom Simpson taped to the top tube of his bike, as though inspired by his late countryman, fighting almost the entire length – or rather height – of the mountain, from the shelter of the trees as the climb got underway, to the bald, lunar-like upper slopes, where Simpson died during the 1967 Tour.

As they ascended into the sky Wiggins was trailed off, but he fought back, only to be trailed off again, only to fight back again – a yo-yo effort that is torture at the best of times, purgatory on a climb like Mont Ventoux. Approaching the summit, and riding past the Simpson memorial statue, and past Simpson's daughter, Joanne, who emptied her lungs to yell 'GO BRAD!', Wiggins dangled just off the back of the Contador-Schleck-Armstrong group, his mouth wide open, his face a picture of agony. After such an effort, and although at the start of the day the podium had seemed a possibility, his fourth place in Paris – equalling Robert Millar's best-ever British performance in the Tour, 25 years previously – could only be seen as a glorious triumph.

Wiggins' fourth-place finish was a game-changer for Brailsford and for Team Sky (and of course for Wiggins). Cavendish, even with his six stage wins, was all but forgotten. With Wiggins now a *bona fide* Tour contender, how could he *not* be in the new British team that was setting out the following season to try and win the Tour? And yet, how *could* he be, given that he was contracted to Garmin for 2010? 'I would have to be clinically insane to sell that contract,' said Vaughters, and he had a century's tradition on his side. Whereas footballers routinely break contracts, and engineer moves to other clubs, such a thing doesn't happen in cycling.

Still, the speculation couldn't be stopped. It was not fuelled by Wiggins, who, when asked, consistently said: 'I'm contracted to Garmin and that's the end of it.'

At least, it *wasn't* fuelled by Wiggins. Not until today, when Brailsford sits down in the Hotel Cadro Panoramica, the British team's base for the World Championships in nearby

Mendrisio, just a couple of hours after Wiggins has given an interview to Jill Douglas of the BBC. Douglas had asked him about the speculation linking him to Team Sky. And ordinarily he would have said, 'I'm contracted to Garmin and that's the end of it.'

But in Mendrisio, following a frustrating ride in the World Time Trial Championship, during which he suffered mechanical problems and tossed away his bike in disgust, Wiggins appears, mid-interview, to disengage the part of his brain that should filter out a remark that he might subsequently come to regret. 'There's a bit of a tug-of-war going on over who Bradley Wiggins will ride for at the Tour next year,' suggests Douglas.

'Yeah, ffffwwoooo,' says Wiggins, affecting a half-frown, half-smile. 'I'll leave it to the experts. It's unfortunate, that. I've had a good year this year at Garmin, but times have changed. The Tour changed everything for me really. We'll see what happens.'

'So,' says Douglas, 'the lawyers will decide?'

'I dunno, I dunno,' says Wiggins, rubbing his chin, biting his bottom lip, looking about as comfortable as a convict – probably because he knows what he's about to say – yet also strangely relaxed, perhaps because he thinks that what he's about to say will be liberating.

'It's a bit like trying to win the Champions League,' he tells Douglas. 'And to win the Champions League, you go to Manchester United. And I'm probably playing at Wigan at the moment. I'll probably have to make that step to do it.' (Amusingly, the next day, Wigan beat the champions-elect Chelsea.)

As Brailsford sits down, he smiles and says: 'No questions on whether we are Man United or Wigan please.'

Now, as the season draws to a close, the British professional team – Team Sky – has never seemed more concrete. Brailsford has been working closely with the team's first appointed *directeur sportif*, Scott Sunderland. Actually, Sunderland will be known as a sports director, not a *directeur sportif*. It is a British team, after all. Sunderland, an Australian ex-rider and previously a director with the Saxo Bank team, has been instrumental in the recruitment process, as he was, briefly, with the Cervelo TestTeam at the end of 2008, leaving to take up the position with Team Sky before a pedal had been turned in competition.

As we sit down with Brailsford in Lugano, Team Sky's first signings have already been named. Brailsford, though, wants to talk buses. 'Twelve months ago,' he says, 'driving down the motorways of Britain, I wouldn't have been able to name you a single [make of] coach. But I guarantee you I could tell you now what they're like, where they're from, who made them – everything.'

He is talking about the new team bus. But as Brailsford explains the thinking that has gone into it, he offers an insight into the detail he is prepared to go into … 'Where do you go to get a coach fitted out?' asks Brailsford. He doesn't wait for an answer. '80% of teams go to two places. We went to those two places and decided it wasn't what we want. We don't want a Belgian bus with little tweaks. We're getting them done by JS Fraser: they make nice buses. But we looked at what they did and thought …' Brailsford sighs. 'It wasn't right. So we got everyone in the next day and looked at it again. We got all our sports scientists, our boffins in, and said: "Right, it's a box on four wheels, how do you get a competitive advantage out of that space, pre-race and post-race? How do you make sure our guys are better recovered by the time they get to the hotel than any other team? What are you going to put in there – that's legal?"

'We're spending that much money on it,' adds Brailsford, 'that it can't be just a billboard – it's got to give us an advantage.'

But if Brailsford is going to this much trouble with the team bus, what does that tell us about his approach to everything else? 'My attitude to the bus is the same as anything else,' he says. 'Where you realise you don't have expertise, you get an expert. So I hired the chief truckie at Honda [Formula One racing team], Gwilym Evans. He's worked in F1 since 1984, starting with Benetton. Anything that didn't walk out of the Honda warehouse was his responsibility – every vehicle. And he's brought new ideas – new for cycling, anyway. He went to a *services des courses* [where bikes and equipment are stored between races and worked on by mechanics] and the first thing he said was: "Lads, paint the floor white." The mechanics are saying, "You can't do that, it'll get dirty." But Gwilym says, "That's the point! We're going to have a clinical environment."

'With the buses, we brainstormed it and figured out what matters. One of the big things is personal space. Ask the riders: they want personal space. They get in the bus in the morning, they're in the public eye straight away, and they're in the public eye all day riding their bike. When they come back, they want personal space. So we wanted to optimise that. On the Tour de France, you've got nine guys. So there are only nine seats.

'But we've got serious technology on there, too. Where the toilet normally goes, we've got a bloody big computer server there. And everyone will have a MacBook Pro console …'

While the image of Brailsford on the motorway, casting his beady eye over passing buses, may be amusing, it seems to be typical of his approach. Nothing is too small or apparently inconsequential to escape his attention, or his quest for 'marginal gains'. A colleague, Ned Boulting, told me of accompanying Brailsford to Quarrata, the Tuscan base of the British Cycling Academy. Brailsford was inspecting a property that had been acquired to turn into an all-purpose, all-singing, all-dancing, Quarrata base for Team Sky, with *services des courses*, treatment rooms and accommodation. It included a self-catering apartment. 'And Dave was trying to work out the optimum layout for kitchen furniture,' says Boulting. 'He then spent a good half an hour discussing with Max Sciandri the importance of getting the access road re-surfaced. It was astonishing that he could spend so long on such a seemingly insignificant thing. But it was all about making life as easy as possible for the rider.'

There's a problem, though. And it has nothing to do with buses, or the layout of kitchen furniture. It has to do with who will lead Team Sky. It is two weeks since the first names were announced. Geraint Thomas, Ian Stannard, Peter Kennaugh – all products of the British Academy – Steve Cummings and Chris Froome are the first British riders named. And there is excitement around some of the overseas riders named – in particular, the Norwegian Edvald Boasson Hagen, one of the most exciting young talents in the sport.

Missing, however, is the British star. There is no Cavendish, no Wiggins. Brailsford has given up on Cavendish – Bob Stapleton is wealthy enough and certainly determined enough not to budge in his commitment to keep Cavendish for the remaining two years of the contract he signed in July 2008. But Wiggins is a different case. He could still be available at a price, though the one recently mentioned by Vaughters seems calculated to deter, or to increase the offer. 'You're risking your title sponsorship if you lose your best GC rider,' said Vaughters. Pressed to put a value on Wiggins, he added: 'Really, you look at the real value, it is probably in line with $15m.' That's a lot of Swiss chocolate.

As he sits down to sign those contracts in Lugano, Brailsford seems unconcerned. He is optimistic and ebullient. 'There are going to be teething problems,' he does concede. 'If it was NASA there'd be teething problems.

'My tendency in a new project is to get involved, to be very hands on, so I have to pull back – and go and speak to Steve

Peters,' he continues. 'I want the people involved, the riders and the staff, to feel that they own a part of this, that it's their adventure; that everyone is there to contribute to the performances of others, so everyone has to feel ownership.

'It's the same as the model at British Cycling. We – the coaching and support staff – are the minions. We're there to help the riders. It's all about the riders. They're the kings and queens of their world.'

CHAPTER 4

THE BEST SPORTS TEAM IN THE WORLD

'You can't teach experience.'

Scott Sunderland

Kilmarnock, 31 October 2009

With one hand, Bradley Wiggins jabs a finger accusingly. With the other, he is holding a bottle of red wine. A straw pokes out the neck of the bottle, bobbing like a cork in a choppy ocean. Wiggins takes a swig (ignoring the straw), then lifts his arm and jabs his finger again.

'You lot just wanna see me fail! You wanna see me fall flat on my face!' he says, addressing a small group of journalists. He is smiling. Joking. Half-joking. Maybe.

The Tour de France, and Wiggins' fourth-place finish in Paris, seems a long time ago. Then again, to Wiggins, lunchtime probably seems a long time ago. It was then that he had boarded a train in Preston, bound for a charity dinner in Kilmarnock, accompanied by his wife, Cath, and armed with booze. (We know this from Wiggins' lunchtime Twitter update: 'On train with @cathwiggins heading to Braveheart doo tonight, Got a bag of Stella and a bottle of red, the day starts here!')

Now it's midnight. But this is the Wiggins of legend, not least of his own legend. As he relates in his autobiography, *In*

Pursuit of Glory, when he's 'on', he's really *on* – no wheat, no gluten, no sugar, no booze. But when he's 'off', he's really *off*, and capable of sinking a dozen pints in his local pub during the all-day sessions in which he said he indulged for a couple of months after the Athens Olympics in 2004. It wasn't unusual, he recalled, for him to follow an all-day session in the pub with a shared bottle of wine in the evening, before polishing off some of the Belgian beer he keeps in the cellar – or *kept* in the cellar, until he realised it was all gone. Tonight, in Kilmarnock, he's most certainly 'off': off season, off the bike, off the leash, off his head, on the lash.

'You-lot-just-wanna-see-me-fail,' slurs Britain's brightest hope for Tour de France glory, the words ceasing to be separate entities and congealing messily. 'You-wanna-see-me-fall-flat-on-my-face.'

At the same time as Wiggins' big night out in Kilmarnock (next day's tweet: 'Braveheart doo done and dusted, great dinner and a great cause. Hungover like a MOFO') – and perhaps even explaining his excess – the will-he-won't-he join Team Sky saga was becoming ridiculous.

Cycling, a sport with no real transfer market, and a noble tradition of riders honouring contracts, had never seen anything like it. The pursuit of Wiggins by Team Sky, who were depicted as arrogantly waving their chequebook in Vaughters' and Garmin's face as they tried to lure their rider, drew criticism, as did their attempted signing of another British rider, the Academy graduate Ben Swift, who had also signed a two-year contract at the start of the 2009 season with the Russian Katusha team.

Still the will-he-won't-he Wiggins affair rumbled on, with Wiggins firing off angry tweets every time the story was reported, as though he wanted it all kept under wraps (and even though most reports were entirely accurate: Team Sky *were* trying to buy Wiggins out of his contract). Wiggins tried to keep out of it, and to get back into training, but the uncertainty was, he later admitted, unsettling; hardly ideal at a time of the year when the party season is supposed to be winding down, and the hard work beginning. On 5 November, 18 days before Team Sky's first get-together in Manchester, and with 17 riders already named, it was reported that a Sky delegation were in New York meeting a Garmin delegation. It was in the hands of lawyers now, it seemed (though the New York story was erroneous).

As urgent as the pursuit of Wiggins seemed – as, indeed, it had become, with so much now riding on the eventual outcome due to the fact that Team Sky had no obvious leader, nor, without Wiggins and Cavendish, either of the British A-listers – contingency plans were drawn and re-drawn throughout 2009. The recruitment of a Tour contender, or at least someone capable of aiming for the podium, was essential, and so it was a topic of regular discussion and debate between the key decision-makers: Dave Brailsford, Shane Sutton and the senior sports director, Scott Sunderland.

Carlos Sastre, the 2008 Tour de France winner, was discussed as a potential signing, and three meetings held with his representatives. Sunderland, who had worked with Sastre at the CSC team, pressed the case for the Spaniard, who, approaching his mid-thirties, could act as a mentor to the younger riders. For one thing, Sunderland said he was confident that Sastre was clean. 'I'd stick my hand in the fire for Carlos,' he told Sutton. (It's a German saying popular in Belgium. Sunderland, an Australian who'd lived in Belgium throughout his racing career, was almost a naturalised Belgian.)

However, with Sastre there was the same problem as with Wiggins: he was under contract for 2010 to the team that Sunderland had helped set up and then left, the Cervelo

TestTeam. Alberto Contador, now a double Tour winner, was also discussed. Again, though, and despite contact being initiated with Contador's manager – his brother, Fran – interest in the Spaniard was dropped before it really developed.

A concrete offer was made to the young Italian rider, Vincenzo Nibali. Nibali, who finished three places behind Wiggins at the 2009 Tour de France, would have earned a salary of €1m had he joined Team Sky. He opted, however, to stay with the Italian Liquigas team. And so the nascent British team still resembled a headless beast: with the infrastructure, the staff and most of the riders in place – but no leader.

Two weeks later, on 20 November, *L'Equipe* reported that Wiggins had signed with Sky. But Vaughters refuted that. 'Brad has a contract with Garmin for 2010,' he told *Cycling Weekly* through gritted teeth. 'That is my statement. If [*L'Equipe*] has such a great source, they should reveal him/her.'

Three days later, 24 riders gathered in a hotel on the outskirts of Manchester for a week-long camp. They included some big names: Tour de France stage winner, cobbled Classics specialist and free spirit Juan Antonio Flecha of Spain; the young, talented, very raw and very shy Norwegian Edvald Boasson Hagen; the Swede with boy band looks, Thomas Lofkvist; Simon Gerrans, an Australian with stage wins in all three Grand Tours, of France, Italy and Spain. But still no Wiggins – and still no leader for the Grand Tours, though Lofkvist was now talking up his prospects in the Swedish press. The Swede assumed that, if Wiggins didn't join, he'd be de facto team leader.

The Manchester camp, held in a hotel just off the M60, was a get-together and a bonding session. It was not a training camp. Which was just as well, since the week provided a stark introduction to Manchester weather: every day featured slate grey skies, driving rain and biting cold. When they weren't in meetings, they mooched around the reception area and the

Starbucks by the entrance, their tans and tracksuits marking them out from the businessmen in suits who hurried past. (Brailsford had been more or less living in a similar hotel nearby for many of the previous months, as he worked around the clock to set up Team Sky, while also fulfilling his responsibilities as British Cycling performance director. His long-term residence at the Holiday Inn led some colleagues to christen him 'Alan Partridge', after Steve Coogan's comic character, who was also a long-term resident in an anonymous hotel.)

But the weather hardly dulled the sense of anticipation. There was a sense that the riders were involved in something new, something different, something exciting. It was infectious.

On the first night a reception was hosted by Brailsford, who called the riders to the stage, one by one. There, he presented them with their new team jersey. It was the first glimpse they'd had of the striking Adidas black-and-blue kit. It was stark, minimalist, far removed from the garish collages of sponsors' names and logos sported by some of the other teams in the peloton; the shorts were retro black, with the shirts featuring black on the front (black disperses heat) and white on the back (white reflects heat) with a thin sky-blue line (symbolising the 'narrow line' between success and failure).

'When we were presented one by one on the stage, and handed the jersey by Dave B, it was pretty emotional,' said the Australian rider Chris Sutton, Shane's nephew. 'It was the first time we'd seen it. It gives meaning to what you do. I wasn't going to cry, but …

'It's blown me away actually,' continued Sutton. 'The way they've organised things, the structure they've set up for this team, and what they want you to achieve. I expected big things but the camp exceeded my expectations. Everyone seems to be on the same wavelength, and to want the same thing. I've known about the British track programme for a long time through Uncle Shane and Dave B. I could see that it was all about the riders – that the emphasis is on them, and they're really supported. It's why I wanted to join the team.'

There were riders involved who'd been in big teams, yet they'd never experienced anything like the buzz of being part of Team Sky. Even little details – sky-blue, Team Sky-branded M&Ms, sky-blue, Team Sky-branded iPhone covers, not to mention the iPhones and laptops – helped foster a sense that this would be, above all else, *different* to other teams. The very fact that the week wasn't a training camp, but a get-together, with the emphasis on talking and planning, was in itself different. 'We had one meeting that lasted five hours,' said Steve Cummings, a straight-talking, down-to-earth Merseysider. 'I still haven't got over it, to be honest.' At school, he admitted, 'I didn't like the classroom, I'd rather be out doing things, playing football, riding my bike.' But he appreciated the need for planning and the attention to detail. He was a professional, now 28, who had also ridden for another team that had upped the ante, Lance Armstrong's Discovery Channel squad. 'Discovery Channel was better than anything else at the time,' said Cummings, 'but this is different, it's more advanced; it takes it up a level. The attention to detail, wanting to go that little step further for every rider …'

For Geraint Thomas, another of the British riders, it was 'a dream'. The Academy graduate had 'dreamed of becoming a pro, and of riding with a British team. We're there now; we're on the map. If we can take the principles from the track team across to the road I don't see why we can't be the best in the world. It's mega. Seeing all the riders come together, the kit, it's really exciting. I can't wait to get going.'

For Serge Pauwels, a Belgian rider who'd signed from Cervelo, another team that had upped the ante when they entered the peloton in 2009, there was a different focus at

Team Sky. 'Last year in Cervelo there was also a lot of attention to detail, but there the focus was on technology, not on performance,' said Pauwels. 'Here, performance is the focus.' And for Michael Barry, an experienced Canadian who'd ridden with Lance Armstrong's US Postal team, and also alongside Mark Cavendish at HTC-Columbia, it was all about the 'philosophy'. 'I've noticed what they've done on the track, what they've accomplished,' said Barry. 'A lot of teams select riders based on their results in the past, and based on their proven potential rather than their projected potential. This team wants to get the most out of every individual, and for an athlete that's the perfect environment to be in. Because we all want to get the most out of ourselves. If we have the support to do that, we can achieve more than we've achieved before.'

Barry, one of the more thoughtful and eloquent members of the peloton – who had written a book about his experience with Armstrong's team – was also attracted to the team's wider goal: its mission to encourage people to ride bikes. Strange as it may seem, promoting cycling is not a common goal for professional cycling teams. In fact, it is unheard of. 'I mean, yeah, we might motivate people to ride bikes by what we do,' said Barry, 'but here there's a direct correlation between the team and getting more people riding bikes. This really appeals to me. Thinking back to when I was a kid, and why I wanted to be a cyclist, it was the interaction we had with cyclists, seeing what they do, being inspired by them. That connection, between racing cyclists and cycling for fun, or for transport, is very rarely made.

'Basically,' added Barry, 'this sounded like a team with a new philosophy and I thought, oh man, I want to be part of it, it sounds exciting. It's about thinking outside the box. Cycling tends to be a very traditional sport. People are scared to make changes or try new things; they're apprehensive. But this team has the personnel and the resources to do that.'

Mat Hayman, an Australian *domestique* and cobbled Classics specialist who had joined Team Sky after 10 years with the Dutch Rabobank team, was similarly impressed. In fact, he had wondered whether the idea he'd been sold had been too good to be true. 'I spent two days trying to get to Manchester,' said Hayman. 'I missed my connecting flight to Europe, and I was trying to phone all the guys – Dave Brailsford, Shane Sutton, Scott Sunderland. All their phones were turned off, and at that moment I was thinking this might be a big hoax.' Hayman's scepticism was understandable. Four years earlier, the legendary Italian *directeur sportif* Giancarlo Ferretti announced that he'd secured sponsorship from Sony-Ericsson and began signing riders, only to then learn that he'd been the victim of a hoax (and not even a very elaborate hoax; Ferretti had concluded the deal entirely by email, with a 'Sony Ericsson' executive using the email address: ronwestland-sonyericsson@hotmail.com).

'At the start some of the things that Scott and Dave were telling me sounded too good to be true,' Hayman continued. 'But what Sky have done, it seems to me, is that they've put their faith in Dave and that British Cycling group. I can imagine those guys walked into a room and said what they want to do for cycling, and that's why they bought into it. They sold it to me on the basis that the riders would have control, which is something I can't see Italian teams going for …

'Listen, this is killing the Aussies,' Hayman continued, 'because we've been trying to get something like this off the ground for years. The British guys don't know how lucky they are, to go in at ground zero on this. There's Russell Downing, he's fought for every minute to get here. It's great for the young guys, they've got the world in front of them, and for Russ, who gets the chance he probably deserved a few years ago.

'It's a British team but a few of us were reflecting, it hasn't been "British this, British that". We're Team Sky. If the Union Jack had been on the kit I'd have got my pen out and added some stars.' They wouldn't be playing 'God Save the Queen' in the bus in the mornings, Hayman added. 'Although the old girl is still my queen, too.'

Dan Hunt, one of the coaches who Brailsford had promoted from his work with the track cycling team (Hunt coached Rebecca Romero to her gold medal at the Beijing Olympics), said that their ambition was no less than 'to become the best sporting team in the world, across all sports'. Barry shrugged his shoulders as he was asked whether that was achievable. 'For sure that is achievable. It's a big reason I came here. There's a lot of work. But I wouldn't want to come to a team that said: our goal next year is to be average.'

Shane Sutton, meanwhile, shed some light on how this might be accomplished. He would be in charge of overseeing the coaches, as he had been at British Cycling. 'Mine is more of a mentoring role to the younger coaches and sports directors,' explained Sutton. 'For us it's about the mission. With the track programme the mission is to win Olympic medals. We're aiming just as high on the road. With the technology we can use, we'll know where the athletes are at every stage of the race in terms of their condition and how they're feeling. We'll have all the scientific data – heart rates, power outputs, all that. A road race is like starting a journey with a full tank of petrol and distributing it evenly over the race, making sure you're empty at the end of it.

'In my days as a rider there was none of this,' continued Sutton, whose career included one start of the Tour de France, with the ill-fated British team, ANC-Halfords, in 1987. 'The game's moved on. But with the association with a company like Sky we could really move it on some more. Look at the sports Sky have been involved with. Football – they've revolutionised it. They've made darts players into household names! They don't do things by halves. We've got the same mentality. Cycling is our life.

'We've done a great job on the track,' continued Sutton. 'Now let's see what we're capable of on the road.

Throughout the week in Manchester Dave Brailsford talked to the riders; he talked to them individually and as a group; he talked and he talked. He infused everyone with his own enthusiasm; he bestrode the gathering like a colossus; he was omniscient. Of course, for successful sports coaches or managers reputation is everything, and Brailsford's – following the success he'd masterminded in Beijing – could hardly have been higher.

Like all the best managers, Brailsford seemed able to get the best out of people. In Manchester he presided over the camp, and the countless meetings, with confidence and a sense of certainty, which fed into and reinforced the aura around him. His staff reinforced it, too. 'People like Dave come along once in a lifetime,' said Sutton. 'I've been fortunate to be in Dave's time. Listen, I think there are three key things behind our success: great leadership, which Dave's given us; a great coaching system; and gifted athletes who want to aspire to achieve things on the big stage. Now we've also got the Sky empire behind us. We're setting out with a full tank of petrol.'

'What's Dave like?' said Dan Hunt, repeating the question. 'Well I've worked with him for just over four years. And I'd say … Fantastic. He's a good boss, a good leader; he's motivational and inspirational. He's hard but pretty fair. I've survived four years, anyway.'

Above all else, though, what Brailsford was in Manchester was in charge. And being in charge is a good place to start.

And yet several of the riders were also surprised by another aspect of the new team. Though Brailsford was in charge, he said he wouldn't be a dictator. Team Sky would be a democracy, he told the riders. They would all have a say in decision-making, just as the track team had done. In fact, this system of management had evolved with the track team, particularly after disputes over team selections. 'What the riders want to know, more than anything else,' said Brailsford, 'is who picks the team, and what are the selection criteria.' After one dispute with the track sprinting team, Brailsford and his team charged *them* with drawing up the selection criteria. 'They went away and tried for hours to come up with criteria they were all happy with, and they couldn't do it,' said Brailsford. 'But at least they understood how difficult it was.' And they felt empowered, he added.

Here in Manchester, as Mat Hayman noted, Brailsford challenged the riders of Team Sky to draw up their own rules – over timekeeping; selection for the Tour de France; whether to have internal drug-testing, or not. 'The riders make the decisions,' said Kurt Asle Arvesen, another experienced rider, and an exile from the Saxo Bank team. 'That's something new for me. I think it's going to be great; we've made our own rules! Now, if we don't follow them, well, they're our rules. We did some of the same things at Saxo Bank, but we didn't go as far as this.'

Then there was the involvement of a psychiatrist. In Manchester, the 24 riders of Team Sky were introduced to Steve Peters.

Peters was the forensic psychiatrist who had been such an integral part of Brailsford's British set-up. In fact, there was surprise in some quarters that Peters remained involved with British Cycling after the Beijing Olympics, and even more that he was now becoming involved with Team Sky. After Beijing, he had been in high demand. His unusual role – no other sports team had a psychiatrist, as far as he knew – saw Peters thrust into the spotlight: his profile rocketed, job offers flooded in. If Beijing established Brailsford as a sporting guru, it also marked Peters, deceptively tall, fit-looking (he's a keen runner, not a cyclist), grey-haired and in his fifties, as someone with special insight and understanding – a Midas touch with more transferable skills than Brailsford, since he had worked across a range of sports and with altogether more complicated cases, including, before he joined British Cycling on a full-time basis, deeply disturbed individuals in Rampton Secure Hospital.

So why did Peters stick with Brailsford and his team, and with cycling? 'After Beijing,' he explains, 'we sat down as a [senior management] team, me, Dave, Shane and Chris [Boardman], and we decided where we were going as a team, and we asked, were we committing to it? Chris Boardman weighed it up and said, "I think I want to step out at this point." Which was fair.' Boardman, it should be pointed out, has six children, a bike business and extracurricular interests such as scuba diving. 'But Dave, Shane and myself said we'd like to go forward to London,' says Peters.

There were 'masses' of job offers, he adds with a smile. As he speaks, Peters is sitting in his grey-walled, windowless office in the bowels of the Manchester Velodrome, which has been fitted out since my last visit in 2007. As well as the desk and plastic chairs, there's a three-piece suite: blue, spongy sofa, and comfortable armchairs. The furniture looks cheap, maybe even the kind you'd buy in a second-hand shop, or rescue from a skip. And it's partly this austere setting that prompts the question: why, when he was in such demand, with some presumably attractive and well-remunerated options, did he turn down the other job offers? 'Em, we've got a job to do,' he says. 'I said I'd run certainly to London and then review it, so it's a four-year cycle. I think it's unfair to athletes to ditch them in the middle of the cycle. There's an expectation of team support. So ... the [job] offers are there. Plenty. It's just a case of saying, well, hang on until after London, and see what I feel then.

'I think the answer to the original question is that it's loyalty and professionalism that keeps me here. I've got a job to do, and it's a four-year job. And I enjoy it. The people are fantastic

… I'm sure there are plenty of psychs [psychiatrists] who'd love to step in and say, "I'll do it if you don't want to do it." And we forget that. You have to remind yourself every so often of the fantastic privilege of being in this team.'

Peters tends to downplay his importance. 'My role is not as significant as Dave's and Shane's,' he says. 'I'm like the icing on the top. It's the cake you really want.'

Peters was involved in rider recruitment for Team Sky. 'But indirectly,' he explains. 'Dave and Shane are the ones who knew about road racing; I'm learning. But it's like with the track – I knew nothing about it when I came in. In any case, that's not what I bring to rider recruitment. It's a culturally diverse team, so that creates new challenges, but the riders were all hand-picked. They're guys who were really into the culture we were trying to create in the team; they bought into that. A number of riders did apply who were rejected. We hand-picked on the grounds that these guys all bought into our principles and philosophy.'

A commitment to anti-doping was central to that philosophy, explains Peters. And this was Peters' responsibility – as well as the psychiatrist, he's the head of medicine. 'We had a lot of medical meetings with [British Cycling's doctor] Roger Palfreeman, myself and Dave, where we looked at riders' records and said, is there any evidence of doping?' says Peters.

'But more than that, when we interviewed the riders, we wanted riders who are so anti … we wanted a culture where they would search out anyone who was doing anything [wrong]. We asked the riders: how do you want to be monitored? And they were actually more rigorous than we would have been.

'It would wreck credibility for every single one of us,' Peters says of the possibility of a positive test, or a Team Sky rider implicated in a doping scandal. 'We could never legislate for it if someone slides through the net, but there wouldn't be any tolerance of them, because we are saying we can do this without any doping. The riders themselves said a lot about this in our interviews with them.'

Over recent seasons, as teams battled to restore credibility, some of them introduced their own in-house anti-doping programmes, recruiting leading anti-doping experts, such as the Dane Rasmus Damsgaard or the American Don Catlin, to oversee additional testing and analysis. When he initially discussed his aim of setting up a professional road team Brailsford said he, too, would have an internal anti-doping programme, operating separately from the UCI.

Indeed, for several months before the Manchester camp Roger Palfreeman, British Cycling's long-standing doctor, had devised an anti-doping programme that Team Sky could implement in addition to the UCI's biological passport programme. But this was a measure that the riders would be given a say on, and in Manchester it was put to a vote. They voted against its adoption.

At least, that is what one insider has said. Peters says it isn't correct. 'No, that's a fallacy,' he says. 'Roger Palfreeman did set up a system and said, "This would be absolutely rigorous." We put Roger's system to the riders but the problem was, the UCI said, "You don't need to be that rigorous; and if you're that rigorous, it's extremely costly and it won't pick up any more [data] than the biological passport." It wasn't that we rejected Roger's plan, or that we wriggled out of it. That's so far from the truth. Roger was perfectly happy with the system we put in place instead, where we do take extra tests but we do it in collaboration with the UCI and WADA [World Anti-Doping Agency].'

Interestingly, in another session at the get-together in Manchester, drugs and doping did feature prominently. In a meeting attended by Robert Tansey, group brand marketing director from the sponsors, Sky, the riders were introduced to a 'fear hat'. They were asked to write, on a piece of paper, any questions or 'fears' they had, and place them in the hat. It was anonymous. '50% of the questions were about doping,' a member of the coaching team later told me. 'The main thing they wanted to know was, what if someone takes drugs? What if there's a positive test on the team? They were told: "You don't have to. You're being paid. You don't need to win. There's no reason to take drugs."' Brailsford had always believed that a culture of 'fear' – or an environment in which riders believe their next contract hinges on winning races – is counter-productive in terms of performance. But fear could also be a staging post on the road to doping. The 'fear hat' was intended to dispel fear.

In Manchester, when he met the riders, Peters says: 'I explained who I was, what I did, what I didn't do.' His approach was similar to that he'd initially taken with the track squad; that is, softly softly. A one-on-one 'session' wasn't compulsory. 'We left it to the riders,' he says. Because some might be fearful of speaking to a psychiatrist, or concerned that a stigma might be attached, each rider was allocated a slot with Peters. It was up to them whether they attended. 'We had 24 riders there,' says Peters, 'and 20 came along for their session.'

They also had one-to-one meetings with the coaching staff, including the man who would act as Team Sky's race coach, Rod Ellingworth.

Though Scott Sunderland was to be the senior sports director, it was clear that Brailsford had big plans for Ellingworth, and hoped he could replicate the magic he'd conjured at the Academy, this time with a group of professionals. Ellingworth's job title, 'race coach', was unusual, if not unique, in the context of a professional road team. 'I don't think any other team has a "race coach",' admitted Ellingworth. 'But that's what it says on my Team Sky business card.'

'When you talk about "coaching", a lot of people automatically take that to mean "training", but there's a lot more to it than that,' Ellingworth explained. 'There are a lot of things that go on in a bike race that have nothing to do with training. "Coaching" isn't sending a bloke a training programme and telling him to get on with it. I'll be talking to the guys face-to-face before and after races, getting them to think about what they're doing, using tools like video analysis. Seven of the guys have their own personal trainers, and we've encouraged them to continue those partnerships. It's logical that we do that, because it's worked so well with Mark [Cavendish] and me, and we thought that was a decent template.

'A good example of the kind of "race coaching" I'm talking about was Mark really focusing on winning the first sprint of the Tour de France this year,' continued Ellingworth, becoming more enthusiastic as he spoke. 'He was fretting about it as the day approached, so I tried to break it down with him and get him thinking about two or three specific areas of the bike race, rather than fifty. I then chatted to his *directeurs sportifs*. That's the key: keeping the message consistent.'

It was clear that Brailsford considered Ellingworth an important member of his team. His role, 'race coach', was perhaps the first and most obvious example of the different approach Team Sky wanted to take to professional road racing. Traditional sports directors have much in common with old-style football managers; the kind who are hands-on in every aspect of the club, from organising training to dictating tactics, to player transfers and handling the media. In cycling, sports directors have similar responsibilities, plus driving the team cars, and in some cases even managing logistics such as travel and accommodation and dealing with sponsors (some *directeurs sportifs* are the point-of-contact with the sponsor, which might explain why they never get sacked: they are effectively their own boss). The race coach, in Brailsford's plan, would not be a glorified driver – as Shane Sutton joked some *directeurs sportifs* were, calling them 'mobile Garmins [sat-navs]' – but someone whose sole concern was performance.

'I see it as being an intermediate role between coach and sports director,' said Ellingworth. 'It's a new role, and in a way it could, in the long term, slightly challenge what is normally expected of a *directeur sportif*. I want to work with bike riders; I don't want to do hotels and logistics. That's someone else's job. That's the idea, anyway.

'I want to focus right in on bike racing, really analysing the racing. My job is to feed in the ideas we've got from British Cycling into the pro team, making sure we instil that ethos and stick to the standards we have at BC of performance planning.'

The main difference for Ellingworth would perhaps be in the age and experience of the riders he'd be working with, from 18-year-olds who'd just left home to – in some cases – 30-somethings with families. Not yet 40 himself, Ellingworth could hardly play the role of father, uncle or big brother to riders just a few years younger than him. 'We all have to listen to each other,' he said. 'There isn't going to be one strong person dominating the show; it's a group. That's what we've created at British Cycling and we want to keep that going.

'I cut my teeth at the Academy,' he continued, 'but of course I'll have a completely different style here. Having said that, the way I've worked with the Academy guys – with Geraint, Cav, Stannard – has changed once they've moved on from the Academy. It has to change. They're men now. I'll still tell 'em [what I think], but I'll make sure they're happy to receive criticism from me. I'm not going to shout and bawl at them. It's not a dictator role I'll have here.

'I was harsh at the Academy at times, I admit that. But I never shouted at them. I wanted to give them the sense not that they'd disappointed me, but that they'd disappointed themselves; it was to put ownership on them, to put the onus on them, so they feel they have ultimate responsibility for their performance.'

Ellingworth and two of the other coaches from the British track team, Matt Parker and Dan Hunt, were the people who Brailsford charged with 'challenging the conventional wisdom'.

Scott Sunderland represented the conventional wisdom. Like most *directeurs sportifs*, he was an ex-rider who had followed the traditional path to a professional career; or as traditional as it gets for an Australian. His father was a racing cyclist, so were his two brothers, and he started racing at the age of seven. As a teenager he worked double shifts in an abattoir close to the family home in Inverell, New South Wales, before travelling to Europe to pursue his dream of becoming a professional cyclist in 1986, aged 19. 'And I never missed a season until I stopped,' he says. He retired at the age of 38.

Still with the lean build, hungry look and sunken cheeks of a professional cyclist, Sunderland had swapped his bike for a place behind the steering wheel of a team car when he retired in 2004. He worked under Bjarne Riis at CSC, the world's number one ranked team, taking special responsibility for the spring Classics in and around Belgium, where he had lived since 1991, and enjoying success with back-to-back wins at Paris-Roubaix (thanks to Stuart O'Grady and Fabian Cancellara). With CSC now re-named Saxo Bank, the team's continuing success in the Classics filled Sunderland with pride. 'I feel that's my legacy, you know?' he said.

Team Sky's second sports director was Sean Yates, a legendary British professional in the 1980s and 90s, and a former Tour de France stage winner and yellow jersey. There could have been a second Sean behind the wheel of one of the team cars, but Sean Kelly, the Irish legend turned TV commentator who was considered for Team Sky, was ruled out on account of Brailsford's zero-tolerance doping policy (Kelly failed two drugs tests in the 1980s).

Sunderland and Yates were joined by two other sports directors: Steven de Jongh of Belgium and Marcus Ljungqvist of Sweden. Both were similarly steeped in European professional cycling, but the role of sports director was new to de Jongh and Ljungqvist; just weeks ago, they had been professional riders themselves, with the Quick Step and Saxo Bank teams. They had been identified by Sunderland as natural leaders; and they would learn about being a sports director under Sunderland and the vastly experienced Yates, whose career as a director also included a stint at CSC, and with Lance Armstrong at Discovery Channel and Astana.

Sunderland, though, was the man in from the beginning, the *senior* sports director, and his role had been to identify riders and talk to them before reporting back to Brailsford and Sutton. Sunderland stressed that it was only 'when Dave and Shane were happy [that] we moved ahead.' 'The riders' personalities were the big thing,' Sunderland explained. 'You could have a whole team of horses, but if they don't work together they'll pull that cart apart.

'We're not going to say that we're going to do everything completely differently,' Sunderland continued. 'But having 12 months prior to kick-off has given us time to think about how we can do certain things in a different way. If we end up reverting to the tried and tested methods, which teams have followed for years, we can say, "Okay, we tried something different …" It's going to be exciting.'

Sunderland relished the responsibility that came with his role. 'For Dave and Shane it's been a big learning curve, whereas for me, I'm doing things I know,' he said. 'As sports directors we're high performance managers. Experience is something you can't learn.'

In many respects Sunderland looked like a good appointment for Team Sky. He was young, ambitious, he had experience. But he was – there was no getting away from it – steeped in a world with a set of conventions that Brailsford was keen to challenge.

Challenging, or undermining, the role of sports director was far from Sunderland's agenda. While helping sign riders for Team Sky he had been involved in another project: a training course for sports directors, held under the auspices of the UCI. It marked a drive to 'professionalise' the role, he said.

As Sunderland told the website VeloNation: 'We're expected to do and to know a hell of a lot … a lot of things that aren't seen. There have been comments from the press that we are merely the chauffeur of the team car. I tell you that it's far from that, and it's really demeaning to us to say that. I think the people making such statements should follow a sports director around during the off-season and up and into the season, and they'd be amazed at all of the tasks that we cover along the way. It's 24 hours a day.'

There seemed a discrepancy between Sunderland's view of the sports director's role – as the most important person in the team – and Brailsford's. But the mood in Manchester at that first get-together was harmonious, happy, excited. The riders mixed easily, even if the French riders, Sylvain Calzati, a former Tour de France stage winner, and Nicolas Portal, and the Italians Morris Possoni and Davide Viganò, struggled to speak English. There was evidence that others were being drawn into the British team, and the British style of doing things. When the hotel bar closed at 11.30 on the Thursday evening Geraint Thomas proposed a night out in Manchester, and was joined by Greg Henderson, Russell Downing and Juan Antonio Flecha, the Spaniard who appeared to have made a positive impression on everyone. With his *joie de vivre* and enthusiasm, even at 32, Flecha summed up the buoyant mood in the camp. But there remained a problem. Team Sky still had no leader.

CHAPTER 5

UNVEILING THE WIG

'I'm staying with Garmin.'

Bradley Wiggins

Manchester Velodrome, 5 December 2009
'Once we're into January and it's apparent I'm still with Garmin, everything will settle down,' says Bradley Wiggins. Wiggins is standing in the track centre of the Manchester Velodrome, the sweat dripping from his lean frame (which isn't quite as lean as it had been five months earlier). A couple of weeks have passed since Kilmarnock, when Wiggins accused journalists of 'wanting to see him fail'.

Does he really think that? He waves his hands dismissively. His mouth flickers into a wry smile. 'I was pissed.'

Tonight he's competing in the Revolution meeting – a popular series that pits composite teams against each other – with Wiggins guesting for the 'Slicks'. He wears a black-and-white Slicks jersey, but with his garish blue-and-orange Garmin kit underneath. For how much longer, though?

Earlier on the same day he told the BBC: 'I have to see my contract out with Garmin [in 2010]. I didn't really have a choice, to be honest. That's why I haven't got too worried about it. In my mind, it was never going to happen, so I never built my hopes up too much. I'll just have to concentrate on what I've got and focus with Garmin, and do the best we can do next year.'

Later, in the track centre, he maintains a steady, steely gaze as he says: 'Yeah, I'm staying with Garmin. Once we're into January and it's apparent I'm still with Garmin, everything will settle down. You'll see.'

Five days later, Bradley Wiggins was unveiled as a Team Sky rider.

As with so much of the saga, the occasion of Wiggins' unveiling was unlike anything previously seen in the sport of cycling, certainly in Britain. There were TV cameras, around 20 reporters … and there, finally, was Bradley Wiggins, striding on to the stage in a private members' club on London's Portland Square, followed by Dave Brailsford. Perched on chairs in front of a gleaming Pinarello bike – one of the official team machines, in black and blue – Brian Nygaard, Team Sky's new press officer (another exile from the Saxo Bank team), introduced the pair.

'It gives me huge, huge pleasure to finally confirm that Bradley Wiggins will ride for Team Sky next year,' said Brailsford. 'It's been a real ambition of mine for quite some time now. Brad and I go right back to the Sydney Olympics. We've worked closely together for all this time; and it became very, very clear to us that he was one of the key people we'd want in the team, at the start.'

Sitting alongside him, Wiggins looked more rock star than cyclist. Specifically, he resembled his idol, Paul Weller, with combed-over-the-ears hair, black velvet jacket, white collarless shirt, jeans and silk, paisley-patterned scarf. Brailsford had gone for the understated look in white shirt, black tank top, with discreet 'Sky Pro Cycling' insignia on the chest, and blue jeans. (Tank tops are *de rigueur* among the squad's coaching and management team.)

Wiggins has signed for four years, says Brailsford. Four years is a long time in professional cycling; four-year contracts are almost unheard of. Brailsford doesn't say what it took to prise him away from Garmin. But that becomes known later: £2m, or the equivalent of £2m including *in lieu* benefits and TV advertising slots (for cycling fans the 2010 season would not have been complete, or perhaps as irritating, without the repetition, in every ad break, during every televised race, of a commercial for Garmin's new co-sponsor, Transitions, starring Tyler Farrar. This advert apparently formed part of the 'package' offered by Sky to lure Wiggins).

On top of all that, there's Wiggins' salary: roughly £1.5m a year (quite a jump from his €350,000 with Garmin, but not, as has been quoted elsewhere, as high as £2m). 'It's not about money,' said Wiggins. 'Money doesn't make you ride faster uphill.' But still, the investment totals around £6m. It's a lot of money. And it does raise an inevitable question: is it too much? As Michael Lewis explains in *Moneyball* – the book cited by Brailsford – a pattern can be observed in baseball, which is 'a tendency to be overly influenced by a guy's most recent performance: what he did last was not necessarily what he would do next.'

That is one view. But an alternative view is also possible. Wiggins had never properly prepared for the Tour de France before. If he did, who knew what he'd be capable of? His margin for improvement could be enormous; his fourth place might only hint at his future potential.

Anyway, perhaps Wiggins' salary, plus the compensation to Garmin, isn't a lot of money for a sponsor like Sky, or for a Tour de France victory. And that is what Brailsford thinks he might be getting. 'Brad will be our marquee rider, and he'll be at home in Team Sky,' says Brailsford, who claims he was '100%' confident, throughout the whole process, that he would get his man. The process to tear up his Garmin contract started, said Wiggins later, 'the minute I stepped off my bike in Paris at the end of the Tour.' (Even later, Wiggins admitted that he had gone for a coffee with Brailsford in Limoges – all the way back to the first rest day of the Tour – and agreed, in principle, to join the new team.)

'I reckon I can be better next year,' says Wiggins now. 'But it's difficult to know. If I'd sat here a year ago and said I want to be top 10 in the Tour de France, everyone would've laughed at me. They did laugh at me.' (It isn't clear who laughed at him. The same people, perhaps, who 'want to see me fail; who want to see me fall flat on my face.')

Alberto Contador will be the man to beat next year, Wiggins concedes. 'I mean, I wouldn't want to wish him to die or anything,' he deadpans, 'but he's the man who's set the bar. It's a bit like Brad McGee was to me on the track. He set the benchmark, and I aimed to be as good as him. Contador is that man; he's proved over the last few years to be pretty invincible. But you never go into bike racing to try and finish fourth or third, so I'll go into next July aiming to be the best I can be. I didn't want to finish fourth this year; I wanted to win the Tour. I wanted to win it when I was 12 years old …' And the bottom line is that with Sky he thinks he'll have a better chance than with Garmin. 'Yeah, if I'm ever going to achieve what I want to achieve, I have to do it in the right surroundings. Doing it with people I've been through three Olympic cycles with, knowing how they work, them knowing me as a rider, how I respond to certain things … I think this is the best place to do it.'

Garmin's 'relaxed' approach had suited Wiggins to a point, he claims. But to step up to the next level, to the podium of the Tour, he is keen to try a different approach; but an approach he's used to. 'Knowing how Dave and his team work, how they got me to the top in track racing – and doing the same on the road – it's quite exciting,' he says.

'There's no way I couldn't be involved with this, leading a British team into the Tour de France,' Wiggins continues, glancing out the window, across Portland Square and in the direction of the Cumberland Hotel. Glancing back, he says: 'I used to work in the Cumberland. I was general dogsbody, a kitchen hand, doing whatever no one else would do: cleaning the floor, cutting up carrots. I never imagined I'd be involved in something like this.'

Later, when Brailsford talks in more detail, it seems that a weight has been lifted from his shoulders. A problem has been solved. And it only happened the previous day, he says. That was when the UCI ProTour council approved Wiggins' move. 'It took a tri-partite agreement,' says Brailsford. 'That's all.'

That's all? 'Well, all three parties had to agree on it – us, Garmin and the UCI ProTour council,' says Brailsford. 'It was pretty straightforward really. It was ratified by the UCI last night.'

And what had it taken for Garmin to agree? 'Commonsense,' replies Brailsford. 'I'm not going to go into details.'

Now that Brailsford's team has its leader he can formulate his plans, and do what he most likes doing: analysing the details, delving into the nitty gritty, boring down, getting towards the essence of the thing. The thing being, in this instance, the Tour de France. But perhaps what Brailsford is most excited about is the unknown. He feels that the kind of approach he and Team Sky are going to take to the Tour has not been tried before. Never mind marginal gains; there is a sense that the margin for improvement could be quite substantial.

Having said that, Brailsford appears to be fascinated by Lance Armstrong, and by what can be learned from the American seven-time Tour winner. Brailsford's gaze focuses on some point in the middle distance as he begins to talk about Armstrong. This could be viewed as a risky strategy; Brailsford could even be accused of courting controversy by invoking the name of Armstrong, who has become the most divisive figure in the sport, around whose feet allegations of doping, though unproven, have danced like the flames of a particularly ferocious fire.*

Yet as Brailsford begins to talk about Armstrong it seems to have nothing to do with strategy or calculation, and everything to do with his natural enthusiasm taking over, prompting him to reveal his and his team's innermost thoughts and their burgeoning plans. 'I don't want to give too much away,' says Brailsford, 'but I think there's quite a lot we can do, to be honest.'

Brailsford's 'I don't want to give too much away' often serves as an introduction to a fascinating insight into what he's been thinking, and the layers of detail he's been peeling away. Here, his eyes narrow, his voice lowers and his shoulders hunch. 'We've studied that race,' he says of the Tour de France. 'And there are things about that race that you look at and think: where are the differences made? How can Lance Armstrong do something like 37,000km [actually it was more like 28,000km in his seven-year winning run] of racing and not put a foot wrong? Why did that happen?

'That's not a fluke, there's a process behind it, so let's figure it out. Armstrong didn't crash. He was always at the front of the bunch. He never had a mechanical [problem]. He rode across a field once [in 2003, when a rider crashed directly in front of him]. And a spectator pulled him off his bike with a bag. But only those things in 37,000km of racing ... there's something in that, for sure.'

The process ... the process. Brailsford is on comfortable ground talking about process. Less so about that stated goal: winning the Tour de France. In some respects, even as Wiggins is unveiled as Team Sky's leader, it is the elephant in the room.

When the question is put to him – 'Can you win the Tour?' – Wiggins might be reading from Brailsford's (or Steve Peters') script, because he switches the focus back to the process.

* This was written in 2011. In 2013 we learned from Armstrong himself that he doped in all seven of his Tour 'wins' (see pp. 370 and 375).

'Results aside, the goal is to be the best we possibly can be, for whatever the goal is,' says Wiggins. 'If the goal is the Tour then the goal, really, is to be in the best possible condition for it; not just me, the whole team, the backroom staff. There's a lot that goes into the Tour de France ...' (Indeed, the backroom staff will eventually number 38, comprising coaches, sports directors, sports scientists, mechanics, operations and administration executives, carers [*soigneurs*], physiotherapists, massage therapists, nutritionist, two full-time doctors, and a chef.)

'Yeah,' says Brailsford, 'I'll reiterate what Brad says: our philosophy has always been about everybody trying to support the riders to be the best they can be. If their best is to win the Tour de France, that's fantastic. It's a dream, and we'll all be there supporting that dream, and looking at ways we can improve. My personal opinion is that the best Brad Wiggins can be is close to the top of the Tour de France podium. Which is very, very exciting.'

Wiggins again: 'Everyone knows where the track team came from. They used to pack their own bikes and go off to the world championships. At the Olympics in Atlanta [1996] they were pretty much paying for themselves ... Yet they went from that to becoming the dominant force in world track cycling. Now Dave wants to take that same philosophy on to the road and try to conquer pro cycling. This team aspires to be the biggest, the best and the most admired pro team in the world.

'I don't like being put on a pedestal,' Wiggins continues. 'This ain't about me. This is about a team that's been picked for their abilities and personalities. The backroom staff too; they've all been picked on their abilities and personalities. Look, we've got an incredibly strong team. We're going to pack 'em up there on the tough days, and if I can't do the job, someone else will.'

'We don't work with results as targets,' Brailsford stresses. 'They're dreams, if you like. So for us a great season would be if we can say that every rider has performed genuinely to the best of his ability. If they do, I'm very confident we'll win bike races. To set a target as [being] an outcome – a result – creates expectations and it's also quite stressful on the riders. All you can do is be the best you can be on the day.'

And beyond analysing how Armstrong completed seven Tours (almost) without incident, Brailsford and Wiggins both talk about the importance of preparation; of innovation; of experimentation. Wiggins mentions one of the two events in which he is Olympic champion, the team pursuit. He recalls that when Matt Parker replaced Simon Jones as the track endurance coach in 2006 he made a suggestion that at the time seemed wacky.

This is an example, though, of the kind of innovative and original thinking Brailsford hopes his coaches – Ellingworth, Parker and Dan Hunt – will bring to road cycling, and to the Tour de France. Parker, now with the job title of 'head of marginal gains' at Team Sky, hadn't been a cyclist; he had been a good footballer, playing for Ayr United in the Scottish Youth Cup final against Hibs, before studying sports science and joining British Cycling's coaching staff. Without the preconceived ideas that come from being steeped in the sport, Parker studied the power output of the riders in the team pursuit, noting their different abilities. One peripheral member of the squad, Ed Clancy, an Academy alumnus, was an interesting and unusual case. So fast was Clancy that he was on the cusp of being a sprint athlete rather than an endurance athlete. He could have gone in either direction; it just so happened he'd gone down the endurance route (perhaps because the British Cycling Academy, set up exclusively for endurance athletes, had given him the opportunity to do so). But Parker could see, studying the huge surge of power Clancy was capable of generating, that he was not a typical endurance athlete.

So Parker suggested a radical change to the way the team pursuit squad rode the 4km race. What was perhaps most remarkable was that this was a team that was already going very fast. They had won silver at the 2004 World Championships and Olympics, gold in 2005, and silver to their perennial rivals, Australia, in 2006.

But as these results – and their times – suggest, they had plateaued. They were no longer improving. And in order to overhaul the Aussies, they had to find some extra speed. So Parker suggested a new approach: instead of the leading rider swinging off after three-quarters of a lap, to allow the second rider to take over the pacemaking, why not leave Clancy on the front for an extra half-lap – for a full lap-and-a-quarter? In that time Clancy could get up to top speed. And it would mean, reckoned Parker, that at the point of the first 'change', when the first rider swung up the track, allowing the second one to hit the front, the team would be travelling marginally quicker. To quote the American writer Daniel Pink: 'Regaining momentum takes three times as much energy as sustaining momentum.' (Pink was talking about writing, but a similar principle applies.)

Parker's suggestion worked. As Wiggins now put it: 'For 40 years everyone had their start rider doing three-quarters of a lap, but when we put Ed Clancy on the front and added a half-lap, we saved six-tenths of a second. Just in that one small change: six-tenths of a second. In a 4km race, that can be the difference between winning and losing.' At the Beijing Olympics, in a team that included Clancy, Wiggins and Geraint Thomas, the British quartet obliterated the world record (going around five seconds quicker than they had been going under their previous coach, Simon Jones) on their way to gold.

'If such a small change in such a short event can make such a significant difference,' says Wiggins, 'then in a three-week race, if you're looking for lots of small gains like that, they can add up to minutes. It's exciting to think about it like that; to have a whole team of people go away and look at ways to go and be better at the Tour.'

An obvious piece of preparation that Wiggins had neglected before the 2009 Tour was the course. He hadn't reconnoitred any of the stages; he hadn't even studied them on paper particularly closely. Again, there could be lessons to be learned from Armstrong here. In his dominant years, Armstrong turned the pre-Tour recce into an art form. Armstrong's recces were legendary – snow-bound ascents of Pyrenean passes; frozen hands unable to change gears; persisting up roads blocked to traffic by adverse weather. It was all there; it all fed into the Armstrong mystique, giving him, if nothing else, a psychological edge.

Wiggins says he'll recce all the mountain stages, as well as the time trial and the – already much anticipated – early cobbled stage in northern France.

But it's not just about the Tour. With Britain's first major professional road team there is an opportunity, Brailsford recognises, to highlight other 'monuments' on the cycling calendar: the Classics like Milan-San Remo, the Tour of Flanders, Paris-Roubaix, Liège-Bastogne-Liège; stage races such as Paris-Nice, Dauphiné Libéré and Tour of Switzerland, not to mention the 'other' Grand Tours, the Giro d'Italia and Vuelta a España. Each of these races has its own rich history, its own romance, its own back catalogue of epic deeds and heroic feats.

Team Sky will compete in around 60 races in 2010. Only one of them will be the Tour de France. 'I'm told 80% of viewing figures are in and around the Tour de France,' says Brailsford. 'But we see with the Olympics that, if we can create heroes – people like Bradley and the other guys – then the rest follows. This nation's a great nation of spectators, of fans. In Britain we enjoy sport and we enjoy winning. If we can start creating some real heroes, and get out there and perform really well and win … sure, it's ambitious. But people like ambition.'

CHAPTER 6

A TSUNAMI OF EXCITEMENT

'Sky have got a strong team, and the coolest bus, but as Christian [Vande Velde] always says, he's had some of the best fun on the shittiest buses.'

David Millar

Millbank Tower, London, 4 January 2010

'It ain't just about me,' said Bradley Wiggins as he was unveiled by Team Sky in December.

And a few weeks later he said so again when, as the clock ticked down to the team's official launch in central London, Wiggins insisted that he didn't want the event to become the Bradley Wiggins show. He objected to his image being in the centre of a montage of the riders' faces. He didn't want to be picked out to stand alone at the front of the stage, in front of his 25 new teammates.

Thus, on the 26th floor of Millbank Tower, overlooking the Thames, and looking down on Whitehall and the Houses of Parliament, Team Sky was officially born at an event befitting the team and its ambitions; it was slick, it was glitzy, it was, more than anything, and certainly as cycling team launches go, *different*. Wiggins *was* persuaded to stand at the front of the stage, but he was joined by five teammates – fellow British riders Geraint Thomas and the latest Academy starlet, Peter

Kennaugh, alongside Michael Barry, Thomas Lofkvist and Edvald Boasson Hagen. Each was interviewed by the Sky News presenter, and keen cyclist, Dermot Murnaghan.

At the entrance to the building were parked the new team cars – Jaguars, no less. And the place thronged with people, from stalwarts of the British cycling scene – scratching their heads, wondering if they were really attending the launch of a British cycling team – to reporters from throughout Europe, from France, Italy, Belgium and Holland. Many had never seen anything like it, not since the notorious Bernard Tapie, owner of the La Vie Claire team in the mid-1980s, held lavish team launches in famous Paris *revue* bars. In general, team launches were not showy or brash, but more like spit 'n' sawdust affairs, without the bling and the glamour of an event that ran to a tight timetable, since it was being broadcast live on the sponsor's sports news channel.

As the 200 guests and media lingered in an anteroom, waiting to be herded into a room that was blacked out and reconfigured into a TV studio, one man seemed to stand apart from the crowd. It was Peter Keen, who'd arguably set this ball rolling by establishing the World Class Performance Plan, almost 13 years earlier. Team Sky, you could argue, was simply a progression, or the latest manifestation – phase three – of the revolution in British cycling that he started. It was the belated entry of British cycling to an area of the sport he'd chosen to spurn, on the grounds that its doping culture made planning for success all but impossible (without doping). That may have been changing. But watching Keen watch proceedings, you wondered what he made of it all.

Now the performance director at UK Sport, Keen had made the short journey across London from his office in Bloomsbury. In some respects it seemed odd that he was just a guest, a spectator at the party; shouldn't he have been up at the front, even on the stage, basking in the reflected glory? He laughed dismissively at the suggestion. 'No, I'm happy in the shadows,' he said. And he was one of the last to file into the studio, claiming a seat at the rear of the room in what seemed a deliberate effort to remain apart, on the outside, looking in.

There were other ghosts from British cycling's past, including Barry Hoban, an eight-time stage winner in the Tour de France in the 1960s and 70s, and Malcolm Elliott, who had ridden for the last British team to ride the Tour, ANC-Halfords – a team that unravelled over the three weeks of the 1987 Tour, and was disbanded in the immediate aftermath. One of Elliott's ANC-Halfords teammates was one of the men now on the stage: Shane Sutton. (The biggest challenge of the day, joked Brailsford, was 'getting Shane in a suit and tie'.)

Two of Team Sky's riders, Wiggins and Russell Downing, were also veterans of the country's last big British professional cycling team, where Sean Yates, now their director at Team Sky, was in charge. That team, the Linda McCartney Racing Team, were worthy successors to ANC-Halfords, being the latest in a long line of ambitious but doomed British squads. It was a team that sounded almost too good to be true. And as with so many things in the sport of cycling which seem too good to be true, it was.

Nine years before the Team Sky launch in Millbank Tower, the Linda McCartney Racing Team staged a similar – well, similar-ish – event on the other side of the Thames, in Trafalgar Square. The previous year they had ridden the Giro d'Italia, the first British team to do so, but in 2001 the plan was to step up another level: the Tour de France was the ambition. To that end, they had new sponsors' names on the yellow-and-black lycra clothing in which the riders stood, freezing, in Trafalgar Square; Jacob's Creek wine; and, like Team Sky, Jaguar cars.

Yet no sooner had the launch finished, and the riders thawed out, than the Linda McCartney Racing Team was exposed as an illusion. It emerged that Jacob's Creek had signed up only to sponsor the team in the first race of the season, the Tour Down Under in Australia. Jaguar, meanwhile, knew nothing of their supposed backing. The agreement had been with a French franchise.

The McCartney debacle – indeed, almost the entire inglorious history of British professional cycling – serves as a sharp contrast to Team Sky. Wiggins nudged Downing as he recalled the Trafalgar Square team launch. 'Mad, isn't it?' he said. After being presented to the audience in their racing kit, the riders changed into the suits supplied by another blue chip British sponsor, Marks & Spencer. Unlike Linda McCartney and ANC-Halfords, nobody could doubt that Team Sky was built on solid financial foundations. The start-up cost was reported by the *Daily Telegraph* as £30m, a figure that was never officially confirmed (nor denied). Apart from an apparent desire for secrecy, one reason could be the difficulty of arriving at a definitive figure; BSkyB own the team, with many of the associated costs – legal, marketing and communications – covered in-house. Whatever the total, it included all the infrastructure – including the two state-of-the-art buses and two fully adapted trucks – and would reduce to around £10m a year in the second year. Given that most major teams operate on budgets of between £6m and £10m, it all suggested that Team Sky meant business. Serious business.

But with their alleged £30m start-up budget, their Jaguar cars, their state-of-the-art buses, their fancy plans and ideas, their emphasis on sports science and their use of a psychiatrist, with their pursuit of Wiggins (and also young Ben Swift, 'poached' from the Russian team Katusha), and their publicly stated aim to do things *differently* and to shake up the small, European-centric scene, Team Sky raised hackles.

The glitzy, glamorous team launch might have been the final straw. Other team launches were held in bland conference centres, middling hotels or the HQ of the sponsor. There was often nothing glamorous or showy about the sponsor, either. But then, look at the sponsors involved in cycling: Team Sky's main competition in their debut season would include teams sponsored by Italian producers of liquified gas (Liquigas), a Belgian laminated flooring company (Quick Step) and a mysterious consortium of Kazakh companies (Astana). Many of the sponsors seemed to be involved not on account of international marketing strategies or visibility, but through the personal interest of the company CEO or marketing director (or in the case of Astana, to try and undo the damage done to a country's image by Borat). For all that cycling might like to think it had progressed, that it was a 21st-century sport that championed technology and innovation, in so many respects it remained a throwback; a sport that held tradition dear and that could appear quite amateur; a sport that resented outsiders, interlopers, *arrivistes*.

According to one journalist the Team Sky launch generated 'a tsunami of excitement' and laid down the gauntlet for the other teams. With the bar raised, it was suggested, others would follow. But there was also evidence of bad feeling and resentment. Apart from Jonathan Vaughters at the Garmin team, Andrei Tchmil, the grizzled former Russian rider, now in charge of the Katusha team, had expressed dismay at the way the new British squad had pursued Ben Swift. 'I think it's very bad that a new team like Sky goes around thinking they can buy up riders who are under contract,' Tchmil told *Cycling Weekly*. 'It's something we never did last year [when Katusha was formed] out of a matter of principle. Contracts exist because they have to be respected. I'll say once and for all: Swift will be part of Team Katusha in 2010. He's not for sale. I don't sell my riders.' (Two weeks later, Swift was unveiled as a Team Sky rider at the team launch.)

As Shane Sutton noted, Sky is a company that doesn't do things by halves. Indeed, when it emerged that cycling was in their sights there was excitement, in some quarters, at the thought of the broadcaster doing for cycling what it had done for football, darts and other sports. Their influence tended to be two-pronged: innovative broadcasting coupled with intense marketing. Cycling, it seemed, was ripe for innovation and experimentation in the way it was presented on television; and few could argue that many of the teams were in dire need of more professional marketing. Perhaps Team Sky, even if they ruffled feathers with their flash launch and grandiose plans, could prove a catalyst for much-needed change.

But a harbinger of change can also represent a threat. And in certain sections of cycling's 'old world' – in mainland Europe – there was interest in the newcomers, but also wariness, suspicion and scepticism. In Italy, *Tuttobici* magazine railed against some of the hype surrounding the team's launch in an editorial headlined, 'Come Back to Earth'. What is interesting is the perceived threat to Italian cycling from Team Sky; that the response to Team Sky amounts to a vigorous defence of Italy's top team, the aforementioned Liquigas. *Tuttobici* claimed that Italy's premier squad, 'though it doesn't have Sky's budget, is still a gem in world cycling, which has invested not only in riders but also in changing this sport, both from a PR and an ethical point of view.' (Yet this was the team that hired Ivan Basso at the conclusion to his doping suspension.) 'That team's move to open its doors to all journalists at altitude training camps is an act of great professionalism and transparency. Sky really is a welcome newcomer to our sport, don't get us wrong. That team represents a wonderful opportunity, something for cycling to brag about, but let's not get carried away.'

A few weeks later, *L'Equipe*, reporting the Team Sky budget as €33m (around £28m at the time), quoted Vincent Lavenu, manager of the French Ag2r team, also warning of the 'danger' of cycling going the same way as football, whose powerbrokers seem not to be the clubs, but agents and players. Such warnings could be interpreted as coded criticism of the new team, given the satellite broadcaster's perceived influence on football's transfer market. Lavenu claimed that his Irish rider, Nicolas Roche, had been the subject of an approach from Team Sky; that he had, in the parlance of football, been 'tapped up'. 'There is a real risk that cycling ends up like football,' said Lavenu. 'These [new] teams do not hesitate to destabilise the market by poaching riders under contract.

'Before, this was not done,' continued Lavenu, who, to use another football analogy, forecast that his team could become a 'selling club' rather than one with aspirations of winning. 'In the future, with a budget of only €7.5m, we can expect to lose riders,' he said. 'We cannot bid on a salary that can be multiplied by three by other teams.'

The *L'Equipe* story was not all negative. It noted that the new team 'intends to apply the methods that have already proven successful on the track', with a supreme focus on 'diet, mental preparation, psychology'. Michel Gros, the agent to one of Sky's two French riders, Sylvain Calzati, was full of praise. 'There is not a training session that was not filmed and dissected and analysed the next day,' he said of Calzati's early experiences with Sky. 'Nothing is left to chance. The Anglo-Saxon teams – Garmin as well as Sky – bring new ways of working, and the French [teams] would do well to follow, without renouncing their own culture.'

On the other hand, there was Marc Madiot, the two-time Paris-Roubaix winner, and manager to one of Wiggins' old teams, the French squad Française des Jeux. If the sport's heartland remained France, Madiot was one of the most obvious representatives; he was decidedly old school. 'Sky have got three times our budget,' Madiot told *L'Ardennais* newspaper. 'Every day there is something new with them: Twitter, the computers, the psychologists, the Jaguars. It's information overload. We too put riders in a wind tunnel to analyse their performance, but we don't make a song and dance about it.

'We're also planning things for the Tour de France,' continued Madiot, really hitting his stride. 'If I've got an image as a guy wearing wellington boots that are stuck in the mud with my puncture repair kit, then that suits me fine. At Française des Jeux we're a bit square. But we've been doing this for 14 years now.'

Madiot also took exception to Team Sky's apparent tendency to 'put out a press release' any time they wanted to make an announcement. 'It is in the English and American culture to have a media plan,' said Madiot. 'In France, we have other advantages. We have a fine heritage of cycling, with the quality of our structure and our races. The bike is anchored deep in our culture. In La Française des Jeux 70% of our riders have come through our own training centre. We are therefore committed to the long-term development of the riders and the sport. I cannot say whether the Anglo-Saxon teams have the same commitment ...'

Another French star, Pierrick Fédrigo, told *L'Equipe* there was beauty in simplicity, in not over-complicating, or over-analysing training. It seemed he attended the same old school as Madiot. 'I want to keep things simple,' said Fédrigo. 'I don't note down how many kilometres I do when I'm training. Perhaps I'm not "professional", but that hasn't stopped me winning races by my own methods.' (Indeed it hasn't: Fédrigo is a three-time Tour de France stage winner, and one of the classiest riders in the peloton.)

* * *

But there is no attack so wounding as from one of your own. David Millar had been spoken about as a potential Team Sky signing from day one. From *before* day one. Back in Bourg-en-Bresse, in July 2007, Dave Brailsford had said that he hoped he could get his new professional team off the ground while Britain's senior riders, Millar and Wiggins, were still competing.

Brailsford and Millar went back a long way. 'Dave's one of my best friends,' says Millar of Brailsford. Indeed, they were together in Biarritz on 23 June 2004, eating in a restaurant and discussing Millar's participation in the Athens Olympics, when their meal was interrupted by three plainclothes policemen from the Paris drugs squad. Millar, a Tour de France stage winner and former yellow jersey wearer, was taken away for questioning and locked in a cell overnight before he admitted to having used EPO, the banned blood booster. He was served a two-year suspension by British Cycling, since national federations have jurisdiction over their own athletes, but Brailsford did not abandon him. Having been questioned himself for five hours on the night that Millar was arrested, he remained in Biarritz while Millar was under police detention and then offered him support as he tried to come to terms with his world collapsing. 'I fundamentally disagreed with what he did,' Brailsford later told Paul Kimmage in the *Sunday Times*, 'and to start with I felt quite betrayed and cheated by it, but ultimately there's a humane aspect to it too.'

Brailsford sought to understand what had led to Millar using drugs; and he came to appreciate the complexities of his case and the pressure he had been under, as well as the endemic nature of the doping culture in professional road cycling. His experience with Millar gave Brailsford, at that time in the process of taking over from Peter Keen as performance director of British Cycling, a valuable insight into Millar's world; a world seemingly far removed from that of track cycling.

By all accounts Millar needed the support of Brailsford and other friends. For a year he drank heavily, thought about where it had all gone wrong, giving much less thought to returning to cycling. But in the second year of his suspension he watched the Tour de France on television 'through the eyes of a child'. His enthusiasm was rekindled; his passion reignited. But he wanted his second career to be very different to his first. He decided to come back, and come back clean, to prove he could win 'on bread and water', as he maintained he had done in the early years of his career. His first Tour de France stage win and spell in the yellow jersey in 2000 had been 'clean', Millar insisted.

Since his comeback – he returned with a Spanish team in time for the 2006 Tour – Millar has become arguably the most articulate anti-doping spokesman in the peloton; he has therefore vindicated Brailsford's initial support. He has acknowledged cycling's deep-rooted problems but also spoken of his love for the sport, its history and romance, of his desire to help clean it up, and his belief that it can become a beacon for clean sport. He has assisted the World Anti-Doping Agency; he has spoken at conferences, offering his own story as a parable of how a gifted, but under-pressure and vulnerable young athlete could become embroiled in a culture of doping. And in 2007, when Jonathan Vaughters, who had ridden as a professional in Europe until 2002, was setting up a team with a strong anti-doping ethos, he approached Millar. 'Jonathan was very forward thinking,' says Millar now. 'When he wanted to set up a team that would give young American cyclists the opportunity to do the sport in a way he never got to, the first thing he did was speak to me. He figured the best way for young riders to learn was from someone who'd made mistakes, and been open about making mistakes. Jonathan knew that because he'd lived it and experienced it – he knew that world.'

Vaughters' team, which became Garmin-Slipstream – and with which, of course, Wiggins would go on to place fourth in the 2009 Tour – was a perfect fit for Millar. In fact, he didn't just join; he became a part-owner ahead of their European debut in 2008. They set out to be different to other teams. 'Having a central base [in Girona, Spain], rather than having riders scattered all over the place, was a key element,' says Millar. 'We set out to do other things differently, taking responsibility for the athletes, rather than just treating them as hired guns.

'Professional cycling teams often had this mercurial atmosphere; 90% of riders are on short-term contracts and they're under pressure to perform; but it's all pressure with no support. The riders are hired guns, contracted workers. This was one of the key things I spoke to JV [Vaughters] and Doug [Ellis – the team's principal backer] about from the beginning. It all stemmed from wanting to create a positive anti-doping environment. But our ideas were quirky and experimental, rather than saying: "We're going to change the sport."'

Despite Millar's attachment to Garmin-Slipstream, he felt an emotional pull to Team Sky when the team began to be assembled at the start of 2009. 'Yeah,' he says, 'it was something I wanted to do. Dave's one of my best friends, my sister [Fran] was working at setting it up. There was a massive personal connection. I was on the phone to them all the time, sharing my knowledge.

'It got closer, but I was so into my team [Garmin], and I'm a part owner … Then again, I began to think, maybe it wouldn't be a bad idea for me to go [to Sky]. And it was kind of fifty-fifty whether I was going or not. At one point I was fairly convinced I'd go. I didn't know what to do, but then the decision was kind of made for me …'

The 'decision was made for him' when Brailsford decided on a zero-tolerance policy towards doping: no one with any doping conviction would be accepted, either as a rider or director. As Brailsford told me: 'I thought about it a lot, but in the end I decided, if you've doped, we can't have you. And at the end of the day, Dave [Millar]'s admitted it. There's no ambiguity there.'

'In a way it helped me,' says Millar of Brailsford's zero-tolerance policy. 'It ended the dilemma I was in.' But the zero-tolerance policy didn't extend to the British team. Indeed, Millar captained the British men's team at the World Road Race Championships in Mendrisio in 2009. 'But Team Sky was a commercial venture, a marketing tool, so the last thing they'd want was a doping scandal,' suggests Millar. 'I think when Dave was selling it to them, I can understand why he'd say he'd have a zero-tolerance policy; he did it on a business, not personal, basis. I can totally understand where he was coming from. But I think that was a bit naive for the sport he was entering into.'

Millar's argument is that a zero-tolerance policy is 'not real world applicable'. He explains: 'It's very hard in the sport of cycling. If you're dealing with anybody over 30 years old, they've encountered doping. Whether they've done it or not, they've encountered it. 100%.'

Despite their employment of the convicted doper Millar, the Garmin team is one of a few in the peloton that boasts a whiter-than-white reputation, owing to their stated commitment to anti-doping, their willingness to speak out about doping, an internal testing programme and no positive tests. Another team with a similar reputation, for the same reasons, is Bob Stapleton's HTC-Columbia team. Yet Stapleton's team also employs people who would not survive a zero-tolerance policy; its directors Rolf Aldag, Brian Holm and Allan Peiper have all admitted to doping during their careers; so has their sprinting coach, Erik Zabel. Stapleton's willingness to retain their services, despite their admissions, amounts to a tacit acknowledgement of what Millar says of the reality of the sport's relationship with doping. 'You can't eradicate the history of cycling and start from year zero,' he says. 'Nobody can do that.' The argument mirrors much of the discussion about anti-drugs campaigns in wider society. Generally, it is now accepted that an approach of zero tolerance – 'Just say no!' – is unrealistic, unworkable, even counterproductive. A more progressive, and arguably more enlightened, approach is to acknowledge the problem, not pretend it doesn't exist. Those, like Millar, who have admitted – or been forced to admit – that they have doped have been able to move on: the truth has set them free. But the *omerta* – the law of silence that prevailed for so long in cycling with regard to doping – means that in other teams riders keep quiet. If a rider at Team Sky has doped in the past then an admission might set him free, but it would also get him sacked. Despite what might seem honourable intentions, *omerta* is upheld.

For Millar, not being able to join Team Sky was a source of some regret, but he could live with it. He was happy at Garmin. 'I love my team,' he says. And it was partly for that reason that he was so unhappy at the manner of Wiggins' departure for Sky. He admits that he was personally hurt by Wiggins' apparent lack of gratitude for what Garmin had done for him in 2009, when Millar and Christian Vande Velde, in particular, turned themselves inside out riding in support of him at the Tour de France.

Millar was hurting in January 2010, when he gave an interview to ESPN and aimed his fire at both Wiggins and Sky. 'I think there are very few people who wouldn't have succumbed to what they offered him,' said Millar of Wiggins' move. 'They threw everything at him. He'd have been an incredible man if he'd said, "No, I'm staying here, I'm doing this." They need him so badly. That's what it's all about. Sky have put so much money into cycling, they can't afford to go to the Tour de France and not have the big British names on their team … I think Brad wants to be a star in England. I think that's very big on his agenda at the moment. He wants to be famous in England ... He wants to be able to mingle with pop stars, to be treated as a pop star. We'll see what that gives him in the long run. I know that's one of his principal reasons for going there.

'I was very pragmatic,' continued Millar. 'Jonathan [Vaughters], on the other hand, wasn't. He had put so much faith in [Wiggins], believed in him when no one else believed in him. Jonathan had a vested personal interest in him. Jonathan fought to keep him, which now in hindsight I have a lot of respect for. I was the first person to say to Jonathan, in July or August, "Let's just sell him and take the money and build and reinforce a team around Christian [Vande Velde]." Jonathan was like, "No. He has a two-year contract. I believed in him. Stand by the contract." It made no economic sense, and it put us in a fundamental endgame situation. But he stood by that.'

In another interview, with *Cycle Sport* magazine, Millar also criticised – perhaps 'critiqued' would be a better description – Team Sky, though this time he appeared a little more detached, with some of his responses laced with humour. Sky, he thought, 'saw a window of opportunity to come in and make cycling a more professional, cutting edge sport ... But they are also bringing in more corporate ethics.

'Sky have got a strong team, and the coolest bus,' added Millar, 'but as Christian Vande Velde always says, he's had some of the best fun on the shittiest buses.'

It is a trademark Millar line; and perhaps a salient point. But now Millar reflects on his 'non-existent' relationship with Wiggins more with sadness than anger. 'We were close,' he says, 'but I was upset he didn't say a nice word about that time [at Garmin], that's all it was. I wanted him to be courteous. We believed in Brad, we worked our arses off for him, he didn't finish fourth in the Tour on his own, and yet it was as if ... he was very disparaging. He said he had to get off our team if he wanted to develop. That was hard to take. Then he killed contact, disappeared. It was just disappointing to have been through so much, and then for it just to end.

'But that's Brad,' adds Millar. 'It's not a surprise. He always gets away with it. People indulge him, which is dangerous. People used to indulge me when I led France's biggest team. I had three phones at one point, but I just let them ring – I thought I was too important to answer any of them. With Brad, I just thought, no – I'm not going to let you get away with this.'

CHAPTER 7

TAKING ON THE MASTERS

'You don't know what you don't know.'

Dave Brailsford

Clare, South Australia, 19 January 2010

Dave Brailsford looks edgy. It's 36 hours after Team Sky's winning debut in the curtain-raiser to the Tour Down Under, but that was only a criterium; only the *hors d'œuvre*. This morning sees the first 'proper' race of the season, a 141km road race: stage one of the Tour Down Under. That could be one reason for his edginess; another might be that his right-hand man is missing. Again.

The stage starts from the small town of Clare, two hours by car from Adelaide. Brailsford hovers on the fringes of his riders as they prepare for the stage, pinning on numbers and pulling on shirts. He studies his phone. As in Rymill Park, before the criterium, it displays a text from the absent Shane Sutton. 'Mechanical problems,' reads the text. 'Loose nut behind the wheel.'

Brailsford laughs. The 'loose nut', he explains, is a reference to Sutton's driver, an old friend from Australia, who had offered Sutton a lift to the start before managing to get lost somewhere between Adelaide and Clare. 'Shane's stuck in a field,' says Brailsford. 'He's got all these stories about getting lost in the Outback as a kid, and how he'd suck the moisture from a stone to keep hydrated. That's what I told him: suck on a stone, you'll be fine.'

Fifty-two-year-old Shane Edwin Sutton's journey from such entirely imaginable escapades as a teenager is as extraordinary as the fact that he has become, as Team Sky hit the road, one of the most respected sports coaches in the UK, and indeed poised to be made an OBE ('Other buggers' efforts,' he jokes) by Her Majesty the Queen. Beijing had in some respects 'made' Sutton's reputation, as it had Brailsford's, but the Australian is somebody who has lived and breathed the sport since he was a kid. And he has always been a lively, larger-than-life presence; a man capable of 'leading 'em into battle' – as he likes to describe his role – and motivating like few others.

In March 2009, outside the velodrome in Pruszków, on the outskirts of Warsaw – scene of the World Track Cycling Championships – I encountered Sutton, hovering by the entrance, his shoulders hunched as he sucked not on a stone but on a cigarette clasped tightly between his fingers. He looked like a wiry, Australian version of Marlon Brando. Adjourning to the velodrome café, with Sutton winking and offering a 'G'day, how ya goin'?' to virtually every passer-by, we sat down and he told me about his journey.

He began cycling in New South Wales with his older brother, Gary, the pair becoming a formidable team in the two-man madison races on the track. Sutton raced both road and track – 'madison, points race, keirin, team pursuit' – but the path to Europe, and the sport's heartland, appeared to be blocked. 'My brother and I had our chances to ride in the six-day [track] races in Europe,' said Sutton. 'They were screaming for the brother combination in those races, but my brother was a bit anti what was going on in the six-days, and what was going on in cycling in general, and he refused to do it.'

Anti what, exactly? 'All the things that went on that shouldn't have been going on,' Sutton says. He means doping and race-fixing, both of which were rife. 'It was a little more mafia-oriented, shall we say.'

Sutton began working for the State Rail Authority in Sydney, but in 1984 came a surprise opportunity to come and join a burgeoning professional cycling scene in a new territory: Britain. Sutton joined a team sponsored by Ever Ready batteries, which contested lucrative televised city centre races. Those races supported a scene that grew exponentially, with professional teams and up to fifty professionals. Sutton became a leading light and prolific winner.

By 1987 he was riding for the most ambitious team to be set up in Britain in years: ANC-Halfords. As noted in the previous chapter, they gained entry to that year's Tour de France – the first and, until Team Sky, *only* British professional team ever to start the Tour – where Sutton made an immediate impression on a journalist embedded with the team, Jeff Connor. To Connor, Sutton, whom he describes as 'a boozer and a brawler', was the team joker. (Sutton is teetotal now.)

Connor also quotes the team owner on Sutton, describing his qualities as similar to those of 'a Welsh miner', asserting that he'd make 'a superb blacksmith … a good bosun's mate … [he's] hard as bloody nails.' Though he only lasted a few days of the Tour ('I'd been ill since March, and was only selected at the last minute'), Sutton was described, even back then, as '*directeur sportif* material'.

Sutton, whose greatest career victory came in the 1990 Milk Race, was a rider 'who you'd always want on your team,' according to a former teammate, Brian Smith. Smith recalls the finish to 'a criterium in Barnsley when one of our riders, Chris Lilywhite, was switched [cut up] on the final bend by another rider. Lilywhite confronted the rider at the finish, and he was arguing with him when Shane, who'd finished near the back and hadn't seen what had happened, just rode up to the pair of them and … he settled the argument very quickly.' With fists, not words.

'He was tough, a bit of a bruiser, and I'm sure back in Australia he'd been in his fair share of scrapes,' continues Smith. 'In the 1993 Milk Race, which Lilywhite won, Shane crashed in Milton Keynes, fractured two ribs and told no one. He rode on the front to help Lilywhite defend the jersey for virtually two weeks, and none of us knew about his fractured ribs until afterwards. It was the same in a stage race in Italy. He fell on his arse and fractured his coccyx and got up and finished the race. But he was always a leader and a captain; those roles came naturally to him.'

Sutton retired as a rider after the 1993 season and became coach to the Welsh team. He made an immediate impression, and was named Welsh coach of the year in 1998, before being drafted into the British team in 2002, to bring order to the group of track sprinters. They had proved difficult to manage, but Sutton sorted them out, moulding them into an effective team.

In Pruszków, I asked Sutton about Team Sky. It was shortly after Brailsford had revealed the team's mission: to win the Tour de France. 'I honestly believe that is possible,' said Sutton, 'and we wouldn't be doing this if we didn't believe it. One thing about Dave is that he doesn't take on challenges lightly. He'll have sat down and thought about it, and he believes there is a possibility of us producing a Tour winner. I believe we have one of the best coaching systems in the world, and I think the pro scene is crying out for that. We have some mouth-watering talent coming through. And on the road, already, I see the fruits of it through the work of Rod Ellingworth with Cav. I think Rod is on his way to becoming one of the best coaches in the world.

'My view,' continued Sutton, 'is that you've got to have your older heads of state to teach these boys their trade, but for me this team should be based around young guns. It's a bit like teaching someone a language: you want to get them young. If we get the young guns we can teach them the way we work and they'll soak it up. You get too many older guys and they're pretty set in their ways. We do need older influences to stabilise us, to ride at the head, for others to follow and learn from; but, for me, it needs to be primarily about young guns, and it needs to be about building a team.

'And we'll do that by setting up a good coaching team, headed by Rod Ellingworth, bringing on Dan Hunt for special projects – time trials etc – and we've got Scott Sunderland, who's been a director with the best team in the world. Rod and Scott have a good feel for what they want. And Dave is a real sponge – he soaks up everything, but he's also an inspirational leader. "DIY Dave" we call him, because he builds things, he makes things happen.'

Although Sutton had travelled to Adelaide for the big kick-off – even if he had managed to get lost on the road to Clare – he said in Australia that he wouldn't be a ubiquitous presence around Team Sky. In fact, there had been rumours immediately after Beijing that he was preparing to step back; there were even rumours that he and Brailsford had fallen out (Sutton claims that he and Brailsford fall out on a regular basis; it's difficult to know whether he's joking). From Adelaide he is planning to head back to Perth, back to the sprinters – Chris Hoy, Victoria Pendleton, *et al.* 'My heart is with those riders and I won't let 'em down,' he said.

Yet his experience, his ability to break down and forensically analyse a race – 'For me,' he says, 'it's all about the methodology of killing off your opponent' – not to mention his presence and his motivational qualities, all make Sutton's involvement in Team Sky a no-brainer. The case becomes even more persuasive when he explains, as he did in Pruszków, about how he would like the team to race: 'I don't want this to be a team that gets a yellow jersey and then their only plan is to sit on the front and close it down. We want to do something different: we want to race. A few decisions might be off the wall at times ... but no stone's going to be left unturned. We're not following the normal model. Training camps won't be about going out and riding 30 hours together with a team meeting in the evening. If we try to model ourselves on any other team we will fail. I'm not interested in other teams. Everything's going to be different.'

And there is yet another compelling case for Sutton's involvement: his relationship with Bradley Wiggins. Sutton had long acted as a father figure to Wiggins, whose estranged father, Gary – also an Australian cyclist, five years older than Sutton, and in his case a confirmed 'boozer and brawler', whom Sutton knew – died in early 2008. It was Sutton who'd called Bradley to tell him his father had been found unconscious, having been beaten and dumped in a street in Aberdeen, New South Wales. But Sutton, it was generally acknowledged, was the one person who was capable of managing Wiggins, who, as I had witnessed at the dinner in Kilmarnock, had a tendency to cut loose; to let his hair down. Sutton was sympathetic to that. 'People have a go at Brad for having the odd drink, and going a bit wild from time to time, but they should try putting themselves in Brad's shoes,' said Sutton.

In Adelaide, though he wasn't there for the duration of the Tour Down Under, Sutton made quite an impression. And not just on the seven riders of Team Sky. 'I don't know that guy,' said Bob Stapleton one morning, as Sutton breezed past in a flurry of wisecracks. 'But he's impressive: I think he's their key guy.'

Yet in Adelaide Sutton made it clear he would not be involved as fully with Team Sky as he had been, and would continue to be, he said, with the track team. He was in Australia to witness the kick-off, and to share the moment with Brailsford, he stressed. But that would be it: afterwards, he insisted, he'd let Sunderland, Ellingworth and the other 'young guns' get on with it, and keep his distance.

After Team Sky's one-two in the criterium in Rymill Park in downtown Adelaide, stage one sees a return to the status quo: HTC-Columbia control the stage and set up an easy victory for their German sprinter, André Greipel, with Henderson only fifth. Greipel is his team's second best sprinter, after Mark Cavendish. But he is also probably the second best sprinter in the world, after Cavendish.

Greipel has a strong team with him, which includes the former World Time Trial Champion Bert Grabsch, Cavendish's lead-out man Mark Renshaw, and another strong sprinter in Matt Goss. They have awesome horsepower, but they also seem to possess levels of organisation and motivation that other teams lack. Grabsch is extraordinary. A squat, powerful figure, the German spends hours sitting at the front of the peloton, almost dragging it along. He sums up the qualities required of a good *domestique*: 'It's easy – work, work, work and then, when you've done that, work some more.'

Grabsch's efforts – he performs a similar job at the Tour de France, usually with another teammate – can keep order in the peloton, discourage attackers, or keep breaks within a manageable distance. When his teammates take over in the final 30km, reeling in any attackers and setting up the sprint for Cavendish or Greipel, their task is that much easier as a result of the work done by Grabsch. Grabsch says he 'enjoys' working at the front, but admits that the prospect, or likelihood, of winning helps enormously. 'You're more likely to work when you think you're working for a good reason. If you're working for a guy who's always finishing fifth, after a while you lose motivation. But if you're working for someone like Cav, who's getting upset when he loses, it makes you much more motivated.'

Apart from Grabsch's tireless and generally unseen work, Stapleton's team has turned lead-outs into an art form. They are as well-drilled as the Red Arrows. In Australia their 'train' sets Greipel up to win stages one, two and four (three is a hilly stage, which doesn't suit the sprinters). Team Sky have come into the race hoping to do the same; they seem keen to take a leaf out of the HTC-Columbia book.

On stage two, into Hahndorf, they do better than on stage one. The Sky train takes on Greipel and co, but Henderson gets 'bashed' from his lead-out man Chris Sutton's back wheel by the Australian sprinter Robbie McEwen. It means Sky's New Zealander is isolated in the final 300 metres, but he spots Greipel charging up the right of the road. 'He came from behind and I went after him but all I could do was get up to his back wheel,' says Henderson, who was second. Until McEwen's roughhouse tactics Henderson reckons the Team Sky train had done its job 'to perfection'. Brailsford is more than satisfied. 'I think it's safe to say we've got the fastest lead-out train here,' he says, 'which is fantastic for our first ride together. Okay, HTC-Columbia did a lot of work during the stage, but I really don't reckon any other team's train is faster than ours in the finale.'

That may be a debatable point, but it is clear – as it had been clear in Rymill Park – that Sky are trying to take it to HTC-Columbia, to beat them at their own game, which is more than most teams are doing. Most don't even try, which has become a problem for Stapleton's team. 'We got to late in the season last year,' he says, 'and no one wanted to ride [at the front]; nobody wanted to sprint against Mark or André. So I think it's good for everybody if there are other teams trying to do what we're trying to do. It's good for our guys to see what

Sky can do; it's good for our guys to know that we need to be as good as we can be all the time.'

The trouble is, nobody else has a sprinter as quick as Cavendish or Greipel. 'Greg's a good guy,' Stapleton says of Henderson, his former rider, one morning. 'He was on our programme for three years. But, you know … he was our fifth best sprinter.' (He was also Greipel's lead-out man, setting him up for 16 of his 20 victories in 2009.) The implication is clear: even with the best lead-out train in the world, trying to win without a Greipel or a Cavendish is like a football team trying to win with the world's best midfield, but without a top-class goalscorer.

In Australia it becomes clear that Team Sky are putting enormous effort into having an organised, slick lead-out train. In the week leading up to the race, they followed training drills drawn up by their race coach, Rod Ellingworth. Ellingworth wasn't in Adelaide, but Yates oversaw the sessions, which had them recce-ing all the stage finishes, and practising lead-outs. Their training rides were short, no more than three hours, and intense; an approach that differs from the traditional approach, which is still favoured by some teams, and can be summed up as miles, miles and more miles. Davide Viganò, the Italian rider, reports that one French squad met in the hotel lobby every morning at 10am before the Tour Down Under, riding for four, five or six hours in temperatures nudging 40 degrees. 'Crazy,' said Viganò, shaking his head.

The idea of practising race drills, or simulating sprint finishes, is alien to many riders and teams (though not HTC-Columbia). 'In theory,' says Sean Yates, 'it's easy to organise a lead-out, but the theory isn't always easy to carry out. It takes a lot of commitment from the individuals involved to form a train: to sit on the wheels like that. It looks easy on TV. But I know that it's stressful, it's nervous, and there's a huge sense of responsibility to your teammates. We'll be analysing it afterwards, as a football team analyses the match. It's logical to do that, though not every team does. HTC-Columbia do it; other teams with sprinters will wise up. But the main thing is commitment: total commitment from the riders.'

But for all their rehearsals, the wheels come off Sky's lead-out train on stage four. It is a stage buffeted by cross-winds, which Lance Armstrong's RadioShack team use to try and split the race. 'It was crazy out there,' says Mat Hayman afterwards. 'It was so windy, I was seeing guys literally being blown off the road – you'd see them landing in the scrub.' But after RadioShack's efforts the race came back together, and Team Sky began to organise their lead-out train for Henderson.

It was going okay until another rider rode into Hayman, the quick release skewer of his wheel ripping several spokes from his front wheel. Hayman stopped, got a new wheel from the following team car, and sprinted back up to regain the peloton – reduced in numbers by the wind – within a kilometre: a remarkable effort. By then, though, Greipel's team had seized the initiative. Hayman couldn't contribute, and, missing arguably the strongest link in the chain, Sky were overwhelmed. Henderson could only manage 13th.

Afterwards, a sombre mood is evident as the Sky riders slump in deckchairs in the shade of the team van, beneath a canopy of trees in the finish town of Goolwa. 'Other days we were beaten,' says Hayman, 'but we were still able to follow the plan and come away with positives. There were none today. We're all very disappointed and dejected.'

Brailsford feels that the team will function better when they get to Europe, and they're able to roll out all the equipment and infrastructure they've put so much time, effort and investment into developing. 'We've put a lot of thought and effort into our support vehicles,' says Brailsford, 'even having systems to understand weather conditions and transmit reliable information directly to the riders. Here [in Australia] we've had to improvise a bit, though it's the same for all the teams, because none of them have their own vehicles. So it's been a case of making do and compromising a bit. But we do think we have things that will add to performance.'

After six days the Tour Down Under finishes back in Adelaide, with another circuit race, this one slightly longer (90km) than the race that had got the team off to such a dream start, with the one-two for Henderson and Chris Sutton. Perhaps that gives the Team Sky riders the confidence to take it to HTC-Columbia once again; on the final lap, they muscle Greipel and his train out of the way. ('I heard guys shouting, "Sky, Sky, Sky!" as we moved up,' says Ben Swift later. 'To hear that put a smile on my face, and it made it easier to move to the front; people give you a bit more space and respect when you're that organised.') They set up the sprint with HTC-esque precision to claim another one-two: Sutton winning this time, with Henderson second. It's good enough for Henderson to claim third overall at the Tour Down Under, behind Greipel and the winner of the previous day's penultimate, hilly stage, Luis Leon Sanchez. Not a bad result in their first ProTour race.

'If you'd told me we'd come away with two wins when we got on the plane to come down here, I'd have taken it with both hands,' says Brailsford.

The week has proved one thing, though. HTC-Columbia remain the masters: they are, indisputably, the best in the world at controlling and winning races. Brailsford's eyes have been opened to that and he speaks in awed tones of 'the grind that people don't see' – mainly the 'dead hours' spent on the front of a road race by the likes of Bert Grabsch. It isn't just about the final 10km, and the lead-out, he admits. 'HTC sat on the front of the peloton all day, and rode hard all day, and still set it up at the finish,' says Brailsford. 'That takes some doing. That's where we've still got some room to develop.'

But Brailsford is searching for solutions, not problems. There is the suspicion that many of the ideas drawn from track racing might not work in road racing, because there are so many uncontrollable variables at play: weather, road conditions, terrain and, most of all, the close proximity of up to 200 other riders.

'No, I don't actually agree with that,' says Brailsford. He is standing by the finish of the final stage, beneath the podium on which his sprinter, Henderson, occupies the third step. Brailsford admits the Tour Down Under has been a learning experience for him; he hasn't interfered in tactics or race strategy, leaving that to Yates. But he has been observing, and discussing with Shane Sutton (who has returned to the sprinters' training camp in Perth). And he is encouraged by what he's seen, and by what he can take to Europe.

'If you actually analyse the number of permutations you can have in a road race, it isn't that many,' insists Brailsford. 'You have a break, you can chase, or you can sit tight: there are only so many cards you can play. There are uncontrollables in that there are more people who can influence the outcome, but it's not that difficult. If we look at the results this week, we can ask: where did we do well, where were we lacking? There are a lot of areas where we can improve. I could be wrong, but it seemed this field was in good shape. The guys went really hard. This isn't a warm-up race. A lot of teams had their A-teams here. So we can be happy, I think.'

Lessons have been learned, though. Brailsford pauses for several seconds as he reflects on the week and searches for the main one. 'The main one,' he eventually says, 'is undoubtedly that in this sport, the greatest strength is in the whole team. You're not going to win anything on your own at this level. Unity is so important, and we've seen it done with the exemplary performance by HTC-Columbia all week, and credit to them. They were brilliant. But our lads today came in with a plan and executed it absolutely to perfection. To finish first and second again is phenomenal.'

If Brailsford is happy, Bob Stapleton is happier. The week has only confirmed his team's pre-eminence, which has reached such a point that he believes other teams are indulging in the best form of flattery. They're copying them.

'Sure, other teams are copying us,' Stapleton says. 'When I came into the sport I looked at the best things other people were doing. I looked heavily at Bjarne Riis, he's been an innovator in technology and other things with his team [CSC and later Saxo Bank], and I looked at what Lance [Armstrong] did at Discovery Channel. You're always going to be copying, so I expect others to copy us. But the challenge now is to find new and better ways constantly. That's what's exciting about it.

'I'm going to keep my eyes on Sky,' Stapleton continues. 'They've got the biggest budget by far, and they've got a lot of expertise from track racing. I want to look at what they do and borrow from them. Right now, I have to say, they look a lot like us. There's a lot of things that are very similar. But one thing that's hard to replicate is the experience of our management team, our *directeurs sportifs*. We have 600 race victories in our management team, and 41 Tours de France. They're from six different countries; they know the races, the athletes, and they've learned how to work together. I feel like we can go toe-to-toe with anybody, even with a budget that's much less than a Sky or a Katusha or others. We just have to work harder and smarter.'

Stapleton is right to say that Team Sky resembles his team: they signed five of his riders, the highest contingent from any team. Yet, for the most part, the Californian will not have lost sleep – they are welcome to riders like Morris Possoni, an Italian climber of limited value to a team increasingly built around its sprinters, Greipel and Cavendish. But there is one that niggles: a rider Stapleton really didn't want to lose. 'I would have loved to keep Edvald Boasson Hagen,' says Stapleton. 'I felt he really blossomed in our programme, but I understand that he should be a key rider there. I think he's the best and most interesting rider at Sky. He'll be someone we talk about for the next 10 years. We did everything we could to keep him; I don't have any regrets that we didn't do something right. But I think he's got everything you could ask for and possibly more. I hope he can make something of it.'

Brailsford shares Stapleton's belief that Boasson Hagen is set to become a major star, but he takes issue with his claims about Team Sky's budget. When they announced their sponsorship, Sky made it clear they would never publicise their budget, but speculation has rushed into the vacuum created by the absence of a reliable figure. 'Everyone tries to big us up in terms of budget,' Brailsford complains in Adelaide. 'How much are they saying it is?'

Well, one Australian newspaper had quoted £33m. 'I wish!' Brailsford splutters. 'We may circulate the UCI list of teams' budgets. We're sixth in the league table. It's a total myth that we're the best funded, and we'll try and put that right by providing some facts. It doesn't do us any favours. Here we are with a team – I mean, Russell Downing spent all last year racing in the UK. He and Ben Swift spent the winter training in Russell's front room in Sheffield because of the weather … We've been the underdogs here.'

The issue of money was not one that was going to go away. Indeed, it was the suspicion that Team Sky is so well funded that explained some of the resentment felt towards them; resentment that stemmed, possibly, from the perceived threat posed by the interlopers. For various reasons, Stapleton was taking a keen interest in Team Sky, its finances in particular. Thinking back to Bourg-en-Bresse in 2007, when Brailsford had explained how a professional team might work, he had kept his options open, saying: 'It'd have to be done as a private enterprise – or as part of the governing body, which would be a first.'

In the event, it had been set up in partnership with the governing body, with Brailsford's argument that Team Sky would complement the British national team, making it stronger, winning the day. But although it forms part of a wider partnership with British Cycling, an important point is that Sky are not mere sponsors: they *own* the team. Tour Racing Ltd is a commercial entity owned by Sky, with a board comprising Sky and NewsCorp executives. As one insider says: 'This gives us a pretty unique set-up and a totally different relationship [with the backer] than teams who operate a traditional sponsorship model.'

The financial arrangements, though, can appear complicated. In an interview published during the Tour Down Under, Brailsford revealed that he had 'no financial or equity stake in Team Sky'. Stapleton, when told this, appeared not to comprehend. 'Why's he doing it then?' he asked with a chuckle.

But Brailsford was drawing two salaries: one from British Cycling for his continuing role as performance director (but on a reduced salary, he has said), the other for his role as team principal for Team Sky. As for other staff and resources, there would be overlap, Brailsford admitted, between the two set-ups. But he was clear: funding allocated to British Cycling for its national programmes would not be directed to Team Sky. Rather, Team Sky would be billed for any 'services' it purchased – which could include staff time, or the use of the Manchester Velodrome – from British Cycling. As Brailsford had said in Bourg-en-Bresse, it was an unprecedented arrangement; but it was also true, as he noted at the time, that 'not many countries have the kind of funding structure for elite sport that Britain has.'

Nevertheless, the Team Sky/British Cycling relationship was untested and new; it would need to be managed, and monitored, very carefully. UK Sport, whose £26m investment in British Cycling in the run-up to the London Olympics was at stake, were watching the situation with interest, and, in some quarters, some skepticism.

Quite apart from the financial arrangements, there were other potential, almost intangible, consequences, and possible conflicts of interest. If, for example, Edvald Boasson Hagen of Norway and Team Sky were to beat Mark Cavendish of Britain and a rival professional team at the 2012 Olympic road race in London, the argument could be made that Boasson Hagen has received more 'help' and support from British Cycling, through Team Sky, than Cavendish.

Certainly it is true that, with Team Sky, Brailsford is venturing into new and potentially dangerous territory. His argument is that the partnership with Sky will benefit British Cycling, not damage it. What's more, he considers it necessary; that such private/public partnerships will become essential, especially in an uncertain financial climate, even more especially in the aftermath of the London Olympics, when public funding of sport is expected to be much diminished. It should be a model for other sports, he thinks. He may even wish in private that certain individuals in certain public bodies shared the 'can do' attitude, and loathing of bureaucratic red tape, of a company like Sky (even if others within those bodies might prefer the description of Sky as 'ruthless, uncompromising and arrogant' to 'can do'). What is certain is that there are significant risks attached to the venture, not least because in some respects Brailsford is on a hiding to nothing. At the Beijing Olympics his British team achieved perfection – or as close to it as is ever likely to be possible.

With or without the challenge of setting up and running a professional road team, the chances of repeating that performance must be slim.

But arguably the worst case scenario is of an overseas Team Sky rider such as Boasson Hagen prevailing over a British rider from a pro team other than Team Sky in the Olympic road race in London. This scenario assumes, however, that Cavendish is not, by 2012, a Team Sky rider. Whenever the possibility was even hinted at in Australia, Bob Stapleton's hackles would rise; his countenance would darken and the easy Californian smile would vanish, replaced by a look of steely determination. In Adelaide it was put to Stapleton that Bradley Wiggins' contract-busting move to Sky could alter the landscape of professional cycling, transferring 'power' from the teams to the riders and their agents, and potentially making such moves commonplace.

'But I think we had a unique situation there,' said Stapleton of Wiggins' move. 'I mean I think Sky was in trouble if they didn't have Wiggins. I think they needed that, for the British market ... they needed a top name British rider. That's reality.'

What of the possibility of a transfer market – similar to football – developing, in which teams can pursue riders, even riders under contract, more aggressively, offering huge financial incentives? 'I don't fear that at all,' said Stapleton. 'Hey, we can play in that game very well. In defence or offence, whatever it takes.'

At the Tour Down Under the burgeoning rivalry between Sky and HTC – or Brailsford and Stapleton – seems set to become one of the fascinating sub-plots to the season, particularly because they appeared to be trying to play the same game. In Australia, Sky's aim appeared clear: to bring the organisation and planning that had delivered such success on the track to road racing, to impose order, and predictability, where there is usually chaos. They might not have had the world's fastest sprinter, but in Greg Henderson they had a rider who could compete, especially if he found himself sitting at the back of the world's best lead-out train.

To some, it was a puzzling tactic. Not many teams would put such efforts, day after day, into trying to set up a 33-year-old sprinter whose previous team regarded him only as a lead-out man (and their fifth fastest sprinter). It also doesn't tally with Team Sky's stated goal: to win the Tour de France, starting with a podium place for Bradley Wiggins in their debut year.

But could there be another reason for putting such emphasis on building an effective and well-oiled lead-out train?

Perhaps the explanation – and the reason – is Mark Cavendish, the one that got away. As Sutton had told me in Pruszków, 'Cav is one reason we need to build a good team. He's happy where he is, but if he ever decides, in the long term, that he wants to come home, we need to be able to accommodate him … and we'd like to think he'll come home.' In other words, Sky's debut season – and their focus on perfecting the lead-out – could form an extended audition for Cavendish, who wouldn't move unless he was sure he'd receive similar support, even a team built around him.

Not that Brailsford is saying so. After the furore over his pursuit of Wiggins, he is saying nothing about chasing contracted riders, least of all Cavendish. Instead, he is stressing, unconvincingly, that creating a fully-functioning team 'will take patience'. Unconvincing, because patience is not necessarily something that comes easily to Brailsford, who is summed up by one of his colleagues in one word: 'intense'. But Brailsford has no choice: he recognises that in an unfamiliar world he has to – initially at least – stand back, observe, learn and, yes, exercise patience.

Unwittingly invoking Donald Rumsfeld, Brailsford explains: 'You don't know what you don't know, but there are certainly things this week in Adelaide that we have learned. It took us 10 years to build the track team, and we're working to that model, creating an environment of trust, understanding and honesty. We're trying to accelerate the process, because we have to. But the best place to do it is on the road, in races.'

Indeed, this was also the *only* place to refine that all-important process. Unlike track cycling, with weeks and sometimes months between major competitions, the road calendar is relentless. After Australia, the races come thick and fast. Next stop, the Middle East.

CHAPTER 8

PISSGATE

*'I don't want to get stuck on this Sky thing. There is no hatred
of Sky. Nobody cares.'*

Roger Hammond

Valencia, 17 February 2010

I'm in a Team Sky Jaguar in Valencia, in the back seat of the car
alongside operations manager Carsten Jeppesen, with the
coaches Matt Parker and Rod Ellingworth in the front. Two
small groups of Team Sky riders are training nearby, and we're
on our way to meet them. Ellingworth has identified a circuit.
He wants to set it up as a race course, complete with finish line,
in order to practise lead-out drills.

But the minds of those in the car are not really on today's
simulated racing; they're 4,000 miles east at a real race, in
Oman. Jeppesen's phone chirrups every few minutes with
updates from Shane Sutton at the Tour of Oman.

After the Tour Down Under, Team Sky travelled with the
rest of the professional peloton to the Middle East, for the next
two races on the ProTour calendar. And they enjoyed a strong
start to their February campaign, Bradley Wiggins making his
debut for the team at the Tour of Qatar, and leading them to
victory in the first stage team time trial in Doha. Edvald
Boasson Hagen had also started to live up to the hype

surrounding him by arriving relatively unfit – after apparently spending much of the winter cross-country skiing in Norway – but taking the leader's golden jersey in Qatar and improving day by day.

Now, in Oman, Boasson Hagen's form has continued to sharpen. He won the previous day's stage and had started today's 187km fourth stage, from Ibri to Nakhal, in the yellow jersey of overall leader.

'All good,' reports Jeppesen, reading Sutton's message. 'There's a break of six, but the boys are chasing.'

The texts keep coming, the message largely the same: 'The break's got seven minutes, the boys are chasing hard and controlling the race.' But then Jeppesen, after digging into his pocket once more to pull out his phone, hesitates before reading the latest Sutton missive. His expression darkens. 'Shane says … Edvald stopped for a pee … there was an attack …,' says the Dane.

'He stopped for a pee and they attacked?' says Ellingworth, turning round.

'Mmm,' says Jeppesen. 'Shane says: "Boys have been flicked."'

What had just happened in Oman illustrated one of the 'uncontrollables' of road racing: when others gang up against you. At least, that is what seemed to happen on stage four, and how it was interpreted by Team Sky. But the circumstances were unusual, the explanation perhaps not as clear-cut as it appeared.

The day had started with a bus transfer for the riders through Muscat's rush-hour traffic to the airport, from where the riders were flown 300km to the isolated town of Ibri. Or so they thought. In fact, when they touched down, already hot, tired and grumpy, at where they assumed must be Ibri, they were actually somewhere else. They were herded on to another bus, and eventually arrived in Ibri an hour after the scheduled start time. By now they were really unhappy. There was talk of protests or go-slows, but any further delay was in no one's interests: they didn't want to prolong the agony. And so, according to Team Sky, another agreement was reached: that all the teams would put two riders on the front to share the pacemaking, control the race and ensure a relatively early finish.

Yet as the stage got underway – 90 minutes late – six riders jumped away to form a breakaway, and the peloton looked at Team Sky to lead the chase. In ordinary circumstances, that would have been logical; it's usually the job of the team with yellow to defend the jersey by chasing. But Sky understood that today would be different, that other teams would help. When they found themselves isolated at the front, they were unhappy.

There was a strange echo with day two of the previous week's Tour of Qatar, when Boasson Hagen was also the overall race leader. On that occasion, Sky opted *not* to chase a two-man break, which escaped early and raced into a huge lead. It was too early, they had felt in Qatar, to assume full responsibility (remember, also, what Shane Sutton had said a year earlier in Pruszków about the tactics the team would deploy: that they would not follow the traditional model; that they would not automatically ride on the front in defence of a yellow jersey; that they would *race*).

But when Sky refused to chase in Qatar they did not endear themselves to the rest of the peloton, or, indeed, to the race organisers (ASO, who also organise the Tour de France). Bad feeling ensued as, on that occasion, the two escapees gained some 12 minutes. And although the lead was reduced to two minutes by the line, it was enough for one of those riders, Wouter Mol, to win the race overall. For everyone else, the race was over. 'Sky messed the whole race up for everybody,' Roger Hammond, the British rider on the Cervelo team, told *VeloNews* at the finish of the stage. 'I guess they knew they weren't very strong when they came here, so they just let the group go. I don't quite know what their tactic was.'

The perception was that Sky had abdicated the natural responsibility that comes with leading the race (though, later on in the stage, Boasson Hagen had struggled in the crosswinds, and punctured, losing 11 minutes). But the incident in Qatar underlined an important, perhaps even defining feature of road racing: the etiquette and unwritten rules that dictate life and behaviour in the peloton. Flout them, as Sky were deemed by some to have done, and there will be payback.

Now, in Oman, with Boasson Hagen again in the race lead, Team Sky began to chase the six-man break. As the break's lead stretched to seven minutes, they asked for assistance. Where was the help they'd been promised by the other teams? Whether Qatar played on their mind, or whether other teams were playing poker – waiting to see if other teams would commit riders before committing riders themselves – was not clear. But the Team Sky riders Juan Antonio Flecha, Mat Hayman, Lars Petter Nordhaug, Ian Stannard, Chris Sutton, Geraint Thomas and Davide Viganò became more and more irritated. And, according to some of their fellow riders, they indulged in some dubious tactics: riding in the gutter, making it harder for the peloton to find shelter behind them; not slowing down as they rode through the feed zone, where the *soigneurs* stand by the side of the road, dispensing *musettes* (food bags).

Geraint Thomas takes up the story: 'There was 55km to go, nothing was happening, and we were on this long, straight road. We'd been on the front for ages. And we were controlling the race. Before the start, after this five-hour transfer, the other teams are giving it all this, saying "We'll put a couple of riders on the front, because we want to finish as early as possible." But the race starts and it's just us at the front. And our attitude was, fair enough, we've got the jersey, so we'll chase. But it meant riding hard all day. A few guys [in the peloton] were saying, "You're putting us in the gutter." And we were saying: "Well, we're not gonna let you have a free ride for 180k – we're not gonna let you just sit there and have a nice easy day."

'Yeah, there was a bit of niggling,' continues Thomas. 'Roger [Hammond] said something … And yeah, we were riding half-road, forcing them [the riders behind] into the wind, 'cos, you know … that's bike racing. But nothing was happening, then Eddy [Boasson Hagen] stops for a piss and it all kicks off. We eased off to wait for him but I got swamped as the guys came past me.'

Two more unwritten rules: don't ride hard through the feed zone; and wait for the yellow jersey if he stops for a pee (this rule also applies if he has a mechanical problem or crashes).

When Boasson Hagen stopped, with 50km of the stage remaining, 'all hell broke loose'. Five Cervelo riders, including Hammond, drove a 41-man break clear of the peloton. Boasson Hagen, back on the move after answering the call of nature, was joined by his teammates, Hayman, Thomas, Sutton and Flecha, and they chased, and chased hard, but they could not catch a 41-man group in which there appeared to be a surprising – and unusual – consensus.

One by one Boasson Hagen's teammates fell by the wayside; only Sutton remained with him by the finish, where he appeared over a minute behind the stage winner, Leigh Howard of HTC-Columbia. The taciturn Boasson Hagen was devastated. 'It was a mistake,' he told reporters, 'but there are more days.'

'That's bike racing,' said Shane Sutton. 'The team rode well and solid, Edvald went to have a natural break, someone reacted to that, and the rest is history.'

Privately, though, Team Sky thought that other teams and riders had combined against them, and taken advantage of Boasson Hagen's pee stop. They suspected that it was the first obvious manifestation of ill feeling that had been brewing against the new team, and to which they were sensitive. 'The general feeling within the peloton was a pervasive sense of resentment at the start,' says David Millar. It owed to the hype around their launch, the level of their ambition, their determination to be different. 'In many ways they came in with the right attitude,' says Millar. 'They were modern in their outlook, they didn't have the baggage of some other teams, and they didn't want it. It was the only way they could do it; it made it very exciting. But they also came in with an attitude that seemed to pooh-pooh the sport. They didn't doff their cap at the traditions. That rubbed some people up the wrong way.'

A couple of days later, Hammond – another high-profile British rider overlooked by Team Sky, as apparently he was deemed 'too negative' by some of the coaching staff – reflected on the events of Oman. He refuted the suggestion that there was ill feeling towards Team Sky. 'You don't want to get stuck on this Sky thing,' Hammond told the Real Peloton podcast. 'There is no hatred of Sky. Nobody cares. Sky are doing their thing. To be honest I find it a little bit disrespectful of the press that they think that I'm going to fly six hours and spend two weeks away from my wife, with the ambition to stop Sky from winning the race. I don't *care* what Sky are doing, so long as we are winning races.' Hammond also pointed out that riding in crosswinds is what he and his Cervelo team do best; that in the Classics of northern Europe, over wind-buffeted, often cobbled roads, they like to tear races apart by riding in the kind of echelon they formed in Oman. The conditions in Oman proved conducive to that, which is why they attacked.

This ties in with another reading of what happened in Oman. According to another witness, there was nothing co-ordinated about the attack that happened to go clear as Boasson Hagen stopped for a pee. 'I don't think teams and riders are organised enough, or united enough, to gang up on one team,' he says. 'It was a mistake by Boasson Hagen to stop so close to the finish – the race is really on at that point – and in those difficult conditions. When he did stop, it was a mess, it was chaotic – riders went to the front and didn't know he'd stopped for a piss. It was just a colossal mistake by him. But Sky were seething, and they were paranoid because they'd shot their mouths off all season about how good they were going to be. A lot of people were amused by what happened, but I don't think there was any conspiracy.'

Yet some other riders clearly did relish what had happened, and felt that Team Sky had got their comeuppance. Robbie Hunter, the South African sprinter with the Garmin team, posted his thoughts on Twitter, making reference to the Tour of Qatar, when Sky also lost the jersey in controversial circum-stances. 'So another good day in the office,' tweeted Hunter. 'Group split in the crosswind & Sky 2 races in a row messed up with the yellow jersey. I'm feeling good.'

With Twitter being the medium of honest communication, Scott Sunderland, Sky's senior sports director, might have been offering a response to 'pissgate' a couple of days later when he quoted the German philosopher Helmut Schoeck: 'The envious man thinks that if his neighbour breaks a leg, he will be able to walk better himself.'

Planning. Attention to detail. Identifying 'controllable' factors; seeking to control them. Analysing data. Logic over emotion. Process over outcome. The aggregation of marginal gains. In the lobby of La Calderona Hotel – Team Sky's training base for the months of January and February – the noticeboards are full of evidence of this attention to detail. A typed sheet of A4 even advises on the dress code for leisure gear: 'Tues 9 Feb: Black & White Polo. Wed 10 Feb: White Polo. Thurs 11 Feb: Black & White Polo,' while a large map has different routes highlighted in yellow, with post-it notes and blue arrows explaining each training ride planned for each day.

In the basement of the hotel, which has become the team's *services des courses*, the bikes are stacked neatly, alongside work stands, spare wheels and other equipment. Signs on the wall indicate bikes that have been prepared for upcoming races. One reads 'Spare Bike Hot Var.' 'Hot' has been scored out, replaced with 'Haut'. It's the spare bike for the forthcoming Tour du Haut Var.

But meticulous planning doesn't always have the desired outcome. Prior to selecting Valencia as the winter training base, Dave Brailsford instructed his scientists and experts to study weather data relating to the entire European continent. They looked at weather patterns over the last 10 years. And their analysis determined that Valencia, on the east coast of Spain, was the driest, warmest and best place to train.

Well, for 10 years it might have been. But in 2010, when the first group of riders arrived in Valencia, they discovered roads blocked by snow. They might as well have stayed in Manchester. ('It was fine,' Brailsford says, downplaying this setback. 'Everywhere in Europe was the same. The main thing was, we didn't lose any training days.')

By the time I get to Valencia, with the training camp entering its seventh week – there's a drop-in arrangement, with riders and coaches coming and going – the weather has improved. A little. It's still cold and grey, with a light drizzle in the air, but the training hasn't been compromised. And as Sutton had promised, the schedule looks very different to a traditional training camp. 'The only thing this team has in common with any other team I've ridden in is that we're riding a bike,' says Simon Gerrans after dinner. 'We're still cycling. That's about the only thing this team is doing that's the same. Everything's different. But the big thing is the support we're getting.'

On the following day's agenda, after a steady two-hour morning ride, is time trial training. En route to the time trial session I find myself in a Team Sky Jaguar again, this time with Sean Yates at the wheel, and Rod Ellingworth and Matt Parker in the passenger seats. Ellingworth has identified a stretch of road that he reckons will be perfect for individual time trial training; he has a 10km course in mind. It's a 20km drive from Valencia, and he's sent a couple of members of staff ahead, to set up a gazebo in the designated start area, sheltering stationary trainers on which the riders will warm up before their effort. The intention is to replicate, as closely as possible, race conditions.

Yates can barely conceal his excitement. He may be laidback and languid, but if one thing can get Yates' blood flowing it's the prospect of a time trial; particularly an event that so closely resembles his first love, which is time trialling in the UK. That is to say, over a fixed distance (of 10, 25, 50 or 100 miles; or, for crazies, 12 or 24 hours – Yates himself competed in a 12-hour when he retired). Other pre-requisites include: an out-and-back course, on flat, featureless stretches of road, often a dual carriageway (preferably with heavy traffic, to increase the 'pull' of the passing vehicles, thus making the course faster), and no spectators. British time trial courses are identified by cryptic codes such as E72 (a notoriously fast 25-mile course east of London) with a church hall or community centre sometimes acting as HQ. Then again, it is difficult to exaggerate the austere nature of the British time trialling scene; at some, an HQ – as in an actual physical building – is a luxury. Riders change in the back of their cars. It can be a joyless experience, and has about as much to do with the glamour of the Tour de France as a kickabout on a housing estate has to do with the World Cup.

But for Yates, a British-style time trial is *real* racing. It is a journey back to his roots. Here in Valencia, he probably disapproves of the gazebo – he'd rather they changed in the backs of cars, and drank tea from polystyrene cups instead of sipping on their fancy post-race recovery drinks.

'You'll love this, Sean, eh?' says Ellingworth playfully. 'It's a straight out-and-back course. Dead flat.'

'Oh yeah, it's a good day, not a breath of wind,' says a chirpy Yates. 'Bit of rain, too – brings the oxygen down. Just need some fucking big dual carriageway with trucks to suck you along.

'But no entries on the line!' he adds, recalling one of the quirks of the British time trialling scene, and spluttering with laughter. 'And send your stamped addressed envelope to the organiser by the closing date!'

We spot the gazebo at the side of the road, and slow down. But Ellingworth, checking his notes, says: 'Oh shit, it's in the wrong layby.'

'Sorry, Gert,' Ellingworth tells Gert, who'd been standing proudly beside the assembled gazebo. Gert looks crestfallen, but gets to work quickly and without complaint, dismantling the gazebo. The impression is that everybody is trying very hard; that even the man tasked with setting up the gazebo is aware of the potential importance of his task. Marginal gains. Ellingworth buries his head in his copious notes. 'We don't like to point the finger here,' says Parker, whose job title is 'head of marginal gains', with a wry smile. 'But that was Rod's fault.'

With the gazebo reassembled in the place Ellingworth had intended, the time trial gets underway. 'Michael Barry and Thomas Lofkvist came back from training this morning talking about the problems of warming up for time trails with the crowds and the bus fumes,' says Ellingworth. 'So we're trying to think of ways around that, of giving them their space.'

'Yeah,' says Yates, 'but the flipside is that's always been part of the attraction – the proximity of the fans, watching them warm up.'

Ten of the 12 riders who are currently in Valencia take part in the time trial. In some ways the atmosphere does resemble a British time trial – it could be the East Grinstead CC (Yates' first club) 'Club 10'. There are no spectators, no closed roads, and tea (albeit honeyed tea) is offered as the post-race drink; but there is also an array of expensive equipment, and no fewer than 13 support staff.

'We're trying to up the ante a bit by having the proper race equipment, the time trial bikes, the skinsuits and a proper warm-up,' explains Ellingworth. 'The whole day is built around the time trial, as it would be in a proper race. So they did a two-hour, evenly paced ride this morning, as they'd do in a stage race.'

With Brailsford and Sunderland also in attendance, but deep in conversation in a car, the riders set out on their ride. They all take the training exercise admirably seriously – and return wheezing and coughing. 'That okay, mate?' Ellingworth asks Morris Possoni, a rider about as comfortable in a time trial as Sean Yates is climbing Mont Ventoux. 'That was hard for me,' says Possoni. 'It's hard for everyone, mate,' says Ellingworth. 'All you can do is thrash it out.'

'Alright, Froomy?' Ellingworth calls to Chris Froome as he starts his effort. 'Get it out!'

Some of the back-up staff have been dispatched to video the riders at the turn, with Ellingworth having explained to them exactly what he wants. 'I want them all from the same angle, get them coming out the apex of the bend,' he says.

Back at the hotel, Ellingworth looks as drained as the riders. He slumps in a seat in the upstairs lobby, among drinks machines and empty tables and chairs, and yawns. But when he starts to talk, describing his role and what he's trying to do, he is reinvigorated. He enthusiastically reflects on the simulated time trial, 'the first session we've done like that'. Michael Barry, an experienced professional, who has ridden with Lance Armstrong at US Postal and Mark Cavendish at HTC-Columbia, says that it was the most seriously he'd ever approached a time trial – and it was only training.

'It was to test everything,' explains Ellingworth. 'It gives us a bit of information on the riders, and it gets them used to the routine. The other day we did hill efforts. We're doing specific work which challenges a lot of them because they're not used to that sort of work. But it's what we're trying to do: challenge them in every way. Getting them up a bit earlier. Having split training days. For the British guys, especially the guys who came through the Academy, it's pretty normal, but for some of the other guys it's challenging.

'The idea is to make it more race-focused,' he continues, 'so it's not just training. Everything shouldn't just be *as it is*, just because *it's the way it's done* in the bike race. Because that doesn't necessarily make sense.

'But I tell you,' he adds with a hint of exasperation, 'it's hard to get a group of guys coming together as a team and to try and please them all in a training camp. Trying to find a happy medium is bloody difficult.

'I'm not trying to force anything on anybody. It's about showing first and foremost that you're there to support them. If they like your ways, they'll end up asking questions.

'Quite rightly, some of them have been a little bit hesitant, but you can't blame 'em. You can't push people. You've got to remember some of them have been let down in the past. Some of them have been promised the earth and it hasn't been delivered … I think that's where we've got to be really careful. But I think we've been lucky. We've got a good group, and they're committing well. There were 10 riders out doing that time trial today, giving it full clout. You have to praise their efforts and their attitude. It was cold out there, it was drizzly, but they all took it seriously. That makes our lives easier.'

Ellingworth says he has work he needs to get on with. But he is one of life's enthusiasts, and an easy communicator, and he keeps talking, wrestling with problems and issues as he does so. 'Some of the foreign lads have got to ask more questions,' he says. 'The British guys are used to it; Cav would phone me at 7am and say he doesn't feel well, and we'd talk about what he should do. I've told them to do that. If they phone me at 7am and I'm asleep, so what? I can handle that. They have to use us. But that's not the environment they're from, it's not the culture they're used to. Some of 'em are too quiet.'

One of Ellingworth's main jobs will be to work directly with Bradley Wiggins in the build-up to the Tour de France. This could be his greatest challenge, if only for Wiggins' tendency to disappear. Journalists have long known that he is virtually impossible to contact by phone, but his elusiveness – or evasiveness – apparently extends to his own team, including his coach. It is Shane Sutton who has worked most closely with him in the past, and who says, 'You've got to let Brad come to you. You can't go to Brad. Sometimes he disappears into the forest, but you've got to wait for him to come back out again. You can't go after him. He'll come out when he's ready.'

Only today, in the team car, Ellingworth and Parker had been reflecting on and laughing dryly at the news that, in Wiggins' new house in Girona, he has discovered that he has no phone signal. As well as Ellingworth, Matt Parker has also been working closely with Wiggins – as he did in the run-up to the Beijing Olympics, and indeed before his fourth place in the 2009 Tour – and recce-ing the roads around Girona, mapping out the best training routes, and the climbs that most closely resemble those he'll encounter at the Tour de France. 'A lot of my work is one-to-one with Brad,' says Ellingworth. 'Matt's from the sports science side, I'm from the racing side, so we're putting it together and I'm delivering his training programme. We're just making sure everything's in place for him, and that he's fully supported in training. A lot of the work is based around what we know of the racing; we're really trying to put some proper race information into training, so it's quite specific.'

But Ellingworth isn't just coaching Wiggins. 'If any of them want information, I'm coaching them,' he says. All 26? 'Well, with most of 'em it's simple programmes, getting them to understand the training efforts. They perhaps haven't had that support in the past. I think there are a lot of areas where we can do more work. It's pretty busy. It's 24/7, really. But it's new and it's not something where we've just plastered a new name across the jersey. We've all got to get stuck in and roll our sleeves up. It's either going to work or it isn't, but we aren't going to use half measures.

'The sports director part, in the car, isn't my favourite part,' continues Ellingworth. 'With the Academy and the Under-23 team, when you were with the team constantly, I did it. But I always preferred the training, getting stuck in there, rolling my sleeves up.'

As Ellingworth is talking a figure appears in the lobby, padding along the carpet in a white bathrobe. It's Marcus Ljungqvist, the new sports director. 'You coming for a sauna, Rod?' asks Ljungqvist.

'Yeah, maybe … er, yeah,' says Ellingworth, glancing at his watch. It is obvious he has no intention of going for a sauna. Then Scott Sunderland appears, also in a white bathrobe. 'You coming for a sauna, Rod?' he asks.

'I want to crack on with some work, to be honest,' says Ellingworth.

* * *

For all of Ellingworth's enthusiasm, you don't have to be Inspector Rebus – or Steve Peters – to detect some tension in the camp, particularly around Sunderland. And it isn't difficult to imagine why.

At the training camp, in particular, it is difficult to know what the sports director's precise role is. Even at races, with Ellingworth drawing up race plans, as he had done at the Tour Down Under, it is easy to see that the sports directors could feel marginalised, and wonder where they fit into the management structure favoured by Dave Brailsford. As Sunderland has stressed, he sees the sports director as the most important role in the team: the man who calls the shots from the team car. At Team Sky, he appears to be undermined.

What doesn't help, from Sunderland's point of view, is Brailsford's deep involvement in the minutiae of running the team. This appears a paradoxical aspect of Brailsford's management style: his ability to empower staff and give the riders a say, while at the same time being so interested, and involved, in most decisions, big and small. One new member of staff, the team doctor Richard Freeman, has an interesting perspective on this. Having worked in football for 10 years, with Bolton Wanderers, Freeman says Brailsford compares favourably with the best football managers. 'He's an excellent man manager. It'd be great to take Dave's model and try it in football, but, then again, I don't think it would work at a football club,' says Freeman. 'It'd be too autocratic. I worked at Bolton with Sam Allardyce, an excellent manager, but he rarely got involved in training, for example. Dave's problem, in a way, is that he loves cycling so much; he wants to be involved in everything. So, in a sense, he's like José Mourinho when he was at Chelsea: he's involved in everything.'

The Brailsford-headed hierarchy at Team Sky doesn't appear to bother the laidback Sean Yates – content to reminisce about British time trials, and much in demand by the riders as an anecdotalist, telling outlandish tales of his own racing career – or the fledgeling sports directors, Marcus Ljungqvist or Steven de Jongh (who is in Oman with Shane Sutton). But it does seem to niggle Sunderland, who takes his role as senior sports director seriously. 'Scott needs to relax,' suggests Brian Nygaard, the team's press officer.

In fact, rumours of problems between Brailsford and Sunderland had been circulating since the start of the year. Sunderland had penned a blog at Christmas that hinted at discord, admitting he'd come close to walking away from the sport in 2009 (while employed by Team Sky). Why, he didn't spell out. But 'those thoughts [of walking away] were fuelled by personal disappointment and frustration generated by different events I had not anticipated.'

Ellingworth – diffident, modest, with no trace of ego – seems perfectly happy, even oblivious to any tension, or resentment. But Sunderland is, to those party to the rumours and gossip, a tinderbox, waiting to explode.

At the heart of the issue is the role of sports director. What is it, and who is he: the most important member of the team, or a glorified chauffeur? Sunderland, as he had said, took great exception to that perception; not least perhaps because he feared – correctly, as it happens – that it was held by some in his own team. 'I think the people making such statements should follow a sports director around,' he had said. 'They'd be amazed at all of the tasks that we cover along the way.'

Two weeks later I'm in the Team Sky hotel in Livorno, three hours before the first stage of one of the early season stage races, the week-long Tirreno-Adriatico. Outside the weather is appalling: bitter cold and heavy rain, mixed with sleet and snow. The riders, including Edvald Boasson Hagen, munch their breakfast in silence, and get up and depart equally silently, leaving behind a scene that looks like the aftermath of a children's party. There are boxes of Alpen and porridge, jars of nutella, honey, ketchup and olive oil (with Team Sky labels, supplied by the team's rider, Dario Cioni, who owns an olive grove in nearby Tuscany). A waitress stands surveying the wreckage with her hands on her hips, shaking her head as Hanlie, the team's *soigneur*, appears with a couple of large plastic boxes and loads them up.

The sheer scale of the Team Sky set-up had been highlighted that morning when I opened the curtains of my room to see the car park taken over with the team bus, the even larger mechanics' truck (with extension bulging from the middle) and three team cars. Minutes later I turned on my computer to see a picture posted by Greg Henderson on Twitter, showing an identical scene: truck, bus and three team cars. But Henderson had taken his picture – from his hotel window – several hundred miles north, as he prepared to ride another stage race, Paris-Nice. In other words, the vast infrastructure that takes over the car park in front of me is merely half the story; an identical scene is playing out in northern France.

The race guide is illustrated by a graphic that shows riders on a road that's flanked on both sides by enormous, threatening waves, which appear to be about to crash down on top of them. Tirreno-Adriatico, a long-established early season stage race, is the race of the two seas. But this sinister, bleak image appears portentous in the current conditions. At the start in Livorno the temperature has risen to 5°C, and the rain still falls relentlessly. A grim-faced Cadel Evans rides past in his predominantly white World Champion's jersey, with so many layers that he looks like a snowman. Fabian Cancellara, another of the sport's superstars, looks as menacing as Darth Vader in a black balaclava. One of the Italian Lampre team's *directeurs sportifs* leans against his car, chewing on a cigar; there is something sinister about this, too – he is like an army general oblivious to the danger he is about to expose his men to.

A red-jacketed official marches through the team vehicles blasting shrilly on a whistle, warning the riders it's time to start. 'This is your weather, man,' Kennet the Belgian mechanic tells Ian Stannard.

'Why does everyone keep saying that?' says Stannard. But it's obvious. The young Briton is 'fresh' from a fine third the previous weekend in Kuurne-Brussels-Kuurne, which had been run off in similar, if not more atrocious, weather. When he finished, Stannard's face was ingrained with grime, he had bags under his eyes and his jaw trembled when he tried to speak. Kuurne-Brussels-Kurne is one of the early season Semi-classics, and it followed the previous day's Omloop Het Nieuwsblad (formerly Het Volk), in which Flecha had scored a splendid solo victory: Team Sky's biggest win to date. It augured well for the full Classics, in particular the Tour of Flanders and Paris-Roubaix, in the coming weeks.

Here in Livorno, Stannard says that it took him several days to thaw out, and to restore his fingers to full working order. And now he's setting off to do it all again.

In the team car Sunderland picks up the radio. 'Michael?' he says. 'Copy,' says Barry.

'Mathew?'

'Eh, yeah,' says Hayman.

'Ian? … Stannard, can you hear me? … Thomas?'

'Yes,' says Lofkvist.

'Edvald?'

'Yes,' says Boasson Hagen.

'Antonio?'

'Hello, hello, hello!' comes the cheerful response from Juan Antonio Flecha.

'CJ?'

'Yup,' says Chris Sutton.

In the neutralised zone Barry and Sutton drop back to the team car. 'It's pretty fucking cold out here,' says Barry. On the dashboard the temperature gauge now reads 3°C. Barry takes another pair of gloves from the car, ripping off the plastic tag with his teeth.

'What do you want, CJ?' Sunderland asks Sutton.

'To stop?' says Sutton.

The race starts, the pace speeds up a little, Sunderland zeroes the mileometer and settles into his place in the convoy.

'So, did you ever get to the bottom of what we're calling pissgate in Oman?' I ask him.

'Yeah,' he says. 'I know what happened there.'

'Was it Roger Hammond – do you think he's a bit aggrieved at all the attention Sky are getting?' I ask, just as a line of riders passes the car, with Hammond among them. Sunderland presses the button on the window. 'Hey, Roger the dodger,' he shouts at Hammond.

'Hey up,' says Hammond and they exchange a few pleasantries before Sunderland's window slides up again. 'Yeah,' says Sunderland, 'I think that analysis is pretty right. I know what happened in Oman, and who was involved. But I told Dave it wasn't worth thinking about; it wasn't worth five seconds' thought. There are bigger fish to fry.'

The radio crackles. 'I feel really good,' says Kurt Asle Arvesen, making a remarkably quick return to racing after breaking his collarbone on day one of the Tour of Qatar. 'We have the hottest wheels, man,' says Barry. 'Bling!' says Arvesen.

One rider, Dmytro Grabovsky – a Ukrainian child prodigy who, on turning professional, went spectacularly off the rails, and lost the previous season to alcohol abuse – is an early attacker. Grabovsky, who still looks more like a rugby player than a cyclist, now has 11 minutes' lead as the race climbs away from the Tyrrhenian coast, into the hills, and into flurries of snow. 'A few teams are riding now,' Hayman's crackly voice comes over the radio. He and Barry, both senior riders and highly respected *domestiques*, are Sunderland's most frequent correspondents. 'They know what's going on and they're good communicators,' says Sunderland.

Sunderland's phone rings – it's Shane Sutton. 'I took the decision to go with CJ today,' Sunderland tells him. 'Edvald's fine with that. I think he wants a bit less pressure on him. At the team meeting, I said: "CJ, you up for it?" He said, "Yeah, I'm up for it." And everyone was right behind him.'

When the call ends the sound of snoring wafts from the back of the car. Kennet the Belgian mechanic is having a nap, his head tilted back, mouth open, but with a spare wheel in each hand. He has the mechanic's trademark trait of appearing laidback and supremely competent. 'If there's a period when you're awake, Kennet, can you get me a coffee?' says Sunderland, peering into the mirror.

'I wonder if we'll have a meeting tonight,' Sunderland says to Kennet as he hands over a cup of coffee. 'We have a lot of meetings. Sometimes it feels like we have meetings about meetings ...' He then says something to Kennet in Dutch.

Barry, meanwhile, reports that the Liquigas, HTC-Columbia and Quick Step teams are chasing. 'With one [rider] each?' asks Sunderland. 'One each,' says Barry.

'Guys, the feed's coming up,' Sunderland tells his riders. 'Edvald, the *soigneur* has special bottles for you.'

'Okay, thanks,' Boasson Hagen replies quickly and Sunderland smiles. 'He's so polite.'

I ask Sunderland how Team Sky was assembled. That was mainly his job, after all – to identify and recommend potential riders to Brailsford and Sutton. 'You can have someone who punches the numbers,' he says, 'but it's about personalities as well. This is different to track racing, where they go away and train for months and come together a couple of times a year. These guys are living together, travelling together. It's different; it's like a different sport. They ride bikes, that's the only similarity.

ABOVE The excitement builds: the glitzy launch of Team Sky in central London, January 2010

ABOVE Team Sky's fleet of vehicles, including Jaguar cars, customised buses and mechanics' trucks, was the envy of the peloton

LEFT Michael Barry and teammates warm up at the Giro d'Italia

RIGHT Not his favourite part of the job: Bradley Wiggins faces the media

ABOVE All aboard the bus: Rod Ellingworth and Sean Yates lead a pre-stage briefing at the Tour de France

RIGHT Simon Gerrans sporting his boxer's look – the Australian added a broken arm to his injuries, forcing him to retire from the Tour

LEFT Mat Hayman, Davide Viganò, Ben Swift and Chris Sutton lead the Sky 'train' at the Tour Down Under

RIGHT A glorious debut: Chris Sutton, Greg Henderson and Ben Swift celebrate Henderson and Sutton's one-two in their first race in Adelaide, Australia

Training in Valencia, the Spanish city chosen for the team's early season training camp on the basis of ten years' weather data

TOP LEFT Juan Antonio Flecha, arguably Team Sky's top performer of their first year, celebrates winning one of Belgium's top semi-classics, Het Nieuwsblad

TOP RIGHT Pretty in pink: Bradley Wiggins in the Giro d'Italia leader's Maglia Rosa after winning the prologue time trial to the Italian tour

ABOVE Scott Sunderland (white T-shirt) addresses his charges during his brief spell as the team's Senior Sports Director

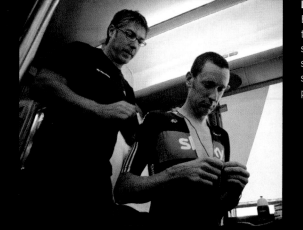

LEFT Txema González helps Bradley Wiggins during the Tour – González's sudden and tragic death six weeks later cast a large shadow over the final part of the season

ABOVE Throughout the Giro and Tour de France Michael Barry's job was to stay close to and look after Bradley Wiggins

LEFT British fans were out in force for Bradley Wiggins and Team Sky at the Tour de France

LEFT The bad weather at the Giro d'Italia symbolised the first part of Bradley Wiggins' 2013 season, prompting him to pull out of the Italian race and fail to defend his Tour title

ABOVE For the second year in a row Team Sky win the Tour de France, this time with Chris Froome. The team's performance was less dominant, but Froome's individual performance more impressive than Wiggins'

RIGHT Dave Brailsford said his 2013 Tour victory could be the first of many for Chris Froome. And with Froome having agreed to stay with the British team until 2016, it could also mean more successes in Paris for...

'Boys,' Sunderland says, picking up the radio again. 'Does anybody need anything? Any food?'

Silence. 'I'll take that as a no, then,' he says, sounding like an irritated parent. The race is in a quiet phase, the lull before the final hour. 'Guys, it's a good time to get rid of any clothing,' Sunderland says. 'Kurt is there at the back if you want to give them to him.'

Arvesen drops back with the layers discarded by his team-mates. 'Been on the Jan Ullrich diet?' asks Sunderland as the Norwegian hands over a rain cape, reaches up his front to pull out two more; then reaches into the rear pockets of his jersey to pull out another three.

'Guys, maybe we should move up a bit, eh?' Hayman says over the radio as Arvesen drops back through the convoy, his job done. The race is on now. Flecha comes back, unclips a foot, raises his leg on to the top tube of his bike and peels off an overshoe. Then he does the same with the other one. It's a complicated operation.

'Guys,' says Sunderland, 'we need to be up the front and together now. From the top of the next climb there's only 20k left. 20k.'

'CADUTA! CADUTA!' comes over the race radio, which has otherwise been quiet. Brakes are slammed on, cars almost sliding as they stop, and mechanics jump out with front and rear wheels in their hands. Kennet is out of the car before it stops, sprinting towards the upended bikes and riders sprawled across the tarmac. Then he's back: no Sky riders were involved. We whiz through the debris and, with a stomach-lurching acceleration, regain the back of the race.

'Were there any riders you'd have liked to sign?' I ask Sunderland.

'A couple of younger guys,' he says. 'Guys we could have developed, but with the British Federation's involvement in this team, that was difficult. I placed one in another team and the director phoned me the other day and said he's doing very well.' Sunderland looks satisfied. 'A lot of directors are asking me how it's going to work with the Federation – at the world championships, for example. It's an unusual situation. Unique.'

Barry's voice comes through the radio: 'Can we start to ride?'

Sunderland: 'If Ian's back isn't hurting, you two can start to ride now.'

On the climb a figure in yellow and white comes back towards us. It's Mark Cavendish, being shepherded by two teammates. He looks stiff, frozen rigid, scowling.

Over the brow of the hill Chris Sutton's voice is almost discernible on the radio, though it's muffled. All that can be made out is: 'Edvald.'

'CJ, are you saying that Edvald should do the sprint?' asks Sunderland, who then turns and asks: 'Did I get that wrong? Is he saying he'll do it?'

Sutton comes back, loud and clear: 'Edvald should do the sprint. I'm not 100%.'

Sunderland: 'Okay, you stick up there with Edvald, do what you can. It's cold, it's fast, no one is at 100% – it's normal. But stay up there, keep talking.'

On the descent we pass George Hincapie, the American champion, standing forlornly at the side of the road, holding a wheel in the air. The run-in to the finish is treacherous. The roads are rutted and pot-holed. On the entrance to the town there's a large speed bump, to which soft tarmac has been added, to smooth the passage for the riders. But in these conditions it's had the reverse effect: it's created a new menace.

Sunderland handles the car like a rally driver down the narrow, twisting roads. I ask him what makes a good sports director – where, for example, do they learn how to drive in the convoy, which seems to have as many unwritten rules as the peloton. 'As pro bike riders we're in the cars all the time, so we see how the convoy works,' he says. 'You learn very quickly what the etiquette is behind the scenes. And we know, when we're behind the wheel [of the car], where the riders are going to go, what lines they take, how much room to give them.' (Not always: Sunderland was infamously, and almost fatally, run over by his former director, Cees Priem, in 1998, suffering terrible head injuries.)

Tom Boonen crashes and we pass him checking his bike for damage. 'That's Boonen, Hunter, McEwen, Cav out the back,' says Sunderland, but not over the radio. 'Most of the sprinters.' On the radio, he says: 'Come on, boys, very good, keep it going.'

'You don't tell them the sprinters have been dropped?' I ask.

'No,' says Sunderland. 'They know. They're pro bike riders, mate. They just know.'

Today the sprinters are foiled. Linus Gerdemann, the German who rides for the Milram team, wins the stage with a late, opportunistic attack. Boasson Hagen, though he will go on to win the final stage of Tirreno-Adriatico, doesn't feature in the top 10. It's murky and bitterly cold in the small finish town of Rosignano Solvay, and the riders perform a U-turn soon after the line to follow the cordoned-off route to the car park and their team buses.

Grim-faced, the Sky riders appear at the bus like miners emerging from a cold and wet underground bunker. Stiffly, and with the kind of audible groans emitted by old men when forced to bend, they dismount their bikes, leaning them carefully against the bus, then slowly straighten their backs and awkwardly mount the steps.

At least today, even if the race hadn't gone to plan, served to highlight – in a literal sense – one of the features that Brailsford had meant when he talked in Adelaide about the advantages conferred by the team's vehicles, with the buses the jewel in the crown. A unique feature, a strobe light – beamed from a three-metre mechanical 'arm' on the roof of the bus – had been deployed in Rosignano Solvay to guide the Team Sky riders to their vehicle. Seconds later soapy water begins to spew out of a pipe in the undercarriage: they didn't win, but at least they are first in the showers.

CHAPTER 9

THE CLASSICS

'This is the first time I got to see the Team Sky bus. I said to Dave Brailsford, I'd been hearing about the darn bus all the time.'

James Murdoch

Bruges, 4 April 2010

It's 7.50am, and rain cascades from the leaden skies that hang low over Markt Square in the centre of Bruges.

But this is Belgium, it's the Tour of Flanders, and the fans – huddled beneath umbrellas – are packed into the cobbled square in their hundreds. It's still two hours before the race starts, so the umbrellas will be there another hour before the team buses arrive and the first riders appear. From their buses the riders will pedal from the car park through a narrow, cobbled and fenced-off corridor into the square ('We are led into the centre like gladiators, and then unleashed,' Fabian Cancellara, the Swiss star also known as 'Spartacus', had remarked). And in Markt Square they will climb on to the stage to wave at the crowds as they sign on for one of the most important races on the cycling calendar and the biggest day of any Flandrian's year: the Ronde van Vlaanderen.

Nowhere in the world are supporters so knowledgeable, though there are no prizes for identifying the first gladiator to appear on this gloomy morning: it's Lance Armstrong. Over the next hour the others appear in ones, twos or threes, bumping down the cobbled, crowd-lined passage, like entrants in a beauty contest, or horses in a paddock. The fans study their heroes as they pass, some clutching newspapers and cross-referencing the numbers, many not needing to. As a rider approaches the sound begins as a quiet murmur: 'Arvesen … Arvesen … HEY, ARVESEN!' (A strong Classics rider like Kurt Asle Arvesen is probably more famous in Belgium than in his native Norway.)

They're not just star spotting, they're gauging each rider's fitness, checking the muscle tone of his legs, the size of his bottom (a bum that wobbles like jelly on the cobbles indicates that a rider is carrying too much fat), and even how much clothing he's wearing. The way a rider is dressed could signify how 'up for it' he is, or isn't. By this measure, the Belgian riders appear most up for it, and expose bare, goose-pimpled flesh. But as well as the actual Belgians, there are adopted Belgians – riders who live there, or who live for their races, including Robbie McEwen, and the Team Sky riders Mat Hayman and Juan Antonio Flecha, both formerly of the Dutch Rabobank team.

Then, as Cancellara said, they are unleashed; and ahead of them lie 260km of racing, much of it on the narrow, twisting roads that criss-cross Flanders, broken by a series of torturously steep, cobbled climbs, each with a phlegm-producing name that evokes so much cycling history: Oude Kwaremont, Paterberg, Koppenberg, Muur-Kapelmuur, Bosberg, Muur van Geraardsbergen, or Wall of Gramont.

After all that – after seven hours of epic, gladiatorial racing – those riders who make it to the finish in Ninove are properly wasted; a kind of wasted that you don't tend to see at any other race, even the Tour de France. On a 'wasted scale' of one to ten, they are 11. 'The lights went out,' Ian Stannard, slumped over his handlebars just beyond the finish line in Ninove, just about manages to say. Stannard, developing into a strong Classics rider, was active in the closing stages, before he suffered the ill effects of not eating or drinking enough early on, and slipped back.

David Millar crosses the line and collapses by the side of the road, slumped on the pavement like a drunk. When he eventually stands up his legs almost buckle under him. He gets back on his bike and goes to move; I walk alongside him, and he leans on me. How does he feel? 'Fucked.' Millar has helped animate the closing miles, chasing after Fabian Cancellara and Tom Boonen, the winner and runner-up. But for him the lights also went out in the closing stages and he slid back to the big chasing group, eventually crossing the line 32nd.

It's been another typical Tour of Flanders, with thousands packing the cobbled climbs that act as launch pads – or torture racks. The atmosphere on the bergs and muurs is febrile, fuelled by chips and mayonnaise and, mainly, beer. 'They lean right into the road, it's incredible, so intense,' says Geraint Thomas. 'I could smell the beer on one guy's breath.'

There had been a point, late on in the race, when Sky had five riders at or near the head of the race. This was the business end of proceedings, when the gladiators emerge at the front – which is no straightforward feat on narrow roads that are no better than farm tracks in places. Yet Arvesen, Stannard, Thomas, Mat Hayman and the team's designated leader, Juan Antonio Flecha, were all there, packing the front of the diminished, bedraggled peloton, and looking strong.

Then it all went wrong. When Cancellara and Boonen launched their attack, others looked around for the previously omnipresent Sky riders, hoping they'd bring them back. But the riders in black-and-blue were nowhere. They also missed Millar's counter-attack, which Philippe Gilbert joined. Their best finisher in Ninove was 13th: a situation that looked so promising ended in disappointment.

'We had numbers in that final group,' said an exasperated Shane Sutton, 'and not one man in the top 10.' He didn't need to add anything else; he just shook his head. Sutton, who hadn't been at the race – who was still trying to stay away, other than being pressed into action at the Tour of Oman – couldn't understand it. He couldn't fathom why the team had been so committed, and ridden so hard on the front before falling out of the picture so completely. The impressive and ever-dependable Hayman was the best finisher, 13th, in Ninove. Thomas was 33rd, Flecha 34th.

The day after the Tour of Flanders, in Team Sky's quiet hotel in a back street near the centre of Kortrijk, Edvald Boasson Hagen pads through the lobby. He'd had to sit out the race with an Achilles injury and he appears as downbeat as you'd expect him to be, stuck in a hotel in the middle of a Belgian town, the centre of which has been wholly taken over by a noisy, chaotic fairground.

A man of few words at the best of times, Boasson Hagen mumbles in response to a question about his Achilles; he is hanging on in Belgium because he still hopes to ride the Scheldeprijs Semi-classic in Antwerp in two days; or, failing that, the Queen of the Classics, aka the Hell of the North – Paris-Roubaix – on Sunday. It's a faint hope. (And it proves futile. Boasson Hagen's injury – a consequence, perhaps, of his winter cross-country skiing – rules him out for most of April and May: a devastating blow for the young Norwegian, and for a team counting on arguably their best prospect.)

After Boasson Hagen exits, Flecha walks past with a bag of laundry, less ebullient today than he usually is. He's an interesting character, Flecha – an Argentinian-born Spaniard who has ridden for several years for a Dutch team (Rabobank), and who, contrary to most of his countrymen, is at home here in Belgium, riding the cobbled Classics of northern Europe. Until his third place in 2008 no Spaniard had ever even finished in the top 10 – the *top 10* – of the Tour of Flanders; none has won Paris-Roubaix, though Flecha has gone close: third, fourth, second and sixth.

'Alright, Flecha?' says Geraint Thomas as he passes. The way the Welshman pronounces his name, it sounds more like the British surname, 'Fletcher'.

He is known only as 'Flecha'. 'If I'm walking along the street and someone shouts, "Hey, Juan Antonio," I know it's not someone close to me,' explains Flecha. 'All my friends call me Flecha, except my mum and my sister. Even my girlfriend calls me Flecha.'

Flecha warms up when he talks. But there are two Flechas: on- and off-duty. In the off-season, Flecha doesn't relax at home (just outside Barcelona), or go on holiday; instead, he takes off in his camper van, parking by beaches and spending the days surfing; or he disappears to his second home in the Pyrenees. If he wasn't a cyclist he'd probably be a surfer or a climber; he'd certainly be a free spirit. 'I like being close to nature,' he says passionately. 'I don't like computers, the internet … for me, these things are not real.'

The other Flecha is the Flecha in race mode. He shuts down, blocks out. 'Overnight, it seemed Flecha's demeanour had changed from a jovial schoolboy's to a man preparing to enter the ring,' wrote Michael Barry, his teammate, in an article about the Spaniard in *Rouleur* magazine. 'The moment he stepped on to the bus he created an invisible cocoon in which he could focus uninterrupted.' The disconnect between the on- and off-Flecha is extreme, it seems.

Flecha, though, is earning his spurs at Team Sky. He is impressing Brailsford and the rest of the coaching staff with his attitude, as well as his riding – he is ferociously strong and loves to attack. He becomes animated, and his eyes sparkle, when he talks about his great love, Paris-Roubaix. 'Ah, I love both races,' he says, meaning Flanders and Roubaix. 'But for me, Roubaix is like going back in history. When I discovered these cobbled races I thought, "This is the kind of cyclist I want to become." It was clear to me; and when things are so clear it is easier. Until then, in Spain, people thought I was a Don Quixote – somebody fighting, trying to do everything, too much. They said, "Flecha wants to do these Classics, but no Spanish guy can do them." But I like the weather, I like the adversity. I even feel now more like a northern European cyclist than a Spanish cyclist.'

There is a technique to riding the cobbles, but Flecha says he does no special training. He shrugs: 'It's all technique; the way you pedal, the way you sit on the bike. It's something natural for me, not something I have to work at.' Flecha seems to be enjoying life with Team Sky. 'I can follow the jokes, the humour, even [Merseysider] Steve Cummings, and Geraint! I can follow their jokes. I even make some of the jokes!'

During the previous day's race it had been Geraint Thomas' job to stay with Flecha, and Thomas now offers an insight into the team's approach to the race. 'We had to watch the breaks at the start,' he explains, 'and if there were any Quick Step, Lotto or HTC riders there, then one of us had to cover it. But when the break went without any of them we could sit back, relax and save as much energy as we could.

'I had to stay with Flecha from the Kwaremont [175km into the 260km race] – that was my job. I had to stay as close to Flecha as I could, because by that stage the team cars weren't going to be behind the main group, because of the narrow roads. After the Koppenberg [185km] we knew it'd have split up, but we rode well to that point – we had five guys there. But coming into the Molenberg [215km], where Cancellara and

Boonen went … Well, I was first in there. But that was the race [over] then.

'To be honest, it was just good to have a real key role to play,' Thomas continues. 'In the past, it's just been about getting round and doing the best you can. Towards the end of my time with [previous team] Barloworld I wasn't even putting my radio on, because there was just no point. But yesterday summed up the difference for me. If you're struggling a bit and you can see three or four of your guys riding on the front, it gives you a massive boost. It's so good for your morale to be at the front setting the pace rather than sitting at the back hurting. The effort's the same. The difference is morale.'

Although the plan had been to help Flecha, Flecha was simply unable to follow Cancellara and Boonen when they attacked. It wasn't a tactical error. 'Flecha didn't quite have the legs,' says Thomas, 'but if we race like that every day, it'll happen for us. I'm sure. We could have quite easily sat back and got two guys in the top 10 – 8th and 10th or something. But what's the point in that? It was about helping Flecha as best we could, really supporting him. And we did that.

'We watched a bit of the race on the bus on our way back to the hotel,' adds Thomas. 'The way Cancellara attacked, and put so much [time] into Boonen, was unreal. Nobody could have followed that. He was on a different level.'

This is true, but I'm still keen to speak to Sunderland about the team's strategy in the Tour of Flanders. As he sits down in a public lounge just off the lobby Sunderland picks up a mandarin orange from a fruit bowl and begins to peel it, eating it slowly. 'The plan for the race,' he says, 'stemmed from knowing the course and knowing the riders … From the beginning, it was to get as many riders as possible over the Koppenberg in the front group, which we achieved. There was a change to the original plan, with Michael Barry crashing. That meant he came into play a bit earlier; he put his hand up and said, "Look,

I'm not sure where I'm at now, so I'd rather do the work early and do something useful."

'When it came down to it,' continues Sunderland, 'the boys were in the right place. We had a few little mishaps. Mat Hayman had a bike change, there were crashes, but there was no panic. So in the run-up to the Kwaremont they were all in a good spot, a good place, and over the Koppenberg we had four guys up there. Then Kurt came back and we had five, which was amazing. If Edvald had been riding, and Barry hadn't crashed, we could've had seven up there …'

An on-form Boasson Hagen could possibly have gone with Cancellara and Boonen. 'Yeah, possibly,' says Sunderland.

'We could have started riding [on the front] a bit earlier, before the Eckenberg [205km – before Cancellara and Boonen's escape] and forced the break to go there,' continues Sunderland. 'But the thing that stopped me from telling them to do that was seeing how Flecha was on the Paterberg [180km]. I had good television pictures in the car and just seeing him up there, I turned to Steven de Jongh and said: "I don't think he's on it today." Steven said, "Yeah, you may be right."

'It was confirmed to me later. I was talking to Flecha but I could also hear, from the lack of communication on his side, that he wasn't really … Although, it was a really hard race, and you've got to be careful in making that judgement. Flecha can do a lot of talking, but at different times, when the race is on, he can go quiet. But body language is a big thing – you can read a rider's body language and know if he's on a good day or not. You've got to know the rider.

'Coming to the end,' continues Sunderland, 'he said he was confident, and he was still the strongest man in the team – that's for sure. So we didn't change the plan; we didn't need to. Geraint and Mat were trying to cover all the moves, and Mat got away in one. The plan was to get one of those guys away, to draw the others out – to put them on the back foot – and allow Flecha to stay in the wheels, following.'

What Sunderland says appears to make sense. The bottom line is, Flecha didn't have the legs. He could have had the strongest team in the race supporting him, and the best possible race strategy; but he didn't have the legs. Sunderland knows this, and he becomes a little irritated at the implication that the team did something wrong; that they failed. 'Look,' he says, 'you can over analyse this. At the end of the day, Flecha wasn't able to go with them. He knows that. Cancellara went, he got the gap, Flecha couldn't close it. He was in the right place. It wasn't a tactical mistake, it was just a question of legs. We did everything right.

'Everything the boys did yesterday pleased me. Geraint and Ian both did a fantastic job. I said to them, in the coming six years they're definitely going to have some results in this race. Mat Hayman did a great job.'

As Sunderland says, Flecha didn't have the legs. Simple. But when he praises his *domestiques* I wonder about Brailsford's quest to find a cycling equivalent of the *Moneyball* formula of analysing, evaluating and assessing baseball players. How does Sunderland know who is a good, or bad, *domestique*? How does he know – given that he can't see much from the car, especially early in the race – that Thomas and Stannard had done a fantastic job?

'I just know,' he says, sounding a little defensive. 'I know what this is … I think that's coming from a world of track cycling, and all the stats and stuff, and you can do all that, but the variables in road cycling are way too immense. I can sit down and probably do it and put it into some kind of formula, but you'd never get it spot on. It's not like soccer, where you can say this guy can pass this many times, have that many assists, all that sort of stuff. There are some stats – with sprinters it's a bit easier, and in time trials you can measure someone's watts. But in the Classics and the Grand Tours, there are so many variables it's not funny.

'Listen, I could put it into … things, but to be honest I don't really want to. I don't need to. I've got that knowledge; that feeling for it, that insight. You can't learn experience, but I've got it.'

Compiègne, 11 April 2010

The only myth about Paris-Roubaix is that it doesn't start in Paris. The others are all true – the severity of the Napoleonic era cobbled roads, known as *pavé*, which shake riders to pieces; the torture of riding over not one or two, but 28 sections, of said *pavé*, sometimes in the rain, sleet, snow, mud – lots of mud – not to mention the freezing cold that can be typical of northern France at this time of year. Paris-Roubaix divides riders, who love it – as Juan Antonio Flecha does – or hate it. 'A race for dickheads,' Bernard Hinault once called it. 'Bullshit,' the great Frenchman described it as on another occasion.

Some love it, some hate it and some seem to love it *and* hate it. It was another 1980s star, Theo de Rooy, who best summed up the ambivalence riders can feel towards Paris-Roubaix. 'It's bollocks, this race,' the Dutchman told a CBS reporter at the finish, in the middle of the Roubaix Velodrome, in 1985. 'You're working like an animal, you don't have time to piss, you wet your pants. You're riding in mud like this, you're slipping. It's a pile of shit.' Would de Rooy ever ride Paris-Roubaix again, asked the reporter. 'Oh sure,' said de Rooy without a moment's hesitation. 'It's the most beautiful race in the world.'

In the grounds of the elegant Château de Compiègne, on the morning of 11 April 2010, the 25 teams invited to Paris-Roubaix begin to arrive in their buses and – in the case of one or two smaller Italian and Belgian teams – campervans. The sun shines brightly, picking out the mist as it rises gently from the grass. It doesn't look like a day of mud, then. Just dust, which will disappoint those, like Sean Kelly, who believe that a Paris-Roubaix without mud is like a beach without sand.

The scene around the Château de Compiègne is in marked contrast to that witnessed in Bruges the previous Sunday. It's not just the weather; the atmosphere is different, too. There are possibly as many fans, but their mood is not as frenzied. And yet, around the Team Sky bus, there is a little pocket of nervousness and anxiety. It owes to the delayed arrival of James Murdoch, son of Rupert, boss of the sponsors. Murdoch's helicopter had been due to land in Compiègne an hour before the start, but he's running late. There are fears he'll miss the start, and his seat in a VIP car with Bernard Hinault, the French legend, five-time Tour de France winner, and hater (but also one-time winner) of Paris-Roubaix.

About 30 minutes before the riders begin to gather for the off in the grounds of the Château de Compiègne, Murdoch's helicopter touches down. He just has time to be introduced to the team. 'This is the first time I got to see the Team Sky bus,' he tells one reporter. 'I said to Dave Brailsford, I'd been hearing about the darn bus all the time.' He is whisked into one of the VIP cars, with Hinault. In the back, alongside Murdoch, is the man who'll act as translator – Brailsford, who is a fluent French speaker. (As an aside, he is also a fluent Welsh speaker, having gone to school there. He once concluded an argument with the Welsh cyclist and Olympic Road Race Champion Nicole Cooke – who isn't a Welsh speaker – by speaking Welsh to her; she had no response.)

James Murdoch is a keen cyclist, having ridden the Maratona dles Dolomites, one of Italy's biggest and toughest 'sportive' rides. But this is his first time at a race with Team Sky. As well as it fitting in with other commitments (he'll fly to New York later today), he had said that Paris-Roubaix was the one he most wanted to witness. Interestingly, according to some who know Murdoch, and who are familiar with his cycling predilections, the Queen of the Classics and the Giro d'Italia are the races that most stir his blood – not the Tour de France.

Sky's involvement in the sport of cycling remains a mystery to some, though many speculate that it owes at least something to enthusiasm for the sport within the higher echelons of the company, James Murdoch included. More important than Murdoch, however, is the company's chief executive, Jeremy Darroch – acknowledged as the driving force behind a project he has described as 'a five-year partnership that focuses on two levels, first on developing elite sport, but it also has a grassroots programme; we see those as two sides of the same coin.' Thus, the company's love affair with the bicycle apparently extends from schemes designed to encourage employees to cycle to work, to their commitment to L'Etape du Tour (125 Sky employees signed up to do the 2010 ride), to the Sky Rides in British cities. Each of these mass participation rides, on closed-road circuits in 11 cities throughout 2010, attracted thousands – London's as many as 100,000 people on bikes. Team Sky's riders were also obliged to attend the Sky Rides, leading to the strange spectacle of a smiling and deeply tanned Juan Antonio Flecha leading a procession of day-glo jacketed leisure cyclists through the streets of Birmingham.

Yet, with a company as big and successful as Sky, there is inevitably suspicion that there is another, so far unidentified, agenda. Are they simply – cynically – hitching themselves to the wagon, and hoping to bask in the reflected glory, of a British sporting success story? Or is their embrace of cycling an effort to 'soften' the image of a company often portrayed as singularly ruthless in its ambition? (In an interview with *Management Today* about Team Sky, Darroch even identified with some of the negative publicity garnered by Team Sky around the time of their launch: 'If you're going to be the new kid on the block, then it's an inevitability. When Sky launched, there were two UK broadcasters. It was very established and we were there to challenge, and that upsets people, it disturbs them. It's the typical behaviour of incumbents who want to defend their position.')

Certainly cycling, especially at participation level, with its 'green' and family-friendly image, could be regarded as a suitable vehicle for perhaps helping to alter the perception of a broadcaster whose reputation still owes so much to its domination of the football market, and their role in transforming a game that – according to popular analysis – has been snatched from 'the people' and turned into an obscenely money-driven industry.

Or perhaps they just want to win the Tour de France. Or, in Murdoch's case, Paris-Roubaix.

Hinault is, claims Brailsford, something of a hero to Murdoch, as the Frenchman is to many in their mid to late thirties. Hinault was so much more than a champion. *Le Blaireau* – the Badger, as Hinault was known – was arguably the last *patron* of the peloton; a rider capable, by sheer strength of personality, of bending a race to his will. When Hinault was riding, the others knew that he was in charge, his authority stemming from his mere presence and his incredible ability, but also owing something, surely, to his legendary temper.

And yet since his retirement, in 1986, Hinault has completed a remarkable transformation, slipping comfortably into the role of glad-handing ambassador; a role that sees him preside over the daily post-stage podium ceremony at the Tour de France, presenting the awards, and introducing the winners to special guests. Now in his mid fifties, Hinault has obviously mellowed. But not entirely. The temper is still there, if provoked – as a couple of Tour de France podium invaders have discovered to their cost in recent years, having their protests interrupted by an aggressive intervention, and a shove from the stage, by the Badger.

At other races organised by ASO, Hinault provides VIPs and guests with an unforgettable 'experience'. At Paris-Roubaix, the plan is for the Hinault-Murdoch-Brailsford car to travel ahead of the race and meet a helicopter, to hover over the race and enjoy an aerial view of the action over some of the famous cobbled sections, before jumping back in the car and racing to the finish in the Roubaix Velodrome.

'This is a huge day,' says the tanned, American-accented Murdoch as he walks from bus to car. 'It's one of the great days on the cycling calendar for any fan, and also for the team. They're looking forward to this. They all seem ready to race and are pumped up.' As for the season so far: 'I can say from Sky's perspective that we're very happy with the results. We're really proud to be associated with a team like this. We're trying to make the best cycling team in the world. We're trying to push the envelope. It's early days, but so far, so good. Dave and everyone in the team are doing a tremendous job. They're juggling a busy calendar but have really high goals. That's what you need to have. I think the guys are progressing really well. Cycling is a complicated sport and it's a big programme but we're getting there.'

In the car, Hinault, Murdoch, Brailsford and the driver set off ahead of the race. Hinault cracks jokes, telling his guests about the film he watched en route to the 1981 Paris-Roubaix, which got him in the mood for a race he would eventually win. 'It was a porn film!' he says with relish. Murdoch doesn't look impressed by the revelation.

But slowly the mood begins to change. Brailsford picks up on some bad vibes between Hinault and the driver. The Badger's body language suggests irritation, annoyance – and anger. '*Putain!*' mutters Hinault, as he realises what has happened. They're lost. And they have missed their meeting point with the helicopter.

This is one of the problems with the Paris-Roubaix route: it uses a twisting, complex network of rarely-used roads. As Hinault begins to openly curse the driver, he relocates the course, but, with the roads lined with crowds and barriers, there's a problem getting back on to the race route, even in an official car. The passage is blocked by a band playing at the precise spot.

The car stops and Hinault storms out of the car and begins remonstrating with those who are blocking the road. It's a disastrous move: everyone recognises Hinault. They clap and cheer. Then the band also recognise the Badger, and begin playing tunes in recognition of their hero. It sends Hinault into a rage – 'his chimp took over,' Brailsford observed later, using Steve Peters' analogy – and he climbs back in the car, muttering '*Putain!*'

'Right,' Hinault tells the driver, 'you are driving through that field.' Unsurprisingly, the driver obliged, gingerly directing the Skoda across a rough field before eventually bumping back on to the road, as the band played on, and the spectators hailed *Le Blaireau*. Fortunately the car containing Hinault, Murdoch and Brailsford was still ahead of the race. But they had missed the helicopter.

At least they made it to Roubaix. There is nothing flash about the velodrome in Roubaix, which has hosted the finish since 1943. It's rudimentary, down-at-heel; a very unlikely venue for an iconic finish, and yet it works. To stand in the centre of the velodrome is, as Flecha has observed, to be transported back in time; it has witnessed victories by Fausto Coppi, Louison Bobet, Felice Gimondi, Eddy Merckx, Francesco Moser ... and Hinault, of course.

Much of the stadium appears to be original, most famously the showers, which are arranged like stalls, but with low walls making them effectively open-plan. Some of the most evocative and, not surprisingly, revealing pictures from Paris-Roubaix are from inside the shower room after the race, when riders scrub the mud and blood from their bodies.

Today, the sense of anticipation, as we await the climax to the race, is tempered by the fact that the winner is known for at least an hour before the finish. Fabian Cancellara, after winning the previous Sunday's Tour of Flanders, is set to do the double, having ridden away from the lead group 50km from Roubaix. It's an extraordinary performance, which had seen him negotiate the final 11 sections of *pavé* alone, and which, as Cancellara approaches the velodrome, is met with a low hum of approval. The hum rises in volume as he races along the road that leads to the velodrome, then increases to a roar as he enters the stadium, and rides on to the track, completing a celebratory lap, arms raised in celebration. The chasers are over two minutes back, but, in the dogfight for the remaining places on the podium, two riders break clear 12km from the end: Flecha and Thor Hushovd.

Now, two minutes after Cancellara, they appear in the velodrome. Flecha leads the Norwegian until the final bend, when Hushovd swoops down the track to claim the inside line and pip the Spaniard for second. Third in Paris-Roubaix is still an impressive result; it's also Flecha's third appearance on the podium. Nobody could beat Cancellara today, as he acknowledges. For Brailsford, though, there's initial frustration at his rider's inability to beat Hushovd for second. Ironically, given that he rides for a team much of whose expertise comes from track cycling, it was Flecha's inexperience on a velodrome – or his lack of what they call 'track craft' – that let him down. Half-walking, half-running from the velodrome to the Team Sky bus, parked with the other buses outside the velodrome,

Brailsford shakes his head: 'There's a few things we could learn about sprinting from the track.'

By 'we' he means Flecha. But then Brailsford stops. 'No, that's unfair,' he says. 'You've got to be happy. For our first outing in Paris-Roubaix, could we have asked for a better team performance? We're a growing team, we're three months in; and Hushovd's a better sprinter than Flecha, let's face it. For Flecha to be there sprinting for second, that's the main thing. That's what we should be focusing on.'

He hadn't had the legs in Flanders, but they returned in Roubaix.

After Paris-Roubaix the Ardennes races finish the spring Classics season: the Amstel Gold Race in Holland, before it's back to Belgium for the Flèche Wallonne and Liège-Bastogne-Liège. They are different kinds of races; hillier, and more for Grand Tour riders and lean climbers to stretch their legs than for bigger, more powerful riders such as Cancellara, Boonen, Hushovd and Flecha.

Bradley Wiggins, his thoughts turning towards July and the Tour de France, rides at Flèche and Liège. He had been due to ride Amstel, but, thanks to ash from the Eyjafjallajökull volcano in Iceland, which grounded planes throughout Europe, he was unable to fly from his new home – the one without a mobile phone signal – in Girona. He kept a low profile in the other two Ardennes Classics, riding for the team, finishing 66th in Flèche Wallonne, and 73rd, three days later, in Liège-Bastogne-Liège. His placings didn't matter: Wiggins' season revolved entirely around the Tour de France in July. Even the Giro d'Italia, in May, was being viewed as purely preparation.

While in northern Europe, Wiggins reconnoitred stage two of the Tour in the Ardennes, finishing in Spa. And the plan, following the Giro, was to recce the mountains – the Alps and the Pyrenees. It was the first time Wiggins had prepared so thoroughly for a major road event; in fact, it was the first time he had prepared at all.

So far, the highlight of Team Sky's leader's season had been at the Tour of Murcia in early March, where he finished third in the time trial, and ended up third overall. It had been billed as a head-to-head with Lance Armstrong, though Armstrong only managed eighth. But Wiggins was a little disappointed; he had fancied winning the time trial. In late March he suffered illness, knocking him out of the Tour of Catalunya, before returning to racing at the hilly, week-long Vuelta al Pais Vasco in early April, finishing 11th in the time trial, 34th overall.

It wasn't until the opening weekend of the Giro, in Amsterdam on 8 May, that Wiggins hit his stride. In the Dutch capital Wiggins roared around the 8.4km time trial course in his all-white British champion's outfit, dodging kerbs and tramlines, to win by two seconds from the American rider, Brent Bookwalter, with other general classification riders – Cadel Evans, Alexandre Vinokourov, Ivan Basso – left well behind. This was, arguably, Wiggins' finest moment in a road race – his first individual stage win in a Grand Tour; his first leader's jersey. 'I realise what I have on my shoulders,' he said in Amsterdam. 'Apart from the Tour's yellow, the pink jersey is the most prized jersey in cycling.'

'It will be on my wall for the rest of my life,' added Wiggins, though it was only on his shoulders for 24 hours. The next day he was held up by crashes; the day after that, with the Giro still in Holland, he was involved in one. Virtually the whole of Team Sky, in fact, came off with 10km to go – a fact, said Wiggins, which made it easier to cope with. 'It wasn't like I was on my own. Virtually all of us [in Team Sky] crashed that day; so it's not like you're alone and sulking. We were all laughing about it that night. What were the chances of that, all of us coming down in one crash? For most of us it was our third crash in two days. It was crazy. But it was quite funny, in a sense.'

It wouldn't have been funny, in any sense, at the Tour de France. The Tour was the be-all and end-all of Wiggins' season. Consequently, he raced at the Giro without pressure. He said later that a strong sense of camaraderie was established among the team – the Canadian Michael Barry performed an outstanding job as the *domestique* who shadowed him most days; Steve Cummings, his oldest friend in cycling, rode strongly; Mat Hayman was powerful and dependable; Dario Cioni, the veteran Italian, shone on the toughest stages, and finished a commendable 17th overall in Verona. Greg Henderson and Chris Sutton also finished, while Morris Possoni and Chris Froome didn't, but the Giro was successful for Team Sky in one important respect. 'The team spirit,' said Wiggins, 'was brilliant. We had great morale.'

Wiggins had faced a dilemma in the final week of the race. It had been a tough Giro, with some atrocious weather and a mountainous route, in which Wiggins yo-yo-ed up and down the General Classification (GC). Having appeared to be out of it, he raced back into contention on a remarkable 11th stage to L'Aquila, over 262km, run off in monsoon conditions. He was in a group that gained over 12 minutes on most of the overall contenders, which meant that, going into the final week, Wiggins was seventh overall. His second top 10 finish in a Grand Tour (in successive Grand Tours) appeared to be within his reach. But it also left him with a big decision.

Should he ride flat out in the Giro's final week in defence of his place in the top 10, or should he ease off, conserving his strength for the Tour? At the back of Wiggins' mind was the conviction that he had not started the Giro in top shape; he was still 2kg over the weight he had been going into the previous year's Tour. And then there was *the plan*: the plan had been to use the Giro as preparation for the Tour.

Wiggins discussed it with Rod Ellingworth and Matt Parker and decided to keep all his eggs in one basket: the Tour. 'It was hard to do,' said Wiggins, 'hard to voluntarily give up a GC spot.' But he eased off and finished the Giro 40th overall.

Team Sky was also swept up, during the Giro, in the scandal that followed Floyd Landis' allegations of organised doping in Lance Armstrong's US Postal team. The winner of the 2006 Tour, who tested positive for testosterone and was stripped of the title, fingered several other riders who'd ridden in US Postal colours – including Michael Barry.

It was Team Sky's worst nightmare: a doping 'scandal' involving one of their riders. In Porto Recanati, before the start of the 13th stage, Barry said he was shocked by Landis' allegation that they had discussed doping as they trained together prior to the 2003 Tour of Spain. 'I found out just before the stage yesterday, and, obviously, I was stunned,' said Barry. 'The stories aren't true, [but] when you see false allegations like that, it is pretty shocking. I was thinking about it during the race quite a bit. It is traumatic, really.'

Team Sky, said Barry, had been 'supportive'. 'The last few years, I have raced with teams with anti-doping stances, and throughout my career I have had a strong anti-doping stance and for clean sport. That was the one big reason I decided to come to Sky. They looked at all the biological passports of the riders. They are contributing to moving the sport in the right direction and that has always been important to me.'

Dave Brailsford, said Barry, 'just wanted to know my side of the story, that was it. They have faith in me, that is why they hired me.'

As for Landis, Barry said that in 2003, before the Vuelta, 'I did train with him for two days. When we were in Girona, I trained with him very little when we were racing for US Postal. Prior to the Vuelta, he was staying up in the mountains and I drove up there with my wife and rode with him for six hours one day and two hours the next day. And then we drove back home. That was it.'

In a statement on his own website, Barry described Landis' claims concerning him as 'completely untrue … I did not share or use any banned substances such as EPO when I was riding with him and am dismayed at his allegations. Landis is either lying or has mistaken me with another rider.' He added that, 'If there are any reviews of this situation, I am happy to participate in any and all of them.'

By this stage of the season things seemed to be going well for Team Sky. They perhaps hadn't made the splash that their launch hinted at, or that was feared by some, worried that the team behind British Cycling's track domination would work their magic on the road. (In any case, as Brailsford pointed out, 'It took us 10 years to get to that level on the track.') They didn't dominate, in other words. But they did win, and did so with consistency. As Mat Hayman, who had emerged, along with Flecha, as one of the team's standout performers, in his case as a work horse, put it: 'I think every race we went into, we affected the way the race was run.' That was more than some teams; more than a lot of teams. And there were some notable successes, not least the first 'European' win by a British rider.

That win came courtesy not of Wiggins, nor Geraint Thomas, but through a rider who, if he was a footballer, would be described as a 'journeyman'. Russell Downing, who had been knocking on the door of the European teams for 10 years, achieved the honour of first British rider to taste individual victory in Team Sky colours on 28 March, when the Yorkshireman won stage two of the Critérium International on the island of Corsica.

Eleven years earlier, when Downing appeared to hit the big time by joining the Linda McCartney team, he had been the country's most exciting talent: the Mark Cavendish of his day, possessed with a similar explosive sprint finish. But Downing was, in a sense, a victim of Peter Keen's decision to focus his efforts and his lottery funding, as British performance director, on track racing. Downing was a good track rider, but his ambitions lay on the road. After the McCartney fiasco he joined Sean Yates' short-lived iTeamNova.com (a member-funded team), and then returned to the UK, riding for a series of domestic teams at a time when the British scene was less than buoyant. Another opportunity eventually came his way in 2007, when the American Health Net team offered Downing a contract; but visa problems left him stranded in the UK, and in 2008 he was back with a small British team.

'I was part of the last big British team, for a day or so,' Downing reflects on the McCartney experience. 'The first guys went to the Tour Down Under, and my first outing was going to be the Tour of Langkawi in Malaysia. I went to the team hotel in London – it was all very similar to the Team Sky launch, in a way. But something wasn't right, the atmosphere was odd. And the next day the rug was pulled.'

In August 2009 the 30-year-old Downing, reckoning – probably accurately – that he was now in the last chance saloon, pulled out the ride of his career, winning the Tour of Ireland. That success made it almost impossible for Brailsford, then assembling Team Sky, to overlook him. 'In Ireland I was thinking: I need to strike,' says Downing. 'It was my last chance to get noticed by a big team. Ireland was my shop window, because all the big teams were there.

'It was just after that Dave B called. I was out on my bike, and I came back and I had a few voicemails from him and others – they were obviously contacting a lot of riders at the same time. I called and spoke to Shane, then Dave rang me back and we had a really good conversation. He popped a few things at me, I popped a few things at him, and it was agreed

I'd join the team. It was a pretty good moment. But I look on this as a bit of a reward for slogging it out, and sticking at it for 10 years.'

And at the end of March came a greater reward: victory in a race that featured the cream of world cycling, including Alberto Contador and Cadel Evans. But Downing's win in Corsica wasn't the only success in the first half of the season: there was Chris Sutton's in the final stage of the Tour Down Under; victory in the team time trial at the Tour of Qatar; Edvald Boasson Hagen's two stage wins in the Tour of Oman, and another at Tirreno-Adriatico; Juan Antonio Flecha's win in the Semi-classic, Het Nieuwsblad; Greg Henderson's in a stage of Paris-Nice; Bradley Wiggins' prologue win in the Giro; Ben Swift's stage win and overall victory in the Tour de Picardie; another stage win for Boasson Hagen, returning from his Achilles injury, on an Alpine stage of the Critérium du Dauphiné; another sprint victory for Henderson on stage three of the Ster Elektrotoer in Holland; and, on the eve of the Tour de France, national titles for Boasson Hagen and Geraint Thomas.

They may have lacked a big one – a Classic victory, or overall success in a stage race – but they were winning, and winning consistently; notching up, before the Tour de France started in July, 15 victories, 13 second-places and 14 third-places.

But there were problems. During the Giro it emerged that UK Sport had commissioned an 'independent review' into the 'operational arrangements between Team Sky and the [British national] squad [and] how the programmes work together'. This review – or, to use a more loaded term, 'investigation' – amounted to a response to deep concern within UK Sport – where of course the architect of British Cycling's World Class

Performance Plan, Peter Keen, was now Director of Performance – at the impact Team Sky might have on the British team, funded to the tune of £26m over the Olympic cycle. 'We invest millions of public money in British Cycling and they will be judged by the medals won in 2012', said a UK Sport spokesman. In fact, phase one of the review, a 'scoping' exercise undertaken by Deloitte, had started in March, with the consultants engaged in 'meetings, finding out how British Cycling and Team Sky work, building up their understanding.' Phase one was expected to last until July, and cost UK Sport £40,000. Then phase two, a more detailed analysis of the financial arrangements, would begin.

News of the 'review' didn't go down particularly well, and it's possible to understand both points of view – UK Sport's and Brailsford's. One of the keys to successful management is autonomy and control – indeed a reason often offered for the success of the British track team, under first Peter Keen and then Dave Brailsford, is the hands-off approach of the board of British Cycling.

The same principle applies in different sports, and it would be interesting to imagine Sir Alex Ferguson running Manchester United on fully accountable public funding. Like Ferguson, Brailsford's instinct is to say, 'Trust me, don't interfere, let me focus on performance, and judge me on that.' But that would make the distributors of the public funding, UK Sport, uneasy; it would also be a dereliction of duty. In this case, they resemble the parent wanting to know how little Jonny is spending his pocket money. And Brailsford is not particularly happy in the role of little Jonny.

For Brailsford the review – which finally, in March 2011, approved the 'operational arrangements' between BC and Team Sky, subject to some recommendations – might have been an unwelcome distraction, but another issue was more immediately pressing. Missing from Italy, and the Giro, was the team's senior sports director, Scott Sunderland. In the short period between the Ardennes Classics and the Giro, Brailsford made a cryptic admission: 'I've got some difficult decisions to make.' He added, 'I think it's time for me and Shane to get more involved.'

Problems between Brailsford and Sunderland had surfaced at the first riders' get-together in Manchester in November 2009. It was there that Brailsford explained his vision of how the team would work, in particular the 'rider-centred' philosophy, similar to the British Cycling model. 'They're the kings and queens of their world,' as Brailsford said, with the coaching staff there to serve them: 'We're the minions.'

Sunderland, it seemed, did not willingly buy into such a model. Virtually from day one there was speculation that his approach was more traditional, or 'old school' and hierarchical than that favoured by Brailsford. Outsiders observed, for example, that Sunderland appeared to identify Edvald Boasson Hagen as the rising star, and seemed on occasions to give him preferential treatment, such as driving him in the team car while other riders went in the bus. Journalists also became aware of apparent breaches in protocol by Sunderland, principally via the medium of Twitter, through which he announced team line-ups ahead of official announcements; again, Sunderland's attitude here honoured cycling's traditions, in which the *directeur sportif* resembles an old-fashioned football manager, involved in everything, from picking the team to talking to the press. Sunderland's team talk before Milan-San Remo may also have been 'off-message'. It apparently focused rather more on Sunderland's own experiences of riding the race than on the Team Sky gameplan for the first major Classic of the season.

After the Classics, Sunderland's days as Team Sky's senior sports director seemed to be numbered, but, with two full years left on his contract, negotiations over his exit were not straightforward. On 22 May a story appeared on the team's website, headlined: 'Senior Sports Director Scott Sunderland has left Team Sky under a mutual agreement.' Brailsford said: 'We would like to thank Scott for his contribution to Team Sky. He helped us get from the drawing board to being a real road team, working with us from the announcement of the project to our first podium finishes. We all wish Scott the very best, personally and for his future career.'

The story included a statement from Sunderland: 'It has been an incredible journey, helping to set up a new, highly professional team from scratch. I'm proud of the team's achievements so far and wish them the best of luck for the rest of the season, their first Tour de France and a successful future.' Sunderland added that his son Tristan's illness – congenital hepatic fibrosis, diagnosed in August 2009 – had been a contributing factor. 'The well-being of our family and in particular the health of our youngest son Tristan asks for me to increase the time and attention I give to my loved ones.'

A friend of Sunderland, meanwhile, complained that he lost a 'power struggle' with Brailsford. 'Brailsford wanted to be in charge of everything, even though Scott was the one with experience. Why give him the job title senior sports director if you're not going to let him direct?'

There was a sense of inevitability about Sunderland's departure. He and Brailsford had been on a collision course, and their strained relationship created tension throughout the team. It seemed a consequence of confusion over the chain of command; in particular over the question of who was in charge. Sunderland liked the 'senior' that prefixed 'sports director'; it was important to him; he insisted on it, even, allegedly, altering internal team correspondence, such as the staff rota, to reflect his status. But Team Sky was Brailsford's baby, not his, and – as the UK Sport investigation inadvertently highlighted – it was Brailsford's reputation on the line, with not only his job as team principal at Team Sky, but also his position as performance director at British Cycling.

Brailsford's method of management is to canvas opinion, not least through the endless meetings that Sunderland took exception to. And while Brailsford liked to describe the team as a rider-centred democracy, when it came to making decisions, he made the call. That could also irritate Shane Sutton on occasions. But Sunderland's frustration at his perception that his voice wasn't being heard, and his resistance to Brailsford's rule, drove a wedge between the pair.

With Sunderland gone, Brailsford turned naturally to his right-hand man and sidekick. Shane Sutton accepted the 'call to arms' with typical bluster, if apparent reluctance. 'Dave wants me to get stuck in with Sky and get me sleeves rolled up,' said Sutton, flicking a cigarette to the pavement.

CHAPTER 10

THE RECCE

'I don't think I'm a normal human being.'

Sean Yates

Geneva, 13 June 2010

'I think Brad's been looking forward to this,' says Rod Ellingworth. 'He's seen the pictures of other riders doing recces of the big Tour stages, and he's been keen to get out here and see what it's all about.'

We're talking in Geneva, the evening before a week-long recce of the Tour de France's crucial mountain stages. It's a fortnight since the Giro, a fortnight before the Tour, and the plan is for Wiggins and the Sky party – two other riders, Steve Cummings and Michael Barry, with seven support staff – to spend two days in the Alps and two-and-a-half in the Pyrenees, before heading to Bordeaux to ride the final time trial course.

'You have to remember that this is all new to Brad,' continues Ellingworth. 'He might be 30, but he's inexperienced when it comes to the Tour. He doesn't even know a lot of these mountains.

'Okay,' adds Ellingworth, standing up and slapping his thighs. 'Wheels rolling at 9am.'

Ellingworth leaves the hotel lobby, walks outside and doesn't return. He, along with the team's performance analyst and physiotherapist, are sleeping not in the hotels in which Wiggins and the rest of the team are staying, but in the large motorhome – christened 'Black Betty' – parked outside in the hotel car park. '*L'entraineur* in the motorhome, not in the hotel?' asks Etienne, a French photographer. His eyes widen and he chops his hands: 'In France *jamais, jamais, jamais!*'

In keeping with the Brailsford 'aggregation of marginal gains' approach, nothing is left to chance in the inaugural Team Sky recce. This much can be gleaned from the support crew: all seven of them – race coach (Ellingworth), sports director (Sean Yates), performance analyst, *soigneur* (masseur), physiotherapist, mechanic and chef – are present. On the first morning the riders clamber into cars to look at the finish of stage seven in the Jura mountains; Yates thinks the view from the car will suffice.

But in the afternoon they will ride, and at midday they convene in a car park on the outskirts of the small Alpine village of Bonne. The motorhome and people carrier are first there, with the chef, Søren Kristensen, donning his apron and setting to work. 'Couscous with mint and apricot, tomatoes, rucola, chicken and melon,' is on the menu for lunch, he says. For the riders, that is. The others devour ham and cheese baguettes.

Tim Kerrison, the team's performance analyst, introduces 'Black Betty,' or, as he also calls it, 'Marginal Gains HQ' – the motorhome that has been his home since he took up his appointment with the team. Kerrison provides a peek inside, pointing out the rolled up specialist 'athlete mattresses', made with 'visco-elastic foam' (or memory foam) by a company in Cheshire. 'They come to your house, and perform a sleep assessment before prescribing the right mattress,' explains Kerrison. 'Brad slept on one every night during the Giro. It makes sense, in terms of aiding recovery, to have a bed that's familiar. All the riders will have their own mattresses at the Tour.'

A quietly spoken, intense Australian, Kerrison is just getting to grips with cycling, having previously worked with rowers and swimmers. It seems that the motorhome is his home: he has been on the road almost non-stop since April. 'We did discuss not branding the campervan,' he says, 'but we decided to do it in the interests of transparency.'

Kerrison obviously knows that cycling is a sport in which team motorhomes can arouse suspicion – especially unmarked ones, which in the past have allegedly been used by some teams to surreptitiously transport doping products. Even branded motorhomes can still arouse suspicion, it seems. 'Driving here, across the Swiss border, we were stopped and the whole van was turned upside down and inside out, by the border police,' says Kerrison. He admits that cycling represents something of a 'culture shock'.

After half an hour the team cars appear in the car park and Wiggins, Barry and Cummings spill out and traipse slowly and silently into the motorhome. People walking dogs linger as they pass; they look surprised to see a fleet of team vehicles taking over the small car park in their tiny village. It's a little like Manchester United dropping by for a training session in your local park, except that cycling and cyclists have always been more accessible, training and racing on public roads. The people of Bonne have probably seen it all before; if they linger, it's maybe because they're trying to identify the riders.

The bikes are removed from the roof of the cars and set up as Burt, the physio, looks on. 'The injuries all come from equipment,' he observes. 'We had fitting sessions in Valencia on a special machine, with 3D motion capture, and we're tracking them all season.' Stepping closer and lowering his voice, he adds: 'They don't know this, but we're seeing if they tinker with their equipment and position – as they all do. And we're seeing how that corresponds to injuries.'

Sean Yates ambles over, munching on his baguette. Still as lean as he was when he was a professional – in fact, leaner – Yates' ideas and methods as a rider were famously extreme. Not necessarily scientific, though. He began his professional career overweight – pictures of him in his mid-1980s Peugeot years show a positively chubby rider – but had an epiphany when he realised that shedding pounds made him go faster. Yates being Yates, he went to extremes after making this connection. 'Sean says he used to do three-hour rides on two spoons of olive oil,' says Burt. 'He's steeped in the old school; in the traditional methods.'

Many of those methods seem radically different to, even incompatible with, the Team Sky *modus operandi*. It makes Yates' involvement in the team interesting. He begins to reminisce: 'When I lived in Nice I used to get up in the morning, have a croissant almonde and an espresso for breakfast, then do six hours on the bike. That was it; didn't eat anything else all day. Maybe some rice or something in the evening.'

Would Nigel Mitchell, the team's nutritionist, approve? 'No,' cackles Yates. 'I don't think so.' Then he stretches, twisting his back, and thinks for a minute. 'But, you know, I don't think I'm a normal human being.'

'That's an understatement,' says Burt.

Yates laughs again, throwing his head back, mouth opening to reveal huge gaps behind his front teeth. He resembles an ageing rocker or roadie, with a large hoop hanging from a stretched earlobe. The earring was his trademark as a rider. He carries on: 'I was lucky to have the constitution to eat like that, train hard, not sleep … You know, I used to ride Paris-Roubaix then fly to Nice and drive up to Courchevel for a week's skiing. I always had a break after the Classics. You imagine Cancellara or someone doing that now. Haha!'

Having finished lunch, the riders emerge from the campervan, Wiggins carrying a box with new shoes. They're patent leather with a red, white and blue Union Jack design; his shoes for the Tour de France. He takes a spin around the car park, and returns with a frown. He gets back off his bike, hands a shoe to Diego, the mechanic, and explains what he wants done. 'Marginal adjustments,' he says.

Then they pedal off with the cars following, leaving Kerrison to pack up and deal with an irate local woman, who thinks that the huge Sky-emblazoned entourage has landed in her village to install satellite television. 'Go away!' she yells.

Driving through the ski town of Morzine, the first, ominously large, blobs of rain begin to spatter the windscreen. And as we begin the 13.6km climb to Avoriaz, where stage eight of the Tour will finish, the heavens open. Earlier, in warm sunshine, we had followed Wiggins, Barry and Cummings as they tapped out a steady rhythm up the little-known Col de la Ramaz; a 14.3km climb, twisting upwards in steady increments – tough enough to be graded 'category one' by the Tour organisers (climbs are graded from four to 'hors'; easiest to toughest). One by one the riders rolled down their arm warmers and opened the zips down the front of their jerseys. 'I've got a bit of a sweat on,' said Cummings as they swung around one hairpin, still in a compact little group, the pace steady.

The idea, Ellingworth had told us, is to increase the intensity on the climb from Morzine to Avoriaz; especially for Wiggins, for whom this is his first serious training ride since the Giro, and the beginning of his final tough week before the Tour. En route to Morzine they pass through Les Gets, 168km into what will be stage eight of the Tour – the first high mountain stage.

But speeding through Morzine, before the final pull up to Avoriaz at 1,800m, the only intensity we're seeing, as we follow the trio, is in the weather. The isolated raindrops quicken their drumbeat until they are ricocheting off the road. Thunder claps in the distance, flashes of lightning briefly illuminate the murky skies, and Wiggins, Barry and Cummings press on, huddled together now, hunched up, heads down. We speed ahead and stop on one hairpin, so we can see the anguished expressions, and the water running down Wiggins' long nose. Perhaps he's thinking of Lance Armstrong's epic recce sessions in the snow. Armstrong always claimed he won the Tour with his recces.

The bedraggled trio pedal on up the mountain, through roadworks – improving the surface ahead of the Tour's visit – and eventually, as the rain eases, they reach the plateau, rising out of the saddle to stretch their backs as they freewheel towards the motorhome. The scene is straight out of Cormac McCarthy's post-apocalyptic novel, *The Road*. Through thick, lifting fog, the high rise and futuristically-designed buildings of the deserted Avoriaz resort, sitting on a ledge high above Morzine, appear to be smouldering.

It only lasts two minutes – long enough for the riders to clamber into the motorhome – before the rain starts falling in rods again. And beneath the shelter offered by a building another Rod, Ellingworth, tells us that another rider had recce'd the climb to Avoriaz earlier on the same day, in glorious sunshine. 'Contador was here,' says Ellingworth, 'with a couple of teammates.'

Wiggins and co had been following in the defending champion's tyre-marks all day, it transpires. It conjures up a wonderful image of Contador as a stealth-like escape artist, elusive and uncatchable. Ellingworth hopes it isn't a portent of things to come at the Tour.

* * *

We follow the Team Sky convoy back down, though it's impossible to keep up with the Yates-driven team car, which hurtles down the mountain. Yates admits later that he might have been showing off, testing the car's limits (and those of the following driver). We continue through Morzine to Cluses, pulling up at the modest Hôtel du Faucigny on the outskirts of town. After having eaten dinner in the motorhome, where Søren makes them salmon with South American quinoa, the riders are now receiving their nightly massage (from the *soigneur*, Garry Beckett), before retiring for the night (on their visco-elastic foam mattresses). Yates, Kerrison, Burt and Ellingworth have all appeared for dinner; Beckett, Diego the mechanic and Søren the chef turn up much later. Søren, of all people, arrives too late for dinner, though an appeal to the kitchen is successful. At the Tour, he explains, he will take over the kitchen in each hotel. He has worked with the CSC/Saxo Bank team for five years. 'I live at Alpe d'Huez,' he says. 'I was chef to CSC's corporate guests one year, and ended up being invited to join the team.' I ask Søren if any of the riders have special diets. While stuffing a piece of bread into his mouth he fixes me with a look that suggests it's a stupid question. 'If they weren't special they wouldn't be riding the Tour.'

Tim Kerrison says that he feels like a sponge, absorbing as much as he can. 'This year for me is a huge, huge learning experience, and sometimes when you're in the middle of that process it's hard to see what it is you can contribute. But I was at the Tour of Switzerland the other day, and I kind of realised: fuck, I've learned so much.'

And on another occasion, just before Switzerland, he had cause to think, 'Fuck, I've still got everything to learn.' It was during the 15th stage of the Giro d'Italia, which finished at the top of Monte Zoncolan. The road to the summit is hideously steep, 22% in places, as well as narrow, and 'Black Betty' fared as badly as Wiggins, who lost 25 minutes to Ivan Basso, the winner of the stage and eventual winner of the Giro. 'We got stuck,' Kerrison smiles sheepishly, before explaining that they got moving again just in time, with the race rapidly approaching and panic rising. There would have been huge embarrassment, not to mention hefty fines and universal opprobrium, had the Team Sky motorhome prevented the passing of the Giro. Disaster was averted just in time, but Kerrison's cheeks flush as he recalls the incident.

'When I met Tim I explained the sport,' says Ellingworth. 'There aren't many sports with this history and structure. It's a funny old game, and you have to really get into the politics of it. The French teams, for example: they have some crazy ideas about diet and so on. A lot of the French teams are still in that mould; that's why a lot of 'em don't move on.'

Ellingworth is right: it is a 'funny old game'. At least, that's one way of putting it. Because for all that there may be marginal gains to accrue, there are also dark arts to understand. How do you legislate for, far less control, events such as those in Oman, when there may, or may not, have been an anti-Sky conspiracy? Road racing is riven with such intangibles; the peloton is a society with its own rules and diktats. It is a sport in which your teammates (and friends) might not be able to ensure that you win, but your enemies (if there are enough of them) can certainly ensure that you don't.

An example of the peloton combining against a rider or team came in 1985, when the British rider Robert Millar lost the Vuelta a España on the penultimate day thanks to an unholy alliance of Spanish teams, who didn't want a foreigner to win their national tour. But there have been numerous other examples of riders failing to win for reasons other than ability, when they have been chased down or worked over in strange, often unfathomable circumstances.

One of the most curious and troubling examples is that of the French rider Christophe Bassons, who was effectively

hounded out of the sport after he made enemies of a significant proportion of the peloton with his anti-doping comments
in the aftermath of the 1998 Festina scandal. While in this
respect the sport may have changed – teams and riders are no
longer afraid to present themselves as anti-doping crusaders
– it remains the case that making friends, or not making
enemies, is an essential part of the game.

Then there are the deals made between teams. A rival team
can be enlisted to help a sprinter's squad to chase down a
breakaway one day, for example, in exchange for an equivalent
favour on another day. But deals can also, allegedly, be made
for hard cash, with races bought and sold. Doping may no
longer be the elephant in the room; but, if some are to be
believed, race-fixing could be.

'It'll take time,' says Kerrison. He is referring to learning
about the sport, not necessarily the dark arts. 'I was involved
with rowing for 20 years, swimming for 15, and so to catch up
to that level will take time. This year for me, as long as everyone around me has the patience to put up with it, it's a learning experience.'

'The same can be said of this recce,' adds Kerrison. 'We talk
about it as a recce for the Tour de France, but it's also a recce
for our future recce's. Everything this year is about learning
how to do it better in the future.'

There is an easy rapport between Kerrison and Ellingworth.
Indeed, Kerrison is in the mould of most of the coaches and
sports scientists employed by Brailsford: conscientious and
diligent, with no discernible ego. And yet, like coaches such as
Ellingworth and Matt Parker, he seems as driven as the riders.
When I ask Kerrison if he's been on the road all year,
Ellingworth laughs. 'Not so much all year,' shrugs Kerrison.

'All year bar two days,' says Ellingworth.

'I have a place in Manchester,' says Kerrison. 'You wouldn't
mind checking my mail, would you?'

So he doesn't have a partner, then. 'Don't be stupid,' says Burt.

'He's got Black Betty,' says Ellingworth.

'At the training camp in Valencia I shared a room with Tim,' says Burt. 'He said, "Do you mind if I do a bit of work?" I said no problem. But I turned around at 4am and he was still working. I had to ask him, "Will you take that out into the corridor?" I had a six-week-old baby. But he works very hard.'

The question is: what's he doing? Kerrison was a coach with the rowing team in Australia, and a performance analyst with the swimmers. Here at Team Sky that's his job title: performance analyst. What does it mean? 'Well, we all had an idea about what our jobs would be, and it's turned out very different,' he says. 'But no one has a problem with that.'

'Same here,' says Ellingworth. 'I said to Dave, it would be wrong to put my role in a box. We call it something but it doesn't have to stay like that. Best to stay flexible.'

'If we were all being assessed based on what our job was supposed to be when we started, we'd be screwed,' says Kerrison. 'It's the happy ant model: everyone moves into the role where they can be most effective.'

'You can't say: "That's not my job,"' says Burt, and Ellingworth admits that he has been on the road more than he expected. His intention at the start of the year was to be based semi-permanently in Quarrata, working with the riders on a one-to-one basis in Team Sky's spanking new base. That has not materialised.

'You get pulled in different directions,' shrugs Ellingworth. 'But that's fine.'

Returning to the question of Kerrison's role as performance analyst, he says: 'The motorhome, the vehicle itself, is the set-up that supports the whole marginal gains concept. So all the things we're trying to do, to get the best out of the athletes – that vehicle supports all that. I mean, just today, how many different functions has that vehicle performed? It's the kitchen where the chef does the cooking; it's where the riders eat; it's our office, where I can study the data from the training and racing; it's where we sleep.'

Yet Kerrison does most of his actual work on a small laptop computer. A big part of what he does is collect and analyse data such as the power generated by the riders on the climbs, in time trials, in road races and in training; he looks at the fluctuations in power, and how the riders respond to those, which includes looking at their heart rates; and he tries to assess their ability to recover, which is a key factor – arguably *the* key factor – in a stage race. He is also, like Wiggins, gathering information about the climbs. But while Wiggins could be said to be collecting 'soft data' – how a climb feels – Kerrison is amassing hard data on gradients, exposure to the wind and likely weather conditions, road surfaces and such like. He was able to collect a lot of physiological data on the riders during the three weeks of the Giro; on this recce, he will add specific knowledge of the course for this year's Tour. It could provide a 'marginal gain'.

'Here we're collecting GPS data,' says Kerrison, 'and then having a debrief afterwards with the riders, about what they think was important. That will all go into the battleplan for that stage of the Tour. We collected a lot of useful information at the Giro, too.'

'Dave was really keen, going into the Giro, not to *say* that it was a recce for the Tour,' Ellingworth chips in. 'But it was. The background staff know that we have to learn. Fundamentally, I think every Grand Tour for the next two or three years is a learning experience. But we probably don't want the riders to think that.

'We're all going to make some mistakes. The important thing to remember is that it's the riders' bike race. So whatever *they* say is important, and it needs to be relayed back and fed in. Tim can use that data, that knowledge, too. But it's not just about giving them info; we need to know what they need. There are times when you're sitting in the car, giving them info … but is it what they need?

'This was one of the things about having Michael Barry here,' continues Ellingworth. 'We were really keen to have him, because he's really detailed. I'm not saying others couldn't do the job. He understands what it is we're trying to do; that some of us are quite naive about what we're trying to do, and that we're learning and trying to gather as much information as we can. Plus, without a doubt, Brad was keen to have Michael along, because a) he's good to ride with and b) he's very experienced and a very good communicator.'

Yet Barry has also, since the Giro, been coping with altered circumstances – the aftermath of the Floyd Landis doping allegations, which implicated him. Ellingworth admits that Barry has been affected. He is not himself, he says. That much is obvious. Normally one of the most generous of interviewees, Barry appears withdrawn and quiet. Whatever lies behind Landis' allegations – whether anything at all – it is easy to see why Barry *would* be affected. He is one of the most thoughtful and erudite members of the peloton; almost as accomplished a writer as he is as a cyclist, with his latest book, *Le Métier* – a ruminative, poetic photographic book with essays by Barry on 'the seasons of a professional cyclist' – recently published. Barry introduces the subject of doping in that book, initially through discussing his friend and training partner, David Millar. What Barry says is cryptic and ambiguous, fascinating and depressing. It also echoes what Millar has said about the reality of riders aged 30-plus (Barry is 34) having 'encountered' doping in some shape or form.

'There are few young cyclists who haven't been manipulated, robbed and cheated,' writes Barry. 'The sacrifice is great, and when an immature adult is pushed to his limits he will buckle. The generation of riders who rode through the 90s doped to win, to survive in the peloton, and to maintain their jobs as professionals.'

Barry illuminates the suffering and the sacrifices of a professional cyclist, especially a *domestique*, investing the profession, and the helper's role, with nobility. The title of the book, *Le Métier*, refers to the 'trade' of cycling; it is also considered, within the sport – and it isn't clear whether Barry intended this or not – to be a euphemism for doping (though it refers to other aspects of the 'trade', too, including perfectly legal, if unusual and certainly unscientific, methods of self-preservation covering diet, rest and training). Accepting the etiquette and living by the rules of the trade are part of becoming a professional cyclist, suggests Barry. 'On a bicycle you can fly like a plane and the following day crawl like a worm, and we rebound because we can only hope it can't get any worse,' he writes. 'But when doping became the norm in the peloton, that hope faded for many, and they were faced with few options: to dope, to pray, to accept defeat, or to retire. Directors, doctors and *soigneurs* told their riders that to race they needed to be professional and take care of themselves: "Il faut se soigner." Drugs were called *les soins*, which made something wrong seem like a necessity for health. Medicine was not pushed for its performance enhancement but as a way to heal the body from the effort.'

When he competed at the 1996 Olympics, the then 19-year-old Barry, about to head to France to pursue his dream of turning professional, was told by his childhood idol, the Canadian rider Steve Bauer: 'I am glad I'm retiring tomorrow and am not in your shoes. The drugs are potent now.'

Barry adds: 'Those words stuck with me, discouraged me, encouraged me, enraged me, frustrated me, and also opened my eyes to the reality of our sport: it had reached a point where no matter how talented a rider was, how much training he did, how fit he was, or how motivated he was, he could not compete with the medicine when the racing reached the extreme … Cycling went from sport to black science.'

Barry's words on the subject, in his book, are thoughtful, thought-provoking and profound. The sport has a black history – dark aspects may still linger on – and it is no use pretending otherwise.

I ask Ellingworth about another sensitive subject: the departure of Scott Sunderland. Ellingworth has mentioned the lack of experience, even naivety, in the camp. Whatever else, Sunderland did have lots of experience. Does his departure change things? 'We've moved on,' says Ellingworth quickly. It is the only time in the evening when he isn't expansive. But he does add: 'I think Sean [Yates] has had to take on quite a lot more. Not more work, but more responsibility.'

'He's the sole source of experience,' says Kerrison.

'And he fucking knows his stuff,' says Ellingworth, lowering his voice to a whisper, partly because Yates is at the other end of the table, laughing and joking with Beckett, a Londoner with a gravelly voice and a penchant for dirty humour. 'Sean's got that British attitude, which is key,' continues Ellingworth. 'The thing for Sean, the track side, the training, the science – he doesn't talk about that stuff, but he knows and loves all that, the method of how you go from A to B as fast as possible. I heard him say to someone, "I've been waiting for this opportunity [to be involved with a British team] for 30 years." And you think, shit, he actually has. He's been so steeped in different ways of doing stuff, but there hasn't been any other way than that, until now.'

Yet Sky will be going to the Tour, I suggest, with only a fraction of the experience of the other teams – Yates will be the only member of the backroom team who's directed a team at the Tour. 'But I think,' says Ellingworth, 'when you actually look at it … I'm not being horrible, but it's not rocket science. I think … Dave's pretty hard on how he does stuff. I don't think you'd have known at the Giro that we hadn't done it before. From the feedback, the lads said it was the best experience they'd had at a Grand Tour, that they'd never got through it in such good nick. And they enjoyed it, as well.'

In many ways Ellingworth straddles the two camps: his background as a rider was on the road; but as a coach he is a product of Britain's track-based programme. Even if he doesn't have experience at this level of racing, he understands the limitations of an exclusively scientific approach; he recognises the infinite variables. 'Unpredictability is the beauty of bike racing,' he says. 'This is where you have to educate the sponsors and everybody else a bit, telling them: this is what can happen. You can't plan everything. In a bike race you may be the best but finish second, third … you can finish eighth and it can be a good ride. There are lots of stories in a bike race. The Giro was full of 'em; full of twists and turns. Some journalist came up to me at the Giro, pushing me to say it was crap, that it shouldn't be in Holland, that it was too dangerous. But our crashes were just bad luck; just bike racing. That's the beauty of bike racing: you don't know what's around the corner.'

The conversation turns to Wiggins. 'Brad's his own person, isn't he?' says Ellingworth, turning to Kerrison.

But there's growing expectation, and pressure, about his prospects for the Tour. Is he comfortable with that? 'I think he does realise that is going to be the biggest challenge,' says Ellingworth. 'He doesn't really like that side of it … well, he likes it and doesn't like it. He doesn't like the time it takes. It's just how he is.

'I've known Brad for a little while,' continues Ellingworth, 'and he's actually quite good at taking people with him. He's not a true leader type person, who really rallies people. Kurt

Arvesen's like that. Brad's not like that, but he can deal with pressure. I mean, he had a week at the end of the Tour last year when there was a lot of pressure.

'He is very good at preparing for an event. He does it all on his own. I don't think anyone can take any credit for Brad being good at certain things. He knows himself very, very well. When he shuts down, you never hear from him – no one can get hold of him – but the thing is, you know he's doing the right thing. The other thing is, if he does want something, he gets on the phone. But he's not reliant, he's pretty self-sufficient.

'It's weird isn't it? Because there are a few things about Brad, when you think … fucking hell. But on other occasions, you think, actually he knows exactly what he wants and he does it his own way. If he wants to perform in one event in two years he'd prepare himself for it. If he turned round and said now that he wants to go back to the track for London, you'd sort of say, okay, and you'd go full hog. You wouldn't think, hmmm, I'm not sure whether he'd commit. He takes a bit of time to make up his mind, but once he does, that's it.'

Turning to Kerrison, Ellingworth adds: 'Brad's pretty good, isn't he? The whole thing is about supporting him; we want to see how he'll perform in the world's biggest bike race. Matt Parker knows Brad well physically. In fact, you'd have made a lot of money if you'd asked him what Brad would do at the Giro – he was bang on.

'Look,' Ellingworth adds, 'there's a lot to learn, a long way to go, and we're far from where we want to be. But we have high expectations; we expect a lot of each other, and we have to be upfront and honest, so we learn from our mistakes. But we're focused on process rather than outcomes … you do have to perform, though, don't you?'

Ellingworth is confident that Wiggins can. 'It's like with the British team. Dave always said, if you're not a podium contender, we don't want you; what are you doing here? But if you are, we'll support you. 100%.'

When Ellingworth finishes talking it's after 11pm and he goes to leave: to Black Betty, but not to bed. 'Got to crack on – work to do,' he says.

At 9am the following morning Sean Yates returns, in full Sky kit, from a training ride. 'Just up the Col de la Colombière,' he says casually. 'Only' a 16km climb; 'only' to 1,600m. And then Wiggins appears in the hotel lobby, swinging a shoe-bag.

He sits down, glancing at his watch as he does so. The Paul Weller hair-do has long gone, replaced with a businesslike – or military-like – shearing. It is part of his preparation for the Tour; when he catches himself in mirrors it reminds him what phase of the year he's in, and what he's preparing for. What does he want out of this week? 'Just familiarity,' Wiggins says. 'Apart from the physical side of it – the training and getting your body right to do what the Tour de France entails – this is like going out to see what you've got to tackle. With the track we'd always try and go out and see an Olympic venue before you raced there, and it's a similar sort of thing but more important because of the climbs, and because it helps to see the run-ins to the climbs, and the descents. Last year I was just guessing. It also helps with gear choices. You'd be amazed how much, in a lot of teams, that comes down to some bloke saying, "Apparently some other bloke knows that climb and he says it'll be hard."'

Yet it's one thing to know the climbs. Racing them in the company of Contador, Schleck, Armstrong *et al*, and being on the limit, must be a very different proposition. The weather had prevented a proper workout the previous day. 'But I'll ride the Madeleine today with a bit of intensity,' says Wiggins.

'This is new territory for me,' he explains. 'I've only got last year to go on, and last year was almost accidental the way I stumbled upon Tour form, in the sense that I wasn't supposed to be there for GC. But after the Giro I got confident, I dropped weight a little bit and ended up thinking I could do something on GC. It was still a big surprise, though. Whereas this year it's all planned, so the expectations are different. I've been higher profile, but we have a plan. And the plan has gone to plan up to now.'

Had he not been tempted, sitting seventh overall going into the final week of the Giro, to fight to retain or improve that position? 'There's always an element of wanting to do more,' he says. 'It was dangerous in terms of, what do we do now? It was tempting. And there was a danger of being distracted. But we decided to stick to the bigger picture, because I'm not sure I can ride two Tours for GC.'

Wiggins describes the atmosphere in the team, and says the British Cycling 'culture' has been reproduced in Team Sky. 'We're not getting everything right, but we're getting there,' he says. Steve Cummings, another stalwart of the British team, says something similar, and that 'Dave's been in contact after the Giro, asking: "What can we do better?" But the Giro was nice to be part of – the staff were good, the riders were good and we raced well together as a team.

'Dave and Shane seem to have got more involved in the last month,' continues Cummings. 'At first they took a backward step, like they were watching what was going on. But I think they thought things could be done better, and they're far more involved now. It's funny: it's made it more like what I thought it would be when I joined.'

Wiggins echoes this. 'Definitely. Dave B and Shane are just good at being around. Dave's not like a boss. You know he is the boss but he's not. In other teams I've been in, when the boss's been around, everyone's been on edge. But Dave's not like that. He's almost like a big brother. He's so supportive of us as riders that it's reassuring when he's around. You feel more confident, rather than "Oh shit, we better do something." He's like the commander. You just know when he's around everything's going to be organised well.'

One of the big questions for Wiggins is how he'll deal with the expectation of leading the team into the Tour. 'That comes with it,' he shrugs. 'To be fair, all the British press, apart from *Cycling Weekly*, are very supportive.' He says this with a straight face, his antipathy towards the cycling magazine owing to its coverage of his move from Garmin to Sky. 'The others want you to do well, the broadsheets I mean,' he continues. 'There's expectation, but I can handle it.'

In the past, some Tour contenders – Lance Armstrong, Cadel Evans – have employed bodyguards. Would Wiggins do likewise? He leans back and throws his hands up: 'That's bollocks, all that. I don't like that air of ... It's creating hostility, having a bodyguard. Once you have a bodyguard you're creating a barrier for something to happen. I've never considered it.

'The easiest way is to stay on the bus until the last minute,' he smiles sheepishly. 'What worked in the past, with Steve Peters, at the Olympics, was going into the arena, seeing all the people, and realising: Okay, this isn't training. You can't make it all go away. You have to accept it. The minute you accept it, and say to yourself, "This is the way it is," you become more relaxed with it. If you try to avoid the press every day it won't work. So do your five minutes. And look on it in a positive sense: they're only there reporting on you because you're doing well. And that's a good thing.'

The paradox with Wiggins is that he seems to enjoy the attention, to a point. His former teammate David Millar had gone further of course, suggesting he wants 'fame' and 'to be a pop star'. Curiously, he *has* had an opportunity to be a pop star, sort of. In 2008 the BBC, ahead of the Sports Personality of the Year awards, tried to persuade Wiggins to play the guitar alongside his idol, Paul Weller. Wiggins, an accomplished guitarist, didn't want to do it. As this perhaps demonstrates, there seems to come a point when Wiggins ceases to enjoy the attention, and a further point where he starts to resent it (his reluctance to play with Weller may also have owed to nerves: he is his idol, after all). But it is hard to know where the cut-off point is. Wiggins doesn't seem to know, either. 'I do kind of enjoy [the attention] in a funny way, especially if you're riding well,' he admits. 'All of a sudden people are listening to what you have to say. For me at the Tour last year there was a fun element, especially with the foreign press, 'cos they kept asking the same questions. You know, "Where have you come from, how are you climbing like this?"' As Wiggins understood, some of the questioning was loaded with innuendo, with the implication that drugs might, or must, have played a part in such an apparently dramatic improvement. (To prove otherwise, Wiggins published his blood data, taken throughout the Tour, online just days after the 2009 race.) 'You wanna show 'em, kind of thing,' he adds.

'This year I'm in a funny situation. I can only lose in many respects. With certain sectors of the press ... well, there's an element of the public and press who want to see if I can back up what I did last year. So if I fail, if I get fifth or sixth it'll be like: "Ah you see, you didn't get on the podium." It'll be seen as a failure. And no doubt some people want to see you fail ...'

It seems curious that Wiggins believes there are people who *want* to see him fail. Who they are, he doesn't say. All he does say, with a sense of grim determination, is: 'I did finish fourth and I have to try and see if I can go better than that. Maybe I can't, who knows? But physically I'm better than last year, and more prepared. The Tour may be harder, the others may be stronger. Who knows? But I have to try.'

Then he grabs his shoe-bag, and strolls out to the car, which is waiting in front of the hotel door, wheels almost rolling.

From Cluses the Team Sky vehicles drive in convoy to the summit of the Col de la Colombière. The climb comes 46km into stage nine, but Wiggins knows it well from last year. So the plan is to ride the three final climbs: the Col des Aravis, Col des Saisies and the 25.5km monster, the Col de la Madeleine. When they stop at the top of the Colombière, and begin to get ready for the ride, sitting on the tailgates of the cars, rolling down compression socks, rolling up leg-warmers, Wiggins begins to chat easily. It's the most relaxed he's seemed in the last two days. He is like a different person, in fact; he is laughing and joking. I ask him about his apparent retirement from Twitter, the micro-blogging site that had provided an outlet during the previous year's Tour for his humorous and irreverent thoughts. The rumour is that he has been 'banned' from it by his bosses at Team Sky – too many 'off message' tweets. 'Nah,' he says. 'It's not that. I'll make a comeback at the Tour.' (He didn't.)

He also admits, though, that it had been a source of stress; that he would find himself drawn to the messages people were sending him, becoming angry and upset by some. Social networking is actually a hot and vexing topic for athletes and for others in the public eye. Later, I asked Steve Peters where he stood on it. 'If someone wants to read it because it's interesting or amusing, then put it away and it has zero effect, then fine,' said Peters. 'But if someone's going to read this stuff as a sounding gauge to where they stand, it's very dangerous. I advise most athletes not to read Facebook or Twitter, or the press. Just don't do it, because if you're sensitive to things, particularly in the middle of a race, it's not doing you any favours if it's likely to upset you.

'What you've got to remember is that there are certain times when you're vulnerable to attack emotionally,' continued Peters. He means in high stress situations, such as riding the Tour, or, conversely, when you're relaxed, such as on holiday. 'In those situations your emotions are less stable, and you let your guard down,' explained Peters. 'When you go on holiday you're much more vulnerable to con artists. You have these holiday romances which, in the cold light of day, are bizarre. But they happen when you have a different perspective on who you are, where you are, what you're up to. The same applies to sports people: your mindset alters when you're in the middle of an intense race. You're far more vulnerable to criticism and comment; your emotions are heightened and less stable and you can suffer horrendous extremes.

'So I say to them, "Put up your guard."'

Wiggins had been working with Peters a lot in the build-up to the Tour. Peters had found, after his initial invitation to Team Sky's riders to speak to him at the first get-together in Manchester, that the interest had not abated. But this created challenges. The geographical spread of the riders, for one thing; but also the sheer number of athletes he was now working with – not only from Team Sky, but from all the British national teams, in every discipline. How did he cope with that? 'I don't sleep,' he joked.

'You have to learn what works for you,' he continued. 'I've got to be realistic. I've got a job here with British Cycling, and I don't want that compromised, and I don't believe it has been. Then I ask myself, can I fit this [work with Team Sky] on top of that, in any gaps that might appear? And the answer is, you can. Because I really do thrive on work. I don't really need holidays. It's not my thing. I'm very happy working. So it's not like I'm burning out. For me to go home, the normal would be for me to do 2–3 hours work at night.'

It was in this window, he said, that he spoke to many of the Team Sky riders, using Skype. 'In the past, if one of the British riders wanted to speak to me, and they were abroad, I'd go and see them. But in the past I might have had to do a single trip to see that rider, which I have done. There was one that asked me to support them in a very important meeting, which involved a 36-hour trip to get to the venue. I was there a day and then I had a 36-hour journey back. Although it was critical to do that, now, with Skype, I've saved 72 hours. And I've spared myself the exhaustion of it.

'There has been a big increase in workload,' continued Peters, 'but you just manage your time better. I call Brad on Skype for specific sessions; I know when he's got an hour, between breakfast and leaving, a window. It could be a one-minute conversation, or 20 minutes. But I make sure that during that hour I'm free.'

Rod Ellingworth is reminiscing as we watch the riders getting kitted up at the summit of the Col de la Colombière. 'I remember we were around here with the Academy,' he recalls, 'and Geraint fell off on one of the descents. He slid down the road on his hands. Took all the skin off, he did. And the next morning he turns up for breakfast, with his hands covered in bandages. He wasn't wearing his racing kit. So I said, "Geraint, where's your kit?" and he looks at me blankly, says nothing. I said, "Come on Geraint, you don't cycle with your fucking hands, do you? You use your legs! Get your kit on!"'

As the Team Sky group – Ellingworth, Yates, Barry, Cummings and Wiggins – mills around the car at the top of the Colombière, stuffing energy bars into pockets, pulling overshoes over feet, Wiggins continues to demonstrate just how relaxed he is. He begins to do what, after cycling, he does best: imitating people. His skills as a mimic are astonishing.

First up is Sean Yates. Wiggins drops a shoulder, just like Yates does, and uses a limp hand to illustrate a point, just like Yates, in his languid way, does. But it is the voice that's the clincher: the sound, the cadence, the accent – all are perfect. He looks and sounds more like Yates than Yates, who wheezes with laughter, like a heavy smoker. From Yates Wiggins segues into Brian Nygaard, the team's now-former press officer (Nygaard had announced his resignation from Team Sky after the Giro, only to later emerge as a driving force behind an ambitious new Luxembourg-based professional team, led by the Schleck brothers); then Wiggins becomes Scott Sunderland.

When Wiggins jokes, the mood lightens. Everyone visibly relaxes. Then he, Barry and Cummings pedal off down the mountain in a blur of jokes and laughter.

But the mood is more serious as they begin the 25km, fog-shrouded climb of the Madeleine. It is the mountain – the final one of the day – that Wiggins had said he would tackle with more intensity.

The fog thickens, the visibility reducing with every metre climbed. Features such as small bridges and villages appear and disappear like apparitions. But adding further to the mystique of the mountain is the intelligence transmitted back to the team car from Tim Kerrison in the motorhome; that Alberto Contador is recce-ing the same stage. Just like yesterday, the Spaniard is riding ahead of the Sky trio with two of his Astana teammates. The news serves, somehow, to raise the stakes. Wiggins, Barry and Cummings climb the lower slopes steadily together, but when the gradient increases, one of them begins to pull away.

But it's not Wiggins. It's Barry.

Barry seems a little embarrassed by this, and not quite sure what to do. He looks around. Then he eases up, and Wiggins catches him. They ride together for a bit, but Barry begins to drop Wiggins again. This time, he carries on. He rides up into the mist as if on his way to a stage win in the Tour. He looks as though he is flying; he appears to be driven and motivated, perhaps by anger over the Floyd Landis allegations, or perhaps simply because he wants to prove that he deserves a place in the team for the Tour (something that is still undecided, in part because the team fears that the allegations will blow up again at the Tour). Wiggins, meanwhile, drops back to wait for Cummings; they complete the mountain at a steady rhythm, chatting much of the way. When they reach the summit, Wiggins climbs off his bike and enters the motorhome without a word. Everyone else is quiet too. Eye contact is avoided. The mood has altered completely.

Another journalist arrives for the second half of the week, in the Pyrenees. It's Paul Kimmage, the former professional rider, now of the *Sunday Times*. Kimmage, through his journalism and his book, *Rough Ride*, has done as much as anyone to expose and battle the scourge of doping, but at considerable cost – he was ostracised by many in the sport, which only increased his resolve, and perhaps also heightened his cynicism. 'I like Paul,' Wiggins told me as he got changed at the summit of the Colombière. 'He's got his opinions, but at least you know where you stand with him.'

Following the recce, I was curious to find out how Kimmage had got on. 'You go first,' he said when I called to ask. I told him that, although I didn't think you could or should read too much into training camps, I had the impression that Wiggins appeared to be struggling to recapture the form he'd had the previous year. 'Yeah, that was my impression,' said Kimmage. He sounded quite deflated himself. 'Very much so. On the climbs you could see he was trying to give it full gas. But whenever the road went up he blew a fucking gasket. Barry was flying ...'

One of the evenings he was there Kimmage sat down to interview Wiggins. 'He was fine,' said Kimmage. 'He's a fantastic talker; fascinating.' But the next morning his mood had altered. A photographer had been flown to the Pyrenees by the *Sunday Times*, but Wiggins wouldn't pose for the portrait he needed. Kimmage was furious. He protested to Ellingworth. But it was no use: Wiggins could not be persuaded.

Kimmage left the recce on bad terms, which was awkward. Very awkward, in fact, because of an agreement he had made with Dave Brailsford. The plan was for Kimmage to travel with Team Sky during the Tour, staying in the same hotels (or the car park – Kimmage had hired a campervan), and enjoying close access to the team and support staff. He had done the same thing in 2008 with Wiggins' old team, Garmin, and the experience proved something of an epiphany for the Irishman. Through his conversations with Jonathan Vaughters, David Millar and Christian Vande Velde, and through observing how they got through that Tour (without doping), Kimmage's scepticism began to fade; he started to believe in professional cycling once again. For the first time in about 25 years he felt his passion for the sport returning.

As well as documenting the British team's debut Tour, he now hoped that process would continue in July with Team Sky.

CHAPTER 11

IT'S ALL ABOUT (THE) BRAD

'Don't do a Boardman.'

Everyone – to Bradley Wiggins

Luxor Theatre, Rotterdam, 1 July 2010

'We're very clear in our minds that we're going with a mission,' said Dave Brailsford as he announced which nine riders would represent Team Sky in their debut Tour de France. 'The mission is to support Brad as far as we can on GC.'

It was a no compromise approach: GC or nothing. And so there was no place for the team's sprinter, Greg Henderson.

Two nights before the Tour gets underway the riders congregate in the Luxor Theatre, in the centre of Rotterdam, host city to the Grand Départ. So much for the glamour of the Tour de France: inside, the scene is anything but. The bowels of the theatre resemble a cattle market. There's even a pen in the middle for the bikes, which are stacked in nines, team by team. Around the periphery, on plastic school chairs and on any spare surface, the riders lounge, looking bored, anxious, or a combination of both, as though contemplating their first day at senior school.

Edvald Boasson Hagen, Juan Antonio Flecha and Simon Gerrans sit with their elbows on their knees. The often gregarious Flecha has entered his pre-race state, locked into his own world, which seems to be a thousand miles away, perhaps on a beach with his campervan, or in his mountain retreat in the Pyrenees. The other Team Sky riders – newly crowned British champion Geraint Thomas; Michael Barry; Belgian climber Serge Pauwels; Thomas Lofkvist – are nearby. But Bradley Wiggins and Steve Cummings are nowhere to be seen. 'They're storming the joint to find a sofa,' explains a member of the Team Sky staff.

Given that the team was built around him, Wiggins had a major say in who would ride. He had insisted on Barry, who had ridden by his side throughout the Giro and would do a similar job here. Only two riders on the team were likely to be given licence to do their own thing on selected days: Boasson Hagen, who was returning to form after his Achilles injury and perhaps, in his debut Tour, would have the ability to contest the bunch sprints; and Gerrans, whose ability to infiltrate breaks and win ('Simon's the sort of guy who can be the third strongest guy in the move, but wins through tactical sense,' as Lance Armstrong said) meant that he might be dispatched to try and claim a stage in the second half of the race. Otherwise, to paraphrase the title of Armstrong's bestselling book, 'it's all about (the) Brad.' To underline the point, while the other eight riders will share rooms, Wiggins will have his own.

On the eve of the Tour, as he announced the nine riders, Brailsford explained: 'This team, Team Sky, the mission behind it, is to perform at the Tour with a British rider. Brad's the leader of the team, and we feel he's in good shape. He's prepared well, and followed a similar pattern to last year. A lot will refer back, and look at what he did last year. But this is a different race, with different people.'

*   *   *

Brailsford admitted that they were going to apply some of the lessons learned at the Giro; and they were going to keep challenging conventional wisdom. 'All year, we've been asking, why the hell do we do that?' he said. 'And people say, "Because of x, y, z …" and some things make sense, but others are done in a certain way because that's the way it's always been done in cycling.'

Some customs appeared minor and trivial. 'For example, eating together: teams always eat dinner together,' says Brailsford. 'After the Giro there were quite long transfers. We often got back to the hotel quite late, then guys would need their massage, and we'd eat, as a group, at 9.30 or 10 at night. Why are we doing that? Everyone knows that if you eat at 7.30 it helps with digestion and you're going to recover better. But no: teams eat *together* – because that's the way it's always been done.

'Another great old wives' tale is that you can't have a massage on a full stomach: it's bad for you. I'm sure the masseurs came up with that one … No, if eating at 8pm means eating on your own, so be it.'

Brailsford also said that he wouldn't want a repeat of the Giro, where they had to defend the leader's jersey on day one. 'Would we want the [yellow] jersey? Yes. Would we want the team to have it on the first day? No.' (Bob Stapleton, the HTC-Columbia team owner, smiled knowingly when told what Brailsford had said. 'Oh sure, yeah. They don't want the yellow jersey. Of course they don't. Seriously, and you *bought* that?')

From backstage at the Luxor Theatre the 20 teams are called to file out one by one, riding through the crowd-lined streets of Rotterdam before being interviewed on the stage set up in the centre of the city. The whole experience is one that the riders, judging from their expressions backstage, generally despise. Forty-eight hours before the toughest race of the year, all they want to do is rest.

Brailsford seems to be relishing the build-up to his team's debut Tour, though. Back in the bowels of the theatre, as his riders wait to be called, he stands, arms folded like a football manager, deep in conversation with Johan Bruyneel, Lance Armstrong's long-time director. When he breaks off, he strolls back towards his riders. He is cheerful, ebullient and chatty. One journalist has coined a nickname for Brailsford: the Pub Landlord. In appearance, with his immaculately shaved bald head, Brailsford does bear more than a passing resemblance to Al Murray's comic creation. It falls down when you understand that the fictional Pub Landlord is known for his anti-European attitudes, with a particular dislike for the French (Brailsford's fluency in French has already earned him much-coveted brownie points with the French media). But the nickname works in another sense, for there is an everyman charm about Brailsford, as there is about the best landlords. He is amiable and approachable, and appears relaxed and laidback.

If that is a myth – laidback doesn't tally with the description of Brailsford offered by colleagues, which is 'intense' – then another is that he is a techno-geek, all about science and 'numbers', and devoid of passion. As his palpable enthusiasm on the eve of the Tour suggests, Brailsford appears to be driven by passion as much as anything else. Indeed, his focus on science, his repeated emphasis of 'logic over emotion', could owe to an awareness of his own weakness in this regard; his tendency to, in the description offered by Steve Peters, be 'hijacked by his emotions'. On several occasions Brailsford has admitted to at times struggling to control his 'inner chimp'. That suggests someone overrun by passion and enthusiasm, not devoid of it.

It is why Peters is such an important member of the team, and not just for the riders. As Peters told me: 'I work a lot with the coaches – a lot. Because I think the coach is a really vulnerable person. And I think that's unfair on the coaches. Most of them are really driven and hard working, but it is thankless in some ways. They get the stick when things don't go right, and I think that's wrong.'

Tonight in Rotterdam, on the eve of the Tour, Brailsford's enthusiasm bubbles up and threatens to spill over. He tries to keep that in check by focusing on the process and the detail, and he avoids projecting ahead, or imagining Wiggins standing on the podium in Paris. 'It's a bit like an A&E ward in a hospital,' says Brailsford, deploying one of his trademark traits: ever more left-field analogies. 'When a body comes in on a trolley, you don't want the doctor to think about the outcome. It's the process he should be focused on.'

But Brailsford hasn't been without his distractions, or worries, in the build-up to the Tour. Wiggins' form and fitness might be one area of concern; Brailsford doesn't say. But the fact that the team – confirmed after the recce – is built around Wiggins suggests that he isn't concerned. He is, however, about the arrangement he'd made with Paul Kimmage, for Kimmage to shadow the team throughout the Tour. The issue with Wiggins during the recce – when Wiggins incurred Kimmage's wrath by refusing to pose for a photograph – is one factor. Another is the presence in the team of Michael Barry. Brailsford knows that Kimmage will quiz Barry on the Floyd Landis allegations. It's a distraction he feels Barry and the rest of the team could do without; and so, just days before the Grand Départ, a member of Brailsford's staff phoned Kimmage and asked if he could join them not at the start in Rotterdam but five days into the race. 'Why?' asked Kimmage. 'Because you make some of the riders edgy,' he was told.

Kimmage, a Brailsford supporter, who clearly wants to believe in Wiggins and Team Sky, and who would doubtless write a series of positive articles about the team's commitment to anti-doping (assuming he sees or hears nothing to trouble him), is not happy about this. He wants to join them in Rotterdam or not at all. Where does it leave him? 'Outside the tent pissing in,' says Kimmage.

It is a curious case; and it seems uncharacteristically badly handled, not least because the prospect of Kimmage standing outside your tent, pissing in, is not an appealing one. He is a journalist who is worth keeping on-side; particularly if, as Brailsford has always insisted, the team has nothing to hide.

But it becomes even more curious just 24 hours before the start of the Tour, when, with Team Sky's pre-race press conference due to be held at 5pm, the entire press pack – travelling to the hotel from the press centre on the other side of the city – is held up in Rotterdam's rush-hour traffic. When they arrive, 13 minutes late, they discover that the press conference has finished. There had been one reporter there, and one question. The reason? The reporter who was there was not Kimmage.

Not that Brailsford, having wrapped up the press conference in record time, doesn't talk. In an upstairs conference room he explains the thinking behind another strange call: the decision to put Wiggins off early in the following day's prologue time trial. This has taken people by surprise. It is traditional for the stars and overall contenders to go among the later starters – Alberto Contador, Lance Armstrong and Fabian Cancellara, to name three, will be among the final 20 – but Wiggins, we have learned, will start in relative anonymity: 41st in the start house, a full two-and-a-half hours before Contador.

Do Team Sky know something – or think they know something – that no one else does? One theory is that the decision is based on a weather forecast predicting rain for the later starters. Is that true? 'Yeah,' says Brailsford. 'You're never sure with the weather. And we know for a fact that Rotterdam has a unique micro-climate, which is quite hard to predict – we know that from our sailing friends – but we think there's a high chance it's going to rain tomorrow. Plus, it could be a bit warmer in the earlier part of the day. And hot air's faster than cold air: everyone knows that.'

Minds were cast back to Chris Boardman in 1995. There, in Saint-Brieuc, Brittany – another northern European town with unpredictable weather, and lots of rain – the conditions altered dramatically midway through the prologue time trial. An early starter, Jacky Durand – no prologue specialist – rode on dry roads and set the standard the later starters, including Boardman, had to beat.

But by the time Boardman began his ride the rain was torrential. And because the event was held in the evening, the light was fading; it seemed that the night was closing in. There was a third factor, too. The course featured hills and corners. And on a descent, on a sweeping bend, Boardman, chasing Durand's time, misjudged his line; he entered the corner too fast, his tyres lost traction, he went down heavily. He was lucky not to be run over by the team car following him – it skidded on the wet roads and stopped just in time. But Boardman broke his ankle: his Tour was over within 8km.

That was the most obvious example of the weather affecting the result of a prologue time trial, though on that occasion it had no material effect on the overall battle for the yellow jersey, because back then the Tour organisers insisted that all the favourites went at the end, and thus tackled the course in the same conditions. That rule had been scrapped. If the same deterioration in the weather happened here in Rotterdam, Wiggins could get the edge on his rivals. It was a gamble worth taking, thought Brailsford.

Did Brailsford have any doubts about Wiggins? If he did, he wasn't letting on. But there had been another behind-the-scenes incident, in addition to the refusal to be photographed for the *Sunday Times*, that might have caused concern. A press day was organised in Girona, where Wiggins is based during the season, with selected journalists and broadcasters invited to the Spanish city to interview the leader of Britain's first Tour de France team in 23 years. But 24 hours before it was due to be held, Wiggins said he didn't want to do it. On that occasion he was told he had no choice: he had to do it. And he did.

'Brad's in better shape now than he was before the Olympics,' says Brailsford now. Psychologically, he was ready. He wouldn't be fazed, adds Brailsford, by the fact that he was starting so early, before the other big guns. 'The good thing about Brad is that he's ridden important Olympic and World Championship qualifying rounds early in the morning in empty velodromes all over the world. I know people say, "But the big guys go at the end, will he not be more motivated then?" But if you're not motivated at the start of the Tour de France, what are you doing here? You also hear people say, "If he knows he's two seconds down [on his main rivals], he'll try harder." But that would mean he wasn't going at 100% in the first place.

'No, come on … Brad's mentality is such that it doesn't make a difference. When he goes off he'll do what he's got to do.'

Rotterdam, 3 July 2010

It's 4.50pm in Rotterdam, on a grey, overcast day with inter-mittent, light rain. Around 10 minutes ago Tony Martin, the young German, crossed the line, at the end of his prologue effort, in 10 minutes, 10 seconds: the fastest time so far for the 8km course. For most of his ride it remained dry, but a few ominous spots of rain fell towards the end. Almost as soon as Martin crosses the line, though, the grey skies open: the deluge begins.

Rain crashes down as Wiggins makes his way from the temporary structure around the Team Sky bus – a perspex cocoon, inside which the riders warm up, shielded from the public – to the start house. In his all-white British Time Trial Champion's skinsuit, he wears an expression of grim concentration. And as he sits in the start house, with his bike held up, and the countdown beginning – '*cinq … quatre … trois …*' – Wiggins begins to look tense and anxious. Sean Yates is behind the wheel of the team car, which waits to the side, and – on '*un*' – accelerates as Wiggins puffs out his cheeks and sprints away from the start house.

Yates slots in behind him. After punching his bike through the lashing rain, getting up to speed, Wiggins settles into his rhythm, arms outstretched on the time trial bars. But approaching the first corner, he sits up, coming out of his aerodynamic tuck, moving his hands to the brakes. It's a sweeping bend that could perhaps be negotiated without braking, but as he approaches the turn Wiggins keeps squeezing the brakes, slowing almost to a standstill. Yates presses his own brake pedal to the floor and crawls round behind him.

Coming out of the bend Wiggins sprints hard and gets back up to speed but then, approaching the next corner, he does the same thing. On greasy roads a bike's tyres are more likely to slip when the bike is tilted, of course. But Wiggins is taking this cautious approach to extremes: he doesn't seem to want to risk tilting the bike a single degree. The curious thing is that Wiggins is an accomplished bike-handler, as any former World Madison Champion must be. He had displayed those skills in another Dutch city, Amsterdam, just two months ago, on the opening day of the Giro. Then, he had fearlessly thrown his bike around corners, skipped over tramlines, kissed the kerbs with his tyres.

Now, it was different. 'It wasn't the speed he was taking the corners at,' Yates says later of Wiggins' ride through the greasy streets of Rotterdam. 'It was the way he was taking them. You could see his upper body was tensed up. He just wasn't in it at all.'

Wiggins is 21 seconds down on Tony Martin at half-distance. He has lost another 25 seconds on the young German by the finish. Here, though, he doesn't apply the brakes. He carries on through the finish area, speeding through a narrow corridor of reporters, taking deep gulps of air. Then he rides as quickly as he can back to the bus, disappearing inside without speaking.

The riders still to go, including Geraint Thomas, are warming up inside the mechanics' truck, which is parked next to the team bus, also inside the perspex cocoon. Taped to the side of the bus is a piece of paper, which reads: 'Sky Warm-Up: 5' easy; 8' ramp to TT pace; 2.30' easy; 2.30' to incl. 2x6" sprints; 2' easy.'

A TV monitor set up outside the cocoon shows the riders inside the truck, from behind, riding their stationary bikes. But the cocoon is proving a controversial innovation. Mentioned in passing by Rod Ellingworth as something they were thinking about back at the training camp at Valencia in February – based on the riders' requests for privacy while warming up – it was first erected at the Giro d'Italia in May. But if it pleases the riders it disappoints the spectators, who are used to milling around the team buses, and observing their heroes in the flesh rather than on a TV screen. There has been one concession, however. At the Giro its plastic walls were black; here they are clear perspex, which at least affords a view of the inner sanctum.

After his warm-down in the mechanics' truck Wiggins re-emerges to talk to reporters. It has stopped raining and Thomas has now finished his ride. And what a ride. He completed the course in 10 minutes, 23 seconds – 13 seconds slower than Martin, and 23 better than Wiggins. He is going to finish among the top riders. But while Wiggins talks, and Thomas warms down outside the bus, the Welshman tilts his head, as though trying to listen to what he is saying; as if he too wants to find out Wiggins' explanation for a performance that puts him among the middle-markers in an event he usually excels at. 'I'm happy with the way I felt physically and with the numbers in front of me,' says Wiggins. 'I didn't want to chance anything. I said all along that the prologue wasn't the be-all and end-all for me, so I'm just pleased to have got round in one piece. I felt good and did what I needed to do.

'Going in a straight line I felt as good as I needed to be. I couldn't push it to the limit in the corners because I couldn't take the risk of losing maybe three or four minutes in a crash.'

Wiggins plays down the loss of time. He doesn't yet know how much he'll concede to the later starters, though he knows he will: the rain has been off long enough for the roads to completely dry. 'It was about getting round,' Wiggins shrugs, 'and about going through the process, and dialling into the effort. The prologue is so insignificant in the three weeks: you can lose seconds here, but [the time differences are] going to be minutes in three weeks' time.

'Now,' he adds, 'I can get back to the hotel and have dinner.'

That's one advantage of starting early. But as Wiggins begins turning to head back into the bus, he is asked a final question. 'Are you hoping it'll start raining again for the later starters?'

'I don't give a monkey's about that, to be honest,' he says sharply.

As expected, Fabian Cancellara, the Swiss specialist and one of the final starters, wins the prologue. Tony Martin holds on for second, David Millar places third, and in fifth place – sandwiched between Lance Armstrong and Alberto Contador – is Geraint Thomas. It's an outstanding performance: his finest ever on the road. Wiggins is 77th, 56 seconds slower than Cancellara.

But Thomas' ride, admittedly on drier roads, differed from Wiggins' in other respects. He was fearless, said Rod Ellingworth, who followed him in the car. 'Gee was hanging off the bike, he nearly hit the barriers at one point,' says Ellingworth. 'Whereas Brad said, "I want to be cautious." But he was over-cautious.'

Later, Ellingworth, his coach Matt Parker and performance analyst Tim Kerrison study the data from Wiggins' ride and they are reassured: physically, there appears to be nothing wrong with him. 'Looking at the data, he lost it all on the corners,' says Ellingworth. 'His peak power was amazing. He's better than last year, no two ways about that. But before he started he said: "I don't want to do a Chris Boardman."'

'We gambled a bit with the weather,' says Brailsford. He's speaking in Rotterdam city centre the day after the prologue. It's midday: stages of the Tour de France start around then, so that they finish between 5 and 6pm, the best time for the TV audience. Brailsford continues: 'The rain came sooner than planned, and everyone kept telling Brad: "Don't do a Boardman." So he didn't commit. He was very, very cautious. Maybe a bit too cautious. He lost all the time on the corners. He was very ... tentative.'

Perhaps there is another explanation for Wiggins' tentativeness. It is linked to the weather, but to something else, too: the sporting equivalent of second album syndrome. The difficulty, in other words, of following an exceptional debut (as Wiggins' 2009 Tour effectively was, given it was the first time he'd targeted the GC).

The case of Boardman in 1995 could offer some parallels. It was Boardman's second Tour. In his debut, the previous year, he'd opened his account with a very loud bang, winning the prologue to claim the first yellow jersey. It marked Boardman out as a prologue specialist, to such an extent that you could almost say his entire 1995 season depended on the 8km prologue in Brittany. The pressure to follow his 1994 performance was immense.

As the rain fell, and the night seemed to close in at Saint-Brieuc, that pressure must have seemed overwhelming. Boardman was not his usual self on the bike; like Wiggins in Rotterdam, he too was tense and nervous. Combined with the fact that he was chasing a fast time, set on dry roads, it was a recipe for disaster. And so it proved.

But in 2010 Wiggins was under even greater pressure. His season had been built around the Tour, and his team – his new British team – had been built around him. And there was evidence to suggest that he wasn't coping brilliantly with that pressure. There was the incident in the Pyrenees with the photographer; his cold feet over the press day in Girona ... He seemed uneasy with his status as team leader and Tour contender. His greatest fear was not crashing, perhaps, but failure. If Wiggins had doubts about his ability to live up to his billing then he might not have fancied a moody close-up of himself with a far-off, thoughtful gaze (possible headline: 'Wiggins Eyes Yellow'), in Britain's biggest selling Sunday broadsheet just six days before the start of the race. Avoiding the photographer and the press might have been a way, albeit a cack-handed way, of trying to dampen expectation and reduce pressure.

'Look, there's no point in dwelling on it,' says Brailsford in Rotterdam, reflecting on Wiggins' disastrous ride in the prologue. Brailsford insists, as Wiggins had done, that in the context of a three-week race it's not a disaster. 'The way to look at it is like an F1 grid. If that's how the riders were lined up now,' Brailsford says, demonstrating with his hands, 'you'd have Armstrong here, Contador here, and Brad ...' – Brailsford pulls one hand back, moving it down the imaginary F1 grid –

'… here. Over three weeks, it's hardly anything.' It also puts Wiggins much further up the grid than another overall contender, last year's second-place finisher, Andy Schleck. Schleck placed 122nd, 1 minute, 9 seconds behind Cancellara.

Rotterdam is hot and sunny. And there is a sense, as there always is for the first road stage, that today is the start proper, with the long 223km leg to Brussels. Sean Yates drives the first of the two Team Sky cars, while Shane Sutton sits in the driver's seat of the second. He is still amused by the news he received just before leaving for the Tour, that he – an Australian who has claimed to have 'yellow and green blood running through me veins' – is to receive an OBE. But in the car seat, on day one of the Tour – his first Tour since 1987, when he was the first rider to go in the prologue time trial in West Berlin – the irrepressible Sutton looks even more edgy than usual. He leans out the window, taking a draw from the cigarette pinched between his fingers, then flicks it to the ground, and sets off, part of the vast and frenetic line of vehicles that follows the Tour's peloton.

It's a stage that finishes in a bunch sprint won by Alessandro Petacchi of Italy, though Thomas again proves in the finale that he is in the form of his life. The Welshman finishes behind the first wave of sprinters, crossing the line 15th. For Wiggins, it's an uneventful day. It's the next two days that he, Sky, and other teams, are worried about. They are far from routine, with Monday's second stage, from Brussels to Spa, featuring roads and hills well-known from the Ardennes Classics. Tuesday's is on another scale: a mini Paris-Roubaix, from Wanze to Arenberg, featuring seven sections of the notorious *pavé*, over 13.2km. It is a stage that has been feared ever since the Tour route was announced the previous October, which has seen all the overall contenders pay visits, in the previous months, to this north-eastern corner of France.

But the mini Paris-Roubaix stage is one that Wiggins and Sky have been looking forward to. Wiggins is an accomplished performer on the *pavé*, even managing a respectable 25th in the 2009 edition of Paris-Roubaix. Thomas is a former winner of Junior Paris-Roubaix. Then there is Flecha, third in this year's race, and Barry, another strong man on the *pavé*. Barry is so far performing the job he is at the Tour to do: to ride by Wiggins' side. At the end of the Ardennes stage, on the run-in to Spa, there was rain and numerous crashes – Wiggins came down heavily in one – but Barry didn't let his leader out of his sight. 'Brad's wing man' is his official title.

Steve Cummings is another with a team role, spending the first two days on 'supplies'. It meant dropping back to the team car whenever there was a lull in the racing, filling his pockets and loading up his jersey with drinking bottles and food, then distributing it to his teammates. Like painting the Forth Bridge, it's a never-ending task; as soon as the final bottle has been handed out it's time to go back for more.

But on the Tuesday morning, when Rod Ellingworth led the pre-stage briefing, Cummings was given a different job. He, along with Simon Gerrans and Serge Pauwels, was to be active and vigilant at the front from the start. It was Cummings' job to follow attacks, Gerrans' and Pauwels' to bring back any moves that didn't feature Cummings. 'I made one effort and was pretty gassed,' said Cummings. 'The second time, I got away.'

When seven riders eventually broke clear, Cummings was among them. They worked well together, in a rotating double-line, all taking turns at the front, patiently building a lead of almost five minutes. Ahead of them lay the cobbles and chaos. Behind, the peloton was nervous; riders began manoeuvring for position, all trying to be close to the arrow-head, among the first 30 or so.

Cummings' group's advantage had been trimmed to three minutes when they reached the first section of *pavé*. Over the first two sections, Ormeignies and Hollain, the peloton rode hard, in a long, thin but unbroken line; it was on the third section, Sars-et-Rosières, where that line was broken; and then, as expected, all hell broke loose. Frank Schleck, one of the pre-race favourites, sitting up near the front – theoretically in one of the safest places – fell heavily, fracturing the lead group, and also his collarbone. The five riders who'd been ahead of him – Fabian Cancellara, Cadel Evans, Frank's brother, Andy, Thor Hushovd and Geraint Thomas – sped clear. Those behind, including Wiggins, picked their way around Schleck, conceding ground in the process.

Today's Sky plan worked perfectly, at least in one sense. With Cummings up ahead, he was perfectly placed to provide assistance to the lead group when it caught him. That it was Thomas, rather than Wiggins, in that group created a dilemma.

Cummings, after doing a double-take when he saw Thomas' British champion's jersey in the elite five-man group, rode alongside his teammate and gave him his bottle. 'My radio isn't working,' Thomas told Cummings. He didn't know whether he should drop back to the chasing group, to help Wiggins. Cummings radioed Yates. 'What should Gee do?' he asked him. 'Tell him to stay where he is,' said Yates.

Instead, Cummings dropped back, though the day's effort was telling. His legs were screaming. When he was swept up by Wiggins' group, which also included Alberto Contador, Cummings asked him: 'How are you?' Wiggins nodded that he was fine. Cummings did what he could, staying with Wiggins for as long as possible, but he couldn't live with an acceleration by Alexandre Vinokourov, and he trailed in alone, having spent the best part of six hours at the head of the race.

Thomas' second place on the stage, finishing narrowly behind the Norwegian sprinter Hushovd, is outstanding. It moves him up to second overall, behind Cancellara, and means that he takes over the white jersey of best young rider.

Wiggins, meanwhile, also fares well. He moves up to 14th overall, leapfrogging a lot of the riders who'd taken time out of him in Rotterdam.

But over dinner that evening there is a discussion over whether Thomas should have waited for Wiggins. On the one hand, he is now in a great position; there's a chance he could even inherit Cancellara's yellow jersey in a few days, when the race hits the medium-sized Jura mountains. On the other, the team's effort is supposed to be all about Brad. Having Thomas in the white jersey won't help Wiggins reach the podium. Indeed, the efforts he's making may even detract from the team effort.

'Was the plan the right plan?' Brailsford reflects the following morning. 'It's always good to have a discussion about that, so you can refine the way you work. I think overall it was good. The whole idea of having Steve up the road was so he'd be in the thick of it when it mattered. It wasn't a case of, will you make the break? It was a case of: Steve, you *are* in the break today. It's about giving them clarity; if the guys have clarity, they'll commit. And the longer he is up the road the longer Brad is protected.

'We did discuss whether Gee [Thomas] should've waited. It could have worked out differently, but they did what we asked of them: that's all we can ask.'

Thomas' white jersey meant one change: the Sky branding on the team vehicles changed from silver to white (there were yellow, green and polka-dot transfers in the mechanics' truck, in the eventuality of a spell in one of the other leaders' jerseys). But Brailsford, keen on clarity, was absolutely clear that the team was not at the Tour de France to defend Thomas' white jersey. How much effort would they commit to defending the Welshman's lead in the young riders' competition? 'None whatsoever. It's not what we're here for. It's fantastic for Geraint, but you end up diluting your efforts and getting indecision. You need clarity. And it's absolutely clear what we're here to do. We're here to help Brad.'

Morzine–Avoriaz, 11 July 2010

On the morning of a stage whose course was ridden only three weeks previously as part of the recce involving Wiggins, Barry and Cummings, the riders of Team Sky recline in their beige leather seats in their team bus, and face the front: it's the pre-stage team meeting. Rod Ellingworth stands facing them, in front of a pull-down white screen. Before other stages they have projected a film of the final five kilometres of the stage, filmed in the morning by performance analyst Tim Kerrison in his motorhome. Not today, though. Mountain stages are not about the final kilometre. The screen says 'Sky Warriors' at the top, and below are mug shots of each rider, alongside his specific role. It amounts to the day's 'Battle Plan'.

At the front of the bus sit Cummings (on the right) and Flecha (on the left); then the order, behind Cummings, goes: Gerrans, Lofkvist, Boasson Hagen. Behind Flecha sit Barry, Thomas and, on his own at the back, Wiggins. Wiggins and Cummings are often the jokers – sometimes video clips of their impressions of teammates are shown on the screen to lighten the mood – but today's a big day: the atmosphere is serious, business-like.

Ellingworth delivers the battle plan. Today is not about selecting a start time for Wiggins; it may not even be about tactics. The mountains just aren't like that. In the mountains, like Flecha at the crunch point of the Tour of Flanders, you have either got the legs, or you haven't. The team will do what it can to help Wiggins, especially in trying to ensure that he arrives at the base of the day's two Alpine climbs in a good position, near the front. The previous day, in the smaller Jura mountains, Wiggins hadn't been so well positioned, and that had a secondary effect: heat. It's hotter among the bodies, cooler up at the front. 'Once the body's core temperature has gone above a certain level you're not going to get it down again,' says Brailsford. 'And then you're in real trouble. Real trouble.'

Ellingworth gives his talk and tells each rider his role. Cummings is on 'ice duty'; the heat is such that, as well as collecting bottles, he collects ice-packed musettes from the car. This is a day when Pauwels – who has been battling illness this season, and was a surprise selection for the Tour – is expected to justify his place by riding up near the front, in support of Wiggins. Lofkvist is another, though the Swede is also, in effect, deputy leader. Barry, Wiggins' wing-man, will stay with him as long as possible. But the key thing is that when the road goes up, Wiggins must be near the front.

And as they hit the Col de la Ramaz, that's exactly where he is. But all the other favourites have the same idea, and the 5km leading towards the first major climb of this year's race witnesses a frantic, chaotic scramble for a place near the front. Crashes are inevitable in these circumstances, and on the approach to the Ramaz Lance Armstrong is one of several fall-ers on a roundabout, with Cummings and Gerrans also falling. But as the climb starts, Sky have men at the front – Flecha, Wiggins, Lofkvist and Thomas, who is first on to the climb itself, trailed by Cadel Evans. Thomas had fallen from second overall the previous day, when he couldn't stay with the lead group in the Jura mountains. He'd also conceded the white jersey. But he'd had an outstanding week; he wasn't disappointed.

Now he was leading his team leader – 'That's what I'm here for, to help Brad,' he'd said the previous day, almost relieved, it seemed, to forget about his personal ambitions – with Wiggins moving smoothly up to third as the Ramaz began to kick up, with Flecha and Lofkvist close by. Now, surprisingly, it is Team Sky who take it on. The first serious mountain of the Tour and the team driving the pace is Sky: Flecha, Lofkvist and Wiggins sitting in a line at the front, with Thomas sprinting back up to join the team effort. It is a bold statement that makes two points: one, the team is strong; two, they have confidence in their leader, Wiggins.

The pace is fast, but controlled, up the Ramaz. Other teams join in at the front – Garmin, Saxo Bank, Astana – while the crash-victim Armstrong, surrounded by RadioShack team-mates, has a torrid time chasing, and failing, to catch the group. It's effectively the end of his Tour. But this is what the mountains do: they deliver a verdict and eliminate contenders with the ruthlessness of an executioner. (Later, Sergio Paulinho, Armstrong's Portuguese teammate, will aim fire at those teams that drove the pace on the Ramaz through Twitter: 'Well done Sky, Astana and Garmin amateurs. Those who laugh last, laugh best.')

Wiggins remains near the front, looking comfortable, looking out, as they approach the summit, for his team's helpers, who hand him ice packs. Next, the climb to the finish, at Avoriaz. Contador's *domestique*, Daniel Navarro, takes over the pace-setting at the foot, as they climb out of Morzine, and whittles the group down. Lofkvist loses contact, so Wiggins is now isolated in a lead group of a dozen riders. The Tour winner will come from this dozen: that is certain. Pauwels has also gone; dropped on the Ramaz, clearly suffering and still not at his best. Michael Rogers, the Australian on the HTC-Columbia team, climbs as though attached to the back of the lead group by elastic. He hangs on, just.

Wiggins looks comfortable, but as they climb towards the 1,800m summit, he begins to concede a little ground. He drops from fourth to fifth wheel; fifth to sixth; sixth to seventh, in amongst the bodies. It is sometimes difficult to tell whether someone is riding conservatively, keeping some fuel in the tank for the final push. More often, though, when a rider loses ground on a climb it's because he is suffering. Wiggins is suffering.

Not for him the Rogers yo-yo effort. When Wiggins goes, he goes. He drops to the back of the group with 3.5km still to race to the summit, past Rogers, the last man, and a gap opens between him, Rogers, and the string of riders. 'Don't unhitch now, Bradley, because you must not let go of that group in front of you,' urges Phil Liggett, the TV commentator. But it is too late: he has unhitched. Wiggins wears a tortured expression as he rides on; as well as the physical pain, there's the knowledge that your dream might be slowly dying.

Wiggins is joined by Lofkvist, who, though he lost contact near the bottom, has ridden at a steady, comfortable rhythm. Lofkvist takes up the pace-setting, helping Wiggins as much as he can. But Wiggins doesn't look comfortable. He is losing ground with every laboured pedal stroke, as, up ahead, Andy Schleck dances away to win the stage, just ahead of Cadel Evans, who takes over the yellow jersey, and Alberto Contador.

Wiggins reaches the summit exhausted and disappointed and 1 minute, 45 seconds behind Schleck. The previous year, on the first major climb – to Andorra – he'd been a revelation even to himself, riding at the front, helping animate the race, finishing among the leaders. That had felt like the beginning of the start of something; it was thrilling and motivating. This feels like the beginning of the end of something; it's depressing and dispiriting. Not that Wiggins is the only one who's had a bad day. Simon Gerrans, whose fall was merely the latest in a series of tumbles, resembles a boxer with his black eyes and his body covered in cuts and bruises. Unbeknown to him, he is also carrying a fractured arm, sustained in the crash, to the summit – he finds that out the next day when he goes for an X-ray. The Australian struggles to the top of Avoriaz, emptying himself of every last ounce of effort and courage and perseverance as he struggles even to stay with the *grupetto*, the large group of non-climbers, which finishes over half-an-hour behind Schleck. The ordeal seems literally to finish him and he slumps over his handlebars just past the line. Team Sky's doctor meets him there and tells him: 'The bus is just around the corner, Simon.'

'I can't fucking ride there,' says Gerrans quietly.

'But it's just around the corner.'

'I can't … fucking … ride.'

Morzine–Avoriaz, 13 July 2010

It's the morning after the rest day, when the Team Sky riders – minus Simon Gerrans, whose Tour is over – ride for 2 hours, 40 minutes on the roads around Morzine. Wiggins had admitted he was disappointed with his ride on day one in the Alps. But he was also defiant, and said he was looking forward to day two, with the long climb of the Col de la Madeleine – the climb on which Michael Barry had ridden away from him on the recce. 'The tougher the better,' said Wiggins of the stage. 'At least you know where you stand.'

He had lost 1 minute, 45 seconds to Schleck on day one in the Alps, prompting *L'Equipe*, on the rest day, to dismiss Wiggins' chances. 'Goodbye podium,' said the French sports daily. 'Yeah, maybe, but that's *L'Equipe*,' said Wiggins. 'Whatever. They're a bunch of wankers, aren't they. No, I mean, whatever.' (He was joking; it was for the benefit of the *L'Equipe* reporter present.) Wiggins conceded he was 'disappointed'; that there was a moment on the climb of Avoriaz, as he became unhitched from the group, that disappointment hit him. His former boss, Jonathan Vaughters, was surprised to see him suffer like that on that particular climb. 'It was Brad's style of climb … So maybe it was the heat that affected him,' Vaughters suggested. 'I'm sure he's going to be strong the rest of the race, but he has been under pressure for a long time now.'

'I'm not going to lie to you,' said Wiggins on the rest day, 'it's not fantastic, is it, but what can I do? Go home, or stay here and battle for the next two weeks and see what happens and get the best out of myself every day? I was sat here last year, [and] no one knew what the next two weeks held. I mean, the Pyrenees is where it's going to be won or lost. By Paris the time gaps are going to be minutes. If we're still 2.45 down in Paris, we're going to be on the podium. So, we'll see.'

In Morzine the following morning the team gathers once more in the bus, and again faces Ellingworth. This is a more difficult meeting than before the previous stage, when everything seemed possible. The screen comes alive, and the words flash up: 'Overall Dream'. This, too, is defiant: 'Podium in Paris'. First, though, there's some discussion of the stage to Avoriaz. 'Does anyone have anything further to say about stage eight?' Ellingworth asks. Serge Pauwels sticks his hand up and apologises that he wasn't there to help out. He'd been suffering from stomach problems.

The discussion turns to the tactic on the Ramaz, to ride hard with Flecha, Lofkvist and Thomas leading the peloton up the lower slopes. That they had all fallen away later, in particular their leader Wiggins, meant that the tactic looked, in hindsight, flawed. It had perhaps been overly ambitious: too bold a statement. 'We took the risk,' says Wiggins, 'and okay, it didn't pay off, but I thought we did a cracking job.' Wiggins urges them to continue to think and race positively: 'If we question every little decision we take, we might stop taking them.'

Brailsford, hovering at the back of the bus, near Wiggins, agrees: 'Let's not over-analyse.'

When the Team Sky riders emerge from the bus they encounter an army of British supporters. Cummings is first, and he is mobbed. 'I think they thought I was Bradley,' he says. Thomas is easily identifiable in his British champion's jersey, and he is also popular – his profile has sky-rocketed in the first week of the Tour. And when Wiggins emerges, he receives the kind of reception afforded a rock star. He grins shyly behind his helmet and sunglasses, and signs autographs. Brailsford, standing by the entrance of the bus, looks on with something like paternal pride. 'I drove up the mountain to Avoriaz,' he says, 'and I couldn't believe it. As a kid, I went out and stood at the side of the road to watch the Tour de France.'

The Alps were where the Brailsford family holidayed; Brailsford's father was, and is, a distinguished Alpine guide (and now lives nearby). 'As a kid, I'd be at the side of the road,' says Brailsford, 'we'd have tents, and you'd think you were going to sleep, but you couldn't, and you'd stand there all day, and eventually the Tour comes past. Brilliant; I loved it, loved it. But at Avoriaz I was blown away. The number of people and the number of Union Jacks and Sky tops in the crowd. Blown away.'

This is the wider context to the Team Sky project, Brailsford points out. 'We want to perform at the Tour de France, but we also want to inspire people to get behind the team, to get cycling.' As for Wiggins, Brailsford claims he's relaxed. 'At this moment in time we're happy where we're at. I'm satisfied. Has Bradley done his best? That's the question I ask myself. Has he given his all? And the answer, unequivocally, is yes. So that's it: what more can the lad do?'

But on the Col de la Madeleine, as Schleck and Contador once again do battle, and Evans, in the yellow jersey – and suffering from a broken elbow, it later emerges – begins to struggle, Wiggins labours as he had laboured to Avoriaz. It's the same struggle, and there's the very real prospect now, and the fear, that the experience is destined to be repeated; that every climb, with the Pyrenees still to come, will involve the same torture, with the same verdict. The verdict in Saint-Jean-de-Maurienne, where the stage finishes after a 30km descent from the summit of the Madeleine, is that this year's Tour is a two-horse race, between Contador and Schleck.

Wiggins arrives in Saint-Jean-de-Maurienne in 30th place, 4 minutes, 55 seconds down; it leaves him 16th, over 7 minutes down on GC. The podium in Paris now seems as vertiginous as the Madeleine.

Before the following day's stage, from Chambéry to Gap, there's another team meeting, but the 'Overall Dream' on the screen at the front of the bus has been changed. It no longer reads 'Podium in Paris.' Now it says: 'Top 10'.

CHAPTER 12

IT'S NOT ABOUT THE BUS

'Want me to be honest with you?'

Bradley Wiggins

Rodez, 17 July 2010

L'Equipe has published a big article about the Team Sky bus. Beneath the headline, '*La Rolls des bus*,' it drools over the vehicle's desirable features, from the technology housed within, to the comfortable seats, to the Bose sound system. 'The high-tech bus was inspired by the world of Formula One,' it says.

I'm in the team car with Sean Yates, though the stage ahead of us is a typical transitional stage between the two major mountain ranges. With the Alps behind, it's a case, now, of waiting for the Pyrenees, which begin tomorrow. The previous day had finished with a short but steep climb, to an airfield high on a plateau above Mende, and it had witnessed a series of small explosions.

In fact, it had been an unexpectedly brutal stage; in Rodez this morning some are calling it the toughest of the race so far. Alexandre Vinokourov attacked early with Ryder Hesjedal and 16 others. Hesjedal, a Canadian former mountain biker, is one of the revelations of this year's Tour and the latest Garmin dark horse to emerge as a GC rider, after Christian Vande Velde in 2008, and Bradley Wiggins last year. Over tough, never mountainous but constantly up-and-down roads, the break piled on the pressure en route to Mende, and the peloton chased, strung out in a long line. There was no respite all day, with the remnants of the breakaway only caught on the final sharp climb to the airfield. There was carnage on that climb: Alberto Contador jumped clear, Andy Schleck set off in hot pursuit; the others were scattered asunder.

Wiggins rode well, not least because he had been an early faller and had to chase hard to regain the peloton – such was the intensity of the day that at one point it looked like he might not make it back. At the finish in Mende he could be proud of his efforts, which saw him cross the line 14th, 31 seconds down on the winner. It was a comeback, of sorts, after the disappointment of the Alps. He was among riders – Cadel Evans, Ivan Basso – who are established Grand Tour contenders, and podium contenders here, but who now find themselves in the same position as Wiggins and everyone else – feeding on the scraps left by Contador and Schleck.

With the clock ticking down to the start in Rodez, Yates checks his radio, checks in with his riders, then pulls away from the bus, driving in a circle around it, trying to work out how to get out of the car park in the middle of the town, and on to the course. 'This is the hardest part of the day,' he mutters. 'Bloody hell. What the …'

On paper the stage doesn't promise too much, featuring gently undulating roads, with minor climbs, including one close to the finish in Revel, not far from Toulouse. Standing by the bus that morning, Brailsford admitted that his riders were so tired they would be riding conservatively today, waiting for the Pyrenees. They had tried the previous day to make it into the 18-man break, but failed. It had been that kind of stage: one of frustration, suffering and survival. Brailsford was keen to take the pressure off today. 'We're not going to try and get in the break today,' he said. 'No point. Cav's team is going to control it and bring it back at the end – they fancy him today.' Cavendish had started the Tour slowly but was getting better with each stage; it took him until day six to get off the mark, but he'd added two more wins since then.

Yates eventually finds his way out of the car park and into the vast, kilometre-long convoy that follows the Tour, blasting his horn as he weaves between the vehicles, working his way up to his allocated slot. The team cars follow the peloton in strict order, the order dictated by where their top rider is placed on General Classification; which means Team Sky is a lowly 13th in line. Race radio crackles into life, with the dulcet tones of the Tour's competitions director, Jean-François Pescheux, who welcomes everybody, and runs through the daily checklist of dos, don'ts and matters arising. Then, in his gravelly voice, and without altering his tone, Pescheux says something that makes Yates' ears prick up.

'I don't know if it's because your bus is too comfortable, or the weather isn't to your liking,' says the dry-as-dust Pescheux, 'but Team Sky, your riders didn't sign on this morning.'

'Fuckin' hell!' mutters Yates, while simultaneously swerving out to overtake the cars in front, and accelerating through the narrow streets of Rodez until he is level with Pescheux's red Skoda, which sits directly behind the peloton. Pescheux slumps in the front passenger seat looking distinctly unimpressed as Yates, in French, and with his left arm dangling out the window, making vague conciliatory gestures, apologises. 'We'll talk to them tonight,' says Yates. 'It won't happen again.' Pescheux barely looks at him but manages a small nod of understanding, and Yates slides back to his rightful place in the convoy.

The race radio provides a permanent aural backdrop. '*Chute!*' We're still in the neutralised zone as we pass a forlorn-looking Lance Armstrong, sitting on the road, looking dazed. In his seven-year winning run, and 28,000km, he had crashed twice, as Brailsford had noted with wonder back in December. But in this, his final Tour, crashing has become almost a daily occurrence. Then again, as Bob Stapleton had presciently noted in January, at the Tour Down Under, 'He's a guy with a lot going on this year.' A US federal investigation into the allegations that Armstrong doped during his seven-year Tour winning run is gathering pace. Some wonder whether this explains his inability to stay upright; they speculate that his mind is elsewhere.

'Dear oh dear,' says Yates as we pass his former teammate. 'I don't think Lance is enjoying himself.' Then Yates holds the radio to his mouth and speaks slowly: 'Be ... Careful ... With ... Big ... Groups ... Guys. Heads up. Keep your eyes open, be reasonably placed and help each other out a bit.'

'They're tired,' says Yates, turning to me. 'Everyone's tired after yesterday.'

As soon as they leave the neutralised zone, and the race is on, the race *is* on. The attacks start immediately. So much for tired. But then, many riders will see collective tiredness as an opportunity to try and break clear; they're not going to let a little tiredness prevent them from trying for a career-making Tour de France stage win. 'These fast starts were my worst frickin' nightmare in my first few years,' says Yates, who rode his first Tour in 1984 (he started 12, finishing nine). 'Used to hate it.'

'*Trois coureurs en tête*,' says race radio – three riders are clear at the head of the race. They have a gap of 100 metres; their numbers are read out: '*vingt-cinq, trente-quatre, cinquante-sept*.' Two Frenchmen: Sylvain Chavanel, winner of two stages already, and the brief holder of the yellow jersey, and Pierrick Fédrigo; and a Spaniard: Juan Antonio Flecha.

It's a strong group, but the presence of Flecha is a surprise, especially after Brailsford's promise that no Team Sky rider would feature in a break. 'It's a good group,' says Yates, 'if they let 'em go.' Ten more riders leave the bunch to chase after them. 'Be vigilant,' says Yates into the radio, 'we need somebody near the front to mark any counter-attacks.'

Still the trio remains *en tête*, driving hard. 'Good job Flecha,' Yates tells his rider. They have 11 seconds on the group of 10; 17 on the bunch. But the group of 10 is re-absorbed, and there's a brief lull before a sudden injection of speed in the peloton. 'Saxo and Columbia are closing it down,' Yates tells Flecha. 'Keep pushing.' And then, abruptly, the peloton fans out across the road; Saxo Bank and HTC-Columbia have decided, or been told, to stop chasing. No one else takes it up. Flecha and his friends (for the day) carry on and the gap expands, from 20 seconds to a minute in no time. 'It's all stopping behind you,' Yates tells Flecha, 'Keep pushing.'

Brailsford phones. Yates hands me the phone. 'When I said we wouldn't have anyone in the break,' says Brailsford laughing, 'I was bluffing.'

'Shane?' says Yates, picking up the radio again. 'It looks like you could be going up front at long last.' For the first time since day four (we're now on day 14) Team Sky has a rider in the day's break. 'Good old Flecha,' sighs Yates after speaking to Sutton. 'He's with frickin' strong riders, so he's gonna have a nice day out.'

Sutton, who drives the second team car, which follows in a second convoy, appears alongside Yates, then pulls ahead and slams on the brakes. Yates stops behind him. Flecha's spare bike is switched from team car one to team car two, and I jump in with Sutton as he races ahead, and pulls alongside Pescheux, at the rear of the peloton. A motorcycle-mounted commissaire sits just in front of Pescheux, ordering vehicles forward when he deems it safe. Sutton must wait for the instruction, which comes with a frantic waving of the hand, when finally the road is wide enough to make it possible to drive through the

170-man peloton. It's a slow, nail-biting passage, though; Sutton grips the wheel tightly and keeps his hand pressed to the horn, but Team Sky's Jaguars are not equipped with the deafening air horns of many of the other teams' cars. Thomas Lofkvist calls out to Sutton as we pass. 'What's that mate?' yells Sutton, glancing to his left. 'Get a new horn!' shouts Lofkvist. 'Fuck off!' yells Sutton.

Once through, and on open roads, as Sutton loosens his grip on the wheel and accelerates up to Flecha's group, he rues the fact that he only has two riders for company. 'Ah, it won't stay,' he says. 'They'll be out there for a long time, but they needed more bodies. I was hoping that group [of 10] would get across.'

Brailsford calls Sutton (as he does frequently during the stage). 'Well, the battle plan's gone out the fucking window,' says Sutton. 'Flecha? … Yeah … Well, I gave him a KitKat at the start.'

We catch Flecha's group, which is followed by Chavanel's Quick Step car and Fédrigo's Bbox car, as well as officials' and guest cars, and 10 motorbikes carrying press, photographers and commissaires. It's a vast flotilla for three riders, who look tiny and vulnerable at its head, as though they are trying to flee, to escape their pursuers (which in a sense they are).

After what he'd told me at the Tour Down Under, where he insisted his involvement with Team Sky would be minimal, Sutton admits he's surprised to find himself at the wheel of a team car in the Tour de France. 'I didn't plan it,' he says. 'But when Scott … Listen, I think Dave and I needed to get our feet in here and sort a few things out. And the riders are happy. You hear all these rumours that our riders are unhappy – that's bullshit. The riders love it.

'It's good to be part of this, but I'm looking forward to going back and working with Sir Chris [Hoy – Sutton insists on the 'Sir'] and Vicky [Pendleton] and the trackies. You build up such an affinity; that's never going to leave me. Hey, I'm at the Tour and I'm thinking of those fuckers. Crazy, isn't it?'

The lead grows to four minutes at 20km, then to six minutes. Sutton begins talking about Wiggins. How he's going to fare in the Pyrenees is a mystery, which creates uncertainty in the team. Everyone's job, after all, is to help him with his objective of finishing on the podium: that was the singular objective coming into the race. But given Wiggins' performances in the Alps, is that still realistic? It could explain why, today, Flecha is the first Team Sky rider to have a proper go at getting away and making it into the day's break. When Cummings was in the move on stage three it wasn't to try to win: it was to help Wiggins. Flecha's move today is unscripted, maybe even spontaneous, but it owes, surely, to his desire to get something out of the race. Is it a sign that the team has lost confidence that Wiggins can deliver?

'Brad's coming around,' says Sutton. 'He was happy yesterday [after the stage to Mende] with his ride at the end. I don't think people realise what a good ride that was. It gives me hope and tells me he could move into the top 10. He's top 10 material, Brad; he should be. The trouble is, he's trying to put himself up there with Contador and Schleck.

'I said to him: "Brad, they're special. You're trying to put yourself where you feel you should be in the Tour – which is fourth or fifth or whatever – but you're trying to ride with Contador and Schleck as well." So we had a real long chat before yesterday's stage, and I said, "Look, mate, you have a fucking certain amount of petrol, and it's how you distribute it. If you keep trying to kick your turbo in, you're going to use it a lot quicker. And that's what you're doing – you're trying to go with the surges of those guys [Contador and Schleck]. But the guy you want to be around is someone like Basso, who's a bit of a diesel, but he's fucking strong." Brad rode that climb yesterday and said he was thinking of what I'd said. And he was there; he was there with Basso. And he was so happy with that. At the finish, he said, "I've been chasing it too much, haven't I?" And I said, "Yeah, Brad, yeah you have. You need to judge your efforts."

'Look, he's got to work his way back into the top 10. It's his first year as a Tour contender. Top 10 would be as good as fourth last year, in a lot of ways.'

Then Sutton picks up the radio: 'Good job Juan, good job mate, just pace your effort.'

Flecha comes back on the radio asking for a drink. 'Sorry mate, you'll have to wait a couple of Ks.' Feeding isn't allowed from the team cars before 50km. Yet when Fédrigo's car pulls alongside their rider they appear to hand him a bottle. 'Expensive drink, that,' says Sutton, peering up the road. 'They'll be fined fifty for that. What do you reckon? Will we take the fine?'

But as Sutton moves forward the commissaire attracts his attention. 'Hey, why were you guys not at the signing [on] this morning?' asks the commissaire in a strong Dutch accent.

'Ah, the bus broke down,' Sutton quips.

'What was the problem?' the commissaire persists. The team will be fined for failing to sign on prior to the stage; but for reasons best known to the riders (and the teams) it seems that one team always fails to sign on.

'I'm going to give our riders a bollocking tonight, I promise,' says Sutton. The commissaire nods his approval, waving us up to Flecha.

Sutton learned on the eve of the Tour of his OBE. 'This bloke said he was calling from the Cabinet Office or something. "Is that Shane Sutton?" But I thought it was Brad winding me up, putting on one of his voices. "Oh yeah," I says. "Yeah, sure mate, whatever." Never got back to 'em. But I kept getting a call, this London number. So I called it and it's Buckingham Palace! "Ah, Mr Sutton, we've been trying to get hold of you. We'd like you to make a decision." 100% I thought it was Brad taking the piss.'

Few are in a position to understand the Wiggins enigma better than Sutton. Sutton, as well as acting as a father figure, remains perhaps his greatest supporter. 'I think Brad's as good if not better than last year,' he says. 'That's not bullshit: that's fact. But there are all these things you have to learn in this new position he's in, as a leader. Last year he was an outsider, everything was a bonus. He was in a situation that was relaxed. This year there's expectation, there's pressure. Look at the situation Dave Millar was in at Cofidis, where he was leader, he had people depending on him. That made Millar revert to what he did [doping].

'So the last thing we want to do is put pressure on Brad,' Sutton continues. 'He's in a non-threatening environment here. Win or lose he'll receive an element of praise because we know he's done his best and he's clean.

'But of course he felt pressure coming in. Of course he did. His performance last year; leading a new team; leading a new *British* team; a team that wants to make a bit of a stir, sponsored by a company that doesn't do things by halves … It's the 12-storey building thing. If you fall from three storeys you're okay, you survive. But if you fall off a 12-storey building you fall pretty hard. Yeah, Brad's taken a bit of a fall and it's hurt him.'

Meanwhile, on the road to Revel, Sutton is proved right: Flecha's group does get caught towards the end, as Cavendish's team leads the chase. 'But having Flecha out there is a good bit of exposure for the team,' notes Sutton, 'and it gives the boys back in the bunch an easier day; takes the pressure off a bit.' As Yates had observed, Flecha was in the company of two of the strongest riders in the race – at least in this type of situation

– and they made for an impressive trio as they raced across the undulating roads, each taking his turn at the front, never shirking, and making the HTC-Columbia-led peloton ride hard to catch them. Perhaps that effort takes something from Cavendish's team, because on the final little rise before the finish they are caught off-guard by Alexandre Vinokourov. Vinokourov, one of the sport's most notorious figures after his blood doping positive during the 2007 race, jumps away and holds on for the victory. Cavendish wins the sprint for second.

'Well done Juan,' Sutton told Flecha towards the end of his great escape, when it became clear he, Chavanel and Fédrigo would be caught. 'Good job ... for a Spaniard.'

'Argentinian,' responded Flecha.

'Remember the Hand of God,' added Sutton, laughing as he let the radio fall into his lap. 'You try and have a laugh with them. This is a riders' team, that's what we want. It's all about the riders. Get them laughing and the next K [kilometre] will go by a bit quicker.'

Ax 3 Domaines, 18 July 2010

'Want me to be honest with you?' asks Bradley Wiggins.

Wiggins is standing at the mist-enshrouded summit of Ax 3 Domaines. He has just finished the first Pyrenean stage, which turned once more into the Alberto and Andy show, with the Tour's leading pair so in control that they could afford to let some of their rivals (if they could still be called rivals) slip away on the final climb as they watched each other. Wiggins struggled. After his disappointment in the Alps he hoped he'd be better in the Pyrenees; hoped he'd rediscover his climbing form of a year ago, when he was able to follow Contador and Schleck, and even, on one or two occasions, attack them.

But in a replay of the climb to Avoriaz in the Alps, on the first of today's two climbs, the monster Port de Pailhères, Wiggins slipped to the back of the Contador-led group, his face contorted with the effort. Then he lost contact, 'unhitched', went backwards. There was no way back. One climb remained, to the finish at Ax 3 Domaines, and for Wiggins that merely prolonged the agony. It also confirmed something else: that Thomas Lofkvist was now riding better than him. The Swede finished 19th on the stage, just a minute and a half behind Contador and Schleck. Wiggins was 36th, almost four minutes behind the favourites, allowing Lofkvist to leapfrog him in the overall standings: he was 16th, Wiggins 18th. Top 10 was looking as distant as Paris, still seven days away.

Wiggins rode through the finish, through all the team vehicles, searching in the thick fog for his own team vehicles. They were right at the end, on the outer edges of the ski resort's car park. There was no bus – the narrow roads prevented the team buses coming to the summit – and therefore no strobe light to help guide him through the murk. When Wiggins reached the team's motorhome, Black Betty, he lent his bike against it. Then he placed his hands against his lower back to help it straighten after five hours on his bike, and he entered the motorhome, the door slamming shut behind him.

A few minutes later he emerges in more clothing: tights and a long-sleeved, windproof jacket. And as he goes to collect his bike, to ride back down the hill (it's the quickest way), he pulls on a pair of gloves, a task he is focusing on to the exclusion of all others. Certainly to the exclusion of the small gathering of reporters who are waiting to try and talk to him. But one of them steps forward. His name is John Trevorrow, otherwise known as 'Iffy'. Trevorrow is an Australian ex-professional, a veteran of the 1981 Giro d'Italia, who now makes irreverent films about the Tour de France. He raced with Wiggins' late father, Gary. And he is a good friend of Shane Sutton; in fact, Trevorrow was the 'loose nut' behind the wheel of the car that got lost on its way to Clare for Team Sky's Tour Down Under debut, back in January.

When Trevorrow steps forward, with his cameraman in tow, Wiggins looks up. 'Brad, were you setting your own pace rather than trying to follow?'

'Want me to be honest with you, Iffy?' Wiggins replies, straightening his back again. 'I'm fucked, mate. I've got nothing. I just don't have the form, it's as simple as that. I'm not gonna lie to you. I'm just trying my hardest, battling on rather than giving up.' Wiggins takes a deep breath – he seems to be battling his emotions, trying hard to appear cool, detached and analytical – and carries on: 'I just haven't got it as I did last year. I don't know why. I'll keep pushing on, trying hard rather than sitting up. I don't really feel any improvement from the Alps. I just feel consistently mediocre. Not brilliant, not shit, just mediocre. I just haven't got it right this year. We thought we had, but we didn't. It's form – it's a funny old thing.

'You do everything right, but I've not got it,' he continues. 'I'm not with the best guys this year, that's obvious. It's a huge learning curve. It's the first year I've really tackled it full on like this. Last year was a bit of a fluke, I think, and it's easy to think you could improve and get it right this year.'

The dam has broken, and as Wiggins' words tumble from his mouth Brailsford appears, patting him on the back, in a gesture similar to a mourner at a funeral, then taking a step back, appearing to concentrate on his phone but listening intently to what his rider is saying. 'I did some good stuff in training that suggested I was pointing in the right direction,' Wiggins continues, 'but it's obviously another thing doing it in racing, day in, day out. It's another thing altogether. And you can't account for what other people are doing … It's disappointing, but that's the reality. There's no point in kidding yourself that it's going to happen. But I think I have a duty to the team and to the race itself, and the support out there is fantastic. I'd hate to give up. I just need to come back next year and try again.'

When Wiggins finishes talking and rides off down the hill, to the bus parked at the bottom, Brailsford steps forward and shrugs. 'You are where you are,' he says, 'and this year Brad's not in that front group. He was just being honest there. You are where you are: it's a brutal sport in that sense.'

Brailsford is at a loss to explain it. Wiggins' preparation was similar to the previous year. It was good. Even in the prologue, although his performance was disappointing, there appeared to be nothing wrong with him physically. The 'numbers' were encouraging – he was producing the same power; he was the same weight as 12 months previously. It doesn't make sense, but Brailsford is in a difficult position; and he knows that, even if Wiggins can be so painfully honest, he can't be defeatist. 'If you drop your ambition in top-level sport you might as well pack it in,' says Brailsford. 'Everything we said from the start still holds: that we were going to commit 100%. And if it's good enough to win, great; and if it's good enough for 10th, great; and if it's good enough for 50th, great.'

With Wiggins, there has always been the suspicion that confidence was a big part of his armoury, as it is for so many athletes. Indeed, most know that confidence and self-belief could be the most potent of performance-enhancing 'drugs'. If you could bottle it and sell it you'd earn a fortune. Wiggins' ride in 2009 owed so much to confidence; confidence that was reinforced with every passing stage, as he found himself matching Contador, Schleck and Armstrong, pedal stroke for pedal stroke. But the corollary to confidence is doubt. 'I think athletes constantly live with self-doubt,' says Brailsford. 'It's that that drives them, no? It's that constant quest to push yourself on. You've just got to encourage them. Tomorrow, when Brad goes out, all he can be is his best. He will be down; he's naturally disappointed. But we'll talk to him tonight and see if we can get him going again.

'The worst thing is, Brad feels like he's let other people down,' continues Brailsford. 'That's crazy – he hasn't. But that's what he feels; I think that's what he's felt here. But he absolutely hasn't. No way.'

But Wiggins' confessional at the summit of Ax 3 Domaines seemed to prove cathartic. The next day he suffered again, losing more minutes, dropping to 23rd overall, but he appeared liberated. At the stage finish in Luchon he sat in the driver's seat in the bus, an unlit cigarette in his mouth, feeding the wheel through his hands, blasting the horn, doing his best impression of the bus driver. Then he emerged with a bundle of team caps and began handing them out to some British fans who had gathered at the entrance. It was the same Wiggins who appeared after the following day's stage in Pau – an easier day, and a better one for Wiggins – when he spent several minutes talking to British fans, handing out hats, posing for photographs. As he signed an autograph he admitted: 'I tell you, the minute I came out and said, "I just haven't got it," it felt like a weight off my shoulders. It's just the way it is. I've accepted it now. I just thought, what's the point of trying to hide the fact? Who am I kidding?'

But had he really meant that the previous year had been a 'fluke'? He shrugged: 'I meant in the sense that I hadn't planned it; it was unexpected.'

For the remaining days of the Tour de France, Team Sky try desperately to salvage something, not least Flecha, who, with Edvald Boasson Hagen, makes it into a six-man move that goes clear early on the final stage in the Pyrenees, finishing at the summit of the Col du Tourmalet. Boasson Hagen had contested the bunch sprints in the first week of the Tour, and although he didn't have the speed to beat Mark Cavendish and Alessandro Petacchi, he placed in the top 10 on four occasions.

Now, however, with time running out for a stage win, a gung-ho spirit seems to infect those members of the team desperate to leave the Tour with something to show.

There was also evidence of some division in the camp, however. With Wiggins' overall ambitions gone, Rod Ellingworth, in his morning team briefings, encouraged the riders to be aggressive and try and get in breaks. It was a tactic supported by Flecha, but one or two other riders – physically exhausted, emotionally drained and wishing the race was over – were reluctant. Perhaps they had been mentally scarred by the tough stage to Mende, when they tried, but failed, to make it into the 18-man move.

Flecha was one rider who was determined to keep trying – hence his attack on the road to Revel; hence his attack en route to the Col du Tourmalet – but there was a heated argument one morning over tactics. Steve Cummings questioned the instructions to attack and to try and initiate a break; it was futile, he said, a waste of effort. Flecha fumed at such defeatism. And later, when Cummings returned from the toilet, he discovered a post-it note on his seat, with a scrawled message from Flecha: 'You will leave your balls on the road today or you will not get back on this bus.'

Simmering tensions were perhaps inevitable in a team whose mission had ultimately failed, but for whom there was no hiding place; who still, day after day, had to go out and compete in the hardest race in the world. Ordinarily in major sporting events, when you fail, you go home. But at the Tour you stay, enduring the agony and the attention. As Brailsford admitted, speaking about Wiggins, 'It's a hard place to be' – but he could have been speaking for the whole team.

In the team's Campanile Hotel in Pau, on the second and final rest day, just four days from Paris, a deflated atmosphere prevailed. The setting suited the sombre mood: a two-star, perfunctory hotel in a drab estate on the outskirts of town.

Cummings admitted that team morale had not been good. 'I don't think this team has clicked so well together here,' he said. 'Hindsight's a great thing, but I think for a Tour team you basically need to know your core riders at the beginning of the season and ride a lot together. I feel that because we haven't raced together we haven't clicked so well. But that's one of the issues with a new team.' Yet perhaps the most revealing thing Cummings said was in comparing team morale at the Giro with the collective mood at the Tour: 'Because Brad was going well [at the Giro], we had really good morale.' It reinforced the impression that Wiggins' mood dictated the mood of the group.

Michael Barry, meanwhile, could reflect on his Tour from a unique vantage point: Bradley Wiggins' side. Barry looked gaunt and drawn as he gingerly sat down in the hotel's dining room. He was still suffering from the injuries sustained in a crash on the road to Spa on day two (as indeed was Wiggins). 'I got road rash right pretty much exactly where I sit on the saddle,' he says. 'I skidded on my butt. It's still tender. It doesn't heal that well when you're sitting on it.'

This Tour, reckons Barry, has been easier than the Giro. He thinks that's why the riders who rode the Giro – Evans, Basso, Wiggins – have failed to shine in France. But it has been more painful in another sense. Having a ringside seat as Wiggins has suffered and seen his dreams of finishing on the podium disappear has been almost as difficult for him as for Wiggins. 'It has been hard. Since the start of the year this has been his big objective, and to see how much effort and sacrifice and planning he's put into that, and see it not really work out, is quite heartbreaking,' says Barry. 'But that's what makes cycling the sport it is. There are a dozen guys out there in the same position.

'It's difficult … as cyclists we always hold hope that tomorrow will be better, you know? And as we were going through the Alps we thought, maybe he'll start getting better. And then I would be hearing on the radio that he was getting dropped, and I felt bad for him. Because all the pressure and everything else aside, I know what he put into this and how hard he worked. It's like, Brad doesn't mess around. He really does his profession 100%. And he's really passionate about it and he cares. So it's difficult to see him struggle like that.

'But, you know … yesterday I was riding in a group with Steve Cummings and we were talking about the race, and Steve said, "You know, I go to bed at night and I sleep really well because I know I've done the best job I can do."

'That's pretty much it,' shrugs Barry. 'You don't sleep well at night when you've screwed up or you've not done your job properly.'

Brailsford appears in the dining room and sits down. In Rotterdam, in a similarly rudimentary hotel, he had seemed like a man in possession of a secret recipe for success; his confidence was infectious. But the last three weeks have been, he admits, a 'humbling' experience. He says he is focused, even as the race is ongoing, on finding out why Wiggins has been so far off the podium, particularly when they had believed, at the start of the Tour, that he was in similar shape to the previous year. 'Our job now is to find out why it hasn't happened,' says Brailsford. 'We have a fair idea, and that's why we have our PhD [the performance analyst Tim Kerrison] in muscle physiology sitting outside in his campervan. That's what he's doing now.' Altitude is suggested as one possible explanation – Wiggins seems to have struggled close to mountain summits (then again, that's where the race tends to be harder anyway).

He and his team would 'work back' to establish a cause, says Brailsford. But he admits there have been other lessons; nothing to do with Wiggins. 'To me, [sport] has always been about performance,' he says. 'But the thing I learned here was to open my eyes, for god's sake. The fans, the British support … I think there's a lot of enthusiasm for what we're doing. There's that engagement with fans, which I'm not used to. People have written to us. A mum wrote to me and said, "Thanks for giving us a team to support. The first thing my kids ask each night is, how did Wiggo do today?" People seem to have an emotional connection.'

The realisation has prompted Brailsford to re-think the perspex box that surrounded his riders as they warmed up for the time trial in Rotterdam. He cringes and shakes his head as he recalls the impenetrable black version at the Giro prologue in Amsterdam. 'From my way of thinking – the Olympic way of thinking – you do what you think is right for the perfor-mance. It's all about performance: everything. And if you win, everyone's happy; nothing else matters. And if you lose, you're fired.

'We built our black box outside the bus,' Brailsford explains, 'because to me it made absolute sense for a rider warming up for a prologue … you give them an environment where they can concentrate and be in the zone. And so the obvious thing to do was to build something around them so people couldn't get at them. But I didn't think what that might look like from the outside.'

And now? 'I totally, totally agree: 100% [with critics of this innovation]. That's where I've shifted. It sounds so naive, such a ridiculous thing to say, but I've spent my life thinking about doing every little thing to win. And if you win it doesn't matter … If you win you'll be alright … And actually I was wrong. It does matter. I have never had a fan base to deal with, or supporters to deal with at close proximity. For me it was: let's win, then everyone will be happy. I was wrong. I was very wrong.'

Longjumeau, 25 July 2010

There is one stage of the Tour remaining, just 102.5km to Paris, and the traditional eight laps in the centre: past the Arc de Triomphe, down the Champs-Élysées, round Les Tuileries and the Louvre and across the Place de la Concorde, then back on to the Champs-Élysées. The previous day Wiggins had ridden out of his skin in the time trial from Bordeaux to Pauillac, and he perhaps would have won had the conditions been different. He was ninth (one place ahead of Geraint Thomas, with another outstanding performance), but he had ridden, like the other riders in the top 30, into the teeth of a strengthening wind. Echoes of Rotterdam: foiled by the weather again. Wiggins was the only rider from the top 30 on General Classification to make the top 10 in the time trial. Rod Ellingworth shakes his head. 'Brad would've been up there, definitely top three, if he'd gone earlier.' But the time trial has confirmed Wiggins' final overall placing: 24th. Lofkvist is Sky's top man: 17th. But there's a yawning gap between them and the champion-elect, Alberto Contador, and the second-placed Andy Schleck.

Ellingworth takes his usual post in the team bus on the final morning. He stands at the front, with Sean Yates lower down, on the steps alongside him, while Brailsford and Sutton linger at the back. The team talk today will focus on perfecting the lead-out for Boasson Hagen, which had been organised and slick two days earlier in Bordeaux. It hadn't quite worked out for Boasson Hagen – who, as well as missing two months of the season, has been ill and on antibiotics for much of the Tour – and he could only finish sixth in Bordeaux, behind Mark Cavendish. But Sky's lead-out had been so impressive that there were even suggestions they'd been riding for Cavendish. In *L'Equipe* the previous morning one headline read: 'Sky, did they ride for Cavendish?'

'A magnificent blue and white train,' the report described the spectacle of Michael Barry, Juan Antonio Flecha, Thomas

Lofkvist, Bradley Wiggins and Geraint Thomas as they flew through the streets of Bordeaux in tight formation, with Boasson Hagen at the rear, waiting to pounce. 'But another rider profited from the British team's train,' it continued. Cavendish, who had for once been left isolated by his team before jumping clear for an easy win, explained: 'It's true, Team Sky were very well organised at the finish, but I think they still need some more experience. But it's nice to see, because they are friends of mine.'

'Okay, lads,' says Ellingworth, clapping his hands and addressing the riders ahead of the final stage. 'It's pretty lumpy at the start. But it's the Champs-Élysées: it's going to be a bunch sprint. Steve and Serge: you guys are the advance guard. The rest of you, you're the hit men. You support Edvald in the final; you take him into the final with the objective of delivering him at *top speed* with 300 to go …'

'That's too far,' Wiggins pipes up.

Yates stands up straight. 'You guys know the circuit, where do you think you should deliver him?' he asks, prompting a lively discussion. Lofkvist and Wiggins are the main contributors; Boasson Hagen, the rider who is to be delivered to the finish, says nothing. 'The key point,' says Ellingworth eventually, 'is that Edvald needs to be delivered fast, and with clear space in the final.' ('He likes to sprint in a straight line,' Brailsford had said of Boasson Hagen, 'he doesn't like getting mixed up with other bodies.') 'Edvald needs to communicate,' Ellingworth continues. 'The key part is, you kill the other teams with your speed at a K to go … But you need to be at the front.'

The plan is agreed. Pauwels and Cummings will be vigilant in the early stages and try to mark breaks. Barry and Lofkvist will take it on 2km from the line, then it'll be up to Wiggins, Flecha, Thomas and Boasson Hagen. Wiggins will lead them through the kilometre-to-go red kite. 'If you can move forward as a team,' says Brailsford, 'that in itself looks ominous, it looks threatening, they know your intent.'

'Come on, lads, last stage,' Yates says as the meeting wraps up. 'It's been a great three weeks. I personally would like to thank you all for your efforts.'

Brailsford: 'I second that, guys. We see you every day but not everyone knows how hard you've tried. Absolutely brilliant. Equally, on behalf of you, and myself, I know how fucking hard Sean's had to work. For three weeks non-stop. I think he deserves a special pat on the back. He's the only guy who's done it before.' With a laugh, Brailsford adds: 'He's had to take a lot of our stupid ideas on board, but he's been very patient, he's taken it, so a huge thank you. I think this team benefits hugely from Sean.'

Three hours later, as they race under the kilometre-to-go kite, Team Sky lead the peloton: Flecha, Thomas and Boasson Hagen. Almost to plan; but the plan had been for Wiggins to lead them under the red kite. Wiggins is missing, and as Flecha peels off, and Thomas takes over, he and Boasson Hagen find themselves overwhelmed by the other teams as they sweep across the Place de la Concorde and on to the Champs-Élysées, where Cavendish, appearing from nowhere, seems to be fired from the head of the peloton like a missile. It's his fifth stage win of a Tour that he started out of shape and out of form; his second consecutive victory on the Champs-Élysées and the 15th stage win of his short career.

Not for the first time, as he strolls past the team buses towards his own, where his riders are being reunited with girl-friends, wives and children, and cracking open bottles of beer, Brailsford might briefly pause to reflect on the unfortunate fact that a British rider who cut his teeth at the British Cycling Academy, who is Ellingworth's protégé, who is a winner and a natural-born leader and who has become a global star, rides for an American team.

CHAPTER 13

SO FAR FROM THE SKY

'I think this year we focused too much on the peas and not enough on the steak.'

Dave Brailsford

'A lot of Team Sky's ideas are brilliant,' says David Millar. 'But the implementation has been wrong, and I think a lot of that came from disrespecting the culture of the sport.

'When I came into pro cycling as a 19-year-old,' continues Millar, who began his professional career in France, 'I thought it was old-fashioned, stagnant, with no scientific basis for anything. It was all *le métier*, all this shit. You'd have these 60-year-old *soigneurs* who had their ways of working from the 1960s, who'd learned from someone who'd been doing it in the 1940s. It made no sense to me, coming from an Anglicised, scientific background of training.

'But over time you realise: he's been doing that for 50 years, and it works. I think this is what it comes down to: it's very easy to think you can control the variables in pro cycling, which I think is what Sky thought they could do – that they could transfer their track knowledge on to the road. And, from a distance, that does seem like it would be easy to do. But when you get into an environment where you have your team doing over 200 days' racing, where you end up being – two months into the year – stretched to your absolute limits, and no matter how many riders you have, or how many staff you have, you're always pushing to the edge, of people being sick, people being tired, people being injured. Science is out the window. It's kind of a game of survival: you race and take care of yourself, just to try and stay healthy.

'I don't think they quite realised that, but how would they?' adds Millar. 'You don't know that until you start doing it.'

From Millar's analysis it is easy to see how and why a doping culture could, and did, develop in cycling. The conditions are ideal, as Millar knows only too well. The *soigneurs*, he suggests, perform a key role in – while also embodying – *le métier*: the traditions, habits and tricks of a century-old trade.

But the word *soigneur* has become a deeply ambiguous one within the sport. Certain *soigneurs* are among the most notorious figures in the sport, caricatured almost as witch doctors or masters of dark arts, with a number implicated in cases of doping – most infamously Willy Voet, the Festina *soigneur* caught with an enormous stash of banned substances on his way to the start of the 1998 Tour de France. Millar argues that this is a simplistic analysis; that – in the modern era, and in teams with a genuine commitment to anti-doping – good *soigneurs* perform a multitude of other vital functions: they are carers, mentors, perhaps even counsellors, and, through massage and their intimate knowledge of the physiology of a cyclist, immensely skilled in helping professional riders, who can race up to 100 days and 15,000km a year, do their job.

Nevertheless, it seemed significant, or merely symbolic, that Team Sky substituted '*soigneur*' with 'carer,' a term that didn't come with the same baggage. Though Dave Brailsford said the terminology was insignificant ('We call them "carers" at British Cycling, so why not here?'), he knew – not least from his experiences with Millar – all about the subject of doping, and the circumstances and environment that could contribute to a doping culture.

Indeed, Brailsford has developed an interesting view on doping, regarding it as a crutch, to prop up riders who might otherwise buckle and collapse, as well as – more obviously – a means of cheating and a shortcut to success. Brailsford's argument has always been that the aggregation of marginal (legal) gains could outweigh the benefits of doping, not least because he believed that many of those athletes who doped could be neglecting other important aspects of performance, such as equipment, diet and even training on the basis that doping has come to be regarded as the magic ingredient: the *panacea*. The success of the British team on the track seemed to support Brailsford's ideas, and he entered road cycling, with Team Sky, with the conviction that a similar approach could work.

Hence the no-stone-left-unturned approach to the Tour, and to Wiggins' challenge for the podium. But it inevitably raised a question at the end of the Tour de France: was he wrong? And if so, does this tell us something about the Tour and cycling, or about Wiggins and Team Sky? But there was another pertinent question, too. If Brailsford's convictions had been challenged and shaken, would they change? Never mind the crutch: would *he* buckle or wobble?

There were echoes of some of Millar's comments on the final day of the Tour, as a hint of *schadenfreude* was detectable in the Paris air. In an analysis of Team Sky's Tour in *L'Equipe* – beneath the headline, 'Sky, so far from the sky' – Bob Stapleton, the owner of HTC-Columbia, said, when asked about Team Sky, 'They are not pragmatic enough. In cycling, everything is not about figures.'

Jonathan Vaughters, of Garmin-Transitions, said, 'The road is very different to the track. On the track you can reduce the unpredictable factors to 1% or 2%; on the road, you can only lower it to 25%. There's always a bunch of stuff that happens that you just can't do anything about ... They say they want to produce a British winner of the Tour de France within five years. Okay, now they have four.'

L'Equipe itself weighed in, noting that the British team 'left Rotterdam with their futuristic bus, their showy Jaguars, their scientific methods and their ambitions to fill their treasure chest ... But at the finish in Paris, it's still empty.'

In *Le Figaro*, beneath the headline: 'The black Sky is black' (a reference to their 'sexy black tops' as they are referred to in the article), more scorn poured forth. Francis van Londersele, the Cofidis team manager, said: 'They are doing their apprenticeship. They have the methods and infrastructure above the others, but it's comforting to see that it's not enough simply to have a large chequebook.'

Then there was Martial Gayant, a former professional and now a *directeur sportif* with Française des Jeux, who shared some damning, if by now familiar, observations, aimed at the 'Anglo-Saxon' culture, but Team Sky in particular: 'The Anglo-Saxons want to impose a new cycling based on new methods of communication. [But] while they are looking at technology, we pedal. In the morning we have breakfast before cycling six or seven hours. They study graphs while asking themselves whether to use the home trainer or the mountain bike.'

It was little surprise that Brailsford, speaking in the team bus before the final stage, did appear to be questioning some of his own principles. 'It's pretty straightforward,' he said. 'You can drink all the pineapple juice in the world; it isn't going to give Bradley the legs he hasn't got at the moment. We can do all the little things we do, but it isn't going to make the difference if you're a chunk away from winning. Those little things can give you an extra 100th ... But unless the engine's fine-tuned ...' Sean Yates echoed this: 'You can be as aerodynamic as you like, but if you ain't got the legs, you ain't got the legs.'

For much of the final week of the Tour Brailsford appeared to be casting around for answers, asking leading questions, posing hypothetical dilemmas, thinking aloud. Millar's point about the relentlessness of the cycling season – and the lack of time for reflection, recovery or even to make simple changes – is a valid one, but it is writ large at the Tour de France, where the public interest and the glare of the media are intense. There is no hiding place.

Yet Brailsford's canvassing of a wide and apparently random range of opinions is, according to team members, part of his normal approach. As one colleague says: 'He talks to a lot of people, gets their views, listens to them, then makes a decision, which can piss off Shane if it goes against his.' A former colleague, the ex-national road manager John Herety, says: 'Sometimes it can seem like Dave is asking daft, or very obvious, questions, but I think that's his way of finding things out from people before he makes a decision.'

Was Brailsford merely thinking aloud – and canvassing opinion through the media – when, speaking to *L'Equipe* in Paris at the finish of the Tour, he hinted at abandoning a policy that had seemed at the very heart of the team? Or was he wondering if, in light of the lessons that seemed to be learned at the Tour, some compromises would be necessary?

'At the start [of setting up Team Sky] I didn't want anyone who'd been caught up in a doping scandal,' said Brailsford. 'But as soon as you look for someone over 35 with lots of experience, you won't find anyone without a few worries. Maybe I will have to reconsider my decision.'

Team Sky's morale was sapped at the Tour de France. But it was destroyed at the next Grand Tour, the Vuelta a España, which got underway in Seville on Saturday, 28 August. It was to be an important development race for three of the team's most promising young British prospects, Ben Swift, Peter Kennaugh and Ian Stannard, and Swift made an instant impact: he was seventh in the bunch sprint that decided stage two. Overnight, however, he and Team Sky's South African climber, John-Lee Augustyn, fell violently ill. Both were sick throughout the night, but they got on their bikes to start the stage on Monday, even though they could barely pedal without retching. Augustyn abandoned early; Swift somehow made it to 100km before he, too, was forced to withdraw.

But Swift and Augustyn weren't isolated cases. Simon Gerrans and Peter Kennaugh also fell ill, and were sick overnight, though they struggled through Tuesday's fourth stage. It was a miracle in Kennaugh's case: the 21-year-old was physically sick throughout the stage. He repeatedly returned to the car to try and keep hydrated, only to vomit the contents of the *bidons* all over his bike. By Wednesday's fifth stage Juan Antonio Flecha was also down with what appeared to be a stomach infection, perhaps caused by food poisoning; the Spaniard was taken to hospital in Lorca, and kept in until 3am, though he too got up the next day and started – and finished – the stage. But by now several members of the backroom team were also ill. Tim Kerrison was badly affected, but the most serious appeared to be one of the team's *soigneurs*, Txema González.

González had in fact fallen ill on the opening weekend in Seville, and was taken to hospital late on Friday evening, on the eve of the race start. By Thursday, after almost six days in hospital, the 43-year-old, an experienced and popular figure on the professional cycling circuit, was believed to be recovering. He was transferred to an ambulance, which was to take him the long journey north to his home in Vitoria, in the Basque country. But after 50km the ambulance turned around and returned to Seville as González's condition suddenly deteriorated.

The Team Sky riders still in the Vuelta were oblivious to the severity of González's illness. All they knew was that he was no longer on the race; that he had been taken to hospital with similar symptoms to theirs. Food poisoning still seemed the most likely explanation. Yet González had fallen ill on the Friday evening, more than 48 hours before the riders began to feel the symptoms.

By Friday, with most of the riders having been affected – or, in Flecha's case, still struggling – with stomach problems, Dave Brailsford, who had been in Britain, was preparing to fly to Spain to deal with what was developing into a full-blown crisis. Then he received a phone call with some devastating news: after returning to the hospital for tests, González's organs began failing. 'And I knew,' said Brailsford, 'that was it. I drove immediately to Liverpool airport, and as I was getting on the plane I got a message to tell me that Txema had died. It was horrendous.'

By now Brailsford and Steve Peters, the head of medicine, had ordered throat swabs, blood tests and urine tests for all staff and riders, and determined that González's condition was unrelated to the riders' illness. While these tests indicated that the riders were suffering from a viral infection, González had developed a sore on his leg two days before he fell ill; from that he contracted a bacterial infection which entered his bloodstream and developed into sepsis (blood poisoning). It was, said the team doctor, Richard Freeman, 'a very unusual and tragic sequence of events.' González died on Friday afternoon, as stage seven of the Vuelta continued with the remaining Team Sky riders, Kjell Carlström, Flecha, Gerrans, Kennaugh, Thomas Lofkvist, Lars Petter Nordhaug and Ian Stannard, still in the race. Flecha remained in a bad way, and finally climbed off his bike during the stage. It meant he was the first to learn of González's death. When his teammates returned to the bus at the finish in Orihuela they found the Spaniard in a distraught state.

'I thought about what we should do on the flight over,' said Brailsford. 'But even when I got there I hadn't decided. I said to Rod Ellingworth, "I need to make a decision." And then I just sat in the hire car thinking about it. I was in there for ages. In the end I thought, I need to show a bit of leadership here. I didn't consult with the riders, as we normally do. But I decided that the whole team should withdraw. One or two of them, like Gerrans and Pete [Kennaugh] had ridden through their illness, and they were looking forward to the rest of the Vuelta. It was difficult. But it was the right thing to do.'

The following morning, at the stage start in Villena, Team Sky's riders appeared in tracksuits, joining their fellow riders for a minute's silence. As the minute drew to a close Flecha raised a race leader's red jersey in the air, and a round of applause broke out. 'It was very moving, and the opposite, in a way, to what had happened in Oman at the start of the season,' says one witness to the ceremony. 'There was a real sense of community, with Team Sky very much part of that community, or family.'

The riders were shocked to the core by González's death. 'It was horrific,' says Kennaugh. 'The Vuelta was strange from the off, with all of us falling ill. I had some really bad days, then I felt I was getting going again. I was really gutted to have to pull out, to tell the truth. But Txema dying was horrific. He was such a nice guy, very quiet but always looking after people.'

In a tribute to González, published on the *Cycling News* website, David Millar, in describing González, also offered a description that might clarify the point he was making about what it is that a good *soigneur* can do for a rider. 'My favourite story of Txema is from when we were at [Spanish team] Saunier Duval,' wrote Millar. 'I was having one of my disillusioned moments and felt very alone, so went and installed myself in the bar next to the hotel, pretty sure that I'd be able to have a bit of personal time and be able to wallow in my self-pity. My massage with Txema was due, so I sent him a message saying I didn't fancy one. Many *soigneurs* would be perfectly happy with this, but no, not Txema. Fifteen minutes later he walked into the bar and sat down next to me. He must have been looking for me all that time, but he didn't bother asking me where I was, he took it upon himself to find me. He ordered a beer and sat with me for 15 minutes and listened, then he told me to get up and come up to have my massage. He sorted me out.'

As Millar also said, the intensity and unrelenting nature of the road cycling season stretches any team to the limit – but the tragedy in Spain exerted unforeseeable pressures on a team in its first year. It also cast a dark shadow over the end of the season, which, to further illustrate Millar's point, resumed, days after González's funeral, in Blackpool, Britain, with the eight-day Tour of Britain. 'It's a game of survival,' as Millar said, and Team Sky seemed now, in common with every other team, to be limping towards the end of a year that would see their 26 riders race in 64 different events, comprising 262 days of racing in 4 continents and 15 different countries. Consider that: 262 days of racing.

And yet the Tour of Britain, in mid-September, was an important race: their home tour. And they lined up with a suitably strong and suitably British-flavoured team, led by Bradley Wiggins, with fellow Brits Geraint Thomas, Steve Cummings and Russell Downing, as well as the dependable Australian *domestique* Mat Hayman and their New Zealand sprinter, Greg Henderson. On paper, the main competition looked familiar: HTC-Columbia sent an ominously strong six-man squad, led by the sprinter André Greipel and all-rounder Tony Martin.

Greipel won the first stage, a mass bunch sprint along the seafront in Blackpool. And for stage two, around Stoke-on-Trent, I joined Steven de Jongh, Sky's Belgian *directeur sportif*, in the team car. It was my third day in the Sky team car in their debut season. And perhaps, in a race of relatively modest importance, the most interesting and revealing.

De Jongh may be your archetypal Belgian ex-pro. Growing up in a country steeped in the sport of cycling, he seems laid-back to the point of appearing blasé. Even though it's his first season as a sports director, he exudes cool competence. But since 2010 has been his debut in the team car, de Jongh has, like the other fledgeling director, Marcus Ljungqvist, been mainly deployed on the 'B' programme, at races such as the Tour of Austria and Tour de Picardie (impressively won overall by Ben Swift) and the Tour de Wallonie (impressively won by Russell Downing).

De Jongh and Ljungqvist had taken the traditional route into the *directeur sportif*'s chair (i.e. behind the steering wheel of a team car), but Team Sky were also blooding their own, British Cycling-groomed coaches, Ellingworth and Dan Hunt, in the role of sports director. At the Tour of Britain, Hunt, who had partnered de Jongh at several of the 'B' events, was driving the second team car, as Shane Sutton had done at the Tour de France.

Hunt admits that he met with some resistance at first. 'Of course,' he says. 'When I started, it was like, "Who the fuck are you? Where are you from?" But it was the same with the track team.' Hunt fits the Brailsford mould for a coach: when he began working with the track team, in 2005, he came from a sports science background. As women's endurance coach, he helped Rebecca Romero master the transformation from Olympic rower to Olympic cyclist, steering her to a pursuit gold medal in Beijing.

'You always have to justify yourself in any new group, but with Team Sky there was some resistance, a little bit of it in-house, from some of the riders,' says Hunt. 'A few snide comments: "It's not like the track," that kind of thing. And you're like, "Yeah, really, no kidding." But actually some of the things we do on the track are a million times better, and some of the things they do on the road are better. It's about taking the best from both, which has got to be better than standing in one world or the other.

'But the first two or three stage races I did were the hardest,' Hunt continues. 'I felt like an outsider looking in, but you evolve into the role and once you gain the riders' respect they start asking you questions.'

Hunt admitted that some aspects of road cycling were still beyond him. The relationships between teams, for example – the fact that some are friends, some hated enemies. And that some teams can become, even just briefly, the common enemy (such as Team Sky perhaps were at the Tour of Oman).

It is also generally understood that 'deals' between teams can be done in races. Teams will sometimes collaborate with other teams, helping them chase, or agreeing not to chase, usually on a *quid pro quo* basis, or perhaps owing to long-standing friendships (or rivalries) between directors. 'Cycling is very much a "what have you done for me lately?" kind of sport,' as one team director puts it. Though it can also work the other way, as Lance Armstrong has memorably described it: 'It is completely ghetto. Everybody looks at the other person and thinks that they're either trying to fuck them over or they're getting fucked.'

Where deals are done between teams, they tend to be discussed and agreed at *directeur sportif* level. It must have been difficult for Hunt to enter this world. In fact, this aspect of professional road racing – the deals, the collaborations, the politics, the games of poker – had opened the eyes of several members of Team Sky's backroom staff, not just Hunt's.

'There's always a bit of other teams asking, "Are you going to ride today?"' says Hunt. 'There are discussions between the directors, not always about collaborating or doing "deals", but more to try and find out what other teams' tactics are. It is like poker. It's not something I've really been involved in, though.'

As we drive out of Stoke-on-Trent, for a lumpy 100-mile stage that will finish back where it started, de Jongh banters easily with his fellow directors; there's a joke here, a smile and a wave there. Then he picks up the radio to address his riders: 'Pay attention to the [HTC-]Columbia ones [riders]. See what they're up to.'

The stage is highly aggressive from the start. Mat Hayman is the rider most often in radio contact with de Jongh; he is fulfilling the role of on-the-road captain again, as he has done so many times throughout the season. He informs de Jongh that two riders have broken clear: a member of HTC-Columbia and a rider from another strong team, Vacansoleil. De Jongh picks up the radio. 'One of you has to jump across, boys.'

There's no need: the race comes back together. There's another flurry of attacks, but the big break of riders that goes clear is more significant – it contains 18 riders. 'How many of us are in the first group, Mathew?'

'Three,' says Hayman. 'Bradley, Gee, Hendy.'

'Okay, guys, that's a good group,' says de Jongh. 'Try to organise the group.'

In fact, the scenario could hardly be better. There's a sprinter, Henderson, and two strong riders, in Wiggins and Thomas, who could challenge for the yellow jersey over the following hilly stages in Wales and Cornwall, before the race finishes in London in six days. HTC-Columbia have two riders there as well – Tony Martin and Michael Albasini – but Sky have the numerical advantage, arguably their strongest riders, and therefore the better cards to play. The peloton knows the group spells danger and chases hard, closing the gap to 22 seconds at one point, but Wiggins and Thomas pile on the pressure and the impetus is lost behind – too many teams are represented in the break, meaning there isn't enough cooperation behind. And as the front group races into a five-minute lead, it becomes clear: the winner of the Tour of Britain will come from this group.

There's a problem when Hunt, in the second team car and driving up to support the front group, punctures. But de Jongh is unflappable. He drives alongside Brian Holm, the HTC-Columbia *directeur sportif*, and tells him: 'We're a car down. You can look after our guys? And I can look after your guys in the front group.' Holm nods; the deal (almost inconsequential, but vitally important, and to each team's benefit) is done.

Brailsford phones de Jongh, and de Jongh tells him: 'It's good for Greg that Geraint's there. They can control it, just ride steady, and maybe Bradley can try something in the final. This is a perfect day for Bradley if he commits to do something.'

The instruction is relayed to Wiggins that he is to try to attack in the final 5km. It's a good plan: if he stays clear, he wins; if he doesn't, if the others chase him down, Henderson should win the sprint. But de Jongh is concerned that Thomas and Wiggins are driving the group too hard – harder than they need to, using up energy they may need later on. He urges them to be careful; not to get carried away. Then Thomas drifts back to the car. 'You okay, Gee?' asks de Jongh.

'Yeah,' says Thomas. 'You think there'll be attacks from this group?'

'Yeah, but you and Brad have to take care of that,' de Jongh tells him. 'Greg can just focus on the final [sprint].'

Later, Thomas drops back again. 'I feel a bit shit on the climbs.'

'Yeah, but these are hard roads,' says de Jongh. 'Concentrate on keeping it together as long as you can.'

Over the radio, de Jongh asks Wiggins how he's feeling – 'Okay,' comes the response – and tells him the plan: that he is to try and attack in the final 5km. Wiggins agrees. But later, with just 15km of the stage remaining, he drifts back to the car and rides alongside de Jongh's open window. 'It's a pretty strong headwind to the finish,' says Wiggins. 'I'm not sure about attacking. Wouldn't it be better to try and control it for Greg?'

De Jongh shrugs. It seems obvious that he still thinks the best tactic, given that Sky have three men in the break, would be to at least try and attack before the finish. Thomas, not at his best since the Tour de France, has effectively been sacrificed, but he's done his job: he's helped the break build a lead that at one point stretched to eight minutes. As de Jongh had said, it was a good day for Wiggins to have a go – it seems he has little to lose, and everything, potentially, to gain. He is the team leader. But he wants to be the teammate.

While Wiggins is riding alongside the team car, and talking to de Jongh, two other riders do attack. They open a gap because Thomas, tired and without Wiggins to help him, doesn't initially chase. By the time Wiggins accelerates back up to the break, the two riders, Heinrich Haussler and Michael Golas, have gained 15 seconds. This puts Team Sky in a bind. The other riders in the break know the Sky riders have to chase, and so they let them do it all, sitting back to watch Wiggins and Thomas bury themselves to bring the two escapees to heel.

Eventually they catch them, but, with 2km remaining, Thomas sits up – the chase has used up his final reserves and he drops out of the break like a stone. Wiggins takes over at the front, keeping the group together for Henderson to finish it off, but as the road begins to climb to the line, he too sits up and drops off the back of the group. 'Oh no,' mutters de Jongh as he drives past Wiggins, 'this is shit.'

Henderson wins the sprint into Stoke town centre, which prompts wild celebrations in the Sky camp. But his success merely papers over the cracks in their strategy for the main prize of winning overall. By sitting up in the final kilometre Wiggins has conceded 1 minute, 16 seconds. From a position of strength, he has conceded too much ground. If Team Sky are going to win overall, it's solely down to Henderson. All their eggs are in the basket of a sprinter who will struggle to stay with the leaders on the climbs.

The following day the folly of that strategy was laid painfully bare in the mountains of Wales. Henderson could not remain at the head of the race on the day's main climb, Black Mountain, and he dropped back. Wiggins was climbing well, and he was with the leaders; so was Michael Albasini of HTC-Columbia, who had been in the break the previous day – but Albasini hadn't lost time to Henderson. What should Wiggins do? Stay with Albasini, or go back and help Henderson? Again he opted to play the teammate card, to sit up and wait, and help Henderson defend the yellow jersey. But it was in vain: Albasini, with his teammate Tony Martin for company, raced into a minute-plus lead to win the stage in Swansea and set himself up for the overall win in London five days later.

'Bradley made the call to wait to help Greg,' said de Jongh at the finish. 'And then they did everything they could to chase, but they couldn't bring it back. We weren't getting time gaps, and there were some mix-ups [on race radio] with names, but it was 40 seconds, 50 seconds, a minute; they were losing time.'

Did he regret the fact that Wiggins sat up and lost time the previous day? 'No, that was a call Bradley made to go for the stage victory with Greg,' said de Jongh.

The next morning, at the stage start in Minehead, one rival team director – who had gained tremendously from Sky's implosion – shook his head as he reflected on how Team Sky had appeared to take such a firm grip of the race on stage two, only to let go towards the end of the stage, and blow it completely the following day. 'Where did they get their tactics?' he asked. 'Benny Hill?'

And yet what had happened on the road to Stoke-on-Trent didn't appear to amount to a tactical failure. Not really. It amounted, instead, to a rider low on confidence, and apparently racked by insecurity, afraid of attacking and being caught. Afraid, in other words, of failure.

'This is Dave's bollocking room,' says a cheerful Gwilym Evans, the Formula One stalwart lured by Dave Brailsford to Team Sky to help develop their fleet of *avant-garde* vehicles. Evans is on bus driving duties at the Tour of Britain, and he shows me into the area at the back, with a small table and, facing each other, two cushioned, bench-style, cream-coloured seats. The hotel car park, deep in rural Norfolk, is dark, the bus eerily quiet, when Brailsford arrives, and steps into this space, also known – apparently – as his 'bollocking room'.

'I don't bollock people,' says Brailsford with a smile. 'I just go intensely quiet and frown.'

Brailsford sits down and rubs his eyes. What's his verdict on Team Sky as the first season draws to a close? He pauses for perhaps a minute. 'It depends which area you look at. We're a new team, in a new environment, and you cannot overestimate the amount of work it took to set all this up: the logistics, race entries, travel, buses, trucks. It's endless, really. It was a massive amount of work in the first period. Then 64 people, 14 different nationalities … It's opened my eyes to how refined British Cycling has become as a working model. It's a pretty well-oiled machine – we're still getting there with this.

'I've heard a few people say they can't wait to get into the winter, to plan properly. But there was such an emphasis on all the setting up, I think it detracted a bit from the emphasis on performance.'

Yet it is this – or the style of Brailsford's emphasis on performance, with his perceived preoccupation with science and 'numbers' – that seems to have attracted some criticism, as well as significant support (the team's popularity was most evident at the Tour de France and Tour of Britain; and by the end of their first year 60,000 people had registered as fans on Facebook).

But criticism has been evident, and it didn't come only from the 'old school'; some of Team Sky's sternest critics seemed to be British cycling fans. In part it could owe, perhaps, to tall poppy syndrome, whereby the successful or ambitious are cut down to size. After Beijing Brailsford was one of the tallest poppies in British sport. But it wasn't just that. The internet – fans' forums, Twitter – had seen, over the course of the year, a stream of seemingly endless opprobrium flowing in the direction of Team Sky and Brailsford himself. There was even a Twitter account, AntiTeamSky, with an explanation that the individual behind it is 'not a Team Sky hater but just a disappointed fan pointing out all the things that Team Sky are doing wrong.'

The premise seems to be this: that Brailsford is trying to apply 'track methods' to road racing. And the aficionados don't like it. 'But I don't think that's accurate,' says Brailsford. 'I don't think my passion for the sport is reflected in that [perception]. Maybe there's too much emphasis on numbers … But I'm hugely passionate about the sport, I can't get enough of it. My background isn't even as a track cyclist. The Tour de France is what got me into cycling.

'But I'm ambitious,' he continues. 'I want to win. Make me performance director of tiddlywinks and I'll want to win. I don't know where it comes from, and why. Sometimes I wish I wasn't like that. I don't know where it comes from, but Shane has exactly the same type of drive.'

Is it a fear of failure? Does Brailsford, for example, ever reflect on his successes – on the Beijing success? 'No, I don't think about Beijing,' says Brailsford, apparently surprising himself with the admission. 'Sad really, isn't it, I suppose. It's something that happened but I just don't think you can rest on your laurels. I think that's what it is. I like the idea … I mean, I am fiercely driven or ambitious for some reason, through whatever it is. I do worry an awful lot. I can be awake all night. When things aren't going right I won't sleep. If I don't think things have been planned properly – if I think it's a bit haphazard, if they're not going as well as they could be – I will lie awake, and be up in the middle of the night, thinking, how do we make it better?

'This week, at the Tour of Britain, is an example,' Brailsford continues. 'Okay, we've identified the problems this week; so how do we go about changing it? What would it take to do it better? Identifying the problem is easy; how do we go about changing it?'

One big issue, Brailsford agrees, is the nature of the road cycling season: those 262 days of racing. 'Once you've set off, once the season has started, it's like trying to turn an oil tanker. That's why we're so looking forward to next winter, to do some preparation and planning and work. Just simple things, like which riders should be doing which races. I'll have a lot more input into that, and it'll be very, very clear. I don't think we've sent optimum teams to the right races; our race selections have been a bit odd at times.'

Then there is the nature of the sport itself – the multiple, uncontrollable variables, and the politics. 'It's true, there are a lot more people, more tactics, more emotions. You know, "He pissed me off today," or "He carried on riding when I stopped for a piss," or "They helped them," or "They raced through the feeding zone" – this is the little soap opera that is pro cycling, and it is quite interesting. And having not been in that, it's taken a season to realise, okay, he likes him, they don't like that, based on something that happened 20 years ago. It is a soap opera.'

'Look,' Brailsford adds, 'a success or a failure ... we won races ... but I think people generally judge success or failure by the expectations they start with. The expectations around us were high, and some of that we generated ourselves. I think that and some of the media that built up around the team created this massive weight of expectation. And against that weight of expectation, we didn't succeed, that's for sure. But if we take the expectation out of it; if we think of ourselves as a new team going straight into the premier league, I think we've done well. We've had a jersey in a Grand Tour, we've won 23 bike races, and our most prolific winner, Edvald Boasson Hagen, was out for two months.

'Success or failure ...?' Brailsford keeps mulling the question over. There is one race that looms larger than all the others, of course. And it certainly looms large in Brailsford's reflection on the season; as sinister and threatening as the iceberg that sunk the *Titanic*. The Tour de France. 'We had a good early season ... we were doing alright in the *pavé* and up to the mountains ... But the second and third weeks of the Tour were very hard for us.' Brailsford pauses for a moment. 'That was tough. And I think a lot of the final assessment, the school report if you like, will be based on that – which we can't complain about.

'I am a ridiculously bad loser,' he continues. 'I beat myself up when things don't go right; I've done it with the British team, with the Olympics. But yeah, the Tour was hard. The incessant day-after-day thing; there was no escape. You have to stand up and be counted, raise morale, show leadership.

'Look,' says Brailsford, 'Brad's had a tough year, but Geraint, Russell Downing, Ian Stannard, Ben Swift, Steve Cummings, Chris Froome – I'd say they've all moved up. The headline is Bradley Wiggins. It's very easy to judge the team on one rider at one event, but that's not really fair. It's like saying the only thing that matters to Andy Murray is Wimbledon. We have to be very careful about that.'

Yet they also have to be careful about something else: being transparent in their commitment to anti-doping. This has been another source of disquiet, ever since it became apparent that Sky, unlike Garmin and HTC-Columbia, would not be running an additional internal anti-doping programme. The handling of the allegations against Michael Barry also attracted justified criticism. When Brailsford talks about his ambition, his desperation to win, the obvious question to ask is, how desperate are you? 'The commitment to being clean, to using science, and alternative methods and the best possible brains as an alternative to doping, that is imperative,' says Brailsford. 'It doesn't stop us wanting to perform. It is a clean team. But we can't say we'll be clean but we won't bother about winning.'

How, though, does he ensure the team *is* clean? 'We've had a lot of discussions with the riders, we're very open and honest; it's not a taboo subject here,' says Brailsford. 'If there's a positive test with a rider on another team, we have a good chat about it. About the line.'

The line? 'You know, where the line is – between what's allowed and what isn't – in cycling it can sometimes be a bit blurred,' says Brailsford. 'But we will not go over it.'

This sounds a little ambiguous, Brailsford's language even seeming subtly different to the language he used 12 months earlier, before his exposure to the world of professional road cycling. At the end of the Tour de France I spoke to the team's doctor, Richard Freeman, who seemed downbeat and not at all confident that the sport has been cleaned up to the extent that some might like to think. Some riders and teams were still indulging in 'dark practices', reckoned Freeman.

And what about Brailsford – has he learned a lot, in the last year, about this dark side of the sport? 'Em, you have to be aware of the world you live in; if you're trying to operate in a society, you have to be aware of the criminal side of society as well as the law-abiding side. Because if we're trying to do something that is completely pie in the sky, we need to know that.

'We need to have knowledge of what all the other riders and teams are doing in terms of performance enhancement – which doesn't necessarily mean doping. But that whole side of the sport is something … It's a topic that is ever present.'

The real question is, are you still as confident in the mission – that it's possible to succeed clean at the highest level? Or is that pie in the sky? 'When you say succeed at top level, can you win Classics clean?' says Brailsford. 'Yes, you can – there's no doubt about that. And you have to believe that it's possible to win the Tour clean. You have to. I believe the guys at that level are going right up to the line, like everyone else. I certainly don't believe there is a clear, systematic doping programme in a team which is allowing those guys to perform that well. But I certainly think they go right up to the line.'

The line: is it significant that Brailsford is talking of 'the line' in this context, given that Team Sky had made so much of the design detail on the back of the team jersey; the narrow blue line signifying the wafer-thin divide between success and failure? That Brailsford is now talking about 'the line' not in relation to winning and losing, but as signifying the divide between doping, and being clean, could be telling. At the very least, it seems symbolic. (Later, I asked Dr Freeman about 'the line' in a doping context; he even spoke of it as 'the blue line'. 'In terms of illegal products it is clear where the blue line is,' said Dr Freeman. 'There is a grey area in terms of injections, for example, but we adhere completely to the WADA [World Anti-Doping Agency] policy on needles. WADA say that if you have to give an injection of something – I mean something legal, like iron or vitamins – then you're allowed to give one injection of up to 50ml every six hours. What some teams do – and I know they do it – is they take a 50ml syringe to squirt one lot in, then another lot, then another. And who's counting? That's an abuse. If our riders need a shot of iron or multi-vitamins they'll get it. But it's one shot of 50ml every six hours.' Freeman adds that, 'If we have a bad rider; if I have intelligence of something going on, I'll tell Mario Zorzoli [the UCI's chief medical officer]. If we have a rider who puts on 5kg of lean muscle, or who dramatically loses fat or puts up [his] wattage … If I have suspicion, I'll pass it on. I think it's getting more difficult to dope successfully, but I also think surveillance is the way to crack drugs now.')

In the team bus with Brailsford, as he stands up to leave, and carefully follows Evans' instructions about turning off the lights and locking up, he manages to distil everything he's said, and the lesson of the year, in one handy soundbite. 'If I can sum it up,' says Brailsford, 'I think this year we focused too much on the peas and not enough on the steak.'

A few weeks later, it emerged that the winner of the Tour de France, Alberto Contador, had returned a positive test. A urine sample on the Tour's second rest day showed traces of clenbuterol. His defence? That he ate contaminated steak. Brailsford's metaphor seemed either eerily prescient, or unfortunate. Such is the minefield of professional cycling.

In the weeks and months after the Tour, Brailsford and Wiggins offered some frank self-assessments as they reflected on year one and began to look ahead to year two. Wiggins admitted that he had been too serious, too caught up in the hype around the team and its stated goal, to win the Tour. The burden was overwhelming, he said as he reflected on 'the first really big public failure of my career'. He told the *Guardian*, 'I ended up my own arse a little.' In another interview he said he and Team Sky had been 'too pompous'.

Brailsford resolved to make changes. The focus would no longer be 'one rider, one race' (Wiggins, Tour). He appointed two new sports directors (Servais Knaven and Nicolas Portal, who retired from competition after a season with Sky) and a time trial coach (Bobby Julich) – all former professional riders. But he also resolved to keep innovating and challenging conventional wisdom; he pointed out that they are at the start of the journey, when the road is rarely smooth – as indeed had proved the case for the track team when they set out on their journey in 1997. Nine years later, they ruled the world.

Yet there are significant challenges ahead, not least in the enormous, all-consuming shape and form of the London Olympics. 'We've had our time,' one British Cycling coach told me towards the end of 2010, acknowledging that in sport things change, eras come and go, and no one individual or team can dominate forever, or even – perhaps – for two Olympic cycles. Event and rule changes also make it all but impossible for Team GB to repeat the success of Beijing. But Brailsford's admission that much of his time and attention was taken up by Team Sky in 2010 led to the inevitable charge that he had neglected the track team. This was fuelled by Jamie Staff, a gold medallist in Beijing, who retired to take up a coaching job in America. 'Dave Brailsford's attention turned to the road, [and] I think it's having an effect on the track team,' Staff said. 'You need a leader. If your leader goes off and leads something else, you get consequences. At the end of the day it comes down to the riders obviously, but having some-one to lead the army is the key. It gives the rider the belief they have the backing. If you remove that and the riders feel like they are on their own, then cracks can appear. I see some cracks appearing.'

Brailsford responded by pointing out that, at the equivalent stage of the last Olympic cycle, between Athens and Beijing, he was also posted missing for large chunks of the year, consumed as he was by the challenge of setting up the British Cycling Academy.

But as 2010 drew to a close the Academy, so successful in its first four years with its conveyor belt producing Cavendish, Thomas, Swift and Kennaugh, was also displaying 'cracks.' These had been evident to me as far back as April when I visited Quarrata and met with Max Sciandri, Rod Ellingworth's successor as Academy coach. 'Cycling's hard and you have to stand back and let them grow a bit,' Sciandri had told me, but he had perhaps stood a little too far back. His laidback approach contrasted sharply with Ellingworth's, and it was perhaps summed up by the large planner pinned to the wall above Sciandri's desk in the Academy house in Quarrata. 'This is the guys' programme for the year,' Sciandri announced as we stood before the messily scrawled-on, plastic-coated planner. Then he stared at it in apparent confusion, as though trying to decipher its codes. 'Oh, this is actually last year's. I haven't got round to doing this year's yet.' (This was in April.)

By the end of the season the Academy riders were complaining about a lack of racing. 'I only raced 20 times,' one rider said. 'I don't feel like I developed at all.' In October it was announced that Sciandri was leaving British Cycling to become a *directeur sportif* with the Swiss team BMC. It had also become apparent that the Quarrata base wasn't working out. Plans for the Team Sky base – in which Brailsford had agonised over the positioning of the kitchen furniture, and which was to form an integral part of his vision of Quarrata as the base for a majority of Team Sky's riders – were abandoned. The Academy house was also closed; 2011 would thus see the Academy, with ex-rider Chris Newton installed as Sciandri's successor, return to first principles, with bases in Manchester and Belgium, and a much heavier programme of racing (or 'learning', as Ellingworth would describe it).

Brailsford was determined to shake up Team Sky as well. 'It takes big people to sit down and say they want to change,' said Mat Hayman, the Australian who, in his role as *domestique* and lead-out man, had inspired several victories and become a lynchpin. 'It's actually easier to say, "I'm right" and be head-strong and keep ploughing on.'

Brailsford appeared, as 2010 drew to a close, to be searching for answers, and – in searching – engaged in a deep examination of his own philosophies, principles and practices. It might be interpreted as an admission of weakness, and – perhaps fatal in sport – doubt. Yet as Simon Barnes, *The Times* sportswriter, noted at around the same time, in relation to another sport: in the aftermath of failure, 'you have two options and the one you take depends on whether or not you are serious about improving. You can accept failure and seek to do it better next time or you can deny that you failed and then fail all over again. The best way to deny failure is to blame somebody else …' Whatever else Brailsford could be accused of, it seemed that he couldn't be accused of blaming others for any mistakes made by Team Sky in their debut year.

In so many ways Brailsford was absolutely right when he sat in the bar in Bourg-en-Bresse in July, 2007, and revealed his plans to set up a professional team. The sport was – is – one that has been crying out for innovation, for a new approach and new people, for years, if not decades. It is in desperate need of modernisation; more than that, it is in desperate need of professionalisation. Through their organisation, planning, presentation and attention to detail, Brailsford and Team Sky could yet prove a catalyst for change; change that, as David Millar would urge, doesn't wholly discard a century of tradition, but somehow marries the best of the old school with a fresh, new approach – as long as it doesn't entail the construction of an impenetrable black perspex box around its riders.

Forty-eight hours after my conversation with Brailsford in his bollocking room, we're standing by the Team Sky bus in Newham, east London, prior to the final stage of the Tour of Britain. A large crowd has gathered, as it has done every day. They appear to be an equal mix of cycling fans, many in Sky shirts, and casual spectators, though even those in the second group are familiar with the people inside the bus. They all know Bradley Wiggins and Geraint Thomas from the Olympics and Tour de France, and many are familiar, too, with Brailsford, the architect of the Beijing success. The reception for Brailsford when he emerges, blinking, into the bright London sunshine is warm, though he is not – like Wiggins and Thomas – mobbed for autographs and photographs. When, a little later, he stands by one of the team cars, several people – older than those waiting for the riders – stand at a respectful distance, but come forward one by one to speak to him. One earnest, middle-aged man shakes his hand as he says: 'Dave, can I just thank you for being an inspiration to young cyclists.'

'Thank you very much,' says Brailsford warmly.

'The cycling club I'm involved with has grown phenomenally,' continues the man, his voice shaking with nerves. 'It's grown from 50 to 250 and it's because of what we see: so many youngsters watching Bradley Wiggins and the others.'

'That's really good to know, really good to know,' says Brailsford. 'It's what we're trying to do, what you're trying to do – it's all part of the same thing, isn't it?'

Then a woman steps forward – she's in her sixties. 'Mr Brailsford,' she says politely, 'I just want to thank you for giving us a team to support.'

'Oh, no, no, no,' says Brailsford.

'Anyway,' she continues. 'I just wanted to say I appreciate what you've done. It's fantastic. I've been watching track cycling from when Hugh Porter was winning. I'm very, very old. It's just fantastic. And it's clean and that's fantastic.'

'It'll stay clean as well,' says Brailsford.

'I can't wait until next year,' she says.

'Well we'll be back,' Brailsford tells her. 'We've learnt a lot. It hasn't been easy, but we've learnt a lot.'

'If it was easy,' she says, 'it wouldn't be worth doing, would it?'

CHAPTER 14

TAKE TWO

'You'd be crazy to sign Mark Cavendish.'

Dave Brailsford

Les Essarts, Sunday 3 July 2011

Dave Brailsford is standing by the Team Sky compound, talking casually in a field on the outskirts of the small village of Les Essarts in western France. It's the scene of stage two of the Tour de France: the team time trial.

Although he is speaking to three journalists, there are no notepads or tape recorders. Brailsford is just chatting; shooting the breeze. He seems unusually relaxed, especially when you consider that today is a stage he has been thinking about, and talking about, for a year. During the 2010 Tour it was the prospect of a team time trial the following year that seemed to act like a light at the end of a very dark tunnel. It's only when the conversation eventually turns to Mark Cavendish that the bonhomie ceases. And, almost imperceptibly, Brailsford withdraws. One of the journalists has mentioned Cavendish because he had been in the press, again. This time, it's because he has posted something on his newly opened Twitter feed.

Cavendish's tweet followed the previous day's first stage, in which Philippe Gilbert, the pre-race favourite, toyed with his rivals on the short rise to the finish – his speciality. Gilbert seemed to be floating, while the others appeared to be wading through treacle. As he drifted towards the front of the thinning line of riders, he glanced at his rivals' pained expressions. He was capable of attacking at will. When he made his move, he left a trail of devastation behind him.

Gilbert's performance – all the more impressive for the fact that it had been anticipated – made a deep impression on everybody who witnessed it, including Cavendish. Although he was too far back to see the attack, he watched the footage later that evening, and was moved to share his verdict with his 100,000+ Twitter followers: 'Just saw today's last kilometre. Gilbert humbled everyone with the equivalent of pulling down his pants to reveal a 13 incher. #YIKES.'

The journalist mentions Cavendish's tweet to Brailsford. He seems to be suffering a sense-of-humour failure – the journalist, that is. He considers it irresponsible; or perhaps it's a cunning ploy to get a reaction, any reaction, from the man who is rumoured to be trying to sign Cavendish.

'No wonder his team's struggling to get a sponsor,' suggests the journalist. 'Sponsors don't want to be associated with comments like that.'

Brailsford smiles politely – ambiguously – but takes this turn in the conversation as his cue, or excuse, to leave. 'Yeah,' he says as he turns for the team bus. 'Mark Cavendish, eh? You'd be crazy to sign him.'

At the end of 2010 Team Sky gathered at the Savill Court Hotel & Spa near Windsor. It was part-debrief, part-bonding, part-looking ahead to 2011. But mainly, judging by the state of some of the team the following morning, bonding. The ritual induction of new signings had involved the consumption of copious quantities of alcohol, and even the old faces had clearly felt compelled to join in.

Next morning, Simon Gerrans sat hunched over a medicinal cup of coffee in the bar. Russell Downing looked as though he'd slept in his clothes, and Dave Brailsford appeared a little the worse for wear. His eyes were bloodshot and his voice croaked: a fitting metaphor at the fag-end of a 'humbling' year. Brailsford was joined by a remarkably clear-headed Sean Yates, who cautiously predicted that the second year 'should, in theory, be more successful. You learn by your mistakes.'

Yates spoke honestly, although there was as much to be gleaned from what he didn't say. The subtext was everything. Had they been unrealistic going into the Tour with Wiggins as leader? 'Unrealistic is a bit harsh,' Yates reflected. 'Brad was fourth the year before, but that was a very controlled Tour; he was incognito and there was no pressure from his sponsors to perform. It wasn't the physical side that was unrealistic. It was the whole thing: the burden that he was carrying, and I think that took a lot away from him physically. We all tried desperately to live up to the expectations. In a way, we shot ourselves in the foot with the big launch. But what are you going to do? You can't go under the radar with a sponsor like Sky.'

Brailsford stressed that a more relaxed atmosphere would prevail in year two. 'We need to have a lot more fun,' he croaked. Yates also said that Wiggins had to 'enjoy the bike racing' more and 'not spend the whole year training for the Tour'.

'"Inspiration" is a good word for next year,' said Brailsford. 'Open, intimate, engaging, inspiring: that's what we want to be next year.'

There were changes to the personnel but there wasn't the clear-out that Brailsford might have secretly wanted. Most riders were on two-year contracts. Sylvain Calzati, however, left for a small French team, apparently unhappy at how little he had raced. And as mentioned in the previous chapter, Bobby Julich, an affable American who had finished third in the 1998 Tour, moved from Saxo Bank, where he was a sports director, to join Rod Ellingworth as a race coach at Sky, with special responsibility for time trialling. (Julich had been a strong time triallist, although he also held a special distinction as perhaps the only rider ever to crash out of the Tour on two occasions, in 1999 and 2006, during individual time trials.) Servais Knaven, Holland's 2001 Paris-Roubaix winner, also joined as a sports director. Among the new riders, the star signing was Michael Rogers, the Australian three-time world time trial champion, with intrigue surrounding the capture of Rigoberto Urán, a Colombian prodigy and climbing specialist. An effort to sign Fabian Cancellara, the Swiss superstar, had failed. But Alex Dowsett, a young British time trial specialist, would be given his chance at Sky.

Speaking to Brailsford in Windsor, looking ahead to the next year, it was almost like a playback of the Tour itself. He still seemed a little humbled; he was certainly less ebullient than he had been 12 months earlier. It was also tempting to consider the security of his position. Had he been a football manager he might, ludicrously, have been sacked (despite a four-year contract with Sky). But cycling doesn't have the same pressures, the same short-termism, the same culture of dispensing with managers. What was Brailsford to do? 'You learn through failure,' he insisted in Windsor. It was unusual to hear someone in his position admit that he had failed; but it was also perhaps the most encouraging sign. He wasn't blaming anybody else.

It was also interesting to note in Windsor that, while most nursed sore heads the morning after the night before, there was one exception. One rider who had resolved that there would be no 'off-season'; and that being the leader of one of the world's top cycling teams meant acting like the leader. For him there was no drinking wine through a straw stuck in the neck of a bottle, or letting his hair down at end-of-season dinners; in Windsor, he did not touch a drop of alcohol and retired to bed early. For Bradley Wiggins, the 2011 season had already started.

Mannum, South Australia, 19 January 2011
The thing about professional road cycling is that it's relentless. It's not like track cycling, with four years from one Olympics to the next, to lick wounds or polish halos. There's always a new race, a new season; an opportunity to re-boot, replenish, renew. Barely a month after the end-of-season get together in Windsor, it all kicks off again in South Australia.

Under the kilometre-to-go banner, on stage two of the Tour Down Under, there's a sweeping bend, and as the close-packed, jostling group of riders swings to the left, one rider skids on the loose gravel and crashes. Others hit him and fall like dominoes. It decimates the front of the peloton, as though a large bite has been taken from it. Mark Cavendish falls hardest, scraping his face on the tarmac. But as the cameras linger on the stricken figures beginning to pick themselves up off the ground, the race carries on, renewing itself, like a river tumbling towards the sea.

At the front, Geraint Thomas emerges with Ben Swift stuck to his back wheel. Previously Mat Hayman had been leading this pair, with the order at the front of the Team Sky lead-out train reading: Hayman, Swift, Thomas and the designated sprinter, Chris Sutton. The first three survive the crash. But when Hayman swings off, his job done, Thomas pulls alongside Swift and tells him that Sutton has hit the deck with Cavendish.

'You sprint, you sprint,' Thomas yells at Swift. Swift nods, accepts the responsibility, and Thomas hits the front, Swift tucking in behind him.

Now, into the final 500 metres, in his white British champion's jersey, Thomas makes a huge effort to give Swift, his young British teammate, the perfect lead-out. He strings out what's left of the peloton, towing them towards the line at close to 40mph; with 200 metres to go he glances briefly over his right shoulder, beckoning Swift through. And as Thomas eases to the left, Swift strikes. He bursts through the centre, out of the saddle, punching the pedals, as he goes head-to-head with Robbie McEwen, now nearing retirement but one of the best sprinters of the past decade. And he holds him off. Swift crosses the line first, hands up, fists punching.

Swift, 23, then won the final stage of the Tour Down Under and notched up another three victories in the early part of the season to earn a call-up to the Tour de France. After Adelaide, Sky had a quiet time in the Middle East, although Edvald Boasson Hagen enjoyed some redemption at the Tour of Oman, the scene 12 months earlier of 'pissgate', finishing second overall to Robert Gesink of Rabobank. Wiggins opened his season at the Tour of Qatar, where he launched an attack at the end of stage four, following some strong work by his teammates to string the field out and break it up in the cross-winds, giving him a launch pad with 1.5km to go. Although he was caught, it was a sign that, as Yates had predicted, Wiggins would be trying to enjoy himself; and showing himself in races other than the Tour de France.

In Qatar, on stages where the peloton ambled through the desert, Wiggins also chatted to Cavendish. The subject of Cavendish's future was in the air. He was out of contract at the end of the season and uncertainty surrounded his team, with HTC threatening to end their sponsorship. Bob Stapleton, the team owner, was no longer such a ubiquitous presence at races; he was spending more time in California, searching for replacement sponsors. But there was another problem: he and Cavendish were not talking.

Relations had been strained for some time, steadily worsening as Cavendish's stock rose while his earnings remained pegged to the contract he signed midway through the 2008 Tour de France. In early 2010 Stapleton tried to get his star rider to commit beyond that contract, travelling with Rolf Aldag, the team's sports director, to Tuscany to woo Cavendish over dinner. During that meeting Cavendish was clear – he wanted a new deal with a salary commensurate to his new status. But Stapleton found himself in a hopeless bind; he could not offer Cavendish a contract without a sponsor. But without Cavendish's guaranteed commitment it would be extremely difficult to attract a sponsor.

Cavendish's frustration simmered, and at the Commonwealth Games in India in October 2010 it bubbled over. Riding for the Isle of Man in Delhi, well away from his employers and the rest of the European racing fraternity, Cavendish let off steam, claiming to be 'kind of abused for what I've achieved, but I've been contracted to do it, so I have to do it'. He complained that he had received 'no bonuses, no goodwill', adding that 'the pressures, the normal person's life that I've lost, you should see the benefits coming with that and I don't get that. I'm disappointed with that.' Yet what was most telling was that this barely veiled attack on his current team, and perhaps Stapleton in particular, was not prompted by any leading or mischievous questions. In fact, it came apropos of nothing in particular. The impression, reinforced by the mischievous twinkle in Cavendish's eyes, was that it was calculated. This was further bolstered by Cavendish's relaxed demeanour in Delhi, where he rode a gutsy road race and then remained to the end of the Games, spending time with his friend David Millar, and helping out the Isle of Man team. A few days after the road race, while walking among the team's pens during the time trial, I was greeted by a remarkable sight: Cavendish, clutching an armful of wheels, jumping into the Isle of Man team car. The world's fastest man was acting as mechanic to his teammates.

His outburst in Delhi hardly improved relations with Stapleton. In Morgan Hill, California, in mid-December, at the first HTC-Highroad get together ahead of the 2011 season, the two were reunited, but they didn't talk. One senior member of Stapleton's team told *Procycling* magazine: 'Whatever Cav wants, Bob has to pay him. If he wants five million, pay him, because he's the most marketable rider in the world.' But there was no reconciliation in California. In fact, Cavendish and Stapleton didn't utter a single word to one another.

And in Qatar, two months later, Cavendish told Wiggins: 'I'm talking to Dave.'

There were rumours that James Murdoch was sceptical about signing Cavendish. A planned meeting between the pair in 2010 did not happen (they would finally meet for the first time in Girona, on the eve of the 2011 World Championships), but Brailsford did not need to be convinced. He wanted Cavendish and spent some time over the winter persuading the decision-makers, including Murdoch, that his signing made sense. And it did. Everybody could see that. In March, a month after his conversation with Wiggins in Qatar, the Team Sky board approved a package – as much as £2.5m a year – to try and lure Cavendish.

Brailsford was confident Cavendish would agree to join. But he and others worried about the possible effect on Wiggins of Cavendish joining Team Sky. Would it seem like a vote of no-confidence in the rider originally signed to lead the team? Would he feel undermined? The pair had had their ups and downs in the past, most notably at the Beijing Olympics. Could Wiggins and Cavendish co-habit?

What seemed certain, as Team Sky's second season entered full swing, was that there was a sea change. Chris Sutton won Kuurne-Brussels-Kuurne, and Swift was prolific, following his wins in Australia with successes in Romandie and California. But it wasn't so much the victories that marked the change. There was a change in atmosphere; a sense of momentum, rather than pressure, was building. Geraint Thomas put it down to the simple fact of people knowing each other better. And he identifies the race at which he feels the team first really 'clicked'. It was Bayern-Rundfahrt, a stage race in Germany in late May. 'It had been building all season, but we had really good morale there,' says Thomas. 'We all knew each other and had spent a lot of time together. We had just been in Tenerife together.' A two-week altitude training camp on the island had been organised in response to Wiggins' failure at the Tour the previous year, in particular his inability to stay with the leaders in the high mountains. 'There was a real good bond between the riders,' says Thomas. 'In the first year we knew each other, but just by name, really, not as people. I think that first year Dave and the staff thought that if they had the right riders and the right system it would just happen. But it wasn't that easy. It's like in football, like Man City, it takes a couple of years. But I think we did it a bit quicker than Man City.'

Wiggins had an early morale boost when he placed third at Paris-Nice, the week-long 'race to the sun', traditionally the first major stage race in Europe. The riders above Wiggins on the podium, Tony Martin and Andreas Klöden, are both major players in such stage races. It was arguably Wiggins' second-most impressive road racing performance, after the 2009 Tour.

But it's little surprise that Thomas singles out a relatively minor event, Bayern-Rundfahrt, as the race when the team finally clicked. He won it. But his victory was part of a strong team performance. Edvald Boasson Hagen, with whom Thomas had by now formed a close friendship, won stage one; Wiggins claimed the stage four time trial and the scalp of the world champion, Cancellara; and Thomas was rewarded for his consistency with the overall win, for *his* greatest-ever road performance. A Sky rider finished in the top three on each of the five stages. The team in Germany contained the nucleus of the Tour de France squad, which had trained together in Tenerife, sleeping in a hotel at 2,150m. Their success boded well for the major Tour tune-up, a week later: the Critérium du Dauphiné.

Wiggins began the Dauphiné tired. For him there was no let-up between Tenerife and Rundfahrt and there would be none, either, after the French stage race, with another altitude training camp, this time in Sestrières. He was following a programme written, with increasing assurance, by Tim Kerrison, the sports scientist who had switched from rowing to swimming to cycling. With Kerrison, the other two members of 'Team Wiggins' were the doctor, Richard Freeman, and Shane Sutton, who Wiggins had turned to in August 2010, when he was at his lowest ebb. 'Shane sorted my life out,' he said. Kerrison then took over Wiggins' training in October. First he had to 'build up a picture' of Wiggins; he recorded his power outputs from every training session, storing it all on his laptop. He found that Wiggins responded well to being told what to do: 'He's very coachable. He's come through the British Cycling system, so he's used to being coached, and following instructions.' The training was 'pretty prescriptive', admitted Kerrison. But Wiggins said that he thrived on it; that he had total trust in the team of people around him, even though Kerrison stressed that he was still on a steep learning curve, and 'turned to Shane a lot'.

Kerrison and Sutton, though both Australians, could hardly be more different. Sutton is combustible, a ball of energy, a rough diamond; Kerrison is reserved, mild-mannered, clean-cut. 'But I've spent my whole career working with coaches from different backgrounds,' says Kerrison. 'Some are science-minded, some are technical-minded, some are old school who coach by feel and get fantastic results. You can still be a great coach. The best team is when you can combine that great intuition with the knowledge and science; when you can make that partnership work.' And Shane was open to his scientific input? 'I'm not sure if he always has been, but we don't have too many disagreements, though we certainly thrash things out. I'll send a programme to him, he'll question it, I'll explain the rationale behind it, and he'll either be okay with it or he'll explain his concerns.'

But Kerrison was keen to apply some of his experiences, especially from swimming, where the training is relentless. Everything on Wiggins' programme had to have sound theory behind it; Kerrison wouldn't accept arguments that were based, in his view, solely on the sport's 'culture of training'. What interested Kerrison was physiology. He acknowledges the 'complex, diverse' nature of the sport of cycling, with 300km one-day races on the one hand, three-week stage races on the other. 'But when it comes to the physical preparation of athletes to meet those demands, physiology is physiology,' he shrugs. 'It doesn't change that much between rowing and swimming and cycling.'

Kerrison had seemed unsure and a little hesitant in the Alps, during the team's Tour recce the previous year. Twelve months later, he seemed more confident. It was difficult to imagine him getting stuck on a mountain in the Giro d'Italia in Black Betty, the camper van that he still called home, as he had done in 2010.

Wiggins also appeared to be growing into the role of leader, and he was oddly reassured by Sutton's regular blasts of honesty. 'When you get to this level of sport very few people can tell you bluntly how it is,' Wiggins said. It wasn't that he previously surrounded himself with 'yes' men, he added. But it sounded as though that's exactly what he meant. For his part, Sutton took some pride in saying that he had no qualms about 'just telling 'em to cut the bullshit and get out and do the hard yards'. He said that his handling of Wiggins varied according to his mood; at times he needed an arm around him, at others he needed a boot in the backside. Sutton seemed uniquely aware of which approach to take, and when.

'Brad's a funny character,' Sutton later told me, in a rare moment of thoughtful reflection. 'When he's on good form you get him in the bus and he's fantastic. But he's also a guy who takes things to heart. He just needs to lighten up a little bit.'

In early June, the Critérium du Dauphiné saw the very best of Wiggins. A race that had previously been won by two British riders, Robert Millar (1990) and Brian Robinson (1961), as well as most of the greats – Anquetil, Merckx, Hinault, LeMond, Indurain, Armstrong – starts with a 5.5km prologue time trial in Saint-Jean-de-Maurienne, where stage nine of the previous year's Tour finished, plummeting into the Alpine town after the Col de la Madeleine, the climb where Wiggins' Tour hopes were definitively extinguished.

Eleven months on, Wiggins is third in the prologue, behind Lars Boom and Alexandre Vinokourov. It bodes well; the previous day, Wiggins had done a five-hour training ride. As if to further illustrate the Dauphiné's place in his priorities, after the prologue, and dope control, he rides a further 80km back to the hotel, in the company of Boasson Hagen.

Over the next two stages Wiggins rides cleverly, among the leaders, even sneaking seconds on some of his rivals when the race splits at the end of a lumpy stage two. And the next day, a 42.5km time trial around Grenoble, on a course that will also be covered by the Tour in seven weeks, he finishes second, just behind Tony Martin, to take the leader's yellow jersey. It's the second time he has led a major stage race, but Wiggins seems unhappy. There had been no carers (*soigneurs*) waiting for him at the finish; he also complained to Sutton about the lack of time checks on Martin, with whom he'd been level with 15 mainly downhill kilometres remaining. The exchange between Sutton and Sean Yates was later reported in *Cycle Sport* magazine: 'He's just had a go at me,' said Sutton. 'He said, "Where were my time gaps to Tony Martin?" and I said, "You can cut that bullshit for a start." We told him he was level at the last time check. What more does he want?'

Sutton's verdict is that Wiggins is frustrated at not winning the stage, although even this leaves him perplexed: 'This wasn't about the stage win!' He is also puzzled by his irritation at the absence of a carer: 'He said he didn't want one. Then he wonders why there isn't one.' As Sutton knows, life is never simple, even when you're winning.

There are another four stages, including summit finishes at Les Gets, Le Collet d'Allevard and La Toussuire. The penultimate stage is brutal, with the Col du Glandon – climbing to close to 2,000 metres – coming before the finishing climb to the Collet d'Allevard. After the time trial, Wiggins has a healthy one minute, 11 seconds' lead over Cadel Evans; much will now depend on how his team rides, although ultimately it will boil down to how Wiggins copes in the high mountains, where he struggled so badly the previous July.

Brailsford arrives for the remainder of the race, but still it's Sutton to whom Wiggins turns – and Kerrison, one of whose innovations is to have Wiggins warm down on a turbo trainer for around 30 minutes after long road stages. While he's riding on the turbo, after comfortably defending yellow on the road to Les Gets, with his team so strong that Johan Bruyneel was moved to congratulate Brailsford ('Basically,' Brailsford said, 'Johan told me: "Your team was fucking brilliant today. You were super strong and everyone's saying it"'), Wiggins chats to Sutton, going over the stage.

He's in new territory. At the Tour in 2009 he was fighting for the podium, but he was never in yellow. Wearing the leader's jersey and battling for the victory is totally different. It brings different pressures and responsibilities, not only to Wiggins but also the team, which is expected to control the race. Sutton tries to reassure him; he tells him not to panic and, on the climbs where he might be isolated, not to respond to every attack or acceleration. To do so, Sutton says, will kill him. 'They'll get 30 metres and just stay there. There's no need to panic.' Perhaps if Contador or Schleck – both pure, explosive climbers – were riding, it would be different. But his main rival, Evans, is a rider more in Wiggins' mould: a diesel rather than a turbo.

Saturday is the decisive stage, with its jagged profile: the Col des Aravis, Col de Tamie, Col du Grand Cucheron and the Collet d'Allevard. This final, relatively unknown climb is especially hard, but when the riders arrive at its base, Wiggins is riding comfortably among the leaders; with his height, and his fluid pedalling style, he has real presence. Boasson Hagen is his last remaining teammate, and he rides out of his skin at the front of the lead group, which is down to 17 riders half-way up the final climb. The tactic works well. Boasson Hagen rides fast enough to discourage the attacks that impose a draining stop-start rhythm on the race; but not so fast that he puts Wiggins in difficulty. In fact, Wiggins looks as composed as another tall rider, Miguel Indurain, did during his pomp, in contrast to the bedraggled-looking riders fighting to remain in contact at the rear of the group, including such strong men as Thomas Voeckler, Ivan Basso and Samuel Sanchez.

When Boasson Hagen swings off, 6.7km from the summit – almost wobbling into the grass verge, such is the effort he has made – Wiggins remains well placed to respond. Initially there's a flurry of attacks; watching on TV in the team bus, Brailsford experiences a moment of panic, especially when first Robert Gesink, then Vinokourov, who is third overall, fly up the road, chased by Joaquim Rodríguez. Following Sutton's advice, Wiggins doesn't panic. Evans has a dig, gaining a few bike lengths, then – just as Sutton had said – he pays for the effort. It takes longer for Vinokourov to begin to pay for his, but eventually he does, letting go of Rodríguez. It's possible to detect Wiggins' confidence mounting as he climbs, past a huge 'Allez Wiggo' banner, and scoops up Vinokourov. By the summit, as he crosses the line in sixth place, 54 seconds behind Rodríguez, who has held on to win, he has managed to claim more time on his nearest challenger, Evans, who is dropped in the final 3km and concedes 15 seconds.

There is still work to do, but the final stage is short, just 118km. It's Rigoberto Uran's turn to play Wiggins' lieutenant. There's a scare 3km from the summit of La Toussuire, where Floyd Landis suffered horribly during the 2006 Tour, losing the yellow jersey, before staging his remarkable recovery to Morzine the following day (then losing the Tour when he tested positive after the stage). Wiggins is dropped from a group containing Evans and Vinokourov. Again he doesn't panic, or alter his pace. He finds his own little group and is paced back up, with some help from one of the HTC riders, Kanstantsin Siutsou. It's rumoured that Siutsou will join Team Sky in 2012, so there might be more to his pace-setting here than meets the eye.

As Rodríguez wins his second stage and Wiggins finishes in the group behind, Wiggins' overall victory, ahead of Evans and Vinokourov, is confirmed. But there's no champagne or wild celebrations. 'It's a bit surreal,' Wiggins says. 'It's over, but it hasn't sunk in that I've won the Dauphiné. The team were fantastic again today; throughout the week they have defended it for me, and been fantastic. I didn't panic on the final climb; I rode my own tempo. It takes a lot out of you to attack and keep it going, and I kept that in mind.'

For Kerrison, too, there is relief that Wiggins has won without going 'too deep'. Kerrison feels confident that there is more to come at the Tour. Wiggins says he feels 'in shape, but not in form'. He started the race tired, is more tired now, and is heading straight for another few days' altitude training in Sestrières. He is the third British rider to win the race; it's far and away the biggest victory of his road career. Yet the sense is that of job done, rather than mission accomplished.

On the final weekend of the Dauphiné, I attended an event in London, a night-time Nocturne circuit race around Smithfield Market. It was won, in dominant fashion, by a Team Sky rider, Alex Dowsett, after he took off on the first lap and lapped the field. But, for me, that was not the most significant Team Sky-related development of the evening. It was a conversation with someone I didn't know, but who said he was connected to one of the team's sponsors. He referred to the recent publication of the first edition of this book. 'I can't believe you wrote a book about Team Sky and didn't mention me!' he said. And as if to illustrate the extent of my folly, he added: 'Of course, you know that Cav's signed up for next year. Confirmed this week.'

'Yeah,' I said. 'I heard about that.' I hadn't.

'Eisel and Renshaw are coming too,' the mystery man confidently added, meaning Cavendish's best friend and loyal *domestique*, Bernhard Eisel, and his lead-out man, Mark Renshaw. It sounded perfectly plausible. Over the next few days I made a few phone calls. It appeared to be true. During the Giro, Cavendish met – again – with Brailsford, and agreed in principle to join Sky (although it was wrong to say that he had 'signed up'). Eisel would probably come with him. Renshaw, however, was doubtful. Apparently there were those within Team Sky who didn't want him.

And so the scoop appeared: 'Cavendish to join Team Sky'. It appeared just after Wiggins' biggest victory, at a time when his position as leader looked secure. Cavendish would bolster the team, not replace Wiggins. The timing might have been ideal, for Team Sky, if not for Bob Stapleton and HTC-Highroad, who were still seeking a sponsor.

Les Essarts, Sunday 3 July 2011

A few weeks later, Brailsford's relaxed mood on the morning of the team time trial is soured only a little by the events of the day. Sky perform well, and Wiggins is outstanding, dragging his team through the closing kilometres. They finish third, although only five seconds separate the first five teams over the 23km, led in by Garmin, followed by BMC. Cavendish's HTC are fifth.

Wiggins rides the first week as a team leader. By keeping him up near the front it should mean that he's out of harm's way. Kerrison is hugely encouraged by his 'numbers'. The difference between 2011 and 2010 is like night and day. Although the main focus is on Wiggins' overall ambitions, the strategy isn't as one-dimensional as simply that – there are other goals too. On day five, in rain-lashed Normandy, after a lumpy stage, Boasson Hagen sprinted to the win after a brilliant lead-out by Thomas. It's the team's first Tour stage; the mood is buoyant.

But 24 hours after Boasson Hagen's win it crashes abruptly to earth. A tumble near the head of the peloton results in several bodies ending up on the road. Similar crashes had been happening daily, particularly in the final hour of the race as the speed increased and teams tried to move their leaders towards the front, where it's generally safer. When riders fall the TV cameramen become like reporters in a war zone in the immediate aftermath of a bomb exploding. Viewers are treated to wobbly camera work; it takes some agility on the part of the cameraman to identify the casualties. They try to focus on the numbers. A number that ends in '1' signifies a team leader. A concentration of riders from one team also suggests that a race favourite has fallen. And here, 40km from the finish in Châteauroux, eight of the Sky riders gather, all staring anxiously at the stricken figure on the tarmac clutching his shoulder. It's Wiggins.

Richard Freeman is one of the first on the scene. He's fairly sure it's the injury all cyclists fear: a broken collarbone. Yet for some reason all eight of his Sky teammates linger on the scene, eventually riding off, but looking lost, directionless. Only when Sean Yates confirms over the radio that Wiggins has indeed broken his collarbone and is out of the Tour do they begin to chase back to the peloton with real commitment, but it's too late and they lose more than three minutes. It was an error to have all eight of Wiggins' teammates wait. It loses Geraint Thomas the white jersey of best young rider, which he'd worn since day one; and it costs Rigoberto Urán, who has been expected to be Wiggins' back-up man in the mountains, any hope of a high overall placing. The explanation for the mistake seems to hark back to the previous year's failings – a lack of confidence in anything other than Plan A.

'It's a devastating day for the team,' says Brailsford at the finish. 'Brad was in great shape. He put so much work into his Tour. It's a shame we never got to see him go into the mountains because he was in the best shape of his life.'

In Châteauroux, meanwhile, where Cavendish won his first stage in 2008, he wins again, for the 17th time. While Wiggins said he 'couldn't get up off the floor for love nor money', his teammates did pick themselves up in the days that followed. Juan Antonio Flecha leads the line, riding aggressively, infiltrating breaks. Two days after Wiggins' crash he's in a breakaway on the road to Saint-Flour when a French TV car, overtaking the group, swerves into the road to avoid a tree and in the process slams into Flecha, knocking him and Johnny Hoogerland off the road as though they were skittles. Hoogerland flies into a barbed-wire fence. When he crawls away from the tangle the wounds on his legs are horrific. Remarkably, both riders get back up and finish the stage, Flecha in a state of anger, Hoogerland in tears.

Then there is Boasson Hagen. Keen to add to his stage win, he escapes with the world champion, Thor Hushovd, and his Garmin teammate, Ryder Hesjedal, on the run-in to the finish in Gap at the end of stage 16. Boasson Hagen against Hushovd is an interesting match-up – both are strong sprinters; both are Norwegian. The main difference is that Hushovd has a team-mate. The obvious tactic, from Garmin's point of view, would be a late attack by Hesjedal, which would force Boasson Hagen to chase. But the attack never comes. Instead, on the wet streets coming into Gap, Hesjedal leads out his teammate – it looks a risky strategy. Boasson Hagen sits second, keeping an eye on Hushovd in third. But coming into the final 200 metres, Boasson Hagen inexplicably switches off. He takes his eye off Hushovd, allowing his gaze to drift down to his bike. It's a momentary lapse but Hushovd seizes on it and jumps. When Boasson Hagen glances back up, he's gone.

In Gap the next morning Rod Ellingworth is bounding through the Village Départ with his usual vigour and enthusiasm. He stops to talk. He says Boasson Hagen had been utterly distraught after his defeat. Normally so mild-mannered, he had never seen him so angry. The last thing he wanted to do was sit down and watch a replay of the stage finish, but that's exactly what Ellingworth made him do. 'Some of these boys,' says Ellingworth, with a hint of exasperation, 'they've got to watch more bike racing.

'You know, every night G [Thomas] and Swifty, they sit down and watch the highlights of the day's stage, 'coz they want to. Cav's the same. They can't get enough of bike racing: even here, halfway through the Tour. But they're not all like that.'

Ellingworth doesn't say it, but Thomas, Swift and Cavendish are, of course, all alumni of the British Cycling Academy.

They're pupils of Ellingworth. As he used to tell his charges, racing is learning. Watching and talking about racing reinforces the lessons. He used to marvel at Cavendish's recall of every detail of race finishes, but it didn't happen by magic. So, the previous evening, he made Boasson Hagen sit and endure the final kilometres of the previous stage. And he was encouraged. From barely able to watch, Boasson Hagen studied the footage, discussed it with Ellingworth and told him that he would not make that mistake again.

The roads from Gap to the Italian town of Pinerolo are similar to those of the day before. A break goes, and it contains Boasson Hagen. Same as the previous day, but with a crucial difference. It's a different Boasson Hagen.

On the climb before the finish he bridges up to a lone attacker, Sylvain Chavanel. And then, just before they are caught, he attacks, with total commitment. He rides up the rest of the climb like a man possessed. But it's a good way to avoid a repeat of the previous day's mistake: win alone. There are 11km left but Boasson Hagen climbs on his own to the summit, then plummets down the corkscrew descent as though on rails. Behind him, numerous riders crash, overshoot corners or end up in driveways. He looks behind only once, briefly, in the final kilometre, then grins widely, throws his arms in the air and celebrates. At the Team Sky bus Brailsford shows him a congratulatory text he has just received from James Murdoch, although it isn't clear if Boasson Hagen knows who James Murdoch is. Ellingworth is nowhere to be seen. But he might allow himself a wry smile. And he'll make Boasson Hagen watch this one, too.

On the Champs-Élysées they're celebrating around the HTC-Highroad bus. Cavendish has just won his fifth stage of this Tour, his 20th in total, his third consecutive victory on the famous avenue. They're sipping champagne but there's a strange atmosphere. Is this a celebration or the prelude to a wake? It had been rumoured that Stapleton would announce a replacement sponsor during the Tour, with the second rest day – in Montpellier in the final week – identified as the day of reckoning. 'On the second rest day of the Tour, we must be told,' Rolf Aldag had said.

The second rest day did witness an interesting development, but not a sponsorship announcement. Around a table in the leafy grounds of the Hotel France in Loriol sur Drôme, a small meeting was convened: Cavendish, Stapleton, Aldag and Cavendish's girlfriend Peta Todd. It was the first time Cavendish and Stapleton had spoken in months. Stapleton had been searching high and low for a new sponsor, and had a meeting arranged in Grenoble with one interested party on the Tour's penultimate day. HTC were still in the frame, although they were reportedly more interested in working with Cavendish than with Stapleton; a personal endorsement deal was one possibility.

During his meeting with Stapleton and Aldag, Cavendish, having agreed to join Sky, might have started to waver. It seemed that the future of the team depended on him. He hadn't signed with Sky yet; he wasn't committed, even if, as far as Brailsford and his team were concerned, there was no way Cavendish would not be a Team Sky rider in 2012. Perhaps, though, he had been hasty; maybe he should continue with the team with which he'd enjoyed such success. Brian Holm, the HTC sports director closest to Cavendish, later said that the meeting ended with Stapleton accepting a deadline of one week to tie-up a new sponsor.

On the Champs-Élysées, a day before that deadline, Stapleton spoke to reporters. 'Nothing has been signed yet,' he said, in his usual cheerful, relaxed way, 'but I am very optimis-tic.' He told *Süddeutsche Zeitung* that he had received enquiries during the Tour and claimed: 'I have two options. We even assume we will have a three-year contract and we will have a larger budget.'

As Stapleton broke away from the reporters, I moved in to speak to him, tape recorder running. I thought I enjoyed a good relationship with Stapleton; most journalists did. He always seemed so genial, but now his eyes narrowed, even as he kept smiling: 'I don't know if I want to talk to you,' he said, addressing me, 'your fact checking is so poor. I've read your Sky book. That's complete horseshit.'

Initially I thought he must be joking, so I laughed. Stapleton also laughed, for the benefit of the crowd around us. And he kept smiling, but he wasn't joking. He carried on: 'Your statements about the history of the relationships are way off. Your recitation of the facts, the numbers quoted, that's all horseshit. So wrong.'

He was talking about the story in this book concerning the contract that Cavendish signed during the 2008 Tour. I reminded Stapleton that I had attempted to contact him on two occasions during the previous winter to check these points with him. Then I said that if he told me the facts, I'd correct them. 'I'm not playing that game,' he responded. 'Whenever you read something that makes me sound stupid you should wonder if that's really accurate or not. Because I'm not a nice person all the time, but I'm never stupid.

'The stuff I've read, that's been published, was targeted to fuck us up,' he added. 'It didn't work.'

Ten days later, Stapleton announced that HTC-Highroad would fold at the end of the season. He claimed he'd had an agreement 'in principle' with a new partner, but he learned that the deal was off during his wife's birthday party. 'That led us to the conclusion to release our athletes and staff to pursue their career options,' he said.

CHAPTER 15

GERBILS ON A TREADMILL

*'There. Is. No. Reason. Why. A. British. Rider. Cannot. Win. A.
Grand. Tour. In. The. Next. Five. Years.'*

Dave Brailsford

As Bradley Wiggins' collarbone healed, and, back at home, he
watched the final 10 days of the Tour with the enthusiasm of
a fan ('Andy Schleck's attack and all that, it was brilliant'), he
fixed on a new target: the Vuelta a España. It could offer him a
glimpse of what he might have done at the Tour, which was
won by Cadel Evans with the Schleck brothers, Andy and
Frank, second and third. Some indulged in speculation that
Wiggins would have challenged at least for the podium,
perhaps even for yellow; others were not so sure, although
Dave Brailsford fell squarely into the former camp. 'Brad
would've gone bloody close,' was his rueful claim in Paris.

The Vuelta would also top up Wiggins' form for the world
championships, which came a little over a week later. For Sky,
the Spanish tour was a race that evoked the very darkest
memories of their debut season, where their *soigneur*, Txema
González, fell ill and died, prompting the team to withdraw en
masse. That had been an act of respect for González, although
it had almost been forced upon them anyway, with the riders
also falling ill. It stood as a bleak and frightening episode in the
team's first year.

When Wiggins was able to return to training it was with the Vuelta – and the Spanish heat – in mind. He prepared on a turbo trainer in his shed with the heaters on full blast. Twelve months after their nadir, Team Sky appeared at the start in Benidorm with the recovered Wiggins, together with a rider who seemed to be on his way out and for whom the Vuelta was less a bike race, more a last-chance saloon.

Chris Froome was described by Brailsford as a 'rough diamond' when he signed him. Born in Kenya to British parents, Shane Sutton identified him as a prospective talent when he saw him compete for Kenya at the 2006 World Championships in Salzburg, where, as though to emphasise just how unpolished he was, he crashed during the Under-23 time trial. In his two seasons with Sky, Froome, who by now had switched his allegiance to Britain, perplexed Brailsford and the coaching staff. In tests he had the 'numbers'. But in races he hadn't delivered.

It should be emphasised that Froome's 'rough'-ness referred purely to his abilities on the bike. Off it, he was friendly, unassuming and unerringly polite; so polite that he seemed almost too nice to be a professional sportsman. At the team's first get together in Manchester, back in 2009, he spoke enthusiastically about his dream of establishing a foundation in Kenya to provide bikes and cycling opportunities for local people. This seemed as, if not more, important to him than any personal ambitions. A couple of months later, at the Tour Down Under, he appeared to struggle to adapt to the role being asked of him by his new team. With his light build, he had a classic climber's frame and wasn't suited to helping with the lead-out train. At times during that first season he resembled a square peg in a round hole. He had previously been in teams with little structure and although eager to fit in – perhaps too eager at times – he often seemed a little out of sorts.

Then, at the end of 2010, he succumbed to a rare infection, bilharzia, which he had picked up swimming in a lake in Kenya. Bilharzia is transmitted by a water-borne parasite or flatworm, and it is, Froome explained, 'very difficult to treat. I think I had had it for just over a year.' The symptoms can be mild, sometimes only a skin irritation, but the effects on Froome were debilitating, with the parasite eating his red blood cells.

'For any endurance athlete it's a nightmare,' he said. 'It's like a virus. You don't sleep properly. You don't recover.' He began treatment in December 2010, to be repeated every six months. It cost him a ride at the Tour de France, but his second course of medicine, after the Tour of Switzerland, seemed to clear his body of the parasite. Now he had a point to prove at the Vuelta. A point he needed to prove, with his contract running out in a few months. Sky had offered him a new deal for 2012 but, at a rumoured £100,000 a year, it was modest. It was worse than that. 'It was effectively "goodbye",' said one insider.

Salamanca, 29 August 2011
The most mountainous Vuelta in years only has one individual time trial, over 47km. It is here, 10 days into the race, that Wiggins is expected to – where he must – lay down a marker. The only other test against the clock, stage one's team time trial, had been a disaster for Wiggins and Sky, with Kurt Asle Arvesen crashing early and the team then imploding on the technical course as four riders, led by Wiggins, became detached at the front, which was a disaster: the time is taken on the fifth rider. What's more, the noise from the crowd meant that Steven de Jongh, the director in the team car, was finding it difficult to relay instructions and tell the front four to ease up. In the end, with Xavier Zando bridging the gap and becoming the fifth man, Sky finished third from last, only managing to beat Geox and the lowly Andalucia Caja Granada, and losing 42 seconds to Leopard Trek.

For a team that specialises in this discipline the team time trial was an out-and-out embarrassment. Chris Sutton restored some pride the next day, winning the sprint into Playas de Orihuela to take the stage, and, in torrid heat, Wiggins then impressed in the mountains that came early in the Vuelta. So did Froome. To the summit of Sierra Nevada, after just four days, Froome set the pace at the head of a dwindling group of favourites, leading Wiggins, who seemed comfortable as they climbed to 2,000 metres. It was early in the race, but in a field that didn't contain any overwhelming favourites – no Contador, no Schleck, no Evans – some already fancied that Wiggins could be the man to beat over the defending champion (and one-time Sky target) Vincenzo Nibali.

Five days later, riding to the finish at the Covatilla ski station, Wiggins did more than follow. Together with Froome he began to string out the lead group, putting strong riders in difficulty on a deceptively tough, crosswind-buffeted drag. He finished fourth and gained precious seconds on Nibali, Denis Menchov and other contenders, prompting the Vuelta director, Javier Guillén, to suggest that Wiggins was emerging as the overall favourite. Twenty-six years after one of the murkiest episodes in Vuelta history, when Robert Millar appeared to be robbed of victory by a Spanish conspiracy on the penultimate day, here, it seemed, was a chance for Wiggins to exact revenge on his countryman's behalf. And it was perhaps a sign of how the sport had changed in the intervening years that Guillén appeared to welcome the prospect.

When Wiggins set off for the next day's time trial, as the fourth last rider to head out on the rolling 47km course around Salamanca, he did so knowing that it was his best chance to gain some serious time and take over the leader's red jersey. The distance and profile were perfect for him – the road climbed steadily from Salamanca towards Morille before looping back to the start. He went out hard, and set the fastest time after 13km, the first checkpoint, passing it a second quicker than Tony Martin. Froome, meanwhile, was also going well, though he trailed Wiggins by 24 seconds.

But the next time check, 17km later, told a very different story: Wiggins was now 19 seconds slower than Martin. More surprisingly, his lead over Froome had collapsed; it was now just one second. Wiggins' distress was barely visible at first, but it gradually became apparent in little tell-tale signs: gently rocking shoulders, face set in an uncomfortable grimace, appearing to gasp for fluid. What began as a challenge for the overall lead became a game of damage limitation; over the final 17km he lost another 1 minute 3 seconds to Martin, and another 33 seconds to Froome. Wiggins would later attribute his decline over the second half to his failure to take into account the fact that the course was close to 1,000 metres above sea level. He rode flat out, he said, and it was impossible to maintain such an effort in oxygen-depleted air. He should have held back.

But one rider who judged his effort to perfection was Froome. While Wiggins wilted, he grew stronger, and at the finish he was second behind Martin, but ahead of Wiggins, who moved up to third overall. And so the rider who became the new overall leader was Chris Froome.

On the podium, where he was presented with the red jersey, Froome looked shell-shocked. In the press conference afterwards he was shaking and appeared to be trembling with nerves. As one journalist observed: 'He seemed to be thinking: what the fuck am I doing here?'

It was a glorious moment for Froome, less so for Wiggins, who finished the time trial in a state of exhaustion, gulping for air like a fish flipped out of the water. The next day was a welcome rest day, when, as well as recuperating, Team Sky could take stock and think about what to do next. Should Wiggins or Froome now lead? Up until now there had been no

Sean Yates, no Shane Sutton, only the relatively junior directors, Marcus Ljunkqvist and Steven de Jongh. On the rest day
Sutton travelled to Spain. For him, the outcome of the time
trial changed nothing. The original game plan would stand.
'It's all about Bradley,' he said.

But that led to a peculiar situation, one that, for some,
offended the sport's etiquette, and disrespected the red jersey.
It would see the leader of the race, who would ordinarily be
protected by his team, effectively sacrifice his own chances for
his team leader. Froome would act as Wiggins' *domestique*,
regardless of his new status. In Froome's position, some riders
would have complained, arguing that they deserved to have
the team at their service. And Froome could have made a good
case; it wasn't as though he had slipped into the red jersey
through luck or chance. On the contrary, he had proved
himself as one of the strongest climbers in the first week and
had claimed the lead in the 'race of truth', a time trial. But
Froome himself echoed Sutton. He said nothing had changed
and that Wiggins was still the team leader.

This led to the arresting spectacle during stage 11 the
following day of Froome, in red, driving the main group up
the final climb to Estación de Montaña Manzaneda while
Wiggins sat comfortably on his wheel, spinning a small gear,
saving his legs for the steeper part of the climb. When that was
reached and the attacks began, Froome chased after them,
absorbing the blows for his team leader, before his legs eventually gave out and he slipped back. At the top, Wiggins finished
in the main 15-man group; Froome trailed in 27 seconds later.
He dropped to second overall. It seemed to matter little at the
time, particularly as Wiggins took over his red jersey. But how
he would later rue those lost seconds. Wiggins, meanwhile,
noted that 'the team did an amazing job all day today' and said
that he 'felt fantastic' and would 'fight every day'. But, he
added, the 'Angliru is probably where it's going to be decided'.

The Asturias climb of the Angliru was added to the Vuelta in 1999 as its answer to the epic climbs of the other Grand Tours: Alpe d'Huez and Mont Ventoux in the Tour de France, the Mortirolo and Passo del Stelvio in the Giro. It isn't the length (12.5km) or the height (1,573m) that makes the Angliru so difficult. It's the steepness – specifically, the severity of the upper slopes. One section, 3km from the top, is 23.6%; the last 7km average 13%. The climb was 'discovered' by Miguel Prieto, who worked for ONCE, the Spanish charity that sponsored the world's best team in the 1990s. In recommending it to the Vuelta organisers, Prieto described 'a mountain whose road is barely marked on maps because it is a cattle road which was only recently paved'; but if included in the race, he added, it was 'guaranteed to leave unforgettable memories burnt into the retinas of the viewers'. The Vuelta organisers were keen. Others were not. Vicente Belda, the Kelme manager, fumed: 'What do they want? Blood? They ask us to stay clean and avoid doping and then they make the riders tackle this kind of barbarity.' In 2002, when it was included once more, this time in driving rain, David Millar, after crashing three times during the stage, stopped before the line and removed his race numbers. 'This is inhuman,' he fumed. 'We're not animals.'

The outcome of the 2011 Vuelta was heading irresistibly towards a showdown on a climb that would come the day before the second and final rest day, and just six days before the finish in Madrid. But before the Angliru there were other ascents. Wiggins feared Nibali, who on one of those days – stage 13 – managed to gain time in a bonus sprint and leapfrog Froome, moving to just four seconds behind Wiggins. But the next day, on another summit finish, Nibali's challenge crumbled. On a new climb, to La Farrapona, Wiggins and Froome managed to clip away from most of the other contenders, finishing in a four-man group 45 seconds behind the winner, Rein Taaramäe of Estonia. This stage to La Farrapona was significant and, because of the severity of the slopes, arguably Wiggins' most telling performance on a mountain stage yet. As Shane Sutton noted, these were not 'Wiggins climbs'. When he had ridden well in the mountains in the past, it had been on long, steady drags where he could use his strength and find a rhythm. Yet here he was taking on, matching and in some cases dropping some of the sport's mountain goats. He was excelling on the kind of steep roads that only pure climbers usually enjoy. Now he led Froome by seven seconds, Juan José Cobo by 55, Jakob Fuglsang by 58, Nibali by 1 minute 25. It augured well for the Angliru.

Approaching the fabled and feared climb, Wiggins was well placed. Froome had again ridden selflessly, not letting his leader out of his sights, marshalling him whenever the road went up. Now Carlos Sastre, the 2008 Tour winner, attacked, beginning the Angliru with a small lead. But this wasn't the Sastre who flew up Alpe d'Huez the year of his Tour victory; he laboured as riders were dropped behind him and the group thinned. Nibali was again in trouble. But Wiggins looked easy and relaxed. Dan Martin of Garmin counter-attacked. So did Igor Anton, causing some chaos and painful changes of pace, but it was another rider who set off alarm bells. Cobo, a Geox teammate of Sastre, moved stealthily towards the front.

Cobo was a pure climber who was less than a minute down overall. He was dangerous but Wiggins was alert. He accelerated smoothly around the outside of the small group, reaching the front, slotting in behind Cobo, marking him. They were 6.5km from the summit and Cobo knew that the road was about to get steeper. Sastre's earlier attack had been a tactic designed to help him. The ideal scenario would see Sastre carve out a lead, Cobo bridge the gap to him and for the two of them to ride together. That might not happen. Sastre was fading fast but Cobo was maintaining the pace. As the slope steepened to a gradient of 22%, he remained in his saddle, pressed a little harder – the slopes of the Angliru are not condusive to dramatic attacks – and opened a small gap to Wiggins.

Wiggins didn't respond. He knew that a big effort here would put him in the red zone, and he would pay for it later. He had to ride at his own rhythm. He had to let Cobo go. But Cobo, whose most notable performance to date had been on the climb to Hautacam during the 2008 Tour de France, was turning the pedals easily. The steepness of the climb didn't seem to trouble him, neither did the banks of supporters, packed on to the narrow road, parting only at the last possible moment. It was reminiscent of that climb to Hautacam, during which he shadowed his flying teammate, Leonardo Piepoli, who won the stage, only to later be disqualified for doping. Cobo would later inherit the victory but his triumph was tarnished when his entire Saunier Duval team was forced out of the race following Riccardo Riccò's positive test, amid suspicion that doping was widespread in the Spanish squad.

As the Angliru wound up the mountain-side, Froome, seeing that Wiggins was isolated and chasing Cobo alone, accelerated to join him. He positioned himself at the front of the group, and in what was becoming a familiar style – hunched back, long arms hooked and grabbing the bars as though he was trying to bend them – he led Wiggins, his leader. The gradient eased to 10%, 11%, and the gap to Cobo, with 3.5km remaining, was 25 seconds. That was manageable. But as the road steepened again and the crowds thickened, Wiggins began to fight his bike. He wobbled. He received a push from a Spanish fan – in stark contrast to Robert Millar's experience in 1985, when he was spat at for daring to challenge a Spaniard. Froome continued to lead Wiggins. The road ramped up again to 20%. Cobo pressed on, still looking strong. There were 2km left and they continued to zig-zag up the lush, green mountain. Behind, through the narrow corridor of spectators, Wout Poels and Menchov – the only riders able to match the pace set by Froome in the chasing group – started to apply some pressure. Froome responded but Wiggins couldn't hold on to him and slipped back. With a kilometre to go Cobo led by 1.10. On the line it was 48 seconds over Poels, Menchov and Froome, with Wiggins a further 33 seconds back. Cobo now led Froome by 20 seconds, with Wiggins in third, a further 26 seconds down.

Now, on the second rest day, there was a reassessment. Was it still 'all about Bradley'? It seemed clear that Froome was better placed than Wiggins to try and win the Vuelta, for one simple reason: he was the stronger climber. The Spanish press agreed, with some commentators questioning the decision to have Froome support Wiggins when the former was in red, and the daily newspaper *As* declaring Froome 'the real strong man of Sky'. So the decision was made: Sky would fight on two fronts, with two protected leaders, but Wiggins was to ride in support of Froome if the current pattern was maintained.

Three days later Froome proved that the Angliru was no fluke; that it did reveal who was the strongest climber. At the end of a thrilling stage, during which Froome launched a 'furious offensive' (*As* again), he and Cobo fought it out at Peña Cabarga, in Cobo's home region. It was the final uphill finish on the longest stage of the race, and it came down, on the short, steep climb to the finish, to Froome against Cobo. As Froome attacked in the final 2km, Cobo struggled to respond, and Wiggins just struggled, slipping out of the back of the group. Slowly Cobo clawed his way back to Froome. But Froome didn't let up and kept the pressure on. And with him the effort showed: he was ungainly, his eyes bulged, he sucked in air, his upper body rocked, and Cobo, though smoother, was forced to dig deep to defend his jersey. As the gap between them opened, and it seemed that Froome might be riding into the lead, there were echoes of past Vueltas, 1985 in particular, as a couple of Cobo fans ran alongside the British rider, yelling into his ear: 'If you win, we kill you.'

Cobo came back to Froome, and went past him in the final 200 metres, only for Froome to respond once more, and take Cobo on the final bend to win the stage. 'One of the hardest days on the bicycle of my life,' he said at the finish. But also the best. 'It was the last mountain-top finish and both Bradley and myself came into the stage trying to do as much as we could,' he explained. Then he shrugged: 'But as you could see, Cobo was so strong and he holds the jersey by 13 seconds.'

As for the team plan: 'Some days Bradley is stronger and other days I'm stronger; the team has been fantastic – it's been a real team effort.' It is 'too easy' to say that if he had not worked for Wiggins, he would have led the Vuelta. 'What I can say is that I learned a lot these last few weeks working for Wiggins. I am very proud. There are no regrets.'

As Froome became the revelation of the Vuelta, there was, inevitably, a sub-plot to his battle for the red jersey. It concerned which team he would ride for the following season, since it emerged that he had not signed a new contract with Sky. Even before the Vuelta finished he had become hot property; not only did he seem to be emerging as a possible Grand Tour contender – of whom there are precious few – but he was, in the process, scooping up enough world ranking points to catapult some teams (were they to sign him) from the lower depths to the upper reaches of the UCI world rankings. For some, signing a rider with Froome's points' tally could be the difference between gaining an invitation to the Tour de France and being snubbed. No wonder there was significant interest. Naturally, Froome was aware of this – and distracted by it. Shane Sutton offered counsel. Froome felt he had some life-changing decisions to make, as well as a Grand Tour to concentrate on. During the Vuelta he was apparently made a tentative offer by RadioShack, worth €750,000 a year; but that was dwarfed by the €1.4m allegedly offered by French team Ag2r, a figure that Astana said they would match. Sky's offer of £100,000 looked derisory.

Meanwhile, the Vuelta was still there for the taking. Froome's final chance to snatch the jersey from Cobo came with two days to go, on the very last climb of the race. Wiggins, now acting in a supporting role, tried to set him up for the attack on the Alto El Vivero, riding hard at the front. Froome tried to repeat his 'furious offensive' but the climb was not hard enough, and Cobo had little difficulty following. In fact, he shadowed him all the way to Madrid, the gap remaining a small but unbridgeable 13 seconds, while Wiggins held on to third, one minute 39 seconds behind Cobo. It was the first time two British riders had finished on the podium of a Grand Tour; indeed, it was the first podium finish for any Brit since Robert Millar's second in the Giro d'Italia in 1987. And yet it was tinged with a little regret. Could Froome have won? Perhaps, if he hadn't been forced to work for Wiggins while wearing the red jersey himself; if he hadn't lost those 27 seconds after flogging himself on the climb to the ski station of Covatilla; if he hadn't expended so much energy helping his leader on the lower slopes of the Angliru, and gone off in pursuit of Cobo a little earlier.

Then again, Froome himself wasn't so sure he would even have been in those positions had he not been there to help Wiggins. 'In a way, riding with Bradley kept me in that lead group without doing any huge efforts to be there,' he said later. 'I think previously if I'd found myself in that position I'd have maybe got excited or carried away and started attacking. I think I need to be a bit more conservative and wait until the last moment to make my move. I actually think Bradley and I work really well together; and maybe by my being there, it takes the pressure off his shoulders a little bit.'

Brailsford and Team Sky thought the same, because they worked hard after the Vuelta to tie Froome to a long-term contract. A five-year deal was rumoured. In the end, he signed for three years, for a rumoured £1.2m a year, 12 times the salary he had been offered just a few weeks earlier.

And what of Wiggins? In Madrid, alongside Cobo and Froome, he hardly appeared delighted with his first-ever podium finish in a Grand Tour. Yet this result confirmed his best-ever season on the road and – following his fourth in the 2009 Tour – it reaffirmed his status as a Grand Tour contender. Fourteen months earlier he had wondered aloud whether 2009 was a fluke; now he had done it twice he knew he could perform over three weeks. But there were still a number of 'what ifs?' And the elephant in the room was the Froome factor. He had been outshone by a teammate; and what's more, a British teammate. That hadn't been in the script. But then, neither had crashing out of the Tour. Wiggins needed to cut himself some slack. Forty-three days before the Vuelta he had been lying on a road in France, nursing a fractured collarbone.

Some weeks later I asked Wiggins about the Vuelta, whether he had come to terms with his result there, and what it meant. 'It gave me a lot of answers,' he said. 'I wasn't at my physical best; I was still nursing my shoulder. It gave us a lot of information.' He was talking like an accountant. But emotionally, what did it mean? 'In terms of performance, it was ...' He paused. 'You look back, it's a great performance for third place, but there's a lot to take from it.' He pointed out that he hadn't prepared for the Vuelta, either physically or mentally; he hadn't even studied the route. That made a difference, he said. 'I think in hindsight I'd have gone and looked at the Angliru and trained for the demands of it because I probably lost the Vuelta there. I'd probably have gone and looked at the time trial and taken into account that it was at 1,000m altitude and not gone out like it was at sea level and blown up.

'And I probably wouldn't have crashed at the Tour and broken my collarbone …'

Brailsford, when I spoke to him, was more effusive. The overall team performance at the Vuelta was, he said, 'massive, massive'. Had Froome's performance surprised him? After all, it surprised a lot of people and it had led, inevitably, to some questions – and even suspicion. The Vuelta had been bedevilled in recent years by drugs scandals. Froome, when asked about this in an interview with *Cyclingnews*, said: 'I'm not bothered by any suspicion, I think it's normal that people suspect and ask, "Where did this guy come from?" But in my mind [drugs] is not even an option for me. I feel really strongly about clean cycling and I very strongly shun anyone who's dragging the sport through the mud.' Indeed, he had direct experience of this at his previous team, Barloworld, when a colleague, Moisés Dueñas, tested positive for EPO during the 2008 Tour. The morning after Dueñas's expulsion, I spoke to Froome, who said he was shocked and that Dueñas seemed 'a nice guy'. He then suggested that jail sentences might be an appropriate punishment for doping offenders.

Brailsford did admit to being surprised by Froome but for very different reasons. 'The question with Chris wasn't "Wow, where did that come from?" It was his performances *before* the Vuelta that didn't stack up. He has outstanding numbers. So the question was: what was stopping him from performing like that before? There was the parasite thing, he was ill; that held him back. But we weren't seeing his physical ability translated into performances.' Brailsford thought that riding in support of Wiggins actually helped him. 'Brad's a master, now, of judging his effort. I think Froomy learned from that and the light went on. The penny dropped.'

Brailsford was more than satisfied to place two riders on the podium in Madrid, albeit he'd have swapped second and third for first. But what about Wiggins? Was he happy? Brailsford paused again. 'Bradley being Bradley, I think … I think he was disappointed. Because he knew how close he came to winning overall. But when he stands back and looks at it, it's a podium. It's a breakthrough for Brad. Everyone says he can only climb 7–8% mountains; people say anything steeper isn't a Bradley climb, but he was holding his own … and he's put to bed the idea that he never attacks.

'It's massive for us as a team,' Brailsford added. 'You want strength in numbers at the end on these mountain stages. The more the better. That's why we want Chris at the Tour de France with Brad.'

For Wiggins, though, the Vuelta was not, he came to feel, the outstanding performance of his 2011 season. 'The best, the one that gave me the most satisfaction, was the world championships,' he would later reflect. 'No one gave us a cat in hell's chance. Even three, four hours into the road race, on the internet forums and all that, they were saying we were a bunch of wankers for going out too hard …'

A couple of days before the men's Men's Road Race at the 2011 Road World Championships in Copenhagen, Rod Ellingworth accompanied Mark Cavendish and the British team on a training ride around the circuit. Ellingworth was on a motorbike, leading them into the final 500 metres at close to race speed.

That evening Cavendish came to speak to Ellingworth. 'I've got to come from further back,' Cavendish said. Ellingworth says now that 'Cav was thinking of the Tour de France stage to Cap Fréhel, which finished up a little drag'. That had been a stage in which Cavendish, without his usual lead-out train, appeared late and from nowhere to pip Philippe Gilbert on a finish that looked tailor-made for Gilbert.

In the hotel in Copenhagen, Cavendish told Ellingworth: 'I can definitely win if I come from behind. If I'm popped up at the front, I ain't gonna win.'

Now, Ellingworth reflects: 'In our pre-race briefing notes it says, very clearly, Mark must be 8th or 10th coming into the final 200, 300 metres.'

The road race got under way with Wiggins having already produced what he calls the time trial of his life to finish second to Tony Martin, beating the four-time world champion Fabian Cancellara for the silver medal. The time trial followed just nine days after the Vuelta, and Wiggins' performance helped him make a major decision. He had been wrestling with a track-versus-road dilemma for 2012, originally imagining that he would form part of the team pursuit quartet who would defend their gold medal at the London Olympics. But Copenhagen changed all that. The gap between the Tour de France and Olympic time trial was roughly the same as between the Vuelta and world championships: 10 days. He had maintained his form for more or less that period between Spain and Denmark, or even improved on it. That gave him a blueprint. He would abandon the track to focus instead on an ambitious double: yellow at the Tour, gold in London.

Four days after the time trial, Wiggins was one of the eight-man British team, led by Cavendish, that began the road race in Copenhagen. When the least hilly course in years had been confirmed a few years earlier, it was identified as one for the sprinters. And as far back as November 2008, with Cavendish having proved himself as the fastest man in the world with his four stage wins at the Tour, it was identified by Ellingworth as one for Cavendish. Ellingworth formulated a plan, dubbed 'Project Rainbow Jersey', with regular get-togethers for prospective team members. At one, he produced a prop: the

1965 world champion's jersey, the very garment won by Tom Simpson, the only previous British winner. 'This,' Ellingworth told his riders, 'is what you're aiming for. It's not just about winning a bike race; it's about making history.'

On the day, there was nothing sophisticated or clever about the British team's tactics. The intelligence had all gone into the planning and taking care of the small details that might make a difference. The clothing, for example, is different at a world championships from the pro team clothing a rider wears all year round. So the riders were issued their British team clothing early, so they could get used to wearing it – especially the shorts.

In the past, the management had also been unfamiliar to the riders, although this was less of an issue in Copenhagen, where six of the eight-man team were from Team Sky. It was a very different set of circumstances to Madrid in 2005, where two of the British riders – Tom Southam and Charly Wegelius – wore GB colours but rode for Italy, and earned themselves a slap on the wrist for doing so from Brailsford. In those days, Brailsford admitted, he and his coaches felt like fish out of water. 'I loved going to the world road championships back then,' said Brailsford, 'because it was such a step up; it's the biggest one-day race in the world and it was an opportunity to be in that milieu. But it wasn't the day job. It feels very, very different now, when it's your day job, and you know the people in that world. It now feels more comfortable; it's like being at one of the big classics.

'But I must admit, with hindsight, you think – in the past – "What was I thinking of?"'

There were plenty of other people, crowded around televisions, who asked the same question – 'What are they thinking of?' – as the Men's Road Race entered its second hour, third hour, fourth hour. Almost since the very start, the race was controlled by one team: Great Britain. Chris Froome and

Steve Cummings were the riders assigned to sit at the front of the peloton in the early part of the race, helping maintain a pace that would keep any breakaways in check. The inevitable early escape contained seven riders; a second move, 140km into the 260km race, contained stronger riders, five in total, including the Paris-Roubaix winner Johan Vansummeren. But the GB game plan was clear: Froome and Cummings were still the men leading, always among the first few riders. Jeremy Hunt shepherded Cavendish, remaining at his side on the circuit's only climb, which was better described as a bump than a mountain. On each 14km lap Cavendish started the climb placed towards the front, easing up as it progressed, until he was close to the rear of the peloton by the top. It allowed him to climb slower than most of the others and it conserved some energy. Then Hunt would escort him back to the front. David Millar, meanwhile, acted as on-the-road captain, communicating with Ellingworth and the coaches, relaying messages to the riders. Into the final hour of the race it had gone exactly to plan. What's more, Cavendish had avoided the big crash that eliminated the defending world champion, Thor Hushovd.

Now the dangerous attacks started. Tommy Voeckler, a hero at the 2011 Tour de France, had a go, and was joined by Klaas Lodewyck of Belgium and Nicki Sorensen of Denmark, but they were kept in check, barely allowed out of sight of the British-led peloton. Millar was spending a lot of time at the front, shadowed by Ian Stannard and Geraint Thomas, the strong men coming to the fore at this late stage of a race for which the schedule had gone out the window – it would finish around an hour earlier than expected. Now Wiggins stepped up and led the chasers for the last time up the drag to the finish, with Cavendish, for once, not slipping back, but remaining attentive near the front. Wiggins almost single-handedly brought Voeckler to heel. Then he swung over, allowing Millar to take over again, before, into the final 12km, he took it on again. His effort here was immense as he sat on the front, stringing the bunch out behind him. A Philippe Gilbert or Fabian Cancellara attack was now expected; it was what Ellingworth most feared. But the only riders waving goodbye to the peloton were dropping out of the back, not attacking off the front. The reason? Wiggins.

Arguably no team had ever ridden the world road race in such a fashion before. Perhaps the Italians in 2002, when Mario Cipollini – the last pure sprinter to win the world road title – enjoyed the full support of the *Azzurri*. Certainly no British team had ridden like this before, and taken it on with such commitment – more than that, with such absolute conviction. Cavendish had told them that if they stuck to the plan and did their jobs, he would win. His confidence seemed to rub off. And now Wiggins was doing the ride of his life to keep it together, to prevent any late attacks and ensure that the riders would all be together for the sprint.

As it wound up, Cavendish was nowhere. It was chaotic, in contrast to the relative order usually imposed by his pro team, HTC-Highroad, upon such finishes. As mentioned, Wiggins would later, much later, observe, 'They were saying we were a bunch of wankers for going out too hard.' How did he know? Perhaps he was told. Or perhaps he trawled the internet forums and Twitter, smiling at what some of the armchair fans had been saying about Britain's tactics. They said it again as the finish approached, and the Australians hit the front, setting up Matt Goss. Thomas and Stannard were up near the front, but where was Cavendish? All that effort for nothing. Five-and-a-half hours of controlling the race, only for the British team to lose the plot in the final 300 metres …

But Cavendish was in eighth place, as he had told Ellingworth he needed to be. Then, suddenly, he appeared, his compact body bent low over the front end of his bike, head down, out the saddle, sprinting, emerging on the right shoulder of his HTC teammate, Goss. The unfamiliar GB team kit made Cavendish difficult to spot. He wore a skinsuit and a helmet that appeared to be covered in cling-film to give him an aerodynamic advantage at precisely this point, as he hit the front for the first time in over five hours. As Goss led, Cavendish came up on his right, sneaking between him and the barriers. Then, only then, did he seem the likely winner. And in the blink of an eye, victory became inevitable. Arms in the air. Cavendish. World champion. Project Rainbow Jersey accomplished.

Finally, 15 days after his world title win, Cavendish's signing for Team Sky was confirmed. It hit some last-minute snags, with problems arising over his long-term personal sponsorship deals with Nike (Team Sky is sponsored by Adidas) and his preference for the Specialized bikes he had spent the previous two seasons on (Sky had a long-term deal with Pinarello). He had also, apparently on the advice of Lance Armstrong, signed with a new management agency, the global Wasserman Media Group. Eight days before the signing was finally confirmed, I asked Brailsford why it hadn't been announced in the days after Copenhagen, in the warm afterglow of a world title win that had seemed to capture the imagination of the British public – with the teamwork behind the victory a source of fascination and bafflement – and catapulted Cavendish into the mainstream, and on to the sofas of some of the country's most popular TV shows. 'I think,' said Brailsford cagily, 'that there's a lot more going on than people realise.'

Finally, though, it was settled. Cavendish batted away questions about the drawn-out nature of the negotiations. He told me it hadn't felt drawn out. 'Not really, I think it was just dragging on for everybody else. But from past experience I have to make sure every single word in the contract is right. Every single word had to be right.' Past experience? He had only signed one significant contract in the past, with Highroad during the 2008 Tour. 'Say something happened,' said Cavendish. 'Say Dave or Rod gets hit by a bus in a couple of years and that's not in the contract; you know, someone else takes over.' So the main thing was that they were in charge? 'Yeah, I know those guys. It's exciting. I'm coming home. They're guys I grew up racing with; the riders and management.'

On 4 January 2012 – two years to the day since Team Sky's glitzy launch in central London – Cavendish was officially unveiled as a Team Sky rider, this time at a low-key press conference staged in a quiet hotel near Heathrow. But the big questions were how he and Wiggins would get on, and how the team would accommodate two riders with such different aspirations, one to win stages of the Tour and the green jersey, the other to win yellow. When he's asked, Cavendish shrugs: 'You should ask Dave that.'

In fact, he and Wiggins hadn't got off to the best of starts as teammates. While Cavendish had woken at 6am to travel to Heathrow from Essex, Wiggins had been late. When he appeared, he didn't have his bike, his cycling shoes or his 2012 team kit for the photo shoot. Cavendish was annoyed and accused him of a lack of professionalism. It hadn't all been Wiggins' fault. He had been booked on the wrong flight, for one thing. But the spat with Cavendish seemed to affect his mood. 'All this crap about goals, and speculation about us going for yellow and green,' he said testily when asked whether it was realistic for the team to target green and yellow at the Tour. 'That might not necessarily be the case.'

He explained: 'It may become apparent in June that I'm not capable of doing that. At this stage it's just way too early to say, "These are the goals, this is what we're going to do." If I crash in the Dauphiné, I might not even be at the Tour.'

Puerto Alcudia, Majorca, January 2012

First thing in the morning, before breakfast, Dave Brailsford gets up, takes his bike and, dressed head-to-toe in Team Sky kit, heads out into the chill Majorcan air. He likes to ride on his own, although sometimes he is joined by Shane Sutton, at other times by Tim Kerrison. After breakfast, when he follows the squad on their training rides, he prefers to drive a car on his own. And when he came to the same island with his partner and daughter for a two-week holiday following the previous year's Tour de France, he rented a house surrounded by high walls. He says he likes to cut himself off. It gives him thinking time.

There's a lot to think about. In the otherwise deserted hotel that Team Sky has taken over, occupying it from December to the end of January, there's a drop-in arrangement. Riders come and go, but you always know when Cavendish is *in situ*. In the evenings his laughter and expletive-peppered banter reverberates from the games room behind the bar, echoing off the polished marble floors. His personality seems to lift the place, and the people, as though the out-of-season resort is transformed from grey to Technicolor.

It seems natural, logical, that the *enfant terrible* has ended up at Team Sky. 'Any team would be crazy to sign Cavendish,' as Brailsford, with heavy irony, had noted during the Tour de France. Yet there is the suspicion that the Vuelta has changed the game again; that the original attraction of Cavendish, with whom negotiations had been going on for the best part of a year, was guaranteed wins and headlines. But now, with Wiggins and Froome, the big prize – yellow at the Tour – might actually be in reach, and earlier than originally thought.

Which raises the nagging question – how to accommodate both Cavendish and Wiggins (and Froome)? Many believe that in the modern era it's simply not possible to double up and go for green and yellow. It divides resources – or spreads them too thinly – and asks far too much of the riders. These days a team targeting general classification rarely takes a sprinter. At HTC Cavendish had a full squad behind him on the flat stages – two riders to sit at the front and control the tempo in the early stages, a five- or six-man lead-out train in the finale – and he will surely desire the same at Sky. But equally, Wiggins – or Froome – will require several strong allies in the mountains and the backing of the full team if either of them finds himself in yellow. Cavendish is bullish. 'If I didn't think it was possible I wouldn't have come,' he insists. Here at the camp he and Wiggins get on well; there's a lot of joking and laughter and opportunities for Wiggins to hone his Cavendish impersonation, which is close to perfect anyway. Yet the camp, and the social aspect to it, also exposes their very different personalities. Like some actors or comedians, Wiggins' impersonations might act as a front for his shyness. At other times he is introverted and happy – when he isn't mimicking his colleagues – to sink into the background. It extends to ceding responsibility for his training and preparation. 'I'm a gerbil on a treadmill,' he says, with the pace of the treadmill controlled by Team Wiggins: Sutton, Kerrison and Richard Freeman. It seems to suit him. 'I find it easier for me,' says Wiggins. 'Doing it all myself in 2010, that's where it all went wrong.'

In contrast, Cavendish is an extrovert, and more comfortable in the role of leader. Responsibility suits him. When I ask him if he ever suffers moments of doubt or uncertainty, his brow furrows. He looks puzzled. Then he replies: 'No.'

In the evening, Brailsford sits in a corner of the bar, beside an un-played piano, looking out through conservatory windows onto a deserted, darkening beach. Sounds from the games room – the clink of balls being smashed on the pool table, the Cavendish banter – interrupt his conversation, but not his train of thought, which is firmly back on track. Team

Sky's second season has restored his reputation and returned his ebullience. As if to demonstrate this, Brailsford mentions some of the 'leaders' he has met and in some cases befriended from other sports, including Billy Beane. Beane, of course, is the general manager of the Oakland 'A's baseball team, as well as the star of *Moneyball*, the book (and now film, starring Brad Pitt) that Brailsford cited as inspiration when he set up Team Sky.

On the Cavendish–Wiggins conundrum, he says he is relaxed. 'Personally I don't think it will be as much of a problem as people make out, I really don't.'

I ask him if he feels vindicated, especially by the double-podium performance at the Vuelta. 'I don't think vindicated is the word. But ... you know when you're really convinced about something because you look at the numbers and the logic, and you work it all out, and think: There. Is. No. Reason. Why. A. British. Rider. Cannot. Win. A. Grand. Tour. In. The. Next. Five. Years, as I said a couple of years back. I really got shot down in flames on this. And when the first year didn't work out, people thought we were a long way off the mark. But now I think people actually think it is possible. Nobody is saying it's pie in the sky.'

But the original aim hadn't been to win a Grand Tour. It was to win the Tour de France. 'Well, at the Tour, I said I thought Brad would have gone bloody close and I maintain that,' says Brailsford. 'The essence is that this is a do-able thing. The Vuelta shows we have the right guys, the right momentum. The question now is, how do we translate that into the yellow jersey at the Tour?'

So that remains the priority? 'Yeah.'

Brailsford identifies Kerrison as the man to talk about how it can be achieved. His has been a remarkable rise, or journey to the very centre of the team. Yet Kerrison remains as reserved and unassuming as he was during the recce in the Alps, in the early days of his involvement, when his learning curve seemed as steep as the Angliru. Now, when asked about that founding mission – having a British rider in yellow in Paris – he raises his eyebrows and measures his words carefully. 'I think,' he says, 'if you'd asked me 12 months ago, after 2010, whether it was possible, I would have wondered whether we had too many things against us. But especially after seeing the events of the last 12 months, seeing the guys race in the Vuelta, and guys like Chris Froome come through this system, and the type of training we're doing, I think, I think, that we aim to be at the forefront of training and support … and I think we're well on our way to achieving that … And I think it is realistic, yes.'

Kerrison says he identified three significant obstacles to that founding ambition: the ability to cope with the heat; the ability to cope with the mountains; and the ability to cope with the altitude. 'British riders are not typically exposed to these things,' he says. 'For me, these are the three key things to performing in a Grand Tour.' It sounds so simple. He shrugs almost apologetically and says something he has told me before: 'Physiology is physiology.'

As ever, there is beauty in simplicity. While sports science is often thought to complicate things, Kerrison – like Ellingworth, in fact, or Shane Sutton – likes to break it all down and make it simple. But his role highlights two consistent convictions of the Brailsford-led Team Sky: the unflappable faith in science and the unerring belief in 'numbers' as holding the key to performance. Allied to an obsession with planning, always looking forward, without pause, letting the momentum carry you – like a gerbil on a treadmill, almost.

Planning, planning, planning.

'We're planning for Rio at the moment,' says Brailsford. Rio? 'The Rio Olympics in 2016,' he says. He's not joking, though most expect Brailsford to step away from the British team after the London Games, and devote all his time to Team Sky. Yet he insists, for the moment, that Rio is on his mind. 'We're spending quite a lot of time on that at the moment, actually. The London Olympics are going to come and go. And while they're going on, you've got to be thinking about the Vuelta and the world championships in the Netherlands.

'You know, I've been to two Olympics now. It's a moment in time, but life goes on.'

CHAPTER 16

LA PROMENADE DES ANGLAIS

Liège, 29 June 2012

'It's amazing how many more of you there are than at the last two Tours,' said Dave Brailsford, surveying a conference room in a hotel on the outskirts of Liège that was teeming with journalists and TV crews. 'I suppose that's a good thing.'

It was the Team Sky pre-Tour press conference. 'As we sit here on the eve of the Tour de France,' continued Brailsford, like a chief executive addressing the company AGM, 'it's a good time to reflect and say that we're ready, we're in great shape, we've assembled one of the strongest teams in the world, and we're looking forward to the next three weeks.'

Alongside Brailsford on the top table were all nine of the Team Sky riders: Kanstantsin Siutsou, Michael Rogers, Richie Porte, Christian Knees, Bernhard Eisel, Edvald Boasson Hagen, Chris Froome and, sitting side by side in the centre of the table, Mark Cavendish and Bradley Wiggins. Unusually it was Cavendish, rather than Wiggins, who seemed self-conscious and awkward. It was the first pre-Tour press conference at which he had not been the centre of attention.

In the weeks leading up to the Tour all the talk of supporting both Wiggins and Cavendish in their ambitions, of going for the yellow and green jerseys, had been quietly shelved. It had never been announced, had barely been acknowledged, but the 200 or so people in the room in the hotel in Liège knew that the subject would be a conversational cul-de-sac. Even Cavendish had been forced to admit in London a few days earlier that yellow would come first. He would be happy to play a supporting role, he said, 'because the yellow jersey is the pinnacle of our sport, and it would be an incredible thing to be part of'. But for him that meant not having a lead-out train. He could still win stages, he said, 'but I won't be guaranteed them'. He would have to use his initiative; he would have to improvise; he would have to take his chances.

The confidence felt by Brailsford and Cavendish in Wiggins and his ability to challenge for yellow was well placed. Wiggins arrived in Liège in the middle of an extraordinary season, having won Paris-Nice, the Tour de Romandie and success-fully defended his Critérium du Dauphiné title. It was a run of victories that not even the great Eddy Merckx had achieved, establishing Wiggins as the best stage racer in the world and the favourite for the Tour. It was a status he appeared to be relishing, which marked a big change from the reluctant leader who lined up for the Tour in 2010. 'I'm very confident of where I'm at,' said Wiggins. 'I'm the best I've been physically. All the tests confirm I'm in the form of my life.'

– In fact, he had made similar noises in Rotterdam two years earlier, claiming his 'numbers' were as good as they had ever been. And maybe they were, but clearly that had not been enough as his challenge collapsed in the mountains. There was something very different about Wiggins in Liège. Even members of his entourage admitted they had never seen him so relaxed. He was Zen-like on the eve of the biggest race of his life, and his words were underpinned by confidence and self-assurance. When he spoke, it wasn't as though he was trying to convince us of something. He seemed actually to believe it.

Whatever happened over the next three weeks, history had already been made. A British rider had never started the Tour as the outright favourite. 'You're not supposed to be a favourite for the Tour de France if you're a kid from Kilburn,' said Wiggins. 'You're supposed to become a postman or a milkman or work in Ladbrokes.'

There was a limit to how much Wiggins relished sitting in a hot conference room discussing all this, though. 'It's all propaganda, isn't it?' he said, throwing up his hands in a gesture that said: give me a break. 'I know you've got column inches to fill, and we could sit here and talk about it all day, but what happens over the next three weeks is what matters, innit?'

Belfort, 8 July 2012

Dave Brailsford looked a satisfied man as he strolled towards the team bus in Belfort. The previous evening had seen Team Sky stay in a hotel overlooking the Village Départ for stage nine, allowing for a leisurely start to the day – transfers are usually an hour or longer. While the riders pedalled to the bus, Brailsford walked, and talked. He couldn't wipe the smile off his face. For the first time, he had a Tour de France yellow jersey on his team. Wiggins had become the fifth British rider – after Tom Simpson, Chris Boardman, Sean Yates and David Millar – to lead the great race after the previous day's stage to La Planches des Belles Filles.

After finishing second to Fabian Cancellara in the prologue time trial, Wiggins stayed out of trouble in the first week. Mainly, he had done this by riding directly behind the giant German, Christian Knees, whose job it was to look after him on the flat stages, as Michael Barry had done in 2010. In head-on shots of the peloton you would often see Knees off to one side, with Wiggins behind him, as though this pair were detached from the others, riding their own race. Knees spent most of that first week riding in the wind. 'But as long as Bradley's happy, I'm happy,' he said.

And Wiggins had avoided the crashes, so he was happy, too. But the team was a man down; Siutsou fell on stage three, breaking his leg. Another setback had been for Froome, who punctured in the closing kilometres of stage one and lost one minute, 25 seconds. It seemed insignificant at the time. It would prove anything but.

Then there was Cavendish. On the first sprinters' stage, to Tournai, he might not have had a lead-out train, but he used all his cunning and guile, as well as improvisational skills, to put himself in a winning position. It involved ducking and diving, jumping from wheel to wheel, disappearing into gaps that other riders don't want you to disappear into, and in the end squeezing out his old nemesis, André Greipel, to win his 21st stage.

The next day he crashed heavily. As well as not winning so frequently, there was always an increased risk of this, too, in the absence of a lead-out train to support and protect him. He picked himself up and finished the stage, scowling, his world champion's jersey torn and bloody, and that night told Rod Ellingworth: 'That's it. I'm not sprinting any more. I'm done.'

A little later Ellingworth asked him if, in that case, he would not be wanting to go over the video of the next day's finish with his coach. He had come round, and agreed to watch the finish and make plans for the next day's expected bunch sprint. But he remained unhappy.

Sky had a plan to strike on stage seven, to La Planche des Belles Filles. They hoped to catch their rivals unawares. It was in the Vosges mountains, the first hilltop finish, but the final uphill was a particular kind of climb: not particularly steep or long, at most a 20-minute effort. On the approach their riders packed the front: Boasson Hagen led on the descent before the road started to rise, then Rogers took over at the foot of the climb, before his fellow Australian, Porte, hit the front and set a pace that put a lot of riders in trouble. Some of the overall contenders began to lose contact, among them Frank Schleck,

Ivan Basso, Levi Leipheimer, Samuel Sanchez and Thomas Voeckler. In the car behind, Brailsford was counting the bodies falling out the back – 'There goes Schleck, there goes Sanchez' – and rubbing his hands.

With 2km to go, Froome took over. Now there were only five riders left in the lead group: Wiggins, the defending champion Cadel Evans, Vincenzo Nibali and Rein Taaramäe. Close to the summit where the road steepened, Evans kicked, but Froome responded, and provided Brailsford with an image he would savour. 'The camera was pointing at the brow of the hill,' he said later, 'and you couldn't see the riders; then you could just see Froomey's helmet rising, like a helicopter gradually appearing in the shot. And I knew, when I saw that. I knew.' Froome won the stage, Evans was second and Wiggins was third, taking over the yellow jersey from Cancellara. 'There's no point in trying to be cocky or smart,' he said in response to questions about whether he had taken it too early and might 'loan it out' to another rider who wouldn't pose a threat over the three weeks. 'We're going to respect the jersey and defend it.'

Wiggins was surprised at the damage his team had done. 'I thought there'd be about 15 guys at the summit. I expected more to be there, so I told Chris to slow down a bit and save something to go for the stage win.'

There's nothing Brailsford likes more than a well-executed plan, of course. It's why he was in such good humour the next morning in Belfort. How had he celebrated? 'I got absolutely plastered,' he said. He was joking but, unusually, he said he was determined to enjoy the moment. He was also realistic: there were still two weeks to go. 'It's like scoring a goal in the first five minutes of a football match, isn't it? The most dangerous thing is that you go to sleep when it kicks off again.

'But I must admit,' continued Brailsford, 'last night we sat back and told everybody: "These things don't come around very often." Over the years of the Olympics and whatnot we've been very quick to move on to the next thing, and we've not stopped and thought about it. Maybe I'm getting older, but last night I said: "Okay, stop. Let's have 10 or 15 minutes to reflect and enjoy this moment." You know, in Beijing I was so worried about the next thing that I didn't enjoy it. You get to the end and it's passed you by.'

After his first day in yellow, Wiggins was asked about rumours that had been circulating on Twitter, alleging that he and Team Sky were doping. The suspicion was mainly aroused by his and the team's performances, particularly their domination of the Dauphiné, in which four Sky riders had finished in the top 10. Cycling fans are inclined to be sceptical when one team appears so much stronger than the others, and, given the recent history of the sport, with good reason.

But there had also been a story in the cycling press in May that gave cause for anxiety and provided fuel for rumour-mongers. The story concerned a Belgian doctor, Geert Leinders, who had worked with Sky on an 80-day-a-year contract since late 2010. Leinders had been appointed after their debut Vuelta, when Txema González died and several riders were struck by an unrelated illness. After that, Brailsford felt he needed a doctor with experience of working with cyclists in a professional team. But in May 2012 it was alleged by the former Rabobank manager, Theo de Rooy, that doping had been tolerated at the Dutch team in the mid-2000s. One of the doctors on that team had been Leinders.

It was a story that had been simmering away in the background. When Brailsford was asked about Leinders at the Tour, he said: 'I categorically, 100% say that there's no risk of anything untoward happening in this team since he has been with us. I'd put my life on it. He's done nothing wrong here, but we have a reputational risk.' To safeguard that, he promised to investigate Leinders' past and take appropriate action.

But when Wiggins faced the press at the finish of the stage in Porrentruy, he was not asked about Leinders, nor was he asked directly about doping. He was asked about people on Twitter who suggested he was doping. He responded with both barrels: 'I say they're just fucking wankers. I cannot be doing with people like that. It justifies their own bone-idleness because they can't ever imagine applying themselves to do anything in their lives. It's easy for them to sit under a pseudonym on Twitter and write that sort of shit, rather than get off their arses in their own lives and apply themselves and work hard at something and achieve something. And that's ultimately it.'

Wiggins went to place the microphone on the table, then picked it back up to add the *coup de grâce*: 'C**ts.'

La Toussuire, 12 July 2012

Day two in the Alps, and after the climbs of the Col de la Madeleine, where Wiggins experienced his nadir at the 2010 Tour, the Col du Glandon and Col de la Croix de Fer, the leaders were climbing to the finish of the 148km stage, to one of the country's uglier ski stations, La Toussuire. There had been a shock on the Glandon, with 56km remaining of the stage, when Cadel Evans attacked. But Michael Rogers, sitting at the front of the bunch, told Wiggins not to panic; that they could ride the climb faster by maintaining a steady tempo, and that Evans, even though he was able to link up with two teammates, would not be able to sustain his effort.

Rogers was right. But on the final climb, as Evans fell back, Nibali, a rider known as 'The Shark' (it being almost obligatory for Italian riders to have nicknames), began to make jabbing attacks. He took others with him as Wiggins and his final remaining teammate, Froome, dropped back. There was no need to panic. The theory was the same: a steady pace is more efficient than sudden accelerations. But as Froome led Wiggins up to Nibali, and then moved to the front of the small group, Wiggins became detached. It was the first time in almost two weeks that he had looked vulnerable. And his weakness had been exposed by his own teammate.

Froome pressed on as Wiggins dropped further back. The gap was growing. The yellow jersey looked to be in trouble. Then Froome lifted a hand to his earpiece, connecting him to Sean Yates in the team car, and reacted immediately to the instruction. He turned around, eased up and allowed Wiggins to rejoin. But the breakdown in communication, and Froome's apparently superior strength on the climb, had people wondering: could Froome win the Tour? Was it the Vuelta – where Wiggins remained the protected rider even when it became obvious that Froome was stronger – all over again?

What happened at the finish was telling. As Wiggins was quickly surrounded and ushered away by members of the team's staff, Froome was isolated as he tried to ride towards the bus surrounded by a swarm of journalists. They crowded in, prevented him from moving, until he had to put a foot to the ground and look up. Blinking quickly as the sweat poured into his eyes, he resembled a rabbit trapped in headlights. The questions came thick and fast. What had happened?

'He asked me to slow down so I waited for him.'

Who asked you to slow down? 'Sean Yates.'

But you could have gone clear? 'Yeah … I mean, obviously Bradley's the priority, and we're here to protect him and keep him up there. But it gives us more cards to play if I'm up there also.'

When you got away were you aware that Bradley was behind? 'Yeah, yeah, I knew Bradley was behind but I, eh, obviously didn't want to put him under pressure. If he was on the wheels and comfortable then it wouldn't have been a problem for me to go off, but, eh, it started splitting up so I sat up.'

But why did you attack? Froome shrugged. 'I felt good, I accelerated.'

'Chris,' a female Dutch journalist addressed him directly, 'do you realise you can win this Tour?' Froome laughed nervously: 'Maybe one day.'

'Why not this year?' she persisted. 'We'll see about that,' said Froome. 'Thank you for the compliment but, eh, yeah ... I think Bradley's in a better position to win the Tour this year than I am, to be honest. I'll follow orders at all costs. I'm part of a team and I have to do what the team asks me to do. Brad is strong in the mountains, and stronger in the time trials.'

Wiggins had convincingly won the stage nine time trial, with Froome second. But the mountains could be more decisive than the time trials. 'It depends how the team rides,' said Froome. 'It depends how they choose to ride, and I stick to that.'

But what did he think of the way they were riding, which was steady, to discourage attacks? 'Yeah,' he shrugged. 'I'm part of a team and I'll stick to ... I'll do what I need to do.'

The Dutch journalist persisted: 'What if, in five or six years, you look back and realise you could have won this Tour, but sacrificed your own chances?'

'Obviously that's a thing I'm going to have to see in five or six years,' said Froome. It was difficult to know what he was really thinking. He was diffident and polite, as he always is. But the way Froome had ridden on the climb, and his hesitant responses, hinted at his ambition and his understanding that this could be thwarted by the fact that he and Wiggins were teammates, and that he had lost time on the first stage. Had he not punctured, he would be sitting only 40 seconds behind Wiggins at the top of general classification.

Later, Brailsford appeared briefly at the door of the team bus, but he was not the relaxed figure he had been in Belfort. Had Wiggins looked vulnerable? 'Vulnerable?' replied Brailsford. 'Oh yeah, he looked vulnerable to me, he looks vulnerable in yellow, he's looked vulnerable all week, he's looked vulnerable all season.' The sarcasm was laid on thick. 'The fact of the matter is it's your job to make as much as you want out of this. We're first and second on the Tour de France and let's look for a scandal.'

Sean Yates' version of events was a little different. 'I think everything's squared up now,' he later said of whatever had happened on the climb to La Toussuire. 'And I think there will be no more misunderstandings, or whatever you want to call it, between here and Paris.'

Brailsford was discovering an aspect of the Tour that makes it vastly different even to the Olympics. With Sky having the riders placed first and second on general classification, and with Wiggins and Froome obviously the strongest in the race, they became the main, almost the only, focus. The race was a three-week narrative, with all the twists and turns, the setbacks and drama, of a blockbuster; and the story would be written at the end, not in the middle. But the plot twists – and the speculation – in the middle were an essential part of the narrative; the final tale would be nothing without them. The biggest difference, however, was the sheer scale of the Tour; instead of having 50 British journalists chasing stories, as Brailsford might experience at an Olympic Games, here there were 500, from all over the world. The scrutiny was relentless and the pressure – clearly – was intense.

The next day there was a fourth British stage win, with David Millar victorious in Annonay. He began each of his post-stage interviews with 'I'm an ex-doper,' using the considerable platform of the Tour to spread his anti-doping message. Then Wiggins appeared, and he also had something to get off his chest. Aware that he had been winning the race but losing the PR battle, with his rant against the Twitterati too easily interpreted as an attack on anyone who might be suspicious, he had written an article for the *Guardian* newspaper that day. In it he nailed his colours to the mast: 'If I doped I would stand to lose everything.'

But what he said after the stage was even more powerful and eloquent: 'I discussed it with my wife the other night, and I asked her: "What is the point in winning the Tour, or attempting to win the Tour, if it's not going to go down in history for the right reasons, or [if people have] suspicion?" If I am to be in this position now for another week, there's no point in me sitting and swearing at the question.

'It hurts me when people say these things. I take it very personally. Perhaps I shouldn't: it's just because of people who've sat here before me. But I want to build bridges to prove I'm doing this with bread and water and hard work, and nothing else.'

Wiggins had turned a corner. He had spoken honestly, without ambiguity, and in doing so had convinced a lot of people that they should have no reason to doubt him. Most of all, he had confronted, head-on, an issue that too few top riders seem willing to address, with David Millar being a notable exception. Doping still remains a taboo. On the first rest day of the Tour I had spoken to Tim Kerrison about the subject. With his background in rowing and swimming, he has never encountered the kind of suspicion that lingers around cycling. He seemed bemused by it. But that could be explained by the fact that he was not steeped in the sport; he had not been lied to by so many former stars, as fans of the sport have been. These people, I put it to him, were entitled to ask questions of the man in the yellow jersey.

'But sport is all about performance,' said Kerrison. 'You have to have more than performance as a basis for your suspicion. We can't be suspicious of everybody who performs without some other reason to be suspicious. I think it's quite sad.' There are no secrets, he said. 'We're open about the process behind what we do. And I think everyone can see that we're prepared to do things that other teams aren't prepared to do.' One small example was the routine the team followed after each stage, which saw them warming down on turbo trainers. 'Every sport warms down,' said Kerrison, 'but it was something that traditionally just wasn't done in cycling. There are other things riders do to recover. But for me the number one thing you must do after a high-intensity effort is to warm down. It took a while to convince everybody that was something we should do, and there are logistical problems of getting turbo trainers to the finish, and holding the bus up for 10, 15 minutes. I could sort of see why it hasn't been done in the past, but to me that was too little of a hurdle to get over to stop us from doing it.'

The warm-downs were now *de rigueur* for Sky. And the interesting thing to note was that they were becoming *de rigueur* for some other teams, too. As the Tour moved towards its conclusion, and the attention on Kerrison and his role increased, I wondered if other teams would soon be looking for their very own Kerrisons. I also thought back to Brailsford's pledge, at the start of his journey to build Team Sky, to try to be 'agents of change' in the sport. Putting science at the centre of a team could fulfil that pledge.

There was an interesting parallel to consider. Towards the end of the 1980s it was doctors who became revered in professional cycling circles and to whom riders went for help when they saw the success they had with other riders. It's perhaps not uncommon for athletes to be more interested in the outcome than the method; mainly, they are interested in people who can help them. And so it was a pity that some of the more notorious doctors of the late 1980s and 1990s, in Italy especially, regarded their clients as medical experiments and paid rather less attention to the anti-doping rules than they should have done. The legacy of that was the EPO generation that dominated and discredited the sport in the 1990s and into the 2000s.

A charge that was levelled against Sky was 'financial doping.' They had filled the team with riders such as Froome, Rogers and Porte, who, on other teams, might have been leaders in their own right, but who, at Sky, were highly paid *domestiques*, or *domestiques de luxe*. It partly explained why they were able to spend all day riding on the front, controlling the race so effectively. Brailsford rejected the charge of 'financial doping.' He preferred 'intellectual doping.'

Peyragudes, 19 July 2012

Two days after Annonay, when an act of sabotage saw tacks scattered on the road to Foix, and Cadel Evans was one of the many puncture victims, Wiggins ordered a go-slow. Now he wasn't *Monsieur Propre* (Mr Clean, as the French media had dubbed him) anymore; he was *Le Gentleman*. But there was another remarkable fact about the tacks incident. As the air filled with the sound of tyres exploding, and the hissing of air deflating, not one Sky rider suffered a puncture. Not one. 'I realised at that point,' said Brailsford later, 'that the gods were smiling on us.'

After a brutal day in the Pyrenees for stage 16 on 18 July, in scorching heat and over four climbs before a twisting descent into the spa town of Luchon, the status quo remained. Wiggins, Froome and Nibali finished together, the top three on general classification confirming they were indeed the strongest in the race. But the next day, on the final climb of the day – of the entire Tour – to Peyragudes, there was a repeat of La Toussuire when Froome's pace on the mountain seemed to put Wiggins in trouble. Again, Froome had responded to a surge from Nibali by taking Wiggins back up to the Italian; but after doing so, and keeping on the pressure at the front, a gap opened between the Sky teammates.

Froome, it later emerged, was desperate to win the stage. Up ahead was a single escapee, Alejandro Valverde, and they were closing on him. But while Froome was capable of accelerating and believed he could bridge the gap to Valverde, Wiggins was comfortable with the steadier tempo. Again the message came over the radio from Sean Yates to Froome: 'Stay together.' And this time Froome made quite a show of easing up, turning round, beckoning Wiggins to join him in pursuit of the leader.

They finished together, second and third on the stage, 19 seconds down on Valverde, but once again the question was asked: was Froome stronger? It wasn't clear. Froome is capable of the stop-start rhythm of the pure climber, but that doesn't mean he could have sustained his effort. Wiggins may well have been capable of reeling him in as he tired. Some were unimpressed by Froome's antics on the climb, *L'Equipe* comparing him to Mr Bean. That was a little cruel. It didn't seem to be calculated on Froome's part, but was rather part of his unpolished charm and occasional naivety. 'He's one of these guys who's really intelligent,' one team insider told me, 'but sometimes lacks common sense.'

On the front page of the French sports daily the next day, meanwhile, was a picture of Froome and Wiggins climbing towards the summit together, having outdistanced Nibali and all the other challengers, and a headline that summed it up: 'La Promenade des Anglais'. There were just three days to Paris. The penultimate stage was the one Wiggins had earmarked as the decisive one. Yet it didn't seem so important now. He had a lead of two minutes, five seconds over Froome. But it was important in another sense; he needed an emphatic performance to put the golden seal on his victory, and to answer those questions about whether Froome, had he been able to ride his own race, might have beaten him.

Wiggins' performance was extraordinary, and more convincing than his win in the first time trial, to Besançon on stage nine. He won the 53km test, beating Froome into second by a minute and 16 seconds. His overall lead had stretched to 3.21. As he crossed the line he punched, and yelled, and was then engulfed in a mass of gendarmes and reporters. 'It was like a mass murderer going into a courthouse,' he reflected later. He was emotional afterwards. He spoke about growing up with his mum in a flat in London after his father abandoned them, and about the grandfather who brought him up and who died during the 2010 Tour. He had been thinking about all of this, he said, as he pounded the pedals. But he also had 'Sean Yates in my ear the whole race, telling me: "This is what it's all been for, this is what it's all about."'

Standing a little apart from the chaos at the finish was Tim Kerrison. He seemed, for once, to be unoccupied, and to be taking in the scene, maybe registering the scale of what had been achieved and which, the next day in Paris, would be confirmed. 'How do you feel?' I asked him. 'You're the numbers guy. But how do you actually feel?'

'It's agonising, it's so drawn out, it's difficult,' he said. He looked in pain rather than happy. 'There's no moment where you can say: we've done it … I mean, my job is to look at things rationally and unemotionally, but all year I've hoped we'd be in this position after this stage. It's agonising, knowing you've got the best guys physically in the race, knowing there's so much that can go not to plan, even though we work so hard to make sure things do go to plan. All the questions people have been asking, sometimes legitimate, through the year: are we peaking too early with Brad? Will he last three weeks? How will he do in the mountains? We planned for all those things: they're the things that make Tour de France champions.

'We know that Froomey's been extremely strong but we continued to back our leader, believing it was the right thing to do, and today confirmed that it was, and that Brad's the strongest rider in the race.'

Can Wiggins do it again; can he sustain his commitment? 'That will remain to be seen. We all believe he's got room for improvement. He knows exactly what he needs to do, and how to do it. But it's not an easy sport. He's seen more of me than his family.'

There was a point, in the final week, when Brailsford, reflecting back to the 2010 Tour, said: 'Fundamentally, people will not change their behaviour unless they are suffering enough or unless the reward is great enough. That's why people have affairs or they stay overweight, because they are not suffering enough to do anything about it. It's the same in sport. For Brad as an individual, for us as a team, certainly for myself, the suffering was agonising in 2010.'

It might have been worse than we realised at the time, with Brailsford said by some to have been on the brink of losing patience completely with Wiggins at the end of the team's first season. The final straw, apparently, was not his failure at the Tour but his failure to turn up at a Sky corporate function. From that low, they sat down and plotted a way forward. The result of that process was here, now, in Paris.

It could be seen not only in Wiggins' historic victory, which he confirmed by riding onto the Champs-Élysées, surrounded by his teammates and resplendent in the sport's greatest symbol, the yellow jersey, but also in the way he now carried himself. On the bike, he was a leader and winner in the great tradition; appropriately, his 13-day spell in yellow was the longest since the great Bernard Hinault in 1981. He rode with great strength and consistency, and he displayed unshakeable confidence. He looked after his teammates, and they looked after him; he even promised to come back and help Froome if the roles were reversed, and Froome found himself in a better position to win. Off the bike, as the race progressed, he showed increasing maturity, intelligence and charisma; or 'bolshy panache', as the writer Graham Robb neatly described it. Where previously some struggled to understand Wiggins' dry humour, now most people seemed to 'get' him. And they liked him; he was likeable. He didn't necessarily smile; but that didn't mean he wasn't joking. It was one of the great legacies of the Tour – not only the fact of his win, but also that finally Wiggins' personality was revealed. He had allowed himself to emerge.

A few hours before the traditional procession onto the Champs-Élysées, for a stage that would eventually be won, for the fourth year in a row, by Mark Cavendish, the winner-in-waiting of the 2012 Tour strolled into the breakfast room of the chain hotel in which he and his team had spent their last night together. It was low-budget, a Campanile on the edge of Chartres; a metaphorical million miles from the splendour of the Champs-Élysées and the prestige of a first-ever British victory in one of the world's great sporting events.

There was nothing remotely glamorous about the setting, but there were reminders everywhere of what Wiggins was on the brink of accomplishing. The livery of his team's vehicles, the bus, lorry, vans and cars that filled the car park, had changed from blue to yellow. The team's 26 members of staff all wore black T-shirts with yellow bands made up of the names of the nine riders who had started the Tour, including the unfortunate Siutsou, who appeared on crutches in Paris.

Wiggins sat down beside Brailsford, who was absorbed in conversation, reflecting, typically for Brailsford, not on the

Tour, or the scenes that were about to be played out in Paris, or on the fact that he was about to achieve his five-year target of winning the Tour in just three, but on how he and Team Sky would retain their hunger, maintain their success and build a dynasty. Minding his own business, Wiggins stared at the table and then distractedly picked up the copy of *L'Equipe* that was sitting in front of him. The entire front page was taken up with a cyclist in yellow, punching the air. 'À l'heure Anglaise', read the headline.

He stared at it with detached bemusement. When he spoke, he brandished the newspaper. 'It's almost a kind of disbelief that this is happening,' he said. He sounded genuinely surprised. 'It's little things like seeing the front page of *L'Equipe*, you know? You don't realise it's you on there. It's strange, really strange.'

CHAPTER 17

FROOME POWER

Porto-Vecchio, Corsica, 29 June 2013

Chris Froome's bid to win the 100th Tour de France could not have started more ignominiously.

Starting as red-hot favourite, having won the Tour of Oman, Tour de Romandie and Critérium du Dauphiné earlier in the year, Froome was the first rider to crash in the 2013 Tour de France. The race hadn't even started and Froome was in the neutralised zone. The riders were trundling through the Corsican town of Porto-Vecchio when he clipped a curb and went down.

It was arguably the worst start for a Tour favourite since 1989, when the defending champion Pedro Delgado turned up over two minutes late for his prologue time trial. At least Froome lost no time; he picked himself up, dusted himself down and was back in the peloton before the official start. But it did not augur well.

Then again, Froome's situation was not as ignominious as that of the defending champion. Bradley Wiggins – now Sir Bradley Wiggins – wasn't at the Tour at all. He was in Majorca, growing a beard and training for the Tour of Poland. A knee injury, sustained at the Giro d'Italia, had ruled him out of a defence.

But it didn't add up. Didn't add up at all. Even on the day his 'non-selection' was confirmed by Dave Brailsford, a full month before the Tour started, Wiggins was reported to be training hard. His team admitted that the injury was minor. According to Team Sky sources, it certainly would not have prevented him starting the Tour the previous year. So why was he not in Corsica?

How fickle sport is. Just a few months earlier Wiggins had been the golden boy, the undisputed leader of Team Sky, the poster boy of the London Olympics. He could do no wrong. Chris Froome, meanwhile, was the outsider. And yet in finishing second at both the 2011 Vuelta and 2012 Tour, Froome had more than proven his ability in a three-week Grand Tour. He deserved his chance.

In January 2013, the press were invited to Majorca to interview Wiggins and Froome, and to hear from Dave Brailsford, Rod Ellingworth and Tim Kerrison. But in an unusual departure, Brailsford, Ellingworth and Kerrison decided to hold a seminar. As Brailsford explained, 'We want to have an informal discussion. We want to give an insight into where we are currently. Lessons learned, if you like.'

There was much to discuss. When Lance Armstrong was finally charged with doping by the US Anti-Doping Agency and stripped of his seven Tour de France titles the previous autumn, it turned up the heat on Team Sky and Brailsford. Partly that was because they were the most recent winner of the Tour; partly it was because they had skeletons in their closet. Michael Barry was one of the riders who testified against Armstrong, admitting at the same time that he had lied in 2010 when he denied using EPO while on the US Postal team.

Brailsford, under pressure from Sky, re-implemented the zero-tolerance policy that had supposedly been one of the team's founding principles. He and Steve Peters carried out interviews with all staff and riders, then asked them to sign a pledge swearing they had no history of doping. 'If you've got anything to say, now is the time to say it,' as Brailsford put it. 'Because the truth will come out.'

Bobby Julich, the race coach, admitted he too had used EPO. So did Steven de Jongh, the sports director. Sean Yates did not confess to having used drugs, but he recognised his previously close association with Armstrong carried a 'reputational risk' to the team, and retired. A more curious case was that of Michael Rogers, who had been such an important member of the 2012 Tour team. The Australian, who admitted to previously working with Armstrong's old coach, Dr Michele Ferrari, but not to doping, was reportedly on the verge of signing a new contract with Sky when he abruptly left and signed instead for Alberto Contador's Saxo-Tinkoff team, a move he later stated was made for financial reasons. (De Jongh also turned up there, and it didn't take long for Julich to find new employment, as a coach at BMC.) Brailsford was also still explaining his decision to hire Geert Leinders, the doctor who had been released and was now under official investigation in Belgium after fresh revelations about his time at Rabobank, although Leinders has always denied any allegations of wrongdoing. 'Hindsight is a brilliant thing,' said Brailsford. 'Had we known then what we know now, we wouldn't have touched the guy. We went through what we thought were the right procedures; we interviewed the guy; he sat down with Steve. With hindsight, we wouldn't have hired him.'

Two months after the clear-out came the seminar in Majorca. It lasted three hours, and in that time, Brailsford, Kerrison and Ellingworth explained their methods. They talked power curves, wattages and VAMs (Mean Ascent Velocity, or the speed of elevation gain – basically, how good someone is at climbing).

It was fascinating, complex stuff. At times Kerrison appeared to be struggling to make it understandable to those of us who are not sports scientists (everyone in the room bar him). But the presentation was, I came to realise later, Brailsford's solution to the pledge he'd made during the previous year's Tour while under siege through Twitter and social media, when accusations of doping were levelled at Team Sky. 'We'll have a conference,' said Brailsford back then. 'Everyone can come to Manchester this winter and learn about what we do.'

The conference did not take place. Instead, this presentation was held in their hotel in Majorca, attended not by the public but by around 20 members of the media. A month or so later, Brailsford and Kerrison did it all again in London for the sports editors of the national newspapers.

Sitting down beside Kerrison and Ellingworth, Brailsford stated that it wasn't just the doping question that gave them pause for reflection over the winter. The goalposts had moved. 'One of the issues with having a results-based goal, as it were, is that once you've achieved it, you think, what next?' he said.

'We wanted to win the Tour in five years, so what next? That's when we came up with the idea of having something that sat just above results. We wanted to be as ambitious as we could be as a sports team. So we got to thinking, what would the most admired sports team look like?

'We broke it down into different areas or aspects: being the best performing team; having the most engaged fans; having the most satisfied partners; and most importantly, that we're recognised as being clean.'

But it was Kerrison, his role, and the journey he had been on since his year of observing the team from his campervan, Black Betty, in 2010, who was the most interesting. Kerrison spoke about the 'gurus' – by reputation, if not in reality – he had encountered: 'We identified early on that there are a lot of gurus in professional cycling, people who have been in the system a long time, who are not necessarily qualified. They [are perceived to] have special skills and powers, which cycling has become dependent on over time.'

Kerrison preferred staff who were 'appropriately qualified', who 'operate in a team environment, [and] have no secrets'. He had also been surprised to find 'no coaching structures' in many teams.

Then they got on to the in-vogue subject in cycling: power data. Estimates of VAM and power-to-weight ratio could be made from timing a rider up a particular mountain. There were two problems: such calculations were based on estimates of such variables as wind speed, road surface, the rider's weight and the effect of slipstreaming. The other was a legacy of the sport's history. The benchmarks for performance tended to be those times – or wattages – set in what is now recognised to have been an era dominated by doping, by the likes of Armstrong, Jan Ullrich and Marco Pantani. And so the question inevitably arose: what conclusions should be drawn if a modern rider's performance was comparable to that of a doped rider? That the modern rider, too, must be doping?

'There's a lot of pseudo-science out there for cycling,' said Brailsford. 'A lot of people who get snippets of info and talk about power-to-weight, VAM and all the rest of it, without truly having the expertise to analyse it. There's a lot of misinformation out there.'

Then Brailsford, standing now beside a whiteboard, sketched a graph and a bell curve. 'This is a simple model, something graphic where riders can see where they currently are,' he said. The curve plotted a rider's power output over time, using figures not calculated from television pictures but from the information collected by the SRM computer fixed to his bike (even this had a margin of error, Brailsford stressed, but since the information was collected over a period of time, rather than on just one particular climb, a reasonably accurate picture could be drawn – or graph plotted).

'You can take any of our riders,' added Brailsford, 'and look at the same day last year, to see where they're at. It's why you hear riders talk with great confidence about being ahead of where they are, or on target; it's not done on feel, it's science. That's something we've integrated into what we do.'

Kerrison interjected: 'But we've got to recognise that riders respond to information in different ways. We had one rider last year who, if you put a graph in front of him, would switch off and walk away. He wasn't interested.'

Kerrison doesn't name the rider but it doesn't take a genius to work out that this was Mark Cavendish, who had, to no one's great surprise, left Team Sky over the winter for the Belgian Omega Pharma-Quick Step team, who promised him greater support in the bunch sprints.

The only moment when Brailsford clammed up and balked at going into more detail was when asked about the content of specific training sessions. Kerrison opened his mouth to speak but Brailsford immediately stopped him. 'If we weren't in the sport we're in we wouldn't be sharing any of this with you,' he said. 'This is our competitive advantage.

'What we're doing here potentially is foregoing a competitive advantage in order to say: "Okay, here's what we do," rather than sneaking around behind closed doors. We realise there's a cost-benefit analysis. We're trying to be open. We're showing people what we do, knowing that our competitors could use it and come back and beat us.'

Kerrison, however, outlined the bind in which he felt himself to be, as well as the inevitable suspicion and scepticism – or even outright cynicism – that would come his way if he did his job successfully.

'Our job is to improve our riders' performance,' said Kerrison. 'And if we do our job really well, which of course we work really hard to do, then we improve our riders' performances quite a lot, and some of the things our riders do are seen as being quite remarkable.

'But remarkable performance does not correlate with doping, necessarily. That's one of the things that I've struggled with over the past year or so; that people assume because we're doing our jobs well, we must be doping. It used to make me really frustrated and angry. But now I think I understand a lot more about what's gone on over the past years of cycling, after the [Tyler] Hamilton book and the USADA documents, and Lance's interview [on *The Oprah Winfrey Show*, where he admitted to doping for all seven of his Tour 'wins']. And I understand now. I understand that people have been reassured time and time again that they were being told the truth, and they've been let down time and time again.'

There was another story in Majorca. A sporting story. Wiggins and Froome. Froome and Wiggins.

Wiggins said he had decided to prioritise the Giro d'Italia – he wanted to win it. But he added that he and Kerrison had, the night before the BBC Sports Personality of the Year Award, in the very same Majorcan hotel, also talked about the Tour. 'Tim said to me, "Why don't you do both the Giro and the Tour?" My thought was, I won't do the Tour, I'll give the space to someone else, but Tim was adamant that as long as we do the right things post-Giro, there's no reason why I can't be even better at the Tour than last year.'

Earlier, Wiggins and Froome had sat together, as requested by the journalists. There were 15 minutes with Froome, 15 minutes of the two together, then 15 minutes with Wiggins. On his own, Froome was relaxed. On his own, Wiggins was relaxed. But the temperature in the room became noticeably cooler when they were together, sitting side-by-side but not once catching the other's eye.

Before Wiggins arrived, Froome said: 'I think we've got a perfectly good working relationship, contrary to what everyone makes out and what the newspapers say.' But were they friends? 'We do what's needed of us,' said Froome. 'I wouldn't say I spend time with him off the bike. For one thing we live in different countries, and he's older than me, he's married ...'

As for the 2012 Tour, 'I know there were moments of miscommunication which could have been portrayed as me going against Brad, but at the end of the day I always did my job. I stayed with him when I needed to, and helped him all the way through. That's our job, and the way it's shaping up this year, our roles will be reversed.'

When Wiggins arrived, he was asked who was in better shape – him or Froome? 'Me, of course.' He laughed – 'Ha, ha, ha' – and Froome smiled. 'But I'm aiming to be ready to go in early April. Chris has got a couple more months before he needs to be ready.'

Sadly for Wiggins – and for the viewing public, perhaps – the question of how he and Froome would co-exist at the Tour did not arise. Wiggins' bid to win the Giro floundered from the very start in Naples. Bad weather affected the race: it rained every day, the temperature plummeted and Wiggins was out of sorts. He crashed on a descent, lost his confidence and then succumbed to a chest infection. By stage 12, to Treviso, as he slid off the back of the peloton and had to be nursed through the sodden streets by his Sky teammates, it was painful to watch. He didn't start the next day's stage.

Despite his bullish talk on the eve of the race of going for the Giro–Tour double (prompting a statement from Froome that urged Sky to confirm his status as leader for the Tour – which Brailsford did), it seemed that Wiggins was bluffing. It was like 2010 and the Tour de France all over again. He knew he wasn't in race-winning shape and tried to will himself into it. But before the Giro he missed one of the Tenerife training camps that had been a cornerstone of his success in 2012. He preferred Majorca, where he had bought some property. It had the advantage of being somewhere he could take his family.

Froome, on the other hand, was as focused as Wiggins had

been in 2012 – and as ready. His build-up was almost identical, as he picked off stage races and established himself as the man to beat.

Nice, 2 July 2013

The team time trial comes four days into the Tour, after three days on the island of Corsica. On the first day, after Froome's innocuous crash in the neutralised zone, Geraint Thomas and Ian Stannard suffer a more serious one. Scans the following evening reveal that Thomas has fractured a bone in his pelvis. On stage two, on the run-in to Ajaccio, Froome attacks on a small rise and rides away from everyone: it confirms his condition and his eagerness.

But the first real test for Froome – and especially for Thomas – comes in Nice. It's a test for the team, too. The Tour's transfer from Corsica has weighed on everyone's mind. While all the riders are to take the plane, the rest of the entourage, including the teams' support staff, will sail to the French mainland on the overnight ferry. Not Team Sky – Brailsford has come up with an alternative plan. 'Fatigue in a race like this is an important thing to try and manage, particularly for the staff,' explains Brailsford in Nice. 'If the fatigue gets on top of you and the staff then you start to lose morale. It's hard, we've learnt that over the years, so we got some drivers to come over [to Corsica] and pick up our vehicles and drive them over, and we all hopped on a plane.

'It was a chartered flight,' he continues, 'but it wasn't that expensive, about €4,000. If you divide that by 14 people, and the amount of expenditure across the whole race, relatively speaking, that's money well spent in my opinion.'

In the team time trial, Sky finish third. A good, solid ride. But for Thomas, who at the start needed to be helped onto his bike and couldn't get out of the saddle, it is, Brailsford later states, 'his defining moment.'

'Geraint said: "I'm going to approach [the first] 700m like it's the Olympic final of the team pursuit." It was like his life depended on it. Everything about him – you couldn't differentiate between that and the morning of the Olympic final.

'His defining moment was from the start ramp to the Promenade des Anglais. Only 700m, but if he didn't get on [and stay with his team], that would have been it. He may have been outside the time limit. All he had to do was a 700m seated acceleration, which he's done in team pursuit training time and time again.

'Sure enough, not only did he get on, but 4km into the race, he gives us the thumbs up, to say, "I'm going through."'

Ax 3 Domaines, 6 July 2013

The first summit finish, a week into the race. The same plan as a year ago. Froome can barely contain his excitement, which rubs off on the team. 'They want to kill it,' says a member of the team.

And kill it they do. Vasil Kiryienka, the tough Belarusian, sits at the front, stamping on the pedals as they approach the Col de Pailhères, then Peter Kennaugh takes over towards the top, with other Sky men in close attendance, notably Richie Porte, who won Paris-Nice earlier in the season and fancies doing what Froome did a year ago, supporting his leader but also finishing on the podium. Here, Sky look in control. Nairo Quintana, the young Colombian on the Movistar team, attacks on the climb, but Kennaugh doesn't panic, sitting at the front tapping out his rhythm, setting up Froome for the next and final climb, to Ax 3 Domaines.

Five kilometres from the summit, Froome glances around. 'I saw the other guys were really struggling on the wheel,' he says later. 'They were hanging in there, and I thought, this is the right moment to push on and get a bit of time.'

When Froome attacks, nobody responds – not even Contador, who once danced so effortlessly up climbs like this. Porte sits behind Froome's rivals, but they're all struggling. Porte lowers his mouth to his chest and talks into his radio: 'They're fucked, they're fucked, all of them.' Then he counter-attacks, and nobody can follow him. At the finish Froome wins alone; Porte is second, 51 seconds down.

Such a dominant team performance is a double-edged sword. Questions are inevitably asked. Froome says he understands this '100%', explaining: 'I think it's normal that people ask questions in cycling. That's the unfortunate position we find ourselves in at the moment. Eyebrows are going to be raised and questions are going to be asked, but I know the sport has changed. There's absolutely no way I'd be able to get these results if the sport hadn't changed. I certainly know the results I get now are not going to be stripped 10, 20 years down the line. Rest assured, that's not going to happen.'

Bagnères-de-Bigorre, 7 July 2013

Team Sky, through Wiggins, took the yellow jersey at exactly the same point the previous year: on the first mountain stage, on the first Saturday. And the next morning, in 2012, Brailsford urged caution: 'It's like scoring a goal in the first five minutes of a football match. The most dangerous thing is that you go to sleep when it kicks off again.'

He doesn't heed the same advice this time. It isn't necessarily that Sky go to sleep at the start of the next stage, with Froome in yellow for the first time – it's that so many other teams go to war. Garmin-Sharp, aiming for the stage win, attack from the gun. So do others. There are five mountains, but the race is stretched from the start, and Sky make the error of trying to control it; of trying to control something that's uncontrollable, which Porte later likens to a fire he once started at his parents' house in Tasmania, which eventually had to be extinguished by two fire engines.

It doesn't help that Sky find themselves a man down before the first climb, the Col de Portet d'Aspet, when Kennaugh collides with Ryder Hesjedal and falls into a ravine. He climbs out, and re-mounts, but never sees the front again. Other Sky riders are below-par: Thomas with his broken pelvis; Kiryienka after his efforts of the previous day; and David Lopez and Kanstantsin Siutsou appear simply off-form.

Mistake number two: Porte tries to cover for all of them, but it's hopeless. As the attacks continue, with the Movistar team of Alejandro Valverde and Quintana particularly aggressive, he can't hold on to the front group. It leaves Froome isolated. And there are 140km still to race.

Porte eventually finishes 18 minutes down, all hopes of finishing on the podium gone. Privately, some in the team are not unhappy about this. At least now the whole team will be focused on one goal: supporting Froome.

Because Froome survives. Although isolated for so much of the stage, and surrounded by large contingents of Movistar and Saxo riders, the other teams seem more interested in killing off Porte than in attacking Froome. He knows whom he needs to follow – Quintana, Valverde and Contador – and whom he can ignore. When Garmin's Dan Martin attacks on the final climb, he lets him go. Martin wins the stage. And Froome, although his team has been exposed, finishes with his rivals, his lead intact.

Still, it's a traumatic day for Sky, capped when Kiryienka is eliminated for finishing outside the time limit. 'We enjoy days like Saturday, but we learn a lot more from days like today,' says Kerrison. But even he doesn't have an explanation for the team's collapse. 'We'll probably go for months from now, and still be mulling over this stage and everything that led up to it, and how we don't make the same mistakes again.'

Mont Ventoux, 14 July 2013

The defining stage of this Tour, and of Froome's career so far, sees him attack 7.2km from the summit after being led up the lower slopes of Mont Ventoux, arguably the most fearsome of all the Tour's mountains, by Kennaugh and Porte. When Froome senses Porte tiring – he had earlier asked him to give everything he had – he accelerates. 'I didn't want to start sitting up and playing games,' Froome says later. 'I thought, now is the time to get rid of Alberto.'

Froome's attack is unconventional: he doesn't get out of the saddle and his legs begin to whir beneath him. It's ungainly, violent, effective. Contador doesn't stand a chance. Ahead of him is Quintana, the smooth-pedalling Colombian, and Froome bridges the gap, rides with him, urges him on, then, with another surge, dispatches him, to win alone at the summit. After that he collapses, needing oxygen. 'This is massive,' he says once he's recovered. 'Everyone wanted to win this stage on Bastille Day, on Mont Ventoux: it really was an epic stage. It's such an emotional win for me. A dream come true. I think every cyclist would dream about winning a stage like today.'

Alpe d'Huez, 18 July 2013

Froome wins his third stage, the hilly time trial held 24 hours before another historic stage, which sees the riders climb Alpe d'Huez twice. This also means a first-ever descent of the Col de Sarenne, a treacherous, twisting strip of road with a sheer drop to one side. It makes Froome nervous, as he freely admits, particularly as Contador now has so little to lose that he seems prepared to take risks. This was evident two days earlier on the descent into Gap, when Froome considered his attacks reckless. The point was proved when Contador came off on one corner, and Froome, shadowing his rival, ran out of road. Both were unhurt but it was a near-miss.

'I personally think he is starting to get desperate and is taking uncalculated risks,' says Froome of Contador.

As he promised, Contador does attack on the descent of the Sarenne, and gets away with his teammate Roman Kreuziger, but this isn't what causes Froome problems. Second time up Alpe d'Huez, with Contador having been caught, Froome's head drops. There are 5km to go. He speaks to Porte, sticks his hand up – does he have a problem with his bike? – then drops back.

He's been unable to get food from the team car after it broke down on the Sarenne, and now he's paying the price with the dreaded 'hunger flat'. The other team car now sits behind Froome's group, but feeding from the car so late in the stage is not allowed. Porte is dispatched to collect some energy gels, which he hands over to Froome, who rips open the sachet and gulps down the sugary liquid. But the race officials, not surprisingly, take a dim view of this. After the stage, both Froome and Porte are docked 20 seconds as punishment.

Meanwhile, Contador's efforts to get away on the descent appear to cost him as he fades. Quintana now seems to be the danger man; as Froome struggles, he can't follow him and concedes a little over a minute. Froome is seventh to the summit, guided in by his faithful *domestique*, Porte. With two more days in the Alps, he leads Contador by 5:11 and Quintana by 5:32. It's a decent cushion, as long as he doesn't suffer another hunger flat.

But by the third week of the Tour there's another talking point: Froome's power data. His performance on Ventoux has inspired sports scientists to crunch some numbers, and some of their estimates have him out-performing a doped-up Armstrong (while some don't, highlighting the difficulties in estimating the figures).

Scepticism is understandable and justified, given the Armstrong revelations; but with Armstrong there was evidence, even as far back as 1999, that he was doping. With

Froome, there are only his performances, which for some are simply too good to be true.

Every day he's asked a version of the same question – 'Are you doping?' He doesn't do what Wiggins did and rant about the anonymous tweeters, but he does appear to lose his patience on the rest day after his win on Mont Ventoux. 'I just think it's quite sad that we're sitting here the day after the biggest victory of my life, quite a historic win, talking about doping. And quite frankly, I mean, my teammates and I, we've slept on volcanoes to get ready for this. We've been away from home for months, training together, just working our arses off to get here, and here I am, basically being accused of being a cheat and a liar and … that's not cool.'

When his frustration bubbled over, Wiggins had also used a c-word. But not 'cool'.

Team Sky do respond to the clamour for Froome's official power data, handing over his files to Fred Grappe, a respected physiologist and Kerrison's equivalent at the FDJ team. Grappe studies the data from the 2011 Vuelta to the 2013 Tour and declares himself satisfied that Froome's performances are consistent – there are no strange spikes – and although his VO2 max must be in the upper range of what is humanly possible, in Grappe's opinion there's nothing to suggest that Froome is doping. Predictably, it satisfies some, but not everyone.

Annecy, 20 July 2013

It's 10.15pm when Chris Froome and Dave Brailsford appear in a small room in their hotel in Annecy. The next day, Froome will win the Tour. But Brailsford is angry.

His belief in Froome, confirmed at the Tour of Oman, seems to have developed into affection, particularly as his performances at the Tour have attracted so much suspicion. 'He's very eloquent, a very bright guy, with a great family background,' says Brailsford, 'and his manners and family values have stood him in extremely good stead here.'

With the doping questions, you mean? 'For someone to be accused of being a cheat with the venom, at times, that he has been, I think is completely unacceptable,' says Brailsford. 'The way he has dealt with that has been absolutely first class. He hasn't snapped. He has been patient and tolerant.

'He will be a lot more experienced, wiser and more robust for this experience. I think he has all the makings, all the ingredients, of a multiple champion. He has all the physical and mental attributes to be competitive in this race, if nothing drastic changes, for quite some time. He's not at his best yet, for sure. He can still reach a better physical condition than he's [in] now.'

Froome, as he has done throughout the Tour – and as he will the following evening in Paris, when he reads a speech in which he makes a point of saying, 'This is one yellow jersey that will stand the test of time' – is calm, humble, gracious and polite. Speaking to just six journalists, as opposed to the hundreds he's addressed daily in the after-stage press conference, he seems more relaxed.

Earlier that day, there had been a moment on the climb to Semnoz, the final climb of the entire race, high above Annecy, when he realised he was going to be crowned champion in Paris in 24 hours' time. Quintana had ridden away to win the stage and Froome allowed himself to briefly switch off, not caring that a fourth stage victory was slipping out of reach. At that moment he looked downwards, shook his head, smiled and allowed the thought to sink in: he was about to win the Tour de France, to become a Tour de France winner.

Froome says he can't really believe it; that it hasn't sunk in yet. Brailsford is also shaking his head. Not smiling, but bullish. 'You all laughed when I told you we were going to win the Tour in five years,' he says. 'If I'd told you we would win it twice with two different riders, you'd have pissed your pants.'

ACKNOWLEDGEMENTS

A previous book, *Heroes, Villains & Velodromes*, was published in June 2008, and in some respects *Sky's the Limit* forms the second instalment to that story. But with a couple of important differences. The first book was subtitled 'Chris Hoy and Britain's Track Cycling Revolution', and, like Ronseal, it did what it said on the tin, with Hoy the central pillar in the story of how the British track cycling team were transformed from perennial no-hopers to prolific winners.

Just after the book came out I met Bradley Wiggins at a pre-Olympic media event in central London. I had a copy of *Heroes, Villains & Velodromes* in my bag, so I gave it to him. I didn't hear if he read it or what he thought of it. He may in fact only have perused the index (it's the first thing they all do), but I did eventually learn, from someone who knows Wiggins well, that he was a little miffed that his rather significant part in the story of Britain's cycling 'revolution' was mentioned only in passing.

This book should redress the balance. It explains how the most popular area of cycle racing – road racing – fitted in to the British cycling 'revolution' – or, rather, how it *didn't* fit in – and how that has changed. But whereas *Heroes, Villains & Velodromes* was written with Hoy's co-operation, I took a different approach to *Sky's the Limit*. Though I mentioned to some of the key people in Team Sky that I was working on a book, I didn't seek their permission. I didn't want it to be the 'authorised' or official story. I figured that, since it's about road racing, there could be potholes, and I wanted to describe them, rather than attempt to fill them in with the kind of gooey tarmac that fools no one.

Given this, access might have proved a problem. But it didn't. Dave Brailsford, the Team Sky principal, and Shane Sutton, the head coach, were admirably accommodating and accessible throughout an interesting – and frequently challenging – first season. I am especially grateful to them, and also to Fran Millar for her invaluable input and insight. Thanks, too, to various other members of the backroom team, in particular Steve Peters, Richard Freeman, Rod Ellingworth, Sean Yates, Phil Burt, Tim Kerrison, Matt Parker, Nigel Mitchell, David Hulse, Corin Dimopoulos, Carsten Jeppesen, Dan Hunt, Steven de Jongh, Helen Mortimer, Gwilym Evans and – while they were involved – Brian Nygaard, Max Sciandri and Scott Sunderland. And thanks to all 26 of Team Sky's riders, in particular Russell Downing, Geraint Thomas, Michael Barry, Mathew Hayman, Chris Froome, Greg Henderson, Simon Gerrans, Nicolas Portal, Juan Antonio Flecha, Ian Stannard, Ben Swift, Peter Kennaugh, Steve Cummings and Bradley Wiggins. For their input I am also very grateful to David Millar, John Herety, Tom Southam and Brian Smith, and – for their help with this book, or merely for their company 'on the road' – to colleagues including Ned Boulting, Brendan Gallagher, Daniel Friebe, Gregor 'Ron Burgundy' Brown, Simon Richardson, Ellis Bacon, Daniel Benson, Stephen Farrand, Owen Slot, Richard Williams, Alasdair Fotheringham, William Fotheringham, Jeremy Whittle, Andy Hood, Jonathan Turner, Lionel Birnie, Jill Douglas, Lia Hervey, Orla Chennaoui, Anthony Tan, Matt Rendell, Paul Kimmage and Matt McGeehan.

Thanks also go to my agent, Mark Stanton, to Tom Whiting and Jonathan Taylor, to my dad, Brian, and brothers Robin and Peter, and, last but most importantly, to Virginie Pierret.

INDEX